Digest of Papers

The Third International Symposium on earable Computers

Thanks to the providers of the wearable photos on the cover, listed in order from left to right:

- Georgia Tech Research Institute
- Neill Newman with the first UK homemade wearable, nicknamed ROME
- Navigator 2, Human-Computer Interaction Institute, Carnegie Mellon University
- Sam Ogden (photographer), Tony Jebara (pictured), and the MIT wearable computing group
- "Touring Machine" prototype combines 6DOF-tracked, see-through head-worn display and hand-held display to present campus information. (c) 1997, Steven Feiner, Blair MacIntyre, Tobias Höllerer, and Anthony Webster, Columbia University.

Digest of Papers

The Third International Symposium on  Wearable Computers

October 18-19, 1999
San Francisco, California

Sponsored by
The IEEE Computer Society

Los Alamitos, California

Washington　·　Brussels　·　Tokyo

Copyright and Reprint Permissions: Abstracting is permitted with credit to the source. Libraries may photocopy beyond the limits of US copyright law, for private use of patrons, those articles in this volume that carry a code at the bottom of the first page, provided that the per-copy fee indicated in the code is paid through the Copyright Clearance Center, 222 Rosewood Drive, Danvers, MA 01923.

Other copying, reprint, or republication requests should be addressed to: IEEE Copyrights Manager, IEEE Service Center, 445 Hoes Lane, P.O. Box 133, Piscataway, NJ 08855-1331.

The papers in this book comprise the proceedings of the meeting mentioned on the cover and title page. They reflect the authors' opinions and, in the interests of timely dissemination, are published as presented and without change. Their inclusion in this publication does not necessarily constitute endorsement by the editors, the IEEE Computer Society, or the Institute of Electrical and Electronics Engineers, Inc.

IEEE Computer Society Order Number PR000428
ISBN 0-7695-0428-0
ISBN 0-7695-0430-2 (microfiche)
Library of Congress number 99-066743

Additional copies may be ordered from:

IEEE Computer Society
Customer Service Center
10662 Los Vaqueros Circle
P.O. Box 3014
Los Alamitos, CA 90720-1314
Tel: + 1-714-821-8380
Fax: + 1-714-821-4641
E-mail: cs.books@computer.org

IEEE Service Center
445 Hoes Lane
P.O. Box 1331
Piscataway, NJ 08855-1331
Tel: + 1-732-981-0060
Fax: + 1-732-981-9667
mis.custserv@computer.org

IEEE Computer Society
Asia/Pacific Office
Watanabe Building,
1-4-2 Minami-Aoyama
Minato-ku, Tokyo 107-0062 JAPAN
Tel: + 81-3-3408-3118
Fax: + 81-3-3408-3553
tokyo.ofc@computer.org

Editorial production by Anne Rawlinson

Cover illustration by Jack L. Moffett

Cover art production by Joseph Daigle/Studio Productions

Printed in the United States of America by Technical Communication Services

Table of Contents

Invited Speakers

Paper Sessions

Session 1: Context-Awareness

Session 2: Systems and Architectures

Session 3: Personal Applications

Session 4: Gadget Show
Don Marinelli, Master of Ceremonies
Director, Entertainment Technology Center, Carnegie Mellon University

Session 5: Posters, Demos, & Reception

Session 6: Hardware Components

Poster Papers

It's my pleasure to welcome you to the Third International Symposium on Wearable Computers. As we approach the end of 1999, several technological developments seem to be converging in a way that is significantly affecting the market acceptance of wearable computers:

- Fast, low-power microprocessors originally designed for use in laptops are being incorporated into wearable systems as well. The price drop in laptops seems to be causing a price drop in wearables.

- High-resolution color miniature flat panel image sources are available in quantity, and head-mounted display vendors are building a new generation of HMDs around them, that are significantly smaller and lighter than the previous generation.

- While previously only startup companies were committed to producing wearable computers, the large-scale computer manufacturers, notably IBM and Sony, have begun to invest in this area.

Quickly, wearable computers are moving into the 'real world.' Industrial and military customers, who used to perceive wearables as a logical next step but not yet sufficiently developed, now see wearables as something that can help them accomplish tasks more rapidly and cheaply today. I have witnessed wearable computer activity in the Boeing Company go from one R&D project to around six application projects in the space of a year. Wearable computers are in everyday use in Boeing's factory in Palmdale, CA, aiding the assembly of Boeing's two prototype Joint Strike Fighter aircraft. Several more production applications appear soon to follow.

But is this an 'industry-centric' point of view? Our colleagues from the MIT Media Lab might retort that their wearable computers have already been in everyday use for years. This discrepancy in views points out that there have developed two quite different models of the way people will use wearable computers in the future. I call them the Tool Model and the Clothing Model.

The Tool Model assumes a vertical, industrial/military market for wearables, where the archetypal application would be as a hands-free digital manual system for aircraft maintenance. In the Tool Model, the wearable contains one application program, it is worn for a specific job, and removed when the job is finished. The precursor of the wearable computer in this model is the rugged, clunky flat-panel computer used for military aircraft maintenance now.

The Clothing Model assumes that the wearable computers is worn all day long, like clothing, and is in constant operation and widely-varied use during that time, as an assistant or adjunct to many of the user's quotidian activities: conversations, making dinner reservations, answering e-mail, remembering an approaching acquaintance's name. Its precursor is perhaps a mix of the laptop, the cellular phone and the palmtop PDA.

I am not advocating a right or wrong here. The growing user market we all anticipate has room for both models; they can coexist. Thomas Martin's insightful comparison of the development of wristwatches and the development of wearable computers, in this proceedings, legitimises this analogy: cooks, physicians, race car drivers and other occupations use watches and other clocks as tools, in specialised ways, while the rest of us use them as functional 'clothing.'

What is important is for us to examine how the research issues and their priority may differ according to which of these usage models we assume.

- Hands-free operation is more important to the Tool Model than the Clothing Model. It is, in fact, critical. If primarily hands-free operation is not required, users will continue to use laptops or handhelds.

- Consequently, user interface design is important to the Tool Model. The systems will be operated hands-free, using speech input and perhaps gaze tracking, by generally less-computer-oriented users. One is tempted to ask whether a Twiddler and an Emacs window comprise the last word in user interfaces for the Clothing Model as well, but at least for the Tool Model, the case for new approaches to user interface design is indisputable.

- New approaches to hardware design, consisting of new ways to incorporate computers into clothing are of greater interest to the Clothing Model.

- Wearable computer software which takes on an 'agent' role—here broadly defined to mean a computation done independently of the user's requests, and possibly without his/her knowledge, Brad Rhodes's Remembrance Agent being the best-known example, is more important in the Clothing Model. The Tool Model assumes a single application use, which will typically entail a user's explicitly controlling computation or data retrieval.

- Position and orientation tracking are of interest to both models, but assumptions differ about how tracking technology will be used, and what its accuracy and range requirements are.

As we come together for this meeting, we're in a unique time. Our technology is poised to 'take off.' Let's talk and think about whether we're meeting the research requirements of both of these usage models. Both are valid; both types of use will occur. The only debatable issues are how large/how soon for each model. Let's try to examine our conscious and perhaps our unconscious assumptions about future wearable computer usage and ask each other, 'Are we doing the right things?'

We should have a good opportunity to discuss these issues and many others at this meeting. I want to thank all the members of this year's organising committee for all the work they did to bring us this symposium. They did all the work, while I hid out in London all summer. My Boeing colleague Chris Esposito, in particular, did lots of heavy lifting in my absence. I also want to express thanks for the advice and assistance kindly provided by my predecessors, Sandy Pentland and Dan Siewiorek.

Enjoy the symposium, and enjoy San Francisco!

David Mizell

It is our distinct pleasure to welcome you to the Third IEEE Symposium on Wearable Computers. We have put together what we think is an exciting and informative program of papers, panels, posters, demos, invited speakers, and another round of the Gadget Show.

It is an interesting time for the wearable computing community—there are more conferences, more applications, and greater diversity of uses and users than we have seen before. We had submissions from 10 countries this year, and expect to have attendees from as many countries.

We have also seen the continuing popularity and increasing capability of handheld devices as they take their place alongside wearables in the non-desktop computing continuum. One of the papers in this volume explores some the relative strengths and weaknesses of these two platforms.

As hardware capabilities rise and sizes fall, devices are increasingly distinguished by human factors, connectivity, and communications. Addressing some of these latter issues, we have invited the chair of IEEE 802.15 to provide an update on significant developments in personal area networks. Communications and collaboration are also the focus of two of the paper sessions in this year's conference.

An area of particular importance is the panel on usability. Measuring system usability is increasingly accepted as a critical activity in the desktop world, and so it ought to be in the wearable world. Just as wearable systems differ substantially in many ways from their desktop counterparts, the ways in which we gather data on the usability of wearable systems also differs from the techniques for desktop systems. This panel explores some of these differences.

We would like to thank the Program Committee for all of the time they have put in working on this conference, and all of the people that have served as paper reviewers for their help in determining the content of the conference.

Chris Esposito & Jane Siegel
1999 ISWC Technical Program Co-Chairs

Commencing three years ago with a series of workshops followed by two successful symposium and through the quiet, efficient effort of several scores of volunteers, a new technical community has been born. In June 1999, the IEEE Computer Society approved the formation of the Technical Committee on Wearable Information Systems (TC WIS). Let's briefly explore the significance of this action.

The IEEE Computer is one of the largest professional information processing societies with over 90,000 members. Computer Society volunteers are organized into over 30 Technical Committees (TCs) to serve more focused communities. The TC's organize workshops and symposiums (125 technical meetings in 1997), publish conference proceedings (147 in 169 volumes totaling nearly 71,000 pages in 1997), and special issues of archival journals.

The TC WIS is devoted to issues concerning the wearing of information based technology on the human body. The TC is concerned with the characteristics of the technology that will be worn, the applications that are appropriate for use on the body, how people interact with wearable information systems, and the ergonomic impact of wearable systems. The TC recognizes that wearable information systems are inherently interdisciplinary and must be addressed in such a manner.

As an interdisciplinary activity, the TC overlaps to some degree with other TCs (Operating Systems, Computer Communications, Distributed Processing, Multimedia, and Security and Privacy) but this TC will focus on wearable information systems and the impact of this wearable technology on people.

We welcome you to become a member of the TC WIS. The TC website (http://iswc.gatech.edu) contains instructions on how to join the Technical Committee, information on upcoming Symposia and workshops, and on-line copies of Proceedings and videos of talks at past symposia.

Please join the TC WIS business meeting associated with the symposium to help plan the future course of your technical community. Also feel free to contact members of the TC organizing committee:

Chairman — Dan Siewiorek, Carnegie Mellon University
Vice Chairman — Alex Pentland, Massachusetts Institute of Technology
Secretary — Chris Thompson, Georgia Tech Research Institute

Steering Committee — Len Bass, Carnegie Mellon University
Hiroshi Ishii, Massachusetts Institute of Technology
David Mizell, The Boeing Company
Alice Pentland, University of Rochester
Rosalind Picard, Massachusetts Institute of Technology
Zary Segall, University of Oregon
Asim Smailagic, Carnegie Mellon University
Thad Starner, Georgia Institute of Technology

Conference Committee

General Chair
David Mizell, *Boeing*

Program Co-chairs
Chris Esposito, *Boeing*
Jane Siegel, *CMU*

Publicity Co-chairs
Thad Starner, *Georgia Tech*
Chris Thompson, *Georgia Tech*

Finance Chair
Paul Jackson, *Boeing*

Local Arrangements Chair
Vaughan Pratt, *Stanford*

Exhibits Chair
Zary Siegel, *U. Oregon*

Program Committee

Co-Chairs
Chris Esposito , *Boeing*
Jane Siegel, *CMU*

Gaetano Boriello, *U. of Washington*
Hans-Werner Gellersen, *University of Karlsruhe*
Robert (Bob) Ianucci, *Compaq*
Noboru Kamijoh, *IBM Japan*
Gerd Kortuem, *U. of Oregon*
Sandy Pentland, *MIT*
Jean Scholtz, *DARPA*
Dan Siewiorek, *CMU*
Chris Thompson, *Georgia Tech*

Chris Baber
Woodrow Barfield
Joel Bartlett
Len Bass
Sumit Basu
Martin Bauer
Michael Beigl
Mark Billinghurst
Staffan Bjork
Gaetano Borriello
Jerry Bowskill
Ed Chang
Andrew Christian
Brian Clarkson
Per Dahlberg
Richard W. DeVaul
Chris Esposito
Jennifica Falk
Erik Geelhoed
Hans Gellersen
Francine Gemperle
Brian Gollum
Jamey Hicks
Pertti Huuskonen
Elaine Hyder
Bob Iannuci
Paul Jackson
Noboru Kamijoh
Sonny Kirkley
Gerd Kortuem

Peter Ljungstrand
Steve Mann
Thomas L Martin
Tom McKlin
Jack Moffett
Dushyanth Narayanan
Jennifer Ockerman
Randy Pausch
Sandy Pentland
Mark Pollard
Steve Poltrock
Johan Redstrom
Steven J. Schwartz
Jean Scholtz
Bernt Schiele
Albrecht Schmidt
Jay Schneider
Jane Siegel
Dan Sieworek
Thad Starner
Desney Tan
Chris Thompson
Carl A. Waldspurger
Deborah Wallach
Lee Weiss
Christopher R. Wren
Jie Yang

Situated Computing:
Bridging the Gap between Intention and Action

Anatole V. Gershman, Joseph F. McCarthy, Andrew E. Fano
Center for Strategic Technology Research (CSTaR)
Andersen Consulting
3773 Willow Road
Northbrook, IL 60062 USA
{anatole.v.gershman, joseph.f.mccarthy, andrew.e.fano}@ac.com

Abstract

Situated computing represents a new class of computing applications that bridges the gap between people's intentions and the actions they can take to achieve those intentions. These applications are contextually embedded in real-world situations, and are enabled by the proliferation of new kinds of computing devices, expanding communication capabilities and new kinds of digital content. Three types of discontinuities give rise to intention/action gaps and provide opportunities for situated computing applications: physical discontinuities, information discontinuities and awareness discontinuities. Several examples of applications that overcome these discontinuities are presented.

1. Introduction

Most people are aware of the increasing pace, and impact, of technological innovations. We believe that three converging trends – the three C's, if you will – are fueling these innovations: (1) *Computing* and sensory devices are becoming cheaper and smaller. (2) *Connectivity* is becoming more widespread, less expensive and multi-modal: from broadband to wireless. (3) Digital *content* and services are becoming more ubiquitous and abundant. Taken together, these trends open the possibility for very different applications of computing – applications embedded into our physical environment and the everyday things we use. These *situated computing* applications will know who we are, where we are, what we are doing, what we want, and how we can take advantage of the resources available in our physical environment. This knowledge will make the new applications vastly more effective in helping us with our tasks both at home and at work.

Other researchers have talked about situated computing [Hull, *et al.*, 1997], but their primary focus was on an architecture to support situated computing applications. Our aim here is to focus primarily on the applications of situated computing, and to provide a conceptual framework that describes how and why these applications are potentially so useful.

We argue that one of the primary impacts of these situated computing applications will be to bridge the gap between our *intentions* – the needs and wants we seek to satisfy – and the *actions* we can take to achieve them. We propose three types of discontinuity that give rise to this intention/action gap – physical, informational and awareness – and describe several prototypes we have built to overcome these types of discontinuity at Andersen Consulting's Center for Strategic Technology Research (CSTaR).

2. The gap between intention and action

At any given time, each of us has a multitude of intentions, both conscious and unconscious, to which we assign varying levels of both importance and relevance to our current context. There often exists a gap between any given intention and our ability to take action to achieve it. These gaps arise for a number of reasons: we may not be in a place where we can take relevant (and effective) action, we may not have the right information with which to direct our action, and/or we may not be aware that an opportunity to take action lies just beyond our immediate focus of attention. Each of these factors is based on a type of discontinuity: physical, informational and awareness. We illustrate each of these types of discontinuity in a separate scenario below.

We are all familiar with some version of the following situation: we are in a store evaluating how well some product would "fit" with our existing possessions. For example, we may be in a furniture store admiring a couch; we think it will match our living room nicely, but we are not sure. Our living room is in one physical location while the couch is in another. We can't be sure about the match unless we see the couch in the living room. This physical discontinuity creates a gap between our intention to improve our living room and our action to achieve it - to buy a couch in this example. If we could overcome this discontinuity, if we could bring the necessary aspects of

3

these two locations together, we would create what business people call a *moment of value*, a window of opportunity within which we can act to satisfy our intentions. This example is not a peculiar case. These physical discontinuities occur whenever we need to decide whether to introduce or remove an object in a physical setting, or alter a physical setting in some way. Such decisions will be based on our capacity to effectively anticipate the resulting state and evaluate its appropriateness. Applications designed to overcome physical discontinuities constitute the first type of situated computing applications that we will discuss.

Another familiar station is seeing (or hearing) a product – an article of clothing, a book or CD – and wanting to buy that product … for the best price, of course. We might be at a friend's house listening to a CD or hearing about their favorite book, and want to get a copy for ourselves, but have to wait until the next time we're at a book or CD store to act on that intention. Or we might even be in a physical book or CD store and wonder if a better price might be found at one of their on-line competitors. In both cases, we know what we want, but we don't have ready access to the information that would help us satisfy our intention. This lack of information where we need it most again creates a gap between our intention and action. In many instances we will not be able to assess the quality of the opportunity without this information. Applications designed to overcome such information discontinuities constitute the second type of situated computing applications.

Finally, the third type of discontinuity that gives rise to an intention/action gap is based on a lack of awareness. For example, we may be walking through a mall, headed for a store to buy a sweater. While doing so we walk right past a store that sells those water filter replacements we've been meaning to get. In this instance we are missing an opportunity to address a longstanding, though not terribly urgent, goal simply because we are not aware the opportunity exists. A key aspect of our planning abilities as humans is to seek and seize opportunities to achieve or further our goals. However due to our various limitations and the constraints imposed by a situation, we will often simply fail to notice and become aware of opportunities that are readily available. Therefore the third class of applications we introduce are those that help address these awareness discontinuities by identifying and highlighting opportunities to address various goals.

3. Overcoming physical discontinuities

In our work we have explored two distinct and complementary approaches to the problem of physical discontinuities. The first approach is embodied in the MAGIC HOME application, which illustrates the furniture shopping example introduced earlier. MAGIC HOME was designed to bring both physical locations – the store and the home – into a common virtual space. In MAGIC HOME, the layout, furniture and other objects in a particular living room are all represented digitally and stored on a smart card, which a furniture shopper brings with him or her to the furniture store. At the store, a wireless bar code scanner is used to select a couch the shopper is interested in. The store has a digital representation of all its merchandise, each identified by bar code, and can merge the digital representation of the shopper's living room with the digital representation of the selected couch. A flat-panel display can be used to depict how the couch would look in the living room, allowing the shopper to rearrange the virtual furniture and even check to see whether the selected couch would fit through the doorways. Figure 1 shows a screen shot from the MAGIC COUCH application.

Figure 1. Magic Home

The capability to merge the content of two physical locations in one virtual location – a virtual house, in this case – has a great deal of potential for creating moments of value. Unfortunately, there are some obstacles to its widespread deployment in today's world. One obstacle is the availability of digital representations of our houses and goods. However, most new houses and manufactured goods are designed on computers, so their 3D renderings are already created during the natural course of the design process, and older homes and artifacts can rely on a rendering technique based on photographing an object from several angles. Thus, in the future, we anticipate greater availability of these models. Even if we can overcome the first obstacle, we are still faced with the problem of updating the position of every piece of furniture every time it is moved. One solution to this problem would be to insert small positioning and orientation sensors into every piece of furniture.

We are exploring solutions to the problem of creating and maintaining digital representations of one's possessions in another project, MAGIC WARDROBE, currently under development at CSTaR. In this application, articles of clothing have embedded smart tags, e.g. in the button of a jacket. When you purchase a new jacket and put it into your wardrobe, the wardrobe immediately recognizes that event and asks if you want to register your purchase with the manufacturer. In exchange, the manufacturer will provide you with a 3D rendering of your new jacket. Now the manufacturer has established a direct relationship with you and you have an updated virtual wardrobe. Next time you go to a different store and want to buy a tie, you can call up your virtual wardrobe to the store's screen and see if the tie goes together with your jacket. Currently, such solutions are prohibitively expensive; however, these sensors are becoming increasingly affordable. Such technological solutions to the physical discontinuity problem will provide a key differentiator for those retailers who are willing to invest in new technologies.

We believe the opportunities afforded by a virtual house justify what are, in the long term, relatively inexpensive investments and surmountable obstacles. Such a virtual house has the advantage of being accessible from anywhere it is needed. Moreover, note that the virtual model does not have to be complete or perfectly consistent to be useful. We don't need to represent the location and orientation of every ash tray in the house to see if a couch would match nicely. And we would probably rather access a representation of our house after it has been cleaned and ordered, rather than a faithful representation of its more likely sorry current state.

MAGIC HOME and MAGIC WARDROBE represent one approach to solving the problem of physical continuity, by merging virtual models of objects from two locations in the physical world. Another approach to this problem is illustrated by one of our augmented reality applications [Dempski, 1999]. IN-HOME SHOWROOM superimposes a virtual model of a selected product over the shopper's view of their physical home using a head-mounted display (HMD). IN-HOME SHOWROOM projects a 3D rendering of the couch I saw in the store or in an on-line catalogue. I can fix the imaginary position of that couch in my room and then walk around it. Using position and orientation sensors built into my HMD, my computer re-renders the couch to provide the correct perspective as I move around the room.

An obvious advantage of this augmented reality approach is that it eliminates the need to render the environment into which the new object is placed. On the other hand, it is hard to "subtract" anything from reality. For example, it is difficult to virtually remove the old couch from my living room before "augmenting" it with the new couch.

We believe that these two approaches for overcoming physical discontinuity have complementary strengths and challenges. The "virtual house" approach is predicated on our ability to automatically synchronize the states of the physical and the virtual worlds. The "augmented reality" approach is predicated on our ability to track our own position and orientation in the physical world.

4. Overcoming information discontinuity

Physical discontinuity involves the problem of merging representations of two or more objects or locations in the physical world. However, another type of discontinuity – information discontinuity – is based on the inaccessibility of information in the digital world in physical contexts where that information would be useful.

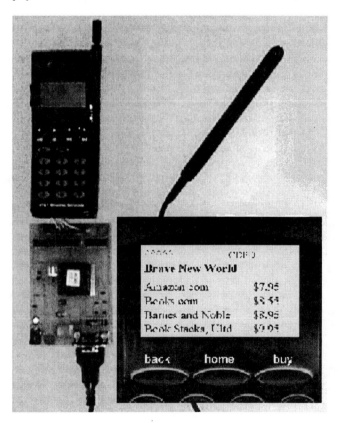

Figure 2. Pocket Bargain Finder

To help the book buyer introduced in Section 2, we developed a device called POCKET BARGAINFINDER [Brody & Gottsman, 1999], which is essentially a portable instantiation of the web-based comparison shopper we pioneered with BARGAINFINDER [Krulwich, 1996], which ran on a desktop machine. POCKET BARGAINFINDER, depicted in Figure 2, is a digital cellular phone with a barcode scanner. You scan the barcode on the back of the book, the device transmits it to a server which checks the prices in several on-line stores and sends them back to you to be displayed on your phone's screen. Technically, it is a fairly simple system, but it sent shock waves through the merchant community [ABC]. It combines the simplest form of physical object tagging (the barcode on the back of the book), a simple sensor (the barcode scanner), the most common wearable computing device (the cellular phone), and the World Wide Web, to connect the physical object and the online information about it. You can use POCKET BARGAINFINDER to buy a book from an on-line bookstore, effectively making the device into a situated cash register for the on-line store. This capability brought together the intention to buy the book at a good price and the action of buying, creating a moment of value.

We can easily imagine many extensions of the same basic idea. When faced with information discontinuity about physical objects, place some remotely readable tags on these objects. Have a wearable or portable device capable of recognizing the tags. Have information about the object relevant to the current context sent to the device and provide the capability to act on this information through the device. Here are some other examples of this idea that we are exploring.

Imagine that you are wearing a jacket with a button containing a "smart tag" discussed in Section 3. If I like your jacket, I can pull out my "smart phone", read the tag and ask my clothier to find me something similar. In this way, the whole world can become a giant showroom.

Or imagine a worker looking at a compressor in the guts of an oil refinery. The sensor in his hardhat recognizes what he is looking at and puts the maintenance records of the compressor and the correct maintenance procedures on a heads-up display.

The second type of a situation where we experience an information discontinuity is familiar to anyone who travels. You are on your way to an out-of-town meeting. You get off the airplane and immediately call your office. Is the meeting still on? Is it at the same time and same place as originally scheduled? Is there any news relevant to the meeting topic? What is the name of the limousine company that you usually use in this city? In other words, you are engaged in a specific task (preparing for the meeting) that requires a variety of types of information. You are mobile but the information you need is in your office, in the head of a colleague, or in some other location different from where you are. A common solution to this problem today is to make a lot of phone calls and check your e-mail all the time, but this is far from optimal.

Our approach to this problem is based on the way that some well-organized high-level executives maintain awareness of relevant information. The process involves two assistants. One assistant is in the home office collecting and filtering the information the executive might need in his or her current tasks. The potentially

relevant information is communicated to the second assistant who is observing the local context and deciding when it is appropriate to communicate this information to the executive. This is a highly effective system, but prohibitively expensive for many executives.

Our goal was to provide a similar functionality automatically by using a combination of an intelligent agent running on the home server (MUNIN) and a personal digital assistant with a wireless communication capability (the AWARENESS MACHINE). The AWARENESS MACHINE is implemented on a Windows CE handheld computer with a built-in wireless modem. It is responsible for communicating the location of the user and other local changes in the user's schedule back to MUNIN. On the home server, MUNIN continuously collects several kinds of information and messages relevant to all the user's interests and tasks, but sends to the AWARENESS MACHINE only the information and messages that are deemed relevant to the current context of the user. It figures out the context based on the user's schedule, time of the day and the location of the user. You could pull the machine out of your pocket, turn it on and immediately see the most important things you needed to know at that moment. Unfortunately, the current generation of hardware makes continuous use of the machine impractical. The communication link turned out to be slow, unreliable and drained the battery too quickly. Ideally, the information should have been trickling in while the machine was not in use, but the current generation of pocket-size machines is not designed to do this. However, in limited contexts, the AWARENESS MACHINE worked well, providing the right information at the right time and in the right place, bridging the gap between our intentions and the actions we can take.

The AWARENESS MACHINE is an application developed as part of our Active Knowledge Management project, in which we are exploring various mechanisms for actively providing the right information at the right time and place. We have experimented with information delivery vehicles other than a pocket-size wireless PDA. One such alternate delivery vehicle, MAGIC WALL, is a large plasma display installed in a high-traffic public place in our Palo Alto office. Your presence near the display is detected by an RF sensor that can read your ID badge within several feet of the display. MUNIN recognizes your presence near a public display and selects the messages appropriate to that context. For example, in the morning when you pass the display on the way to your office, it reminds you of your next appointment. In the evening, when you are on your way out, it displays the traffic report along your usual route home.

Another application that seeks to overcome the information discontinuity problem is the MAGIC MEDICINE CABINET [Wan, 1999], a situated portal to online health information embedded in a medicine cabinet. One door of the cabinet contains a traditional mirror, the other door houses a flat screen that displays a personalized selection of health care information. The MAGIC MEDICINE CABINET also has a camera (for face recognition capabilities), a microphone and speakers (for speech-based interaction), a computer with an internet connection, and a variety of devices related to health maintenance. This on-line medicine cabinet also knows something about your health. For example, if you have allergies, it monitors on-line resources that measure the local pollen count and warns you to take your medicine. If you suffer from hypertension, the cabinet reminds you to take a blood pressure reading and automatically communicates the results to the doctor's office. Through the use of sensors and smart labels on pill containers, the cabinet also knows what medicines are inside and which one has been taken out, warning you if you pick up the wrong one. It can establish real-time connections to your doctor, pharmacist and other providers of health care related services when the situation calls for it.

A working prototype of the MAGIC MEDICINE CABINET is depicted in Figure 3. As with many of our applications, the technologies employed in the prototype are still a bit too expensive for widespread deployment, but the price-performance curves in the computing and communications industries will bring the costs within the mass-market range in the next few years.

Figure 3. Magic Medicine Cabinet

5. Overcoming awareness discontinuity

The first two types of discontinuity discussed so far assume that we have already identified the specific focus of our intentions, e.g., we know that we want to buy a couch or a book, we need to get to a specific meeting. A third type of discontinuity arises in connection with opportunistic behavior. At any given time, we have many different goals or intentions. While a small number of them may be in the foreground at a particular time – getting home from work, buying a jacket, writing a business proposal, etc., the other goals or intentions persist in the background. Our immediate goal may be getting home from work, but if we see an interesting shoe sale advertised at a store along the way, we may stop and explore this opportunity. We continuously scan our environment, consciously or unconsciously looking for opportunities to satisfy one or more of our intentions. However, if we are not aware of an opportunity, we cannot take advantage of it. In our laboratory, we are exploring several ways in which technology can greatly expand our awareness of the opportunities available in our environments.

SHOPPER'S EYE is an application that addresses the problem of shoppers' lack of awareness of buying opportunities [Fano, 1998]. The system maintains the user's shopping list and preferences on a wireless hand-held computer with a Global Positioning System (GPS) receiver. As the user travels around a shopping mall, the system makes the items on the list available to the local stores, which in turn make bids for the user's business (the latter part was simulated). In essence, SHOPPER'S EYE sends a message to the merchants saying: "There is a customer 75 feet away from your store who wants to buy what you sell. Do you have anything to say to him?" A similar system could be installed in a car, greatly expanding the driver's awareness of the surrounding businesses, such as potentially interesting shoe sales.

While SHOPPER'S EYE focuses on the consumer at the shopping mall, the AQUARIUM application [Bryan & Gershman, 1999] focuses on the consumer at home. The AQUARIUM, depicted in Figure 4, uses a large, flat-panel display to present pictures of your favorite products, animals, places, etc., appearing in the back, floating up to the front and then disappearing. The mix of objects on the screen is constantly changing, governed by the system's perception of your interests. At any time, you can touch an object on the screen and say "more of this," or "less of that." The system will adjust the mix of products based on your preferences. In this way, the AQUARIUM helps consumers "discover" more of their needs and intentions. If you do nothing, the system will gradually sift through its entire database while still showing you mostly the kinds of things you like. If you want to buy something you see, tap on it and say "buy". The AQUARIUM creates an awareness of buying opportunities for products of interest to the user, bringing their intentions to the surface and enabling them to act immediately.

Obviously, the awareness discontinuity is not limited to shopping. Imagine a technician walking through a plant on the way from lunch. The equipment that needs a quick adjustment may be a few feet away, but the technician would not know it. This would be different if the equipment could sense the technician's presence and opportunistically request service while he or she is nearby.

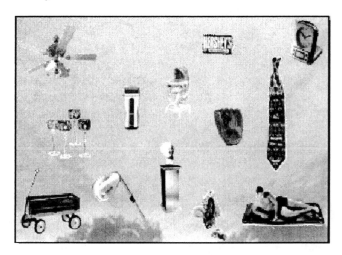

Figure 4. The Aquarium

So far, we discussed the awareness discontinuity related to specific products or. Another important class of awareness discontinuity arises in a corporate environment with respect to knowledge management. In a large global organization it is very difficult to know if someone else has been working on topics related to yours. For example, if you are writing a proposal for an electronic commerce system and mention computer security considerations, your proposal might be greatly enhanced if you could cite the work done at one of your company's other clients or get advice from your company's security guru. For this to happen, you have to be aware that computer security is an important topic and that your company has the relevant experience. In a large organization, it is very difficult to maintain awareness of all the topics for which the company has one or more experts, or all the topics that may be relevant to a proposal. The INFOSCOUT project [Prasad & Anagnost, 1998] addresses this problem.

INFOSCOUT is a proactive recommender agent designed to watch a user performing a particular task and suggest other people and resources that could potentially be of help. For example, as you are writing your proposal and type "computer security," InfoScout automatically identifies this phrase as an important concept, and collects pointers to relevant documents and people. INFOSCOUT

can also be used to read your incoming correspondence, suggesting documents and people related to the concepts mentioned in the messages.

The last type of awareness discontinuity that we will discuss in this paper is related to the awareness of people within the physical environment. I have a good sense of awareness of when my colleagues that are immediately adjacent to my office are available, but have very little awareness of the availability of colleagues just two or three doors away. Although various methods exist for contacting these people in the electronic realm (electronic mail, telephone, voice mail), there exist certain kinds of issues for which face-to-face interaction is necessary. For example, when I want to ask a colleague about how to solve a problem, and I'm not quite sure how to describe the problem, real-time interaction is necessary.

Several research labs are looking at how to support collaboration across remote sites, but we are looking at how we can better support collaboration among physically proximate colleagues. One application we have developed, ACTIVEMAP [McCarthy & Meidel, 1999], shown in Figure 5, superimposes images of coworkers over the locations in which they were last seen (or rather, the locations in which their infrared badges were last detected). The system uses a variety of mechanisms to represent the freshness of the location information, so that users can make inferences about the potential availability of colleagues. The most common use of the application is in a kiosk installed in a hallway in the CSTaR work area, where people can track someone down when they can't find them in their office.

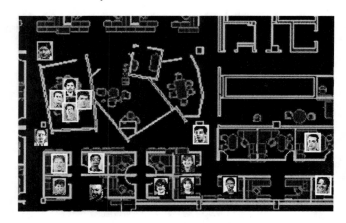

Figure 5. ActiveMap

In addition to its use as an awareness mechanism for physically proximate colleagues, the tool is also proving useful for distributed workers. I can login into the system from an outside location (e.g., home, another office, etc.) and easily see "what's going on" – who is in the office, who is talking to whom, who is attending a meeting, etc. If I want to reach a person, I can send a message to be read through the loudspeaker nearest to that person's current location. I can also set up automatic rules that would be triggered by specific events such as someone returning to his or her office.

Although there are privacy issues involved in this work, as well as most other situated computing applications, people are generally willing to give up some of their privacy for commensurate benefits, as evidenced by the widespread use of credit cards. Thus far, we have managed to provide a level of benefit that is perceived to outweigh the loss of privacy in ACTIVEMAP; however, we readily acknowledge the need to be vigilant about this issue in our efforts to develop other situated computing applications.

6. Conclusion

We believe that Situated Computing represents an important new class of contextually embedded applications – providing computing, connectivity and content in physical situations where they are most needed, i.e., when there exists a gap between a person's intentions and ability to act. We have defined three types of discontinuity – physical discontinuity, information discontinuity and awareness discontinuity – that give rise to such gaps, and highlighted a number of applications that attempt to close these gaps. As this collection of applications demonstrates, situated computing has the potential for defining entirely new "moment of value" opportunities, enabling people to achieve their intentions more frequently and more successfully.

While much attention is currently devoted to businesses that deal exclusively in the virtual domain, the most significant business opportunities in the future lay in the convergence of the virtual and physical worlds, in applications that take full advantage of what each world has to offer. Situated computing applications take this one step further, by tailoring the best of this convergence to the specific contexts in which people have opportunities, currently unrecognized or unavailable, to achieve specific intentions.

As we have shown in this paper, we are engaged in a number of projects that explore what kinds of contexts might provide important applications for situated computing. We will continue to push on in this area, identifying new contexts and new technologies that can be used to fit into and take advantage of these contexts. After all, despite all the advances in the virtual world, we still live in the physical world, and as we enhance situations in the physical world with relevant connections to the virtual world, our experiences will be greatly enriched.

7. References

ABC World News Tonight, November 12, 1998.

Adam B. Brody and Edward J. Gottsman. 1999. Pocket BargainFinder: A Handheld Device for Augmented Commerce. To appear in *Proceedings of the International Symposium on Handheld and Ubiquitous Computing (HUC '99)*. Karlsruhe, Germany.

Doug Bryan and Anatole Gershman. 1999. Opportunistic Exploration of Large Consumer Product Spaces. To appear in *Proceedings of the ACM Conference on Electronic Commerce (EC '99)*.

Kelly L. Dempski. 1999. Augmented Workspace: The World as Your Desktop. To appear in *Proceedings of the International Symposium on Handheld and Ubiquitous Computing (HUC '99)*. Karlsruhe, Germany.

Andrew Fano. 1998. Shopper's Eye: Using Location-based Filtering for a Shopping Agent in the Physical World. *Proceedings of the Second International Conference on Autonomous Agents (Agents '98)*, Minneapolis, MN. pp. 416-421.

Richard Hull, Philip Neaves and James Bedford-Roberts. 1997. Towards Situated Computing. In *Proceedings of the First International Symposium on Wearable Computing (ISWC '97)*. Cambridge, MA.

Bruce Krulwich. 1996. The BargainFinder Agent: Comparison Price Shopping on the Internet. In *Bots and Other Internet Beasties*. J. Williams (ed). SAMS.NET.

Joseph F. McCarthy and Eric S. Meidel. 1999. ActiveMap: A Visualization Tool for Location Awareness to Support Informal Interactions. To appear in *Proceedings of the International Symposium on Handheld and Ubiquitous Computing (HUC '99)*. Karlsruhe, Germany.

M. V. Nagendra Prasad and Theodore Anagnost. 1998. InfoScout: An Active Recommender Agent. In *Proceedings of the AAAI-98 Workshop on Recommender Agents*, Madison, Wisconsin.

Dadong Wan. 1999. Magic Medicine Cabinet: A Situated Portal for Healthcare. To appear in *Proceedings of International Symposium on Handheld and Ubiquitous Computing (HUC'99)*. Karlsruhe, Germany.

Solutions for the Last 10 Meters:
An Overview of IEEE 802.15 Working Group on WPANs

Robert F. Heile
GTE Technology Organization
bheile@bbn.com

Abstract

Wireless personal area networks will proliferate in the next millennium. In response, the IEEE 802.15 Working Group for Wireless Personal Area Networks (WPAN's) was formed to develop standards for these short range wireless networks. The group is closely following the emerging industry specifications, viz. Bluetooth and HomeRF, and realizes that it is important to build on the work of these groups as they enjoy significant market interest and industry participation.

This talk describes why WPANs are important, the history of the group and the standards process, the known candidate radio transmission technologies that the Working Group, via peer review and formal balloting, will choose from for their first draft standard, and a discussion of the issues of coexistence and interoperability.

One of the primary motivations for this Working Group is to ensure the best use of a shared medium.

We believe that the IEEE 802 Committee provides the best forum for consensus open standards and that this process will provide for a rock solid, market accepted WPAN technology.

Bob is a 20 year veteran in the field of data communications and wireless data. He is the chair of 802.15, the IEEE working group on Wireless PANs, and is a part of the GTE Technology Organization, which acquired BBN in mid 1997. Bob joined BBN in early 1997 as Vice President, Engineering and Manufacturing for Internetwork Technologies with the mission of commercializing wireless ad hoc networking and wireless personal area networking technologies. From 1990 to 1996, he served as Vice President of Engineering and Business Development for TyLink Corp, a bootstrap start up specializing in high speed digital access products and network and circuit management software, and was a co-founder of Windata, Inc., a developer and manufacturer of wireless local area networking equipment. From 1980-1990, Bob was with Codex Corporation, a subsidiary of Motorola, Inc. where he was Vice President/General Manager, Transmission Products, the company's largest and most profitable business unit. Bob holds a Bachelor of Arts degree from Oberlin College, and Master of Arts and Doctorate degrees in Physics from The John Hopkins University.

Wearable Computing: An Overview of Progress

Ellison (Dick) C. Urban
Deputy Director
Microsystems Technology Office (MTO)
Defense Advanced Research Projects Agency (DARPA)
3701 North Fairfax Drive
Arlington, Virginia 22203-1714
(703) 696-2251 (phone)
(703) 696-2206 (fax)
email:eurban@darpa.mil

Mr. Ellison (Dick) C. Urban manages the Smart Modules and Distributed Robotics programs in DARPA's Microsystems Technology Office.

From 1972 to 1981, Mr. Urban was a design engineer and Branch Head in the Microelectronics Division at the Naval Ocean Systems Center (now NRad). He later became Deputy Director of the Navy manufacturing Technology Program at the Naval Air Systems Command. Mr. Urban served as the Deputy for Electronics and Physical Sciences in the Office of the Assistant Secretary of the Navy (Research, Engineering, and Systems). Prior to joining DARPA, he was Chief of the VHSIC and Electron Devices Division (DTAO) in the Office of the Director of Defense Research and Engineering.

Mr. Urban received a B.S. in Electrical Engineering from San Diego State University in 1972, and an M.B.A. from National University in 1974.

Virtual Information Towers - A Metaphor for Intuitive, Location-Aware Information Access in a Mobile Environment

Alexander Leonhardi, Uwe Kubach, Kurt Rothermel, Andreas Fritz

University of Stuttgart
Institute of Parallel and Distributed
High-Performance Systems (IPVR)
Breitwiesenstr. 20-22
70565 Stuttgart, Germany
Phone +49 711 7816-236
Fax +49 711 7816-424

E-mail: Alexander.Leonhardi@informatik.uni-stuttgart.de

Abstract

This paper introduces Virtual Information Towers (VITs) as a concept for presenting and accessing location-aware information with mobile clients. A VIT is a means of structuring location-aware information, which is assigned to a certain geographical position while having a certain area of visibility. A user equipped with a mobile, wearable computer has access to the VITs which are "visible" from his/her current location. The architecture and protocols of a system are described, which allows its users to create VITs and to access the information on them using Internet mechanisms. We have implemented a prototype of this system and a VIT client for a wearable computer and will present some aspects of this implementation.

1 Introduction

Mobile information access is an important field of application for wearable computers. In a mobile environment much of the accessed information is location-dependent, i.e. the content of the information or the user's interest in the information depends on the user's current location. For example, if a tourist is looking for a restaurant, he will be more interested in restaurants that are close to him than in restaurants that are at the other end of the city, he/she is visiting. Recently, so-called location-aware applications have been developed, which take into account the user's geographical position when answering information requests [5]. In order

to determine the user's geographical position GPS-based or IR-based [10] positioning sensors are used.

In this paper, we present Virtual Information Towers (VITs) as a metaphor for making location-aware information access more intuitive to the user. In [8] an electronic equivalent to Post-It notes has been suggested. However, this approach is limited to attaching textual information to certain locations. VITs are more flexible as they support different content types and visibility ranges together with hierarchical document structures. As the area of visibility of a VIT should approximately describe the geographical region the information attached to it is associated to, only relevant VITs are presented to a user according to his/her position.

The remainder of this paper is structured as follows: in Section 2 we present the basic concept of the VITs. Section 3 describes the main components of a VIT system for the Internet and their interfaces. Some details of the implementation of a first prototype of this system and of a client application for a wearable computer are described in Section 4. In Section 5 we reflect the related work. Finally, we conclude our paper in Section 6 with an outlook to future work.

2 The Concept of Virtual Information Towers

VITs have been created as a rough electronic equivalent to real-world advertising columns. Therefore, each VIT is positioned at a fixed geographical location and has a certain "height". The height of a VIT determines the range within the VIT is visible. The higher a VIT is, the bigger is its visibility range. When a user enters the visibility range of a VIT, the VIT will appear on his/her display and he/she can access the information provided by the VIT. Additionally, the items of information attached to the VIT can have their own area of visibility inside the area of the VIT. Their visibility can further be restricted to users approaching from a certain direction (see Figure 1), e.g. to create a sign that points at a certain building.

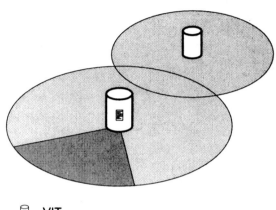

🛢 VIT

◯ visibility range of the VIT

◔ restricted visibility range

Figure 1. Visibility range and restricted visibility range of a VIT

In contrast to virtual Post-It notes [8], VITs have a more permanent character as the users will remember a certain VIT even if its information changes. The purpose of virtual Post-Its is mainly limited to annotate real world objects or places with simple textual notes. A VIT, however, is a more complex object, which may host a complete hierarchy of information objects, so called posters. Posters can be of different types, e.g. audio, video, or image posters. They can also be used to provide access to existing services and information systems, e.g. the World-Wide Web. A poster can even include program code, which allows to develop special VIT services such as a ticket office. It is also possible for the users to annotate information on a VIT or a certain poster, if the access rights of the VIT permit that. This allows the users to make annotations as with virtual Post-Its.

Due to the flexibility achieved by supporting different types of posters, VITs can be used for many different applications. For example, a mobile tourist guide system can be based on VITs. At every place of interest, e.g. a historic building, a VIT provides information about this sight. If the VITs are arranged as a guided tour, each VIT gives the directions to the next sight. For a public transportation system VITs at bus, train or subway stations can display the corresponding timetables. The presented timetables can be modified according to the station and the current time. A VIT in front of a cinema or theater can be used to buy tickets and make reservations.

As most VITs will have a certain purpose, e.g. provide information about transportation or a historic sight, the contents on a VIT are summarized by a profile. A simple form of such a profile would be a list of keywords. The profile can be used to search for VITs that contain information about a certain topic or to filter the VITs presented to the user by automatically matching it to the his/her profile.

3 A System for VITs in the Internet

In this section a distributed system is described, which permits its users to create and to access VITs in the Internet. A prototype for this system [2] has been developed as part of the initial work for the project Nexus [7].

The main components of the VIT System are shown in Figure 2. A user accesses the system via a VIT Client mainly from a mobile computer, where his current position is determined through a GPS sensor. The client, which is based on a Web browser, allows its user to view the contents of a VIT and in some cases to attach his/her own posters. A global VIT Directory is used to find the appropriate VITs, e.g. all VITs within 50m, and the VIT Managers to get the contents of a certain VIT. In the remainder of this section, the data structure describing a VIT and the interfaces of the VIT Directory and the VIT Manager are described.

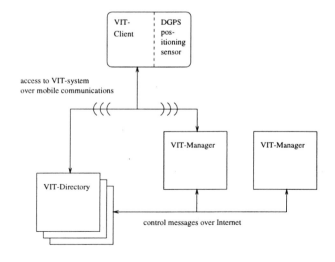

Figure 2. Components of the VIT architecture

16

3.1 Location Model

To define the geographical position and area of visibility for the VITs we use a simple location model based on coordinates of the geographical coordinate system WGS84 [1] that is used by GPS. The data-type *location* consists of one such coordinate and represents a certain geographical position. A geographical region is described by the data-type *area* which is either a circle defined by its center and radius or a polygon, which is specified by the coordinates of its corners. The location model also defines a set of predicates that e.g. test a position for inclusion in an area, test for overlapping areas or calculate the distance between two positions. For a detailed description of such predicates see [4].

3.2 Attributes of a VIT

This subsection shows the main attributes of the VITs which are stored in an XML data structure on a VIT Manager (see below). The information that is attached to this VIT is organized in a hierarchy of folders and items. Folders are used to group related information, e.g. to realize a blackboard to which users can attach their own information items as a message for other users. All items are URLs pointing to (multi-media) documents, which are either in the WWW or are stored on the VIT itself, like the notes of the blackboard.

The VIT itself has the following set of attributes:

- Each VIT is identified by a **name**, which is unique in the context of its VIT Manager. Globally unique names can be created similar to a URL by concatenating the local name of the VIT with the name of the server (e.g. vit://cembalo.informatik.uni-stuttgart.de/CS-Index).

- A VIT contains information related to a certain geographical region, which is defined by its **area of visibility**. Normally, a VIT is only visible for a user when he is inside this area. Additionally, an exact geographical position of the VIT can be specified for visualization.

- To specify which users or groups of users are allowed to access the information of a VIT, its **owner** and **access rights** can be set by the corresponding attributes. These settings become the default settings for the folders and items on this VIT.

- The attributes **time of last modification** and **time of expiration** give the last time the VIT has been modified at and if available how long the information of this VIT is expected to be valid. These attributes are used by the clients to determine how long this data structure can be cached.

- Finally, a **main folder** contains the content of the VIT starting at the top-level folder.

The folders and items on a VIT have their own set of attributes, which are similar to those of a VIT. They can have their own access rights and owner, as the blackboard e.g. should be permitted to be written by everybody, whereas the other information of the VIT can only be modified by its owner. Items and folders can also have their own location and area of visibility inside the area of a VIT. This visibility can be further restricted to a certain direction given by a segment of the compass. This is e.g. useful when creating a virtual signpost with signs pointing in the correct direction from all sides of the VIT. Important items of information can also be marked as active and are presented to the user as soon as he comes near to it.

Figure 3 shows an example of the configuration for a VIT, which can be placed in front of the building of the Faculty of Computer Science at the University of Stuttgart.

3.3 Interfaces

The following subsection describes the VIT-System in more detail by explaining the network interfaces of the basic components.

Each **VIT Manager** stores and manages a number of VITs. Like a Web Server, the VIT Managers are intended as organizational units, which are managed by a single administrator. As mentioned above, each VIT on a VIT Manager is identified through its locally unique name. VIT Clients use the following protocol for accessing the items of information attached to a VIT:

- **getvititem**: vitname, itemname, userid, location → (item/nak)
  Get the contents of the item with the given name and VIT if it is visible from this location (see above). The name of the item consists of a hierarchical path including the name of its folders. Through the userid the VIT Manager determines if the user has the right to access this item, otherwise or if the item does not exist a negative acknowledgment (nak) is sent.

- **putvititem**: vitname, itemname, item, userid → (ack/nak)
  Attaches an item to the VIT. The item is included in the folder, which is specified as the path in the itemname. The contents of the item to attach are contained in this message. An ack-reply is sent if the request was successful, otherwise a nak-reply.

- **removevititem**: vitname, itemname, userid → (ack/nak)

```
<VIT>
  <NAME>CS-Index</NAME>
    <AREA>
      <LOCATION type="WGS84">
        48.72100N, 9.12710E
      </LOCATION>
      <RANGE unit="meters">300.0</RANGE>
    </AREA>
  <DESC>
    Main VIT for the the Faculty of Computer
    Science of the University of Stuttgart.
  </DESC>
  <MODIFIED>10:10 26.04.1999</MODIFIED>
  <EXPIRATION>10:00 27.04.1999</EXPIRATION>
  <OWNER>Alexander Leonhardi</OWNER>
  <ACCESS>
    </READACCESS all="true">
    </WRITEACCESS owner="true">
  </ACCESS>
  <FOLDER>
    <NAME>Index</NAME>
    <ITEM>
      <NAME>Plan of building</NAME>
      <DESC>
        A plan of the building of the
        Faculty of Computer Science of
        the University of Stuttgart.
      </DESC>
      <LINK>
        http://www.informatik.uni-stuttgart.
        de/plaene/gebaeude.html
      </LINK>
    </ITEM>
    ...
  </FOLDER>
</VIT>
```

Figure 3. Example for the XML-code defining a VIT for the building of the Faculty of Computer Science at the University of Stuttgart

Removes an item from a VIT, if the access rights of the user permit that.

- **getvitfolder, putvitfolder, removevitfolder**:
  These messages are similar to the ones above, but are used to get, create and remove a folder.

The **VIT Directory** is a distributed service, comparable to the Domain Name System (DNS), which stores the name, area of visibility, some keywords and the address of the corresponding VIT Manager for all existing VITs. The VIT Directory is structured hierarchically and each server is responsible for the VITs in a well-defined area. Requests are routed to the appropriate server or servers by a mechanism similar to Geographic Routing [6]. The VIT Directory is updated by the VIT Managers, whenever a VIT is created, changed or deleted, by sending the following messages:

- **addvit**: vitname, area of visibility, keywords, expiration date, address of vit manager → (ack/nak)

Creates a new VIT with the given name and area of visibility. The message also specifies the address of the VIT Manager the VIT is stored on, and an expiration date after which the VIT can be deleted if no change message has been received.

- **changevit**: vitname, area of visibility, keywords, expiration date, address of vit manager → (ack/nak)
  This request is similar to addvit and is sent when attributes of a VIT have changed or the expiration date has been reached.

- **removevit**: name, address of vit manager → (ack/nak)
  Removes the VIT with the given name and VIT Manager from the directory.

Clients use the VIT Directory mainly to determine the VITs that are visible at a certain location. Normally, this is the current position of the user. The number of VITs that are returned could be further reduced by specifying a domain, like "public transport" or a maximum size for the area of visibility, if only local VITs are of interest. The VIT Directory can also be used to search for a VIT with some given keywords or to get a map of an area.

- **getvits**: location, cache size, max area of interest → (name, area of visibility, address of vit manager)*
  Returns a list of all VITs whose area of visibility includes the given location. If the parameter cache size is set, a look-ahead is specified. The VIT Directory then returns information about as many of the nearest VITs as fit into the cache of the client (limited by its maximum area of interest), so that it does not need to send this request continuously.

- **searchvits**: location, range, keywords → (name, area of visibility, address of vit manager)*
  Similar to getvits, this message searches for all VITs which match the given keywords.

- **getmap**: area → coordinates, map file
  Returns a graphic file with a section of a map, which best fits the requested area, and the coordinates of its corners.

Usually as an extension or in combination with a WWW browser, the *VIT Clients* are used to access the VIT system and to view and modify their contents. The VIT Client are intended to run on a mobile computer, which communicates with the VIT system over a wireless network and has access to a positioning system like GPS. It can be used on a stationary computer as well, when the position the user is interested in is entered manually or selected on a map. The VIT Client uses the VIT Directory to find the appropriate (i.e. nearest) VITs and notifies its user or other applications of changes. To avoid constant polling, it caches this information by using a look-ahead defined by the size of its VIT cache (see above). The VIT Client also handles the registration of a user at the VIT Managers and allows them to access the information which is stored there.

4 Implementation

Together with the prototype for the VIT system we have implemented a first VIT Client for the Xybernaut MA IV wearable computer. In comparison to the alternatives, a PDA and a Notebook, it has more computing power than the PDA and is much easier to use while walking around than the Notebook. The prototype connects to the Internet either over GSM (9.6 kbit/s) or over a Wireless LAN (802.11, 1-3 Mbit/s). For positioning a Differential GPS system is used that has an accuracy of 2 to 5 meters. We do not use the height information provided by the GPS sensor as it has proved to be comparatively inaccurate differing in a few cases by some hundred meters. Figure 4 shows the user interface of the VIT Client, which is running inside a Web browser.

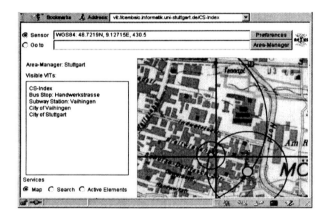

Figure 4. User interface of the VIT client

In the prototype the VIT Directory exists only in a simple form. A single server of the VIT Directory is called an Area Manager and is responsible for all VITs in a certain area. The appropriate Area Manager has to be selected manually in the VIT Client. This makes moving between areas with different Area Managers difficult, as the user has to know their addresses. Also, if the areas of two Area Managers overlap, only one of them can be used at a certain time. Because many location-aware applications with distributed components require something similar to the VIT Directory, we plan to develop a general, distributed, hierarchical Area Service Directory, which efficiently maps location-related services to certain areas. The VIT Directory will eventually be integrated into this more general directory.

5 Related Work

In the past few years a number of location-aware information systems have been developed, e.g. [5], [9]. However, most of these systems do not use any metaphors in order to support the user with this new kind of information access. An exception is the Stick-e notes project at the university of Kent [8]. The aim of this project is to realize the electronic equivalent to Post-It notes. A user can make notes at an arbitrary geographical position. The notes are stored together with the position information and can be displayed if the same position is re-encountered later. Our metaphor is more focused on providing access to existing information than managing user entered information.

The idea of integrating virtual objects in a real world environment is not new and can be found in many Augmented Reality systems. An application example is a system that allows a worker to "see" power lines and water pipes, which run in the walls of a building. However, the information access in such systems is usually especially designed for a certain application and does not provide a generic metaphor for different kinds of information.

6 Conclusion and Future Work

In this paper, we have presented the idea of Virtual Information Towers (VITs) as a metaphor for publishing and accessing information that is related to geographical locations or areas. We have shown some possible applications for VITs and have described a system that integrates VITs into the Internet. A simple VIT Client has been developed for a wearable computer, which has proven a suitable device for viewing and interacting with VITs. We have implemented a prototype of the VIT system which will be further improved and enhanced.

VITs are only one possible metaphor for attaching information to geographical positions or physical (here stationary) objects. Depending on the application, they have their strengths, e.g. the integration of existing information, and weaknesses, e.g. information can not directly be attached to certain objects of the real world. The VIT system uses a relatively simple model of the real world which only consists of VITs, i.e. virtual objects which have no corresponding objects in the real world. To attach information items directly to a (mobile) object a more detailed model, that includes real world objects, is needed. With the Nexus project [3] we have started to develop a platform which offers a generic support for location-aware applications. The Nexus-platform will maintain a distributed augmented model of the world containing real as well as virtual and mobile as well as stationary objects. All available information about the state of the real world, e.g. about the position of mobile objects, will be used to update the model.

The platform will also support different types of virtual objects, which can be created and modified by users and applications. Besides VITs this could be Virtual Post-Its notes for example, which can be attached to any object. A VIT system can then be implemented based on the Nexus platform. All functionality that is related to location-awareness, like finding the nearest VITs and providing maps, that is currently done by the VIT Directory will then be performed by this platform.

References

[1] DoD World Geodetic System 1984, its definition and relationship with local geodetic systems. Technical Report 8350.2, Third Edition, National Imagery and Mapping Agency, 1997.

[2] A. Fritz. Positionsabhängiger Zugriff auf WWW-Inhalte. Master's thesis, University of Stuttgart, 1999. (in german).

[3] F. Hohl, U. Kubach, A. Leonhardi, M. Schwehm, and K. Rothermel. Nexus - an open global infrastructure for spatial-aware applications. In *Proceedings of The Fifth Annual International Conference on Mobile Computing and Networking (MobiCom '99)*, Seattle, WA, USA, 1999. ACM Press.

[4] U. Leonhardt. *Supporting Location-Awareness in Open Distributed Systems*. PhD thesis, Imperial College of Science, Technology and Medicine, University of London, 1998.

[5] S. Long, R. Kooper, G. Abowd, and C. Atkeson. Rapid prototyping of mobile context-aware applications: The cyberguide case study. In *Proceedings of The Second Annual International Conference on Mobile Computing and Networking (MobiCom '96)*, pages 97–107, Rye, NY, USA, 1996. ACM Press.

[6] J. Navas and T. Imielinski. Geocast - geographic addressing and routing. In *Proceedings of the Third Annual International Conference on Mobile Computing and Networking (MobiCom '97)*, pages 66–76, Budapest, Hungary, 1997. ACM Press.

[7] Nexus. Nexus project pages. University of Stuttgart, http://www.informatik.uni-stuttgart.de/ipvr/vs/projekte/nexus.html, 1999.

[8] J. Pascoe. The stick-e note architecture: Extending the interface beyond the user. In *Proceedings of the International Conference on Intelligent User Interfaces*, pages 261–264, 1997.

[9] B. Schilit, N. Adams, and R. Want. Context-aware computing applications. In *Proceedings of the First IEEE Workshop on Mobile Computing Systems and Applications*, pages 85–90. IEEE Press, 1994.

[10] R. Want, A. Hopper, V. Falcao, and J. Gibbons. The active badge location system. *ACM Transactions on Information Systems*, 10(1):91–102, 1992.

The Conference Assistant: Combining Context-Awareness with Wearable Computing

Anind K. Dey, Daniel Salber, Gregory D. Abowd
GVU Center, College of Computing
Georgia Institute of Technology
Atlanta, GA 30332-0280
+1 404 894 7512
{anind, salber, abowd}@cc.gatech.edu

Masayasu Futakawa
Hitachi Research Laboratory
7-1-1 Omika-cho
Hitachi-shi, Ibaraki-ken, 319-1221, Japan
81-294-52-5111
futakawa@hrl.hitachi.co.jp

http://www.cc.gatech.edu/fce/contexttoolkit

Abstract

We describe the Conference Assistant, a prototype mobile, context-aware application that assists conference attendees. We discuss the strong relationship between context-awareness and wearable computing and apply this relationship in the Conference Assistant. The application uses a wide variety of context and enhances user interactions with both the environment and other users. We describe how the application is used and the context-aware architecture on which it is based.

1. Introduction

In human-human interaction, a great deal of information is conveyed without explicit communication, but rather by using cues. These shared cues, or *context*, help to facilitate grounding between participants in an interaction [3]. We define context to be any information that can be used to characterize the situation of an entity, where an entity can be a person, place, or physical or computational object.

In human–computer interaction, there is very little shared context between the human and the computer. Context in human-computer interaction includes any relevant information about the entities in the interaction between the user and computer, including the user and computer themselves. By improving computers' access to context, we increase the richness of communication in human-computer interaction and make it possible to produce more useful computational services. We define applications that use context to provide task-relevant information and/or services to a user to be *context-aware*.

Context rapidly changes in situations where the user is mobile. The changing context can be used to adapt the user interface to an application, providing relevant services

and information to the user. While context is important to mobile computing in general, it is of particular interest to wearable computing. This is evident from the number of papers dealing with context-awareness in the previous Symposiums on Wearable Computers.

Rhodes [13] presented a list of defining characteristics for wearable computers. In each of these features, context plays an important role.

Portable while operational: A wearable computer is capable of being used while the user is mobile. When a user is mobile, her context is much more dynamic. She is moving through new physical spaces, encountering new objects and people. The services and information she requires will change based on these new entities.

Hands-free use: A wearable computer is intended to be operated with the minimal use of hands, relying on speech input or one-handed chording-keyboards and joysticks. Limiting the use of traditional input mechanisms (and somewhat limiting the use of explicit input) increases the need to obtain implicitly sensed contextual information.

Sensors: To enhance the explicit user input, a wearable computer should use sensors to collect information about the user's surrounding environment. Rhodes intended that the sensors be worn on the body, but the real goal is for the sensed information to be available to the wearable computer. This means that sensors can not only be on the body, but also be in the environment, as long as the wearable computer has a method for obtaining the sensed environmental information.

Proactive: A wearable computer should be acting on its user's behalf even when the user is not explicitly using it. This is the essence of context-aware computing: the computer analyzes the user's context and makes task-relevant information and services available to the user, interrupting the user when appropriate.

Always on: A wearable computer is always on. This is important for context-aware computing because the wearable computer should be continuously monitoring

21

the user's situation or context so that it can adapt and respond appropriately. It is able to provide useful services to the user at any time.

From a survey on context-aware computing [6], we found that most context-aware applications use a minimal variety of context. In general, the use of context is limited to only identity and location, neglecting both time and activity. Complex context-aware applications are difficult to build. By complex, we mean applications that not only deal with a wide variety of context, but also that take into account the contexts of multiple people or entities, real-time context as well as historical context, that use a single piece of context for multiple purposes, and that support interactions between multiple users, mobile and wearable computers and the environment. This family of applications is hard to implement because there has been little support for thinking about and designing them.

This paper describes the design of a complex context-aware application that addresses these issues. We will present the Conference Assistant, a context-aware application for assisting conference attendees and presenters. We demonstrate how context is used to aid users and describe how the application was built. In particular, we will present some concepts that make it easier to design complex context-aware applications.

2. The Conference Assistant

In this section, we will present a complex prototype application, the Conference Assistant, which addresses the deficiencies we pointed out in previous context-aware applications. The Conference Assistant is a context-aware application intended for use by conference attendees. We will describe the conference domain and show why it is appropriate for context-awareness and wearable computing and provide a scenario of use. We will then discuss the context used in this application and how it was used to provide the user benefit. We will end with a discussion on the types of context-aware features the Conference Assistant supports.

2.1. Conference Domain

The Conference Assistant was designed to assist people attending a conference. We chose the conference domain because conferences are very dynamic and involve an interesting variety of context. A conference attendee is likely to have similar interests as other attendees. There is a great deal of concurrent activity at large conferences including paper presentations, demonstrations, special interest group meetings, etc., at which a large amount of information is presented. We built the Conference Assistant to help users decide which activities to attend, to provide awareness of the activities of colleagues, to enhance interactions between users and the environment, to assist users in taking notes on presentations and to aid

in the retrieval of conference information after the conference concludes.

A wearable computer is very appropriate for this application. The Conference Assistant uses a wide variety of context: time, identity, location, and activity. It promotes interaction between simultaneous users of the application and has a large degree of interaction with the user's surrounding environment. Revisiting Rhodes' list of wearable computer characteristics, we can show how the domain is applicable for wearable computing.

Portable while operational: During a conference, a user is mobile, moving between presentation and demonstration spaces, with rapidly changing context.

Hands-free use: During a conference, hands should be free to take notes, rather than interacting with a computer to collect context information.

Sensors: Sensors in the environment can provide useful information about the conference to the user, including presentation information and activities of colleagues.

Proactive and Always on: In a conference, a user wants to pay attention to what is being presented while maintaining an awareness of other activities. A wearable computer can provide this awareness without explicit user requests.

2.2. User Scenario

Now that we have demonstrated the utility of context-awareness and wearable computing in the conference domain, we will present a user scenario for the Conference Assistant. A user is attending a conference. When she arrives at the conference, she registers, providing her contact information (mailing address, phone number, and email address), a list of research interests, and a list of colleagues who are also attending the conference. In return, she receives a copy of the conference proceedings and an application, the Conference Assistant, to run on her wearable computer. When she starts the application, it automatically displays a copy of the conference schedule, showing the multiple tracks of the conference, including both paper tracks and demonstration tracks. On the schedule (Figure 1), certain papers and demonstrations are highlighted (light gray) to indicate that they may be of particular interest to the user.

Figure 1. Screenshot of the augmented schedule, with suggested papers and demos highlighted (light-colored boxes) in the three (horizontal) tracks.

The user takes the advice of the application and walks towards the room of a suggested paper presentation. When she enters the room, the Conference Assistant automatically displays the name of the presenter and the title of the presentation. It also indicates whether audio and/or video of the presentation are being recorded. This impacts the user's behavior, taking fewer or greater notes depending on the extent of the recording available. The presenter is using a combination of PowerPoint and Web pages for his presentation. A thumbnail of the current slide or Web page is displayed on the wearable computer display. The Conference Assistant allows the user to create notes of her own to "attach" to the current slide or Web page (Figure 2). As the presentation proceeds, the application displays updated slide or Web page information. The user takes notes on the presented information using the Conference Assistant. The presentation ends and the presenter opens the floor for questions. The user has a question about the presenter's tenth slide. She uses the application to control the presenter's display, bringing up the tenth slide, allowing everyone in the room to view the slide in question. She uses the displayed slide as a reference and asks her question. She adds her notes on the answer to her previous notes on this slide.

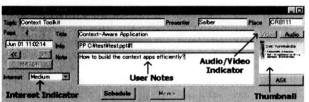

Figure 2. Screenshot of the Conference Assistant note-taking interface.

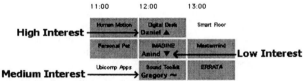

Figure 3. Screenshot of the partial schedule showing the location and interest level of colleagues. Symbols indicate interest level.

After the presentation, the user looks back at the conference schedule display and notices that the Conference Assistant has suggested a demonstration to see based on her interests. She walks to the room where the demonstrations are being held. As she walks past demonstrations in search of the one she is interested in, the application displays the name of each demonstrator and the corresponding demonstration. She arrives at the demonstration she is interested in. The application displays any PowerPoint slides or Web pages that the demonstrator uses during the demonstration. The demonstration turns out not to be relevant to the user and she indicates her level of interest to the application. She looks at the conference schedule and notices that her colleagues are in other presentations (Figure 3). A colleague has indicated a high level of interest in a particular presentation, so she decides to leave the current demonstration and to attend this presentation. The user continues to use the Conference Assistant throughout the

conference for taking notes on both demonstrations and paper presentations.

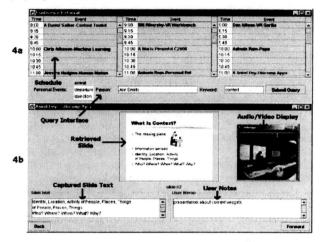

Figure 4. Screenshots of the retrieval application: query interface and timeline annotated with events (4a) and captured slideshow and recorded audio/video (4b).

She returns home after the conference and wants to retrieve some information about a particular presentation. The user executes a retrieval application provided by the conference. The application shows her a timeline of the conference schedule with the presentation and demonstration tracks (Figure 4a). The application uses a feature known as context-based retrieval [9]. It provides a query interface that allows the user to populate the timeline with various events: her arrival and departure from different rooms, when she asked a question, when other people asked questions or were present, when a presentation used a particular keyword, or when audio or video were recorded. By selecting an event on the timeline (Figure 4a), the user can view (Figure 4b) the slide or Web page presented at the time of the event, audio and/or video recorded during the presentation of the slide, and any personal notes she may have taken on the presented information. She can then continue to view the current presentation, moving back and forth between the presented slides and Web pages.

In a similar fashion, a presenter can use a third application to retrieve information about his/her presentation. The application displays a timeline of the presentation, populated with events about when different slides were presented, when audience members arrived and left the presentation (and their identities), the identities of audience members who asked questions and the slides relevant to the questions. The interface is similar to that shown in figure 4. The presenter can 'relive' the presentation, by playing back the audio and/or video, and moving between presentation slides and Web pages.

2.3. Use of Context

The Conference Assistant uses a wide variety of context to provide both services and information to users. We will first describe the context used in real time to assist a conference attendee during a conference and then will describe the historical context used after the conference by a conference attendee and a presenter.

When the user is attending the conference, the application first uses information about what is being presented at the conference and her personal interests to determine what presentations might be of particular interest to her. The application uses her location, the activity (presentation of a Web page or slide) in that location and the presentation details (presenter, presentation title, whether audio/video is being recorded) to determine what information to present to her. The text from the slides is being saved for the user, allowing her to concentrate on what is being said rather than spending time copying down the slides. The context of the presentation (presentation activity has concluded, and the number and title of the slide in question) facilitates the user's asking of a question. The context is used to control the presenter's display, changing to a particular slide for which the user had a question.

The list of colleagues provided during registration allows the application to present other relevant information to the user. This includes both the locations of colleagues and their interest levels in the presentations they are currently viewing. This information is used for two purposes during a conference. First, knowing where other colleagues are helps an attendee decide which presentations to see herself. For example, if there are two interesting presentations occurring simultaneously, knowing that a colleague is attending one of the presentations and can provide information about it later, a user can choose to attend the other presentation. Second, as described in the user scenario, when a user is attending a presentation that is not relevant or interesting to her, she can use the context of her colleagues to decide which presentation to move to. This is a form of social or collaborative information filtering [15].

After the conference, the retrieval application uses the conference context to retrieve information about the conference. The context includes public context such as the time when presentations started and stopped, whether audio/video was captured at each presentation, the names of the presenters, the presentations and the rooms in which the presentations occurred and any keywords the presentations mentioned. It also includes the user's personal context such as the times at which she entered and exited a room, the rooms themselves, when she asked a question and what presentation and slide or Web page the question was about. The application also uses the context of other people, including their presence at particular presentations and questions they asked, if any. The user can use any of this context information to

retrieve the appropriate slide or Web page and any recorded audio/video associated with the context.

After the conference, a presenter can also use the conference context to obtain information relevant to his/her presentation. The presenter can obtain information about who was present for the presentation, the times at which each slide or Web page was visited, who asked questions and about which slides. Using this information, along with the text captured from each slide and any audio/video recorded, the presenter can playback the entire presentation and question session.

2.4. Context-aware Features

Pascoe [11] introduced a set of four context-aware capabilities that applications can support. We will present each capability and will show how the Conference Assistant supports each one.

Contextual sensing: A system detects context and simply presents it to the user, augmenting the user's sensory system. The Conference Assistant presents the user's current location, name of the current presentation and presenter, location of colleagues, and colleagues' level of interest in their presentations.

Contextual adaptation: A system uses context to adapt its behavior instead of providing a uniform interface in all situations. When a new presentation slide or Web page is presented, the Conference Assistant saves the user's notes from the previous slide and creates an empty textbox in which notes on the new current slide can be entered.

Contextual resource discovery: A system can locate and use resources that share part or all of its context. When a user enters a presentation/demonstration area, the Conference Assistant creates a temporary bind to the presentation server in the local environment. The shared context is location. This binding allows the application to obtain changes to the local presentation/demonstration.

Contextual augmentation: A system augments the environment with additional information, associating digital data with the current context. All the notes that a user makes on presented information are augmented with contextual information (location, presentation title and presenter, and time). This augmentation supports retrieval of the notes using context-based retrieval techniques.

The Conference Assistant exploits all four of the context-aware capabilities presented by Pascoe. These capabilities are used to provide substantial benefits to both conference attendees and presenters.

3. Application Design

In this section, we describe the design of the Conference Assistant. We illustrate the software architecture of the application, as well as the context-aware architecture it was built on top of. We discuss the concepts the architecture supports that make it easier to build and evolve context-aware applications. Finally, we also describe the hardware used to deploy the application.

3.1. Software

The Conference Assistant is a complex context-aware application. It uses a wide variety of context, supporting both interaction between a single user and the environment and between multiple users. This application would have been difficult to build without a great deal of underlying support. It was built on top of an architecture designed to support context-aware applications [5]. We will first briefly describe this architecture and then will show how the architecture was used to build the Conference Assistant.

3.1.1. Context Architecture[1]

In previous work [5,14], we presented an architecture and toolkit that we designed and implemented to support building of context-aware applications. We will briefly discuss the components of the architecture and its merits.

The architecture consists of three types of components: widgets, servers, and interpreters. They implement the concepts necessary for easing the development of context-aware applications. Figure 5 shows the relationship between the context components and applications.

Context widgets encapsulate information about a single piece of context, such as location or activity, for example. They provide a uniform interface to components or applications that use the context, hiding the details of the underlying context-sensing mechanism(s).

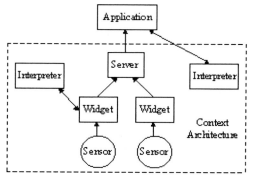

Figure 5. Relationship between applications and the context architecture. Arrows indicate data flow.

A context server is very similar to a widget, in that it supports the same set of features as a widget. The difference is that a server aggregates multiple pieces of context. In fact, it is responsible for all the context about a particular entity (person, place, or object). Aggregation facilitates the access of context by applications that are

---

[1] For more information on the context architecture, see http://www.cc.gatech.edu/fce/contexttoolkit

interested in multiple pieces of context about a single entity.

A context interpreter is used to abstract or interpret context. For example, a context widget may provide location context in the form of latitude and longitude, but an application may require the location in the form of a street name. A context interpreter may be used to provide this abstraction.

Context components are instantiated and executed independently of each other in separate threads and on separate computing devices. The architecture makes the distribution of the context architecture transparent to context-aware applications, mediating all communications between applications and components. It supports communications using the HyperText Transfer Protocol (HTTP) for both the sending and receiving of messages. The language used for sending data is the eXtensible Markup Language (XML). XML and HTTP were chosen because they support lightweight integration of distributed components and facilitate access to the architecture on heterogeneous platforms with multiple programming languages. The only requirements on devices using the architecture are that they support ASCII parsing and TCP/IP. These minimal requirements are particularly important for mobile and wearable computers, for which communications support tends to be small.

The context architecture promotes three main concepts for building context-aware applications: separation of context sensing from context use, aggregation, and abstraction. It relieves application developers from having to deal with how to sense and access context information, and instead, concentrate on how to use the context. It provides simplifying abstractions like aggregation and abstraction to make it easier for applications to obtain the context they require. Aggregation provides "one-stop shopping" for context about an entity, allowing application designers to think in terms of high level information, rather than low-level details. The architecture makes it easy to add the use of context to existing applications that don't use context and to evolve applications that already use context. In addition, the architecture makes context-aware applications resistant to changes in the context-sensing layer. It encapsulates changes and the impact of changes, so applications do not need to be modified.

3.1.2. Software Design

The Conference Assistant was built using the context architecture just described. Table 1 lists all the context components used and Figure 6 presents a snapshot of the architecture when a user is attending a conference.

During registration, a User Server is created for the user. It is responsible for aggregating all the context information about the user and acts as the application's interface to the user's personal context information. It subscribes to information about the user from the public

Registration Widget, the user's Memo Widget and the Location Widget in each presentation space. The Memo Widget captures the user's notes and also any relevant context (relevant slide, time, and presenter identity).

Table 1. Architecture components and responsibilities: S = Servers, W = Widgets, I = Interpreters

Component	Responsibility
Registration (W)	Acquires contact info, interests, and colleagues
Memo (W)	Acquires user's notes and relevant presentation info
Recommender(I)	Locates interesting presentations
User (S)	Aggregates all information about user
Question (W)	Acquires audience questions and relevant presentation info
Location (W)	Acquires arrivals/departures of users
Content (W)	Monitors PowerPoint or Web page presentation, capturing content changes
Recording (W)	Detects whether audio/video is recorded
Presentation (S)	All information about a presentation

There is a Presentation Server for each physical location where presentations/demos are occurring. A Presentation Server is responsible for aggregating all the context information about the local presentation and acts as the application's interface to the public presentation information. It subscribes to the widgets in the local environment, including the Content Widget, Location Widget, Recording Widget and Question Widget.

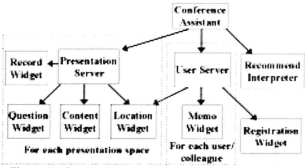

Figure 6. Conference Assistant capture architecture.

When an audience member asks a question using the Conference Assistant, the Question Widget captures the context (relevant slide, location, time, and audience member identity) and notifies the local Presentation Server of the event. The server stores the information and also uses it to access a service provided by the Content Widget, displaying the slide or Web page relevant to the question.

The Conference Assistant does not communicate with any widget directly, but instead communicates only with the user's User Server, the User Servers belonging to each colleague and the local Presentation Server. It subscribes

to the user's User Server for changes in location and interests. It subscribes to the colleagues' User Servers for changes in location and interest level. It also subscribes to the local Presentation Server for changes in a presentation slide or Web page when the user enters a presentation space and unsubscribes when the user leaves.

In the conference attendee's retrieval application, all the necessary information has been stored in the user's User Server and the public Presentation Servers. The architecture for this application is much simpler, with the retrieval application only communicating with the user's User Server and each Presentation Server. As shown in Figure 4, the application allows the user to retrieve slides (and the entire presentation including any audio/vide) using context via a query interface. If personal context is used as the index into the conference information, the application polls the User Server for the times and location at which a particular event occurred (user entered or left a location, or asked a question). This information can then be used to poll the correct Presentation Server for the related presentation information. If public context is used as the index, the application polls all the Presentation Servers for the times at which a particular event occurred (use of a keyword, presence or question by a certain person). As in the previous case, this information is then used to poll the relevant Presentation Servers for the related presentation information.

In the presenter's retrieval application, all the necessary information has been stored in the public Presentation Server used during the relevant presentation. The architecture for this application is simple as well, with the retrieval application only communicating with the relevant Presentation Server. As shown in Figure 4, the application allows the user to replay the entire presentation and question session, or view particular points in the presentation using context-based retrieval. Context includes the arrival and departure of particular audience members, transitions between slides and/or Web pages, and when questions were asked and by whom.

3.2. Hardware

The Conference Assistant application is being executed on a variety of different platforms, including laptops running Windows 95/98 and Hewlett Packard 620LX WinCE devices. It was not actually run on a wearable computer, but there is no reason why it could not be. The only requirements are constant network access and a graphical display. For communications with the context architecture, we use Proxim's RangeLAN2 1.6 Mbps wireless LAN for WinCE devices and RadioLan's 10BaseRadio 10 Mbps wireless LAN.

The retrieval applications are running on desktop machines, under both the Windows 95/98 and Solaris operating systems.

The context components were executed on a number of different computers running different operating systems. This includes Powermac G3's running MacOS, Intel

Pentiums running Windows 95 and Windows NT, and SPARC 10s running Solaris.

To sense identity and location of the conference attendees and presenters, we use PinPoint Corporation's 3D-iD™ Local Positioning System. This system uses radio frequency-based (RF) tags with unique identities and multiple antennas to locate users in a physical space. Although, it can provide location information at the resolution of 6 feet, we used coarser-grained information to determine when users entered a room.

4. Related Work

In this section, we will discuss other work that is relevant to the Conference Assistant, in the areas of conference assistants, context-aware tour guides, note taking, and context-based retrieval.

There has been little work in the area of context-awareness in a conference setting [10]. In the Mobile Assistant Project, Nishibe et al. deployed 100 handheld computers with cell phones at the International Conference on Multiagent Systems (ICMAS '96). The system provided conference schedule and tourist information. Social filtering, using the queries of other conference attendees, was used to determine relevant tourist information. The system supported community activity by allowing attendees to search for others with similar interests. Context was limited to "virtual information" such as personal interests, not taking into account "real information" like location.

Somewhat similar to a conference assistant is a tour guide. Both applications provide relevant information about the user's current context. The context-aware tour guide application is, perhaps, the canonical context-aware application. It has been the focus of much effort by groups doing context-aware research. Feiner et al. developed a tour guide for the Columbia University campus that combined augmented reality with mobile computing [7]. Fels et al. and Long et al. built tour guide applications for visitors attending an open house at their respective laboratories [8,2]. These systems use static configurations and can not deal with changes to tours at runtime. In contrast, the context aware architecture used in the Conference Assistant is able to make runtime changes transparent to the application.

There have been a number of systems that support individual users in taking notes on presentations. The Classroom 2000 project used an augmented classroom that captured audio, video, web slides visited and whiteboard activity to make the student notetaking activity easier [1]. The NotePals system aggregated the notes from several notetakers to provide a single group record of a presentation [4]. Stifelman built an augmented paper notebook that allowed access to the audio of a presentation during review [17]. The context most extensively used in these applications is time. The Conference Assistant expands the range of context used.

One of the most important projects in context-based retrieval was the Forget-me-not system from Lamming and Flynn [9]. It kept a record of a person's activity throughout the day in a diary format, allowing retrieval of the activity information based on context. Rhodes' wearable Remembrance Agent used context information about notes a user wrote, such as co-located people, location, and time to allow automatic retrieval of those notes that most closely matched the user's current context [13]. Rekimoto et al. used an augmented reality system to attach notes to objects or locations [12]. When users approached those objects or locations, the note was retrieved. This is similar to the Locust Swarm project by Starner et al [16], which allowed the attachment and retrieval of notes from infrared-based location tags.

5. Conclusions and Future Application Work

We have presented the Conference Assistant, a prototype mobile, context-aware application for assisting conference attendees in choosing presentations to attend, taking notes, and retrieving those notes. We discussed the important relationship between context-awareness and wearable computing. We demonstrated this relationship in the Conference Assistant. We showed how the Conference Assistant made use of a wide variety of context, both personal and environmental, and how it enhanced user interactions with both the environment and other users. We discussed the important concepts that our architecture supports, that make it easier to build and modify complex context-aware applications: separation of sensing and using context, aggregation, and abstraction.

The Conference Assistant is currently a prototype application running in our laboratory. We would like to deploy the application at an actual conference. This would require us to provide many handheld devices (in case the conference attendees do not have their own wearable computers), a wireless LAN, and an indoor positioning system. This would allow us to perform a realistic evaluation of the application.

There are also additional features that we would like to add to the Conference Assistant. The first is the addition of an improved assistant for demonstrations. Currently, the application doesn't treat paper presentations any differently from demonstrations. We would like to enhance the application when a demonstration is being given, by providing additional information about the demonstration. This includes relevant web pages, research papers, and videos.

Currently, the Conference Assistant only uses information about PowerPoint slides and Web pages being presented. We would like to extend this to use other presentation packages and mediums. This will require no change to the application, but will require the development of additional context widgets to capture the presentations and relevant updates.

Other features to add deal with access to information about the user's colleagues. Presently, at registration, users indicate the colleagues about whom they would like to receive information on. This is actually the opposite of how we should be approaching this problem, from a privacy point of view. At registration, users should actually indicate who is allowed to access their information (location and level of interest). This allows users to manage their own information. A related feature is to allow users to access their colleagues' notes with the retrieval application. This would provide additional information that would augment the user's own notes on a presentation and would be a source of notes for presentations that the user did not attend.

A final feature to add to the Context Assistant is an interface that supports serendipitous information retrieval relevant to the current presentation, much like the Remembrance Agent [13]. Potential information to retrieve includes conference and field-relevant information.

We would like to add a third retrieval application for conference organizers. This application would allow them to view anonymized information about the number of people at various presentations and demonstrations and the average amount of time attendees spent at each.

Acknowledgements

We would like to acknowledge the support of the Future Computing Environments research group for contributing to the ideas of the Conference Assistant. We would like to thank Thad Starner for his comments on this work. This work was supported in part by an NSF CAREER Grant # 9703384, NSF ESS Grant EIA-9806822, a Motorola UPR and a Hitachi grant.

References

[1] G.D. Abowd et al., "Investigating the capture, integration and access problem of ubiquitous computing in an educational setting", in Proceedings of CHI'98, April 1998, pp. 440-447.

[2] G.D. Abowd, C.G. Atkeson, J. Hong, S. Long, R. Kooper and M. Pinkerton, "Cyberguide: A mobile context-aware tour guide", ACM Wireless Networks, 3(5), 1997, pp. 421-433.

[3] H.H. Clark and S.E. Brennan, "Grounding in communication", in L.B. Resnick, J. Levine, & S.D. Teasley (Eds.), Perspectives on socially shared cognition. Washington, DC. 1991.

[4] R. Davis et al., "NotePals: Lightweight note sharing by the group, for the group", in Proceedings of CHI'99, May 1999, pp. 338-345.

[5] A.K. Dey, D. Salber, M. Futakawa and G. Abowd, "An architecture to support context-aware applications", submitted to UIST '99.

[6] A.K. Dey and G.D. Abowd, "Towards an understanding of context and context-awareness", submitted to HUC '99.

[7] S. Feiner, B. MacIntyre, T. Hollerer and A. Webster, "A Touring Machine: Prototyping 3D mobile augmented reality systems for exploring the urban environment", in Proceedings of the 1st International Symposium on Wearable Computers, October 1997, pp. 74-81.

[8] S. Fels et al., "Progress of C-MAP: A context-aware mobile assistant", in Proceeding of AAAI 1998 Spring Symposium on Intelligent Environments, Technical Report SS-98-02, March 1998, pp. 60-67.

[9] M. Lamming and M. Flynn, "Forget-me-not: Intimate computing in support of human memory", in Proceedings of FRIEND21: International Symposium on Next Generation Human Interfaces, 1994, pp. 125-128.

[10] Y. Nishibe et al., "Mobile digital assistants for community support", AAAI Magazine 19(2), Summer 1998, pp. 31-49.

[11] J. Pascoe, "Adding generic contextual capabilities to wearable computers", in Proceedings of 2nd International Symposium on Wearable Computers, October 1998, pp. 92-99.

[12] J. Rekimoto, Y. Ayatsuka and K. Hayashi, "Augment-able reality: Situated communications through physical and digital spaces", in Proceedings of the 2nd International Symposium on Wearable Computers, October 1998, pp. 68-75.

[13] B. Rhodes, "The Wearable Remembrance Agent: A system for augmented memory", in Proceedings of the 1st International Symposium on Wearable Computers, October 1997, pp. 123-128.

[14] D. Salber, A.K. Dey and G.D. Abowd, "The Context Toolkit: Aiding the development of context-enabled applications", in Proceedings of CHI'99, pp. 434-441.

[15] U. Shardanand and P. Maes, "Social information filtering: algorithms for automating 'word of mouth'", in Proceedings of CHI'95, May 1995, pp. 210-217.

[16] T. Starner, D. Kirsch and S. Assefa, "The Locust Swarm: An environmentally-powered, networkless location and messaging system", in Proceedings of the 1st International Symposium on Wearable Computers, October 1997, pp. 169-170.

[17] L.J. Stifelman, "Augmenting real-world objects: A paper-based audio notebook", in Proceedings of CHI'96, April 1996, pp. 199-200.

Indoor navigation using a diverse set of cheap, wearable sensors

Andrew R. Golding and Neal Lesh.
MERL - A Mitsubishi Electric Research Laboratory
201 Broadway, Cambridge, MA 02139
{golding,lesh}@merl.com

Abstract

We apply machine-learning techniques to the task of context-awareness, or inferring aspects of the user's state given a stream of inputs from sensors worn by the person. We focus on the task of indoor navigation, and show that by integrating information from accelerometers, magnetometers, temperature and light sensors, we can collect enough information to infer the user's location. However, our navigation algorithm performs very poorly, with almost 50% error, if we use only the raw sensor signals. Instead, we introduce a "data cooking" module that computes appropriate high-level features from the raw sensor data. By introducing these high-level features, we are able to reduce the error rate to 2% in our example environment.

1 Introduction

Context-awareness — the ability to detect aspects of the user's internal or external state — is essential for many applications of wearable computing (Pascoe, 1998). Applications include automated tour guides that augment the user's view of whichever attraction she is currently looking at (Feiner et al., 1997; Long et al., 1996); and systems that use different modes of communication depending on whether the user is engaged in a conversation (Clarkson and Pentland, 1998). In this paper, we apply machine-learning techniques to the task of inferring aspects of the user's state given a stream of inputs from sensors worn by the person. We are especially interested in integrating information from the diverse set of cheap, wearable sensors that are now available, including accelerometers, temperature sensors, and photodiodes.

We have focused on indoor navigation, the task of interactively guiding the user to a desired indoor destination. For example, the user may be looking for a certain conference room in a convention center, or a train in a large underground train station. This task requires, minimally, that the computer be aware of the person's location. Global Positioning Systems (GPS) cannot provide this information indoors or in crowded urban areas. One might, instead, use active badges (Want and Hopper, 1998; Lamming and Flynn, 1994) or beacon architectures (Long et al., 1996; Schilit, 1995), but installing and maintaining such systems involves substantial effort and expense.

Instead, we have explored the other extreme of not modifying the environment and using machine-learning techniques to infer a person's location from naturally-occurring signals in the environment. These include characteristic magnetic fields from steel beams in the walls, fixed arrangements of fluorescent lights, and temperature gradients across rooms. Additionally, the user herself provides distinctive acceleration patterns by walking up or down staircases, or riding an escalator or elevator. Figure 1 shows our initial research prototype. The user wears a "utility belt" which holds several sensor boards and a battery. The outputs from the sensors plug into a laptop, which performs the actual navigation function.

A central challenge that arises in this application, and is likely to arise in related ones, is that the raw sensor signals are unsuitable for use as direct inputs to a machine-learning algorithm. The reason is that there is too great a distance between the raw signals and the high-level inference that we wish to make. To address this, we introduce a "data cooking" module that computes high-level features from the raw sensor data. These high-level features do not add new knowledge to the system; they simply reformulate existing information into a form that the machine-learning algorithm can use more effectively. Introducing these high-level features improved performance on the indoor-navigation task dramatically. Currently, we handcraft a set of appropriate high-level features; however, we are interested in algorithms for discovering useful features through search.

The main contributions of this paper are to show that (1) by integrating information from diverse sensors, we can collect enough information to perform context-aware tasks such as indoor navigation, and (2) "cooking" the low level sensors is necessary in or-

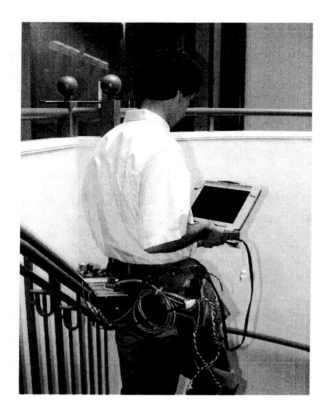

Figure 1: Initial prototype of wearable navigation system. User wears a "utility belt" which holds the sensor boards and a battery. The outputs of the sensors feed into a laptop on which the navigation program resides.

der to make the information they contain accessible to machine-learning algorithms.

The rest of this paper is organized as follows. In Section 2, we describe the hardware platform and sensors we have been using. In Section 3, we describe our navigation algorithm. In Section 4, we describe our experiments. Section 5 discusses related work, and Section 6 concludes.

2 Hardware

The guiding principle in choosing sensors was that they be small, lightweight, low-power, cheap, and preferably non-directional — all properties intended to increase practicality for a wearable application. We currently have four types of sensors:

- 3D accelerometer: Detect the user's acceleration in three dimensions. Implemented using two 2D accelerometer boards (ADXL 202 EB from Analog Devices, Inc).

- 3D magnetometer: Detect magnetic fields in three dimensions. Our magnetometer (Honeywell HMC2003) uses three permalloy magnetoresistive transducers to measure the strength and direction of a magnetic field.

- Fluorescent light detector: Works by extracting the 60 Hz component of the signal from a photodiode aimed at the ceiling. Responds primarily to fluorescent lights, which flicker at this rate.

- Temperature sensor: Measures ambient room temperature. (We used TMP37 GT9 from Analog Devices, Inc.)

The sensors are mounted on several circuit boards and attached to a utility belt worn by the user. This arrangement (approximately) fixes the orientation of the sensors with respect to the user, circumventing problems of orientation drift (for the accelerometers and magnetometer), and aiming directional sensors as needed (the light sensor is aimed at the ceiling).

The analog outputs of the sensors are fed into an A/D card (PCM-DAS 16/330 from ComputerBoards, Inc) which plugs into a PC/MCIA slot on the laptop. Our navigation program resides on the laptop and samples the digitized signals roughly every 50 msec.

3 Navigation System

Given the view of the world provided by the sensors, the task of the navigation system is to (1) Learn a model of the world at training time, and (2) Use this model to infer the user's location at run time.

The structure of the navigation system is shown in Figure 2. The **data acquisition** module reads a tuple of sensor readings roughly every 50 msec, converting the input voltages into canonical units. The **data cooking** module augments these raw readings with *computed features*; for example, one computed feature is the variance of the user's Z acceleration. The remaining two modules, **data modelling** and **navigation**, perform the two tasks stated above: learning a model of the world at training time, and using this model to infer the user's location at run time.

The following sections describe the modules in greater detail. We first describe the representation of the world that our navigation system uses, and then discuss the data acquisition, data modelling, and navigation modules. Because the data-cooking module is best understood in the context of how the navigation algorithm works, it is presented last.

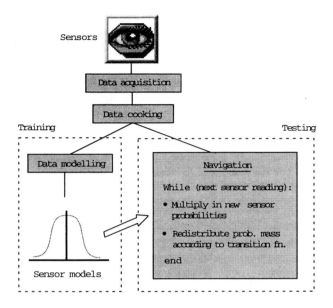

Figure 2: Structure of navigation system. The system samples the sensors roughly every 50 msec. At training time, it uses the sensor readings to learn a model of the world. At testing time, it infers the user's location from the sensor readings.

3.1 Representation

We formulate the navigation problem in terms of the "world" in which the navigation system will operate. Figure 3 shows the environment used for the experiments reported here. It contains five "locations": office, arch, upstairs, downstairs, and ping pong room. We put "locations" in quotes because a location does not correspond to a point in the world, but rather to a *transition* between points. For example, the upstairs "location" corresponds to the transition from the bottom of the stairs to the top (it could more properly be called the "going upstairs" location). This allows us to distinguish between upstairs and downstairs, which occupy the same physical space. A location such as the office corresponds to starting in the office doorway, walking around inside the office, and returning to the doorway.

3.2 Data acquisition

The data acquisition module is responsible for continually reading tuples of sensor readings, and converting them into canonical units. A tuple is read roughly every 50 msec. Table 3.2 lists the 9 sensors currently in use and their canonical units of measurement.

Table 1: Sensors read by the data acquisition module.

Sensor	Description	Units
Left X acc.	Acceleration to user's right (measured at user's left hip)	G
Left Y acc.	Acceleration forward (measured at user's left hip)	G
Right X acc.	Acceleration to user's right (measured at user's right hip)	G
Right Z acc.	Acceleration upward (measured at user's right hip)	G
Comp. X	Component of magnetic field pointing to user's right	gauss
Comp. Y	Component of magnetic field pointing forward	gauss
Comp. Z	Component of magnetic field pointing upward	gauss
Temp.	Ambient room temperature	degrees (F)
Lights	Strength of 60 Hz component of overhead lights	volts

3.3 Data modelling

The navigation system needs a model of the world, or, more particularly, a model of what its sensor signals look like throughout the indoor environment.

Training proceeds as follows: the user is given a set itinerary to traverse through the environment. He proceeds along the itinerary, clicking a handheld button once when entering and once when leaving each location. In this way, the system is kept informed of the user's true location in the world. In addition, the system samples the sensors every 50 msec, as usual, and performs its customary conversion to canonical units and augmentation with computed features (described below). The result is a set of training data in the form of a sequence of augmented sensor tuples, each accompanied by a training *label* that specifies the location at which it was collected.

From these labelled tuples, the data-modelling module learns a model of the world. The data-modelling module lumps together all readings for a given sensor at a given location, and constructs a *distribution* of these readings. The gross characteristics of the location show up in the shape of the distribution. For example, the magnetism of the arch will show up in the Compass Z distribution as an elevated mean and standard deviation compared to the Compass Z distribution of other locations. The overall model of the world produced by the data-modelling module takes the form of a set of distributions over the possible values of the sensors — one distribution for each ⟨sensor, location⟩ pair.

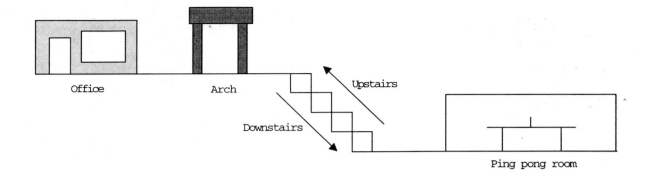

Figure 3: Example indoor environment consisting of five "locations": office, arch, upstairs, downstairs, and ping pong room.

The remaining question is what *type* of distribution will best model a set of sensor readings at a location. We tried two types: gaussians and histograms. Gaussians are appropriate under the assumption that the observed sensor values were generated by the cumulative effect of numerous random processes. Histograms test this assumption by modelling the data without making any assumptions about the type of distribution; the trick with histograms, of course, is choosing an appropriate bin width. We used a cross-validation approach, which starts by splitting the set of observed sensor values into a training set and a holdout set. The intuition is that an appropriate bin width will have the property that if we form a histogram out of the training set using that bin width, then the histogram will be highly predictive of more data from the same distribution — namely, the holdout set. Thus our approach is to try a variety of bin widths, and to select the bin width w that maximizes the probability of the holdout set, where the probability of the holdout set is calculated using a histogram probability density function constructed from the training set with bin width w.[1] Figure 4 shows examples of both gaussian and histogram distributions for the data for four sensors collected at the arch. Informally, it can be seen that the gaussian approximation is reasonably well-justified in most cases. We have therefore used gaussian models in the work reported here.

---

[1] More specifically, we used leave-one-out cross-validation; that is, given n sensor values to model, we did n iterations, designating each value in turn as the (singleton) holdout set, and the remaining $n-1$ values as the training set. The probabilities of the holdout set from all iterations were combined by taking the product. We chose this style of cross-validation because we found that it outperformed other styles (e.g., 2-way cross-validation) on synthetic datasets.

3.4 Navigation

The navigation system brings two types of knowledge to bear on the task of inferring the user's location. First, it has knowledge of the distribution of signal values throughout the environment, as learned at training time. For example, if it observes large Compass Z values, it can infer that the user is likely to be at the arch. Second, the system has dead-reckoning knowledge — rough knowledge about the user's change in position from one time step to the next, as inferred from accelerometer and compass readings.

The navigation algorithm incorporates these two types of knowledge in an iterative, Markov-model-like, two-step algorithm, as seen in Figure 2. The algorithm starts with some initial probability assigned to each location. Each time a sensor tuple is read, the algorithm incrementally updates the probabilities.

The first step of the update incorporates the sensor information. This is done using Bayes' rule. Let the augmented tuple of sensor readings be $S = \langle s_1, \ldots, s_n \rangle$. Then for each location ℓ, we calculate the posterior probability that the user is now at that location (given that we have observed the new sensor readings) using Bayes' rule with the conditional independence assumption:

$$P(\ell|\langle s_1, \ldots, s_n \rangle) = \left(\prod_{1 \leq i \leq n} P(s_i|\ell) \right) \frac{P(\ell)}{P(\langle s_1, \ldots, s_n \rangle)}.$$

The $P(s_i|\ell)$ terms are calculated using the model learned at training time for the ith sensor at location ℓ. The prior probability, $P(\ell)$, is the probability assigned to location ℓ before the update. The $P(\langle s_1, \ldots, s_n \rangle)$ term is omitted; instead, we scale the probabilities for all locations to sum to 1.

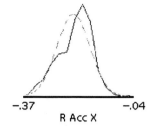 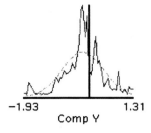 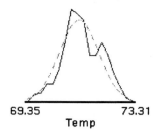 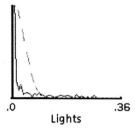

| −.37 R Acc X −.04 | −1.93 Comp Y 1.31 | 69.35 Temp 73.31 | .0 Lights .36 |

Figure 4: Gaussian (dashed) and histogram (solid) models of the data for four sensors collected at the arch. The bin width was set separately for each histogram using a leave-one-out cross-validation procedure.

The second step of the update incorporates the dead-reckoning information. This step attempts to transfer probability mass in the same direction and distance that the user moved since the last sensor readings. For example, if we had perfect dead-reckoning information that the user moved east by 5 feet, then we would transfer 100% of the probability mass from each location to the location 5 feet to the east of it. In practice, of course, we have only rather vague dead-reckoning information, and thus we are reduced to spreading out the probability mass in a less focused manner. In particular, our current dead-reckoning information consists simply of footstep detection.[2] When a footstep is detected, we spread out probability mass from a location by retaining some fraction p_{stay} of its probability at the location itself, and distributing the remaining $(1 - p_{\text{stay}})$ fraction of its probability equally among all adjacent locations. The value p_{stay} is the probability that a single footstep will not carry the user outside of her current location, and is estimated from training data.

3.5 Data cooking

The preceding sections describe our basic algorithms for training and running the navigation system. If we apply them to the raw (unaugmented) tuples of sensor readings, however, they perform rather badly. We can, however, improve the performance to high levels (see Section 4) by introducing computed features that add no new information at the knowledge level, but simply reformulate the existing information into a form in which it can be used more effectively. Below we discuss the specific problems that we identified with using the raw sensor readings for navigation, and the computed features that we developed to address these problems.

One problem that quickly became apparent was that of overcounting evidence due to excessive independence assumptions in the Bayesian update part of the navigation algorithm. Not only are all features in a tuple assumed to be conditionally independent, but consecutive tuples are assumed independent as well. Thus if the user stands under a light, we find that the algorithm quickly comes to believe she's in whichever room was best-lit during training. The solution is to add a computed feature that triggers only when the lights go from off to on, rather than responding whenever the lights are on.

A second problem concerns absolute versus relative measurements. Sensor readings are often subject to drift for various reasons; for example, an accelerometer may shift around somewhat on the utility belt, thereby changing the perceived value of gravity (which nominally has a Z acceleration of −1 G). Clearly it is bad for the navigation algorithm to depend on the absolute Z accelerations that are read. To address this, we compute a feature which, for each accelerometer, reports the delta between the current value and a running average of the last, say, 10 minutes' worth of readings.

A third problem arose in the context of the Z acceleration sensor: we observe that when a user walks down stairs, the amplitude of the oscillations in the Z acceleration increases. This effect does in fact show up if one looks at the distribution of Z acceleration values for the downstairs location: the distribution has a wider shape than the Z acceleration distributions for other locations. However, this is still not enough of a clue for the navigation algorithm to latch onto easily. If we make the information about wider shape available *directly*, however, by adding a computed feature for the *variance* of the Z acceleration, then the algorithm becomes able to discriminate the downstairs location reliably. Figure 5 displays the raw Z acceler-

---

[2] We detect a footstep iff the the Z acceleration is greater than 0.05 G after being less than 0.05 G for at least 250 msec.

ation feature together with the variance of Z acceleration feature. The latter, cooked feature is much more obviously correlated with walking down stairs.

A final problem concerns noisy or unreliable sensor distributions, a difficulty which occurs frequently in the navigation domain. For example, the Compass Z sensor often hovers in an intermediate range indicating a fairly weak magnetic field. Such a value is not particularly indicative of *any* location; yet the value will inevitably turn out to favor one location over another (perhaps by a small amount). Incorporating this kind of evidence into the calculation is never good; it introduces noise, and the noise does not always balance out across locations. There are several ways to clean up such evidence; the approach we have adopted is to establish an *in-bounds range* for each sensor. If a sensor value falls outside this range, it is ignored (i.e., not used to perform Bayesian updates). For example, the Compass Z in-bounds range is above 1.2 gauss or below -1.2 gauss. If a weak Compass Z value, such as 0.3 gauss is read, it is discarded. That is, the algorithm does not use this reading of the Compass Z sensor in the Bayesian update step. Currently the ranges are set by hand, but we are considering methods for setting or adjusting them automatically.

4   Experiments

We were not able to develop a single metric by which to measure the performance of the navigation algorithm. One possible metric is the percentage of time that the navigation algorithm "knows where it is", i.e., that the location it reports as most likely is, in fact, the location it is in. However, not all errors seem equally important. For example, when one first enters an office, it seems reasonable for the navigation algorithm to not immediately report that it is in the office. This error seems less significant than, for example, suddenly reporting that it is going downstairs in the middle of a visit to an office.

We divide each visit to a location into a *header* and a *body*. The *header* is the time from the point the person enters a location until the navigation algorithm first reports that it is in any location other than the one it was reporting at the very beginning of the visit.[3] The *body* is the remaining time spent in that location. We measure three aspects of the performance of the navigation algorithm: (1) the average length of the header, (2) the number of errors, i.e., the number of times the algorithm changes the location it is reporting

---

[3]However, if the navigation algorithm reports the same location throughout a visit or is already reporting the correct location at the beginning of a visit, then the header size is 0.

Table 2: Performance results.

high-level features	restricted ranges	time until first guess	errors per visit	error rate
yes	yes	4.8 secs	0.3	2%
yes	no	2.0 secs	2.6	33%
no	yes	3.4 secs	10.1	52%
no	no	2.1 secs	10.5	49%

to a wrong answer, and (3) the error rate, i.e. the fraction of time (within the body) that the algorithm's prevailing guess is wrong.

We trained the navigation algorithm a total of 28 visits to the locations in our test environment and tested the algorithm on a set consisting of 19 visits. A typical visit to a location lasted about 20–30 seconds. We handcrafted the set of high-level features and ranges used by our navigation algorithm on some of the training data, prior to collecting the test data.

As shown in Table 2, our navigation algorithm had very low error rates when we used both the cooked features and the restricted ranges on the features, although it took an average of almost 5 seconds to recognize a location once the person entered it. The algorithm's performance degraded to unacceptably high error rates if we turned off the computed features or the restricted ranges, or both. These results show that the machine-learning algorithm could not use the raw signals effectively, unless the information they contain was reformulated in terms of the computed features.

The performance of our system degrades even further if we do not make use of the history of sensor readings, but try to guess the location of the user only based on the current sensor readings. Although not shown in the table, without the extra features or the ranges, the navigation algorithm using only the current sensor readings has a 55% error rate and makes 52 errors, on average, per visit. With the extra features and the ranges, but only using the current sensor readings to guess where it is, the algorithm has a 49% error rate, and an average of 5.5 errors per visit.

5   Related work

While we have focused on the task of inferring state information about the user by combining information from the available sensors, much previous work has investigated the *desirability* of obtaining this information. Pascoe (1998), for example, generally considers the value of context-aware computing, and describes a case study of incorporating GPS information into a system that assists a field worker who is observing

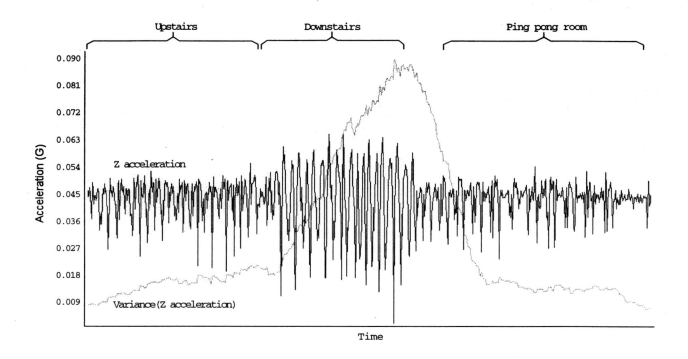

Figure 5: The Z acceleration feature (black) versus the Variance(Z acceleration) feature (gray). The features are shown over time as the user walks upstairs, downstairs, and into the ping pong room. Variance is computed over the last 100 readings.

giraffes. Feiner et al. (1997) and Long et al. (1996) describe automated tour guides that augment a person's view of the attractions that they are viewing. Ertan et al. (1998) and Ram and Sharf (1998) describe systems that provide navigational assistance for visually impaired people.

Our work is close in spirit and objectives to work being done by the Technology for Enabling Awareness group (http://www.omega.it/research/tea) which is developing hardware and software to enable portable devices, such as loptops, to have a higher degree of awareness of their user's context such as location and activity. Additionally, previous work has made use of the diverse variety of sensors that are available, using them to detect a variety of aspects of the user's internal and external state. For example, Picard and Healey (1997) describe how to use wearable sensors to detect the wearer's affective patterns such as expressions of joy or anger. Similarly, Myrtek and Brugner (1996) investigate the correlations between physiological parameters (heart rate, physical activity) and psychological parameters (excitement, enjoyment). Additionally, van Someren et al. (1998) use

actigraphy (processed accelerometer readings) for detailed and long-term measurement of hand tremors to help Parkinson patients manage their symptoms. Blood et al. (1997) compare three wearable sensors for the task of detecting when a person is sleeping. Teicher (1995) shows correlations between levels of activity and mood disorders and attention-deficit hyperactivity disorder.

Finally, previous work has used video and audio sensors to provide context-awareness for wearable computers. Starner, Schiele, and Pentland (1998) tackle the problem of indoor navigation using the output of two cameras worn on the heads of MIT students playing a game called Patrol. They use Hidden Markov models (HMMs) with a small number of states trained on a feature vector derived by sampling various regions from the images returned by the cameras. They obtained encouraging results (82% on their scoring system, which is not directly comparable to ours), and discuss possible improvements such as incorporating optical flow or inertial sensors in order to decide when to process frames. Similarly, Clarkson and Pentland (1998) train an HMM on an audio signal to detect whether or not a person is engaged in a conversation so as to decide how to notify them of an incoming message. In contrast, we have focused on combining evidence from different sensors rather than optimizing one source of evidence. Additionally, our algorithms model the world directly (i.e., one state for every location) and thus produce a probability distribution over all possible locations. Of course, the work we have described in this paper is complementary with a video- or audio-based one. For example, we could use video or audio as additional sensors. We chose not to in our initial design because we suspected the video images would vary wildly based on the orientation of the person in the rooms.

6 Conclusion

The work reported here addresses the problem of enabling a wearable computer to be context-aware — that is, to take into account aspects of the user's internal or external state. We focus on the task of indoor navigation, where the particular aspect of the user's state that is of interest is the user's physical location. By affixing a diverse set of cheap, wearable sensors to the user, including accelerometers, magnetometers, and temperature sensors, and applying machine-learning techniques, we find that we are able to infer the user's location quite accurately in a simplified office environment. However, this high accuracy was obtained only when we augmented the representation with "cooked" versions of the original sensor readings; the raw sensor readings were too low-level to be used directly to perform the high-level inference. Two conclusions emerge: (1) By obtaining high accuracy with our cooked representation, we have demonstrated that our approach of integrating information from a diverse set of low-level sensors is adequate to obtain enough raw knowledge to perform context-aware tasks such as indoor navigation; and (2) The raw sensor values must be "cooked" appropriately to put the knowledge in a form that is accessible to machine-learning algorithms. Currently, we have handcrafted the definitions of our cooked features; a direction for future work is to develop methods for discovering such feature definitions automatically or semi-automatically.

Acknowledgements

This project would not have been possible without the help of Darren Leigh, who designed and built the hardware sensors, as well as being a good all-around source of ideas. We would also like to thank Bill Yerazunis and Baback Moghaddam for their helpful thoughts and comments on the project.

References

Blood, ML., RL. Sack, DC. Percy, and JC. Pen. 1997. A comparison of sleep detection by wrist actigraphy, behavioral response, and polysomnography. *Sleep*, 20(6):388–95, June.

Clarkson, B. and A. Pentland. 1998. Extracting context from environmental audio. In *Proc. of the second international symposium on wearable computers*, pages 154–155, October.

Ertan, S., L. Clare, A. Willets, H. Tan, and A. Pentland. 1998. A wearable haptic navigation guidance system. In *Proc. of the second international symposium on wearable computers*, pages 164–165, October.

Feiner, S., B. MacIntyre, T. Hollerer, and A. Webster. 1997. A touring machine: Prototyping 3D mobile augmented relatiy systems for exploring the urban environment. In *Proc. of the first international symposium on wearable computers*, October.

Lamming, M. and M. Flynn. 1994. Forget-me-not: Intimate computing in support of human memory. In *FRIEND21: international symposium on next generation Human interface*, pages 125–128.

Long, S., R. Kooper, G.D. Abowd, and C. G. Atkeson. 1996. Rapid prototyping of mobile context-aware applications: the cyberguide case study. In *Proc. of the second ACM international conference on mobile computing and networking*, November.

Myrtek, M. and G. Brugner. 1996. Perception of emotions in everyday life: studies with patients and normals. *Biological Psychology*, 42(1-2):147=–64, January.

Pascoe, J. 1998. Adding generic contextual capabilities to wearables computers. In *Proc. of the second international symposium on wearable computers*, pages 92–99, October.

Picard, R.W. and J. Healey. 1997. Affective wearables. *Personal Technologies*, 1:231–240.

Ram, S. and J. Sharf. 1998. The people sensor: A mobility aid for the visually impaired. In *Proc. of the second international symposium on wearable computers*, pages 166–167, October.

Schilit, W. 1995. *System architecture for context-aware mobile computing*. Ph.D. thesis, Columbia University.

Starner, T., B. Schiele, and A. Pentland. 1998. Visual contextual awareness in wearable computing. In *Proc. of the second international symposium on wearable computers*, pages 50–57, October.

Teicher, MH. 1995. Actigraphy and motion analysis: new tools for psychiatry. *Harvard Review of Psychiatry.*, 3(1):18–35.

van Someren, EJ., BF. Vonk, WA. Thijssen, JD. Speelman, PR. Schuurman, M. Mirmiran, and DF. Swaab. 1998. A new actigraph for long-term registration of the duration and intensity of tremor and movement. *IEEE Transactions on Biomedical Engineering*, 45(3):286–95.

Want, R. and A. Hopper. 1998. Active badges and personal interactive computing objects. *IEEE Transactions on Consumer Electronics*, 38(1):10–20.

Realtime Personal Positioning System for a Wearable Computers

Hisashi Aoki[◊], Bernt Schiele and Alex Pentland
MIT Media Laboratory
{aoki,bernt,sandy}@media.mit.edu

Abstract

Context awareness is an important functionality for wearable computers. In particular, the computer should know where the person is in the environment. This paper proposes an image sequence matching technique for the recognition of locations and previously visited places. As in single word recognition in speech recognition, a dynamic programming algorithm is proposed for the calculation of the similarity of different locations. The system runs on a stand alone wearable computer such as a Libretto PC. Using a training sequence a dictionary of locations is created automatically. These locations are then be recognized by the system in realtime using a hat-mounted camera.

1. Introduction

Obtaining user location is one of the important functions for wearable computers in two applications. One is automatic self-summary, and the other is context-aware user interface. In self-summary, the user is wearing a small camera and a small computer, capturing and recording every event of his/her daily life. The computer might be able to summarize the recorded data and eventually producing a "diary" [1,2]. For example, "At 8:15, left home. At 8:17, happened to meet Bob on the street. At 8:44, arrived at the office..." The computer might be also able to navigate the way to an unknown place. Furthermore, important reminders might be shown on one's worn display when the user is in a particular location, such as supermarket [3,4,5,6].

As for context-awareness, Thad Starner et al. discussed the following example [7]:

> *"For example, if the user is in his supervisor's office, he is probably in an important meeting and does not want to be interrupted for phone calls or e-mail except for emergencies."*

To realize these functions, a computer needs to know user's locations. Outdoors, a Global Positioning System (GPS) may track movements. Indoors, active tags may take this role [8,9,10], however, sticking transmitters on all the doors is obviously a difficult task, and GPS is not available inside buildings.

The other approach to recognize location is to use a camera. If barcodes are stuck on every door, the computer may find the place easily by reading the code [10]. Even if there is no barcode, object recognition or text recognition may help the computer detect the place [11]. However, many of these computer vision approaches analyze still pictures. So accurate segmentation of object or character is needed. Starner et al. showed a place detection method by introducing an HMM of transition of rooms [7]. Clarkson et al. showed a method to segment and label audio-video sequences from a worn camera and microphone [12].

In this paper, we propose a realtime personal positioning system that only uses a small wearable camera as shown in Figure 1, and a standalone PC.

In previous work [13], we demonstrated that a dynamic programming algorithm [14], can be used to recognize not only the user's location but also the approaching trajectory. In [13], we tested the accuracy of the system with about 100-second video sequences that were manually chosen and segmented. The images were handled off line on an SGI workstation.

In this paper, practical changes have been done added to the previous work to run on wearable computers. Firstly, the proposed system runs at about 7 frames per second, on a standalone PC such as a Toshiba Libretto without wireless communication to remote database. This overcomes delays caused by database reference over limited bandwidth. Secondly, no segmentation of the video sequences is needed. Thirdly, we introduce a method to choose suitable trajectories for the "location dictionary" automatically. And at the recognition stage,

---

[◊] Now at Toshiba Corporation R&D Center, Japan

the user doesn't need to tell the system when to look up on the dictionary. Lastly, larger sets of training and test data are used for the evaluation. The dictionary is extracted from a real video sequence of 16 minutes and 30 seconds, and testing is done with independent video sequences of a random walk of 7 minutes and 30 seconds. We introduce and use accuracy scales similar to the ones used by [7].

Figure 1   A small wearable camera.

In the following section, an overview of the system is given. In Section 3, the histogram calculation of each frame and the similarity measurement of video segments are explained.   Then in Section 4, the method to automatically select a location for the location dictionary is discussed. The experimental results are shown in Section 5.

2. System Overview

The system consists of a notebook PC, PCMCIA video capture card and wearable camera (see Figure 1 for the wearable camera). It completely runs in realtime on a standalone PC and does not need access to a remote server. User operates the system in two phases, which are training phase and recognition phase. Between these two phases, the location dictionary is calculated offline. At training phase, while the user is walking about in a building, a chromatic histogram is calculated and recorded for every frame (Figure 2). After recording, the program looks for suitable segments for the trajectory dictionary in the histogram sequence. From the top of list, trajectory segments are stored in the dictionary. This process is discussed in Section 4.

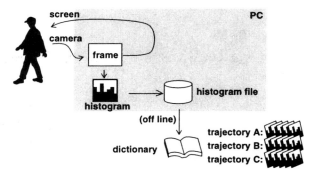

Figure 2   Data flow at recording mode.

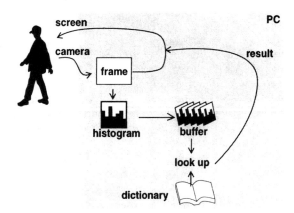

Figure 3   Data flow at analysis mode.

Subsequently, the user walks about in the recognition phase. Again the chromatic histogram is calculated and matched to the trajectories in the dictionary. When a trajectory is similar enough to the recent frames, the system tells the user that he/she has walked through there before, and shows him/her the image of the detected location (Figure 3).

We use an ordinary notebook PC that has an Intel Pentium 166 MHz processor and supports MMX instructions. Training and test video sequences are recorded by a camcorder to allow repetitious analysis and evaluation. However, the system layout is compatible and substitutable with a small computer such as Toshiba Libretto and a camera shown in Figure 1. Libretto 100CT has the same processor speed as the notebook PC we used.

The program is written in C++ and partially in assembly language to provide faster access to MMX instructions. Since MMX supports 64-bit calculation at a time, histogram and some other calculations can be done as fast as 10 Hz.

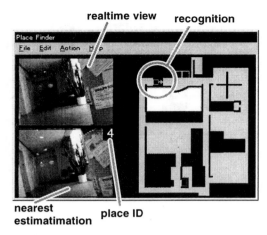

Figure 4　Screen shot of the proposed personal positioning system.

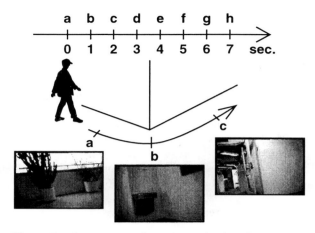

Figure 5　Sparse sampling causes bad performances.

3. Histogram Similarity

In order to implement a vision system onto a wearable computer, we have to keep in mind the following:

- The system should be robust against brightness and noise.

- Calculation for each frame should be fast enough in order to enable high rate of sampling.

- Representation of each frame should be as compact as possible.

The frame representation should not be affected by brightness since lighting can be different from time to time, day or night, even indoors. The second point concerns speed. If the calculation is so heavy that the system can handle only one frame in two seconds, the image sequences can be very different even if the user is passing through the same path at training phase and at test phase. For example in Figure 5, dictionary trajectory for location A is made out of frame (a), (c), (e), (g) and test sequence is sampled as (b), (d), (f), (h). If the sampling frequency is high enough, (a) and (b) are expected to be similar and the system may succeed in matching the two sequences. But if the gap between (a) and (c) is two seconds, (a) and (b) can be quite different which will cause the system to fail.

Frame features are stored in a location dictionary. This means, due to limited space of storage, the smaller the size of feature is, the more locations can be stored. Also, the larger the size of the feature, the slower the performance of the system will be.

3.1 Hue histogram

We calculate hue histograms as frame features. Pixel values are represented by hue (H), saturation (S), and brightness (B). HSB, YUV and RGB units are converted to each other. We linearly translated RGB unit to YUV, and then calculated H value by taking the arctangent of (U,V). The hue (H) histogram is used as a frame feature. We calculate 36-bin histogram, resulting in a 36-dimensional feature vector **f** for each frame.

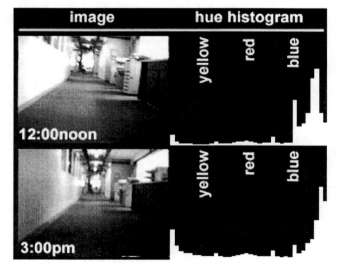

Figure 6　Chromatic (hue) histogram

Figure 6 shows the example of chromatic histogram. As seen in Figure 6, chromatic histogram is robust against angle of camera and time of day [15].

A sequence of **f** represents sequentially incoming video frames. We denote a sequence of **f** as **F**:

$$\mathbf{F}_{se} = \left(\mathbf{f}_s, \mathbf{f}_{s+1}, \ldots, \mathbf{f}_e\right)$$

where $\mathbf{f}_s$ is the chromatic histogram of the s-th frame and $\mathbf{f}_e$ of the e-th frame.

In the system, a histogram element is represented in a byte (8-bit). Therefore, $\mathbf{f}$ occupies 36 bytes in the memory. The system uses a table of tangent value for 5, 15, 25, 35 degrees to calculate to which histogram bin a pixel belongs. This part of the system is implemented in MMX without using floating point calculation. This calculation runs at about 10Hz on 166MHz PC.

3.2 Video segment similarity

Once $\mathbf{F}_{se}$ is calculated, similarity between two segments is calculated in the following way. The distance matrix between segment i and segment j is introduced as:

$$\mathbf{D}_{ij} = \begin{pmatrix} d\left(\mathbf{f}_{s_i}, \mathbf{f}_{s_j}\right) & d\left(\mathbf{f}_{s_i+1}, \mathbf{f}_{s_j}\right) & \cdots & d\left(\mathbf{f}_{e_i}, \mathbf{f}_{s_j}\right) \\ d\left(\mathbf{f}_{s_i}, \mathbf{f}_{s_j+1}\right) & \ddots & & \vdots \\ \vdots & & & \vdots \\ d\left(\mathbf{f}_{s_i}, \mathbf{f}_{e_j}\right) & \cdots & \cdots & d\left(\mathbf{f}_{e_i}, \mathbf{f}_{e_j}\right) \end{pmatrix}$$

where

$$d\left(\mathbf{f}_k, \mathbf{f}_l\right) = \left|\mathbf{f}_k - \mathbf{f}_l\right|^2$$

If segment i and j are the same, diagonal elements in $\mathbf{D}_{ij}$ are 0.

If the user passed through the same location at the same speed in segments i and j, the diagonal elements in $\mathbf{D}_{ij}$ are expected to be small.

If the user passed through the same location in segments i and j, but the user was slower in j than in i, $\mathbf{D}_{ij}$ would have the form of Figure 7.

Therefore, the similarity between segments i and j should be calculated along corresponding elements, which are not necessarily on diagonals. We search a path from the (1,1) element to the $(e_i\text{-}s_i, e_j\text{-}s_j)$ element of D_{ij} under the constraints:

- proceed from (m,n) only to $(m+1,n)$ $(m,n+1)$, or $(m+1,n+1)$.

- along the chosen path, the sum of the elements is minimum.

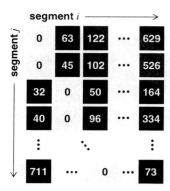

Figure 7   Difference in speed.

The path chosen in the above way is called minimal path, and the sum of elements along the minimal path is denoted as $\mathbf{T}_{ij}$. For example, if $\mathbf{D}_{ij}$ is;

$$\mathbf{D}_{ij} = \begin{pmatrix} 0 & 3 & 2 & 9 \\ 3 & 4 & 5 & 2 \\ 7 & 9 & 2 & 0 \end{pmatrix}$$

Here, the minimal path is (1,1)-(2,2)-(3,3)-(3,4) and $\mathbf{T}_{ij}$ is 0+4+2+0 = 6. (2,2) is chosen even if it is greater than (1,2) or (2,1), since along paths via (1,2) or (2,1), the sums of elements are greater than via (2,2). Dynamic programming frequently used in speech recognition can be used to find the minimal path [16]. Dynamic programming finds the correspondence of frames in segments even if speed is different or not stable.

The proposed system uses 40 frames for each trajectory or video segment. When the location dictionary has 16 trajectories, the dictionary actually holds 40x16 = 640 histograms. When a sequence of histograms for a location P is denoted as $\mathbf{F}_{dict(P)}$, and a sequence of histograms for recent frames at time t is denoted as $\mathbf{F}_{test(t)}$, we note the following incremental comptation of $\mathbf{D}$:

$$\left(\mathbf{D}_{dict(P)test(t)}\right)_{kl} = \left(\mathbf{D}_{dict(P)test(t-1)}\right)_{k,l+1} \qquad \left(l < e_{test}\right)$$

Therefore, only $\left(\mathbf{D}_{dict(P)test(t)}\right)_{k,e(test)}$ is calculated whenever the system receives a new frame. The cost per frame is one histogram calculation, 40x16 = 640 similarity $\left(\mathbf{D}_{dict(1..16)test(t)}\right)_{k,40}$ calculation, and 16 searches for minimal paths.

4. Trajectory Dictionary

Not all locations are suitable for the trajectory dictionary. For example, when a video segment is recorded while the user walks 20 feet in a monotonous hallway, and another segment is recorded of another 20 feet of the same hallway, it is impossible to differentiate the two sequences. Only discriminative segments are suitable to be chosen for the trajectory dictionary. Therefore, a measurement of distinctiveness will be introduced in the following.

We calculate $\mathbf{T}_{ij}$ for all the combinations of segments in the test data with segments partially overlap to each other. Distinctiveness measurement (M) for segment i is introduced as follows:

$$M_i = \sum_{all\_j} \mathbf{T}_{ij} / (number\_of\_segments)$$

In the training data, the same location can be visited more than once. Ideally, segments from the same location should be eliminated from the calculation of M_i. However, the number of segments to be eliminated is relatively small with respect to all the segments. And it is difficult to eliminate them without having a priori association of location and training video sequence.

After M_i is calculated, the system shows the distinctive locations by using the order of M. This list can contain segments too close to each other. For example, if the segment from frame 301 to 340 is on the top of list, segment from 302 to 341 may be listed on the second or third. Therefore by eliminating overlapping segments from the list, the system creates a trajectory dictionary of the most distinctive locations in the environment.

5. Experiments

A training video sequence and a test sequence are taken in the MIT Media Lab Building. The training sequence is 16 minutes and 30 seconds in duration, and the test sequence has 7 minutes and 30 seconds. Both sequences are taken by walking mainly around the third floor. However, in both cases, the user walked on the other floors too. Sequences are taken at the different days. The training sequence is taken at night and the test sequence is taken during the day. Trajectories for the dictionary are only chosen in the third floor. Figure 8 shows an approximate topological map of the third floor and trajectories chosen for the dictionary. These trajectories are chosen from the top of the list as described in Section 4. The order is 13, 9, 11, 4, 14, 5, 8, 6, 10, 16, 2, 1, 7, 15, 12, and 3. Trajectory 8 and 16 are the same, but taken at different visits in the training sequence. The dictionary is made by picking up 9 to 16 trajectories from the top of list.

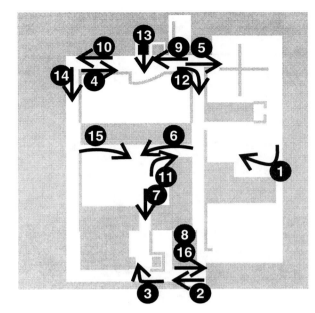

Figure 8   The floor plan and chosen trajectories.

Figure 9 shows the path of the test walk. The solid line indicates the first part of the test walk (3 minutes). The broken line indicates the last part (2 minutes 30 seconds). Between these two parts, the user went down to the ground level by stairs, walked around the ground level, went down to the lower level by stairs and came back to the third floor (2 minutes). These three parts are consecutive. Figure 10 shows detection result of the system. Numbers in normal letter indicate correct detection. Reversed letters indicate substitution error. Blank black box indicate deletion error. Numbers in box indicate insertion error. Blank areas are the gaps between two trajectories in the dictionary. For example, trajectory 6 on the first column is correctly detected at anytime. Trajectory 7 on the second column is correctly detected when the dictionary has 16 trajectories. When the dictionary has 15, 14 or 13 trajectories, the system fails to detect (deletion error). The dictionary doesn't contain trajectory 7 when it has 12 or fewer trajectories, therefore, failures of detecting trajectory 7 are not considered as errors any more.

As for the second part of test walk (out of the third floor), nothing is detected as expected.

41

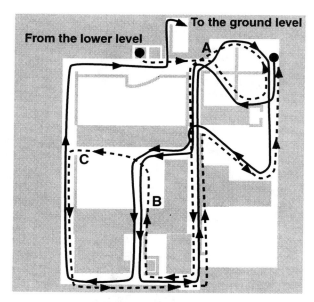

Figure 9 The test walk.

$$Acc_T = \frac{T - D - S}{T}$$

$$Acc_G = \frac{G - I}{G}$$

#	T	T-D-S	D	S	$A_{ccT}\%$
16	12	9	3	0	75.0
15	11	8	3	0	72.7
14	11	8	3	0	72.7
13	11	7	3	1	63.6
12	9	7	2	0	77.8
11	8	6	2	0	75.0
10	7	6	1	0	85.7
9	6	5	1	0	83.3

#	G	G-I	I	$A_{ccG}\%$
16	12	2	10	16.7
15	12	1	11	8.3
14	12	5	7	41.7
13	12	6	6	50.0
12	10	4	6	40.0
11	9	4	5	44.4
10	8	4	4	50.0
9	7	4	3	57.1

Table 1 System performance (#: number of trajectories in the dictionary)

Table 1 shows the numerical evaluation of the system. We use similar evaluation as Starner et al. [7]. T and G are the total numbers of trajectories and gaps in the test sequence. G includes the gap between trajectories 4 and 13 (the second part of test sequence, of the third floor). D (deletions) is the number of trajectories not detected, S (substitution) is the number of trajectories falsely detected, I (insertions) is the count of false detection in gaps, which are not supposed to be detected. Accuracy Acc_T and Acc_G are given as follows:

Figure 10 The results.

As described in [7], Acc_G can be negative when many insertions are detected. D and I are related to each other. When the parameters are set to minimize I, D goes up.

Table 1 shows that the system performs best when 9 or 10 trajectories are chosen for the dictionary.

As seen in Figure 10, location 5 has not been detected. This is because door A was open when training data was taken, and it was closed during testing. The system is confused when the user passes through from point B to C. This is because the color of the whole image is stable for 4-5 seconds in this area, and the path from B to C is similar to 6,7 and 15. The other confusion around 2,3,8,16 was caused by the same reason. There was no salient object in this hallway and this caused the mismatch. This means, 6,7,11 and 15 are very salient to any other segments except 6,7,11 and 15. The same holds for 2,3,8, and 16.

6. Results

We proposed a location recognition system which runs on a wearable computer. Recognition is done in realtime on a standalone PC, and the system doesn't require any wireless communication. The experiments showed that the system recognized locations in relatively good accuracy from the previous work. In addition to the proposed method, we suppose that the introduction of a topologic grammar will solve many problems especially during the insertions. Currently, we are also working on different means to automatically choose the location dictionary. We are considering more discriminative frame representations by changing adding frame features and/or using multiple subregions of each frame.

References

[1] M. Lamming and M. Flynn. *Forget-me-not: intimate computing in support of human memory.* In Proceedings of FRIEND21 International Symposium on Next Generation Human Interface. pp. 125-128. 1994.

[2] B. Rhodes and T. Starner. *Remembrance agent: a continuously running automated information retrieval system.* In Proceedings of the First International Conference on the Practical Application of Intelligent Agents and Multi Agent Technology (PAAM '96).

[3] M. Weiser. *The computer of the twenty-first century.* Scientific American, 1991.

[4] S. Kakez, C. Vania, and P. Bisson. *Virtually documented environment.* In Proceedings of the First International Symposium on Wearable Computers (ISWC '97).

[5] J. Rekimoto and K. Nagao. *The world through the computer: computer augmented interaction with real world environment.* ACM UIST'95, 1995.

[6] J. Rekimoto and K. Nagao. *Agent augmented reality: a software agent meets the world.* In Proceedings of Second International Conference on Multiagent Systems (ICMAS-96).

[7] T. Starner, B. Schiele, and A. Pentland. *Visual contextual awareness in wearable computing.* In Proceedings of the Second International Symposium on Wearable Computers (ISWC '98).

[8] R. Want and A. Hopper. *Active badges and personal interactive computing objects.* IEEE Trans. on Comsumer Electronics, 38(1):10-20, Feb. 1992.

[9] J. Orwant *For want of a bit the user was lost: Cheap user modeling.* IBM Systems Journal, 35(3), 1996.

[10] T. Starner, S. Mann, B. Rhodes, J. Healey, D. Kirsh, R.W. Picard, and A. Pentland. *Augmented reality through wearable computing.* Presence 6(4): 386-398, 1997.

[11] B. Schiele and J. Crowley. *Probabilistic object recognition using mutltidimensional receptive field histogram.* International Conference on Pattern Recognition (ICPR '96) B:50-54, 1996.

[12] B. Clarkson and A. Pentland. *Unsupervised clustering of ambulatory audio and video.* In Proceedings of the International Conference on Acoustics, Speech and Signal Processing (ICASSP '99).

[13] H. Aoki, B. Schiele, and A. Pentland. *Recognizing personal location from video.* In Proceedings of the Perceptual User Interfaces Workshop (PUI '98).

[14] H.Ney. *The use of a one-stage dynamic programming algorithm for connected word recognition.* Readings in Speech Recognition: 188-196. 1990.

[15] H. Aoki, S. Shimotsuji, and O. Hori. *A shot classification method of selecting effective key-frames for video browsing.* In Proceedings of ACM Multimedia 96: 1-10. 1996.

[16] H. Sakoe and S. Chiba. *Dynamic programming algorithm for spoken word recognition.* Readings in Speech Recognition: 159-165. 1990.

Co-Modal Browser – An Interface for Wearable Computers

Jonny Farringdon, Vanessa Oni, Chi Ming Kan, & Leo Poll

Software Engineering & Applications Group
Philips Research Laboratories
Cross Oak Lane, Redhill. Surrey. RH1 5HA. UK

farringdon@bcs.org.uk   Vanessa.Oni, Chi.Kan, Leonard.Poll @philips.com

Abstract

This paper describes user tests on a co-modal browser, a general interface for wearable devices that can communicate through a browser. The co-modal browser is a Handheld Device Markup Language (HDML) browser with fully integrated visual display, synthetic speech, voice command, short sounds and buttons. The browser was tested for hands-free, eyes-free, and hands & eyes-free use. Usability test results are presented here of use to wearable computer researchers concerned with hands & eyes-free use. The co-modal concept is demonstrated as viable on an HDML browser.

Keywords— *co-modal, eyes free, hands free, HDML, multimodal interface, usability, WAP, wearable, WML*

1. Introduction

The co-modal browser addresses the changing circumstances and contexts in which the mobile user finds themselves. The aim is to allow a user to access an application seamlessly as their circumstances and their environment changes by displaying information and controlling the device in co-existing modalities.

A first prototype co-modal browser has been developed in software, based upon the Handheld Device Mark-up Language (HDML) [4]. HDML is a Web like mark-up language initially aimed at addressing web browsing issues for mobile phones. Our HDML browser utilises synthetic speech, voice control, non-speech sounds, a small visual display, and push buttons.

Usability trials have been carried out to identify issues concerned with using the browser under conditions of restricted modality. Specifically hands free, eyes free, and hands & eyes free use. The usability test results are feeding into the development of a second-generation co-modal browser.

Here we describe our HDML browser and the co-existing modality "display" and controls, together with results from the usability trials.

2. Handheld Device Markup Language - HDML

The co-modal browser is a custom designed handheld device mark-up language (HDML) browser using a small visual display, control buttons and "soft buttons" (programmable buttons), together with fully integrated synthetic speech, voice command recognition, and short non-speech sounds.

HDML is a counterpart to the better known internet web-site mark-up language HTML. HDML is optimised for a small display such as those on mobile phones where a normal HTML web page could not be accommodated.

HDML was the precursor to the Wireless Application Protocol (WAP) which is currently the subject of an industry standardisation activity. WAP forum members include Unwired Planet (UP), Nokia, Motorola, Ericsson & Philips [6].

The co-modal browser implements a partially compliant HDML browser. The HDML specification was not fully implemented for a number of reasons. This software was to use multiple modalities, and the specification makes no reference to multiple modalities. Also certain aspects of HDML were not considered to be "user centred." An example of this is the ability of content providers to destroy the users browsing history. This feature can be misused to lock users into a web site.

3. Co-Modal Interface

The co-modal interface uses three different modal methods for communicating from the device to the user, and two methods for the user to communicate with the device. The user can look at the small visual display, can hear short non-speech sounds, and listen to synthetic speech. To control the device the user can push keys (buttons) and speak commands. A screen shot of the browser is shown in Figure 1.

Previous relevant work is use of an audio-only wearable computer by Roy, Sawhney, Schmandt, & Pentland showed that "it may be socially unacceptable to speak at certain times so a secondary method of input (for example using a keypad or some tactile device) should also be considered." [1]. The audio-only wearable is developed and used "on the run" by Sawhney & Schmandt, [3].

A speech enabled web browser was developed by Rudnicky, Reed & Thayer, [2], who added spoken language and speech generation code directly into the NCSA Mosaic browser. Language specific information was added to hypertext documents by extending HTML.

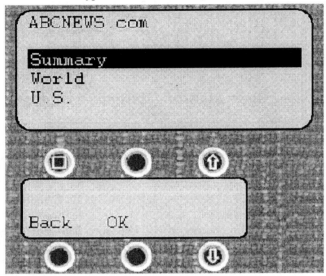

Figure 1. On-Screen simulation of HDML browser window and control buttons

3.1. Visual Display

The visual display consists of four lines of text, 21 characters in length. Typically the heading of a list and three of the items (sub-headings) in that list are displayed. The size of the screen is comparable to a small personal device such as a mobile phone or wristwatch display.

3.2. Keys (Push Buttons)

Six buttons are present on this particular display though only five are used. Three of the buttons have symbols printed upon them (symbols for STOP, UP & DOWN) while two of the buttons are "soft" labelled. The up and down arrows move a highlight bar through any lists of choices. The "stop" button will stop all actions by the browser. In this version of the software there is also one button left unlabelled. The soft labels are programmable by the content provider and can change from page to page. When left blank, the browser system makes use of the left soft button, labelling it BACK, this acts like the back button on a web browser taking you to the previous page.

3.3. Non-Speech Sounds

Non-speech sounds are used to give the user feedback and to paint an audio-picture as to what is happening on the screen. For example, there is a "woosh" (golf-club swinging sound) used to signify the start of a page, and a male voice "clearing his throat" just before reading the text.

3.4. Synthetic Speech

Synthetic speech is presented in the form of a male voice, with an American accent. The speech system used was Microsoft Speech SDK 4.0, from Microsoft Research. This contained a high quality voice (called Mike). It also enabled the use of simultaneous synthetic speech and voice recognition, something some other speech systems would not allow on a single PC sound card. For more information see http://research.microsoft.com

3.5. Voice Control

Speech recognition was set up before the start of the experiment to recognise the subject's voice depending on gender. Also, a single voice control parameter was adjusted during a practice session by changing the sensitivity of the speech recognition. This was done in order to minimise false positives (registering a positive word recognition, when this was not the case). False positives had a more serious effect on navigation than false negatives (where the user would say a word, nothing would happen, and they would have to repeat the word). A strong regional accent could require the sensitivity value to be changed.

The speech recognition was set to look for the following words, occasionally similar sounding non-words were also used. To improve performance of the speech recognition, words and non-words that the system was required not to respond to, were also listened for. For the "up" command two words could be spoken, both "up", and "previous". Additionally, a maximum of two words could be set by the content of the HDML page for the two soft buttons. As these words were not known beforehand no variations were included in the system.

- *Stop* from the word and phonetic variations: "stop", "stopp", "sto", "stap", "stup"

- *Down*, "Down"

- *Up*, "Up", "upp ", "uup ", "uupp ", "previous"

- *OK*, "okk", "ook", "awkay", "owkay", "oky"

- *At*, "at", ignore this word

- *Cup*, "cup", ignore this word

- *On*, "on", ignore this word

- *Back,* "Back"

3.6. A UI for Changing Contexts of Use

The co-modal browser addresses the problem of using your device on the move, walking, driving, running, sitting on a train, at a desk, while shopping, and so forth. Switching between interaction modalities to suit the situation is recognised as crucial in the broader scope of future information delivery, [5]. Using the co-modal browser it is possible to access information and switch between interaction styles

- Using the small visual display and push-buttons (in the traditional way)
- Hands free, using voice command
- Eyes free, using the synthetic speech and short sounds
- Hands & eyes free, using voice commands and synthetic speech

For the purposes of the usability tests, the latter three interaction modes were used in isolation.

4. Usability Tests

These lab-bound usability tests aimed to identify the major usability issues of the first co-modal browser implementation. Results will feed into the development of a mobile co-modal browser and mobile tests.

4.1. Subjects

The trials included 18 subjects, 9 male subjects (average age 30.3 years) and 9 female subjects (average age 31.4 years). In each experimental condition, 50% were male and 50% female, 6 subjects per condition. Subjects were all employees of Philips Research Laboratories, Redhill. At this first stage in the usability development process using in-house subjects was deemed satisfactory.

Concerning their use of related technologies, 6 of the subjects currently used a mobile phone, while 3 subjects had used mobile phones in the past. Of the 18 subjects, 17 had regular access to the internet. None of the subjects currently used a pager but 3 subjects had used pagers in the past.

4.2. Experimental Conditions

There were three experimental conditions in this experiment. A *hands-free* condition, using voice command to interact with the browser while having visual access to the information. An *eyes-free* condition, using buttons to interact with the browser and having the information presented through synthetic speech and short sounds. A *hands* and *eyes-free* condition, using voice commands to interact with the browser and having the information presented through synthetic speech and short sounds.

4.3. Tasks

Seven browsing tasks were given to each subject. An example task is "find the news about Greenspan", where there was a single ABC News page about an announcement Greenspan had made. Six tasks were chosen at random plus a terminating task, which was the same for each subject. The complexity of the set of tasks was the same for each subject.

The experiment used live pages from existing internet web sites. The "jukebox", pages were bespoke using commercially available music CDs.

4.4. Test Procedure Summary

The co-modal browser software and both a video camera and recorder were set up before the subject arrived. Once the subject arrived they were introduced to the test environment and the purpose of the test was explained. The subject was given a questionnaire and asked to fill in some basic personal details. After this, the subject was given a written description of the co-modal browser and a set of practice tasks to perform. On finishing the practice tasks, the subject was given the real tasks to perform and the video camera was switched on to record the session. The software also logged mouse clicks and (recognised) spoken commands. After the seven tasks had been completed the subject was given the second part of the questionnaire to fill in and a brief interview was conducted. The subject was then thanked for having taken part and the need for confidentiality was stressed.

5. Usability Test Results

5.1. Subjective Results

The responses given by the subjects in the post experiment interview were evaluated and are presented in the graphs below. Subjects were encouraged to give their spontaneous opinions on the browser and the experience of using it.

Positive experiences with the browser are shown in Figure 2. Using speech input to interact with the browser was considered enjoyable. Some found that the browser became easier to use after an "initial learning period". Some subjects also commented positively on the music from the "jukebox" pages. The feedback from the sounds was well received and the speech synthesiser used was considered acceptable.

Figure 3 shows features that subjects disliked about the browser and where they had difficulty in using it. Some subjects found the browser frustrating to use after a while or found that it needed some getting used to initially. There was a delay in recognising commands and some subjects found this laborious. It was hard for subjects to visualize the information and structure in the live web pages, especially those in the eyes-free condition. Subjects had some difficulty finding the items in the tasks they were given. Most subjects had difficulty with the American accent used for the speech synthesiser.

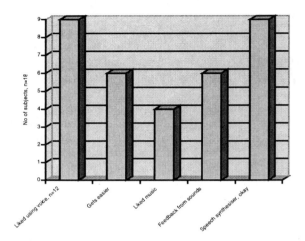

Figure 2. Subjects' overall positive experience and opinion of the browser (18 subjects).

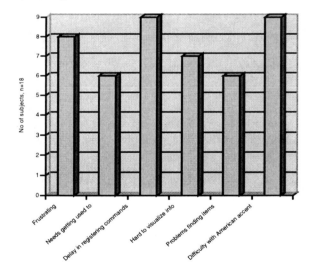

Figure 3. Subjects' overall negative experience and opinion of the browser (18 subjects).

5.2. Trial Observations

The software being used in the trials produced datalogs, and these together with the video tapes of the trials allowed for the observation and quantification of usability behaviour.

The main usability issues which were derived from the observations are shown here. This first graph, Figure 4, shows the average time taken to complete the tasks between the subject groups. All subjects were given the same instructions, "do the tasks in your own time, this is not a competition or a race."

Figure 4 shows that subjects in the *hands-free* condition took the shortest time on average to complete all seven tasks, 18.5 min. Subjects in the *eyes-free* condition took 23.8 min. on average, while subjects in the *hands* and *eyes-free* condition took the longest on average to complete all seven tasks, 30 min.

Subjects in the *hands-free* condition probably took the shortest time because when you are presented with information visually, it is easier to search for information and remember where you are in the "tree structure of pages". However, it must be taken into consideration that subjects were told to perform the tasks at their own pace.

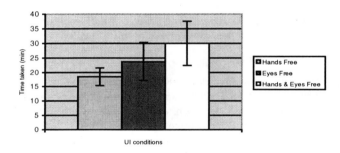

Figure 4. Average time taken in the three user interface conditions to complete all seven tasks. Subjects were told that time was not important, "this is not a race."

To examine whether there was indeed a significant difference in the time taken by subjects in the three user interface conditions, an unrelated one-way ANOVA (Analysis of Variance) was carried out. There was a significant difference for the time taken by the subjects in the three User Interface conditions ($F_{(2, 15)} = 5.436 > p = 0.05$). We have a confidence level for these results of 98.3%.

Figure 5 shows that subjects in the *hands-free* condition used STOP the least on average. Being able to press the key resulted in the STOP key being pressed more frequently. The other groups appeared to be less inclined to use the stop facility if they had to say the word STOP.

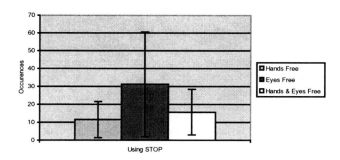

Figure 5. Pressing or saying STOP, for the three user interface conditions over all seven tasks.

Initially it appeared as if the STOP key could be removed, saving space and cost in the construction of a co-modal browser device. However, statistical tests showed that there was no significant difference in using STOP between the different UI conditions.

To examine whether there was indeed a significant difference in using STOP between the three user interface conditions, an unrelated one-way ANOVA (Analysis of Variance) was carried out. There was no significant difference for the use of the STOP command between the three User Interface conditions ($F_{(2, 15)}$ = 1.722 > p = 0.25). With a confidence level of 79% the differences in behaviour between the groups is not considered significant.

Like traditional web browsers such as Netscape and Microsoft Internet Explorer, the co-modal browser has a BACK facility that takes you back to the previous web page visited. The co-modal browser also has up and down facilities for navigating lists of links within a page.

Figure 6 showed that subjects in the *hands & eyes-free* group used BACK when they wanted to issue an UP command more frequently than subjects in the other conditions. While subjects in the *hands-free* condition did this the least.

A reason for this could be that when you see a list of items, the words up and down correspond with your visual representation (it being easier to perform spatial reasoning when the information is presented to you visually). Whereas the groups with no visual display had to construct their own model of the page structure and more readily confused the semantically similar commands BACK and UP. The group using buttons pressed the arrow keys and made this error less frequently than those who had to speak commands, again suggesting that the visual arrows on the buttons, pointing up and down, helped them identify the correct command for navigation.

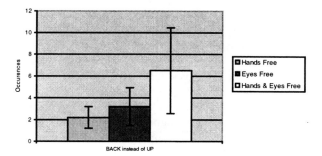

Figure 6. Non-optimal behaviour, confusing the BACK and UP commands, and navigating in the wrong direction, for the three user interface conditions.

To examine whether there was indeed a significant difference in using BACK instead of UP between the three UI conditions, an unrelated one-way ANOVA (Analysis of Variance) was carried out. There is a significant difference for using BACK instead of UP between the three User Interface conditions ($F_{(2, 15)}$ = 4.768 > p = 0.05). We have a confidence level for these results of 97.5%.

Occasionally subjects who wished to navigate down further into a web site would end up going up and across into another branch of the tree, in practice ending up in a different web site altogether, see Figure 7. Subjects in the *hands* and *eyes-free* group were most likely to move out of a site while subjects in the *hands-free* condition are less likely to do this. Again, the fact that some subjects could see a visual representation of the content meant that they were less likely to navigate in the wrong direction.

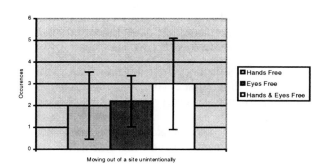

Figure 7. Moving out of a web site unintentionally. The user intended to move down a tree of pages in a particular site but unintentionally moved up and into another web site.

To examine whether there was indeed a significant difference in moving out of a web site unintentionally between the three UI conditions, an unrelated one-way ANOVA (Analysis of Variance) was carried out. There is no significant difference for moving out of a web site unintentionally between the three User Interface conditions ($F_{(2, 15)} = 0.632 < p = 0.25$).

Further observations from the trials are recorded in Figure 8. While browsing for information, subjects often forgot the commands needed to navigate through the web pages and one introduced their own commands. Some subjects using the speech input often had to repeat a word before the browser recognised it. Also, some subjects did not realise that a given task had been completed. Most subjects tended to interrupt the browser as it was responding to a previous command. The content providers used a certain menu structure to trap users in their web pages which resulted in some subjects getting stuck in loops.

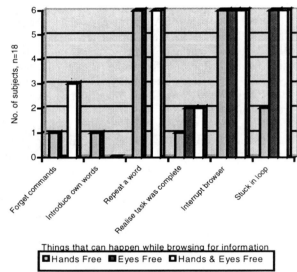

Figure 8. Co-modal browser user behaviour for the UI conditions.

5.3. Trials Summary

Usability trials conducted on the first co-modal browser prototype highlight issues concerning hands and eyes-free browsing. Significant observations regarding usability are listed here.

- Time required to complete browsing tasks is dependent upon the user's method of interaction with the browser. *Hands-free* group were the fastest, then *eyes-free* group. The slowest were the *hands & eyes-free* group.

- Navigation is equally difficult using a small browser, *hands*, *eyes*, or *hands & eyes-free*. Unintentionally navigating out of a site was common for all three conditions, with no significant difference between them.

- Semantically similar commands were easily confused, "BACK" (move back to a web page), and "UP" (move up one item in a list), were often confused. This was particularly the case for *hands & eyes-free* subjects.

- Simultaneous voice command input and speech recognition is crucial. All subjects interrupted the browser.

- Speech recognition often required subjects to repeat commands as the browser did not recognise them initially.

- *Eyes & hands-free* users enjoyed using the device more than *eyes-free* users who controlled the device by pushing buttons.

- Those using the *eyes-free* version were three times more likely to get stuck in loops made by content providers, compared to those using the *hands-free* version.

- Synthetic speech and voice control were particularly enjoyable features.

6. Future Work

These usability tests produced detailed user feedback about the browser that is guiding development of a mobile prototype. Figure 9 shows the mobile prototype which runs on a WinCE palm PC platform. Some of the initial usability improvements include:

- Distinguishing "links" from "text" on screen

- Distinguishing "links" from "text" in audio by using different voices

- Speeding up system reaction times

- Adding a dedicated back/undo button

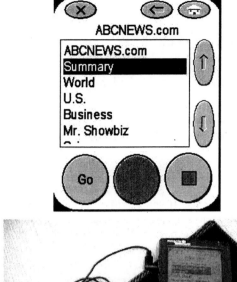

Figure 9 Co-Modal Browser on WinCE palm PC. Screen shot (above), and browser with combined microphone & earpiece (Jabra), and wrist strap (below)

7. Summary

The modalities of a visual display, synthetic speech, short sounds and buttons co-exist in the co-modal browser.

The co-modal browser is a web browser and general wearable interface for devices with small screens and only a few buttons such as mobile phones or wristwatch displays, with fully integrated synthetic speech, voice command, and non-speech sounds. Such a browser can form the basis for a general user interface for mobile and wearable devices.

The HDML browser we have developed can be used hands and eyes free. This is a considerable achievement as the HDML specification [4] does not account for these features. The co-modal browser addresses the problem of using your computing devices on the move, walking, driving, running, sitting on a train, at a desk, while shopping, and so forth. Using the co-modal browser it is possible to access information and switch between interaction styles

- Using the small visual display and push-buttons (in the traditional way)
- *Hands free*, using voice command
- *Eyes free*, using the synthetic speech and short sounds
- *Hands & eyes free*, using voice commands and synthetic speech

We have proven that a co-modal HDML browser is a viable proposition. The co-modal browser has been successfully used and tested hands-free, eyes-free and hands & eyes-free. The co-modal browser techniques transfer to WAP technology [6] which is already appearing in mobile consumer devices such as the Ericsson R380 "smart cellphone" and the Nokia 7110, the first "WAP- GSM" phone. The usability test results can be used by other wearable computer researchers concerned with hands-free and eyes-free use.

Acknowledgements

With particular thanks to David Pearce for his exemplary software engineering on WinCE, and David Yule for support with HDML.

References

[1] Deb Roy, Nitin Sawhney, Chris Schmandt, & Alex Pentland. *"Wearable Audio Computing: A Survey of Interaction Techniques."* Perceptual Computing Technical Report #434. MIT Media Lab, MA, USA. 1997. http://nitin.www.media.mit.edu/people/nitin/projects/NomadicRadio/AudioWearables.html (Last visited 10th August 1999).

[2] Alexander I Rudnicky, Stephan D Reed, & Eric H Tayer. *"SpeechWear: A mobile speech system."* School of computer science, Carnegie Mellon University. 1996. http://www.speech.cs.cmu.edu/air/papers/speechwear/speechwear.html (Last visited 10th August 1999).

[3] Nitin Sawhney, & Chris Schmandt. "Speaking and Listening on the Run: Design for Wearable Audio Computing." In proceedings of *The Second International Symposium on Wearable Computers*. IEEE. Pittsburgh, Pennsylvania, USA. October 19-20 1998. pp 108–115

[4] Unwired Planet, Alcatel Alsthom Recherche, AT&T, GEMPLUS, Mitsubishi Electric Corporation, Sun Microsystems Corporation, & Tandem Computers Inc. 1997. "Handheld Device Markup Language Specification." 9th May 1997. http://www.w3.org/TR/NOTE-Submission-HDML-spec.html (Last visited 10th August 1999).

[5] Greg C Vanderheiden. "Anywhere, anytime (+anyone) access to the next-generation WWW." *Computer Networks and ISDN Systems* (Netherlands). No 29. Pp 1439-1446. Elsevier, 1997. Also in proceedings of *Sixth International World Wide Web Conference*. Santa Clara California. April 7-12 1997. http://www.scope.gmd.de/info/www6/technical/paper253/paper253.html (Last visited 12th August 1999).

[6] *"The WAP Forum"*. http://www.wapforum.org (Last visited 10th August 1999).

MEX: A Distributed Software Architecture for Wearable Computers

Juha Lehikoinen, Jussi Holopainen, Marja Salmimaa, Angelo Aldrovandi

Nokia Research Center, Tampere, Finland
{juha.lehikoinen, jussi.holopainen, marja.salmimaa, angelo.aldrovandi}
@nokia.com

Abstract

A new dynamic software architecture for wearable computers is proposed. Key properties of this MEX architecture are examined and compared to some other existing software architecture. One application utilizing MEX, called WalkMap, is presented. The aim of the applications currently under development is to enhance the communication and cooperation of the users utilizing wearable computers in their daily lives. Based on that the software components needed to access context information anywhere and the hardware requirements arising from constant usage are considered. The hardware platform for the software architecture developed is briefly described.

1. Introduction

A major challenge in building wearable systems is to develop flexible configurations for several user groups and applications. The basic building blocks, both in hardware and software, need to be adaptable and easily reconfigured. Basically, a wearable system should fulfill at least the following E^3 criteria originally presented by Steve Mann [6]:

1. Eudaemonic criterion. The system is a seamless part of the user.

2. Existential criterion. The locus of control is within the user's domain and the system behaves as an extension of the user's mind and body.

3. Ephemeral criterion. Interactional and operational delays are nonexistent and the system is always active when worn.

The untethered nature of wearable systems and the freedom to move are key issues usually mentioned in articles describing the development of the hardware for wearables. If the goal is to develop versatile wearable systems, not only the hardware but also the software has to be done such that it is adaptable to several configurations and environments. If the environment consists of several intelligent senders ubiquitous in a certain area, the software architecture should be able to answer the requests of these devices. On the other hand the peripherals of the wearable may vary depending on the operating situation of the user. The aim of our work is to assure that the software we develop for a wearable system can fulfill these requirements.

The software architecture for the wearable computer should be both adaptable and adaptive. An adaptable system is easy to configure and change. Adaptive systems, on the other hand, are able to change their behaviour automatically according to the system's context.

1.1. Our design goals and principles

We have an ongoing research project on wearable computers, called NetWalk. Our goal is to find concepts and techniques for a wearable computer, targeted towards a general audience for everyday use. This goal sets quite demanding requirements for many aspects of a wearable computer. In this paper, we will propose a software architecture for such a wearable computing concept.

Our aim was to have an open, dynamic software architecture for our wearable computing project. We wanted the architecture to reflect the fundamental idea behind wearable computing in general – small footprint, mobility, connectivity, and dynamic changes in the using environment. The absence of such an architecture made us design and implement one of our own. We named our architecture MEX (MessageEXchanger).

Our current software is written completely in C and C++, and the network technology is based on TCP/IP. It can be run on any platform with a decent C/C++ compiler, while the applications running on MEX can be written in any programming language providing support for inter-process communication.

In the design phase, we set the following requirements for our architecture:

1. It should allow the different applications in a wearable computer to communicate with each other.

2. It should allow the applications to communicate with the ubiquitous environment.

3. It should allow the applications to communicate with some other applications in some other wearable computer.

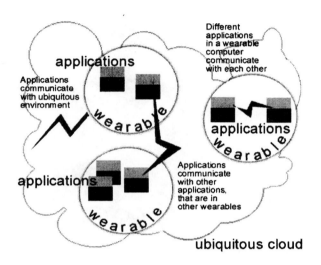

Figure 1. Communication goals.

These first three goals, depicted in Figure 1, fulfill the need for mobile, continuous and flexible communication between users. They also make it possible for an application to query for information about the environment.

In addition to these three goals, we also defined some goals concerning dynamical changes:

4. It should allow dynamic removal and insertion of individual applications.

5. It should allow dynamic changing of a module of an application (including user interface).

6. It should allow the applications to use services provided by the other applications, no matter whether local or remote, without knowing the exact provider of the service.

7. All these operations should be autonomous, requesting actions from the user only when needed (for instance, a decision has to be made).

These goals ensure that the changes in the environment and local conditions will be reflected in the user's machine in an invisible, natural way. They also allow loading of applications over the network, and when combined with the goal three they also allow the user to use an application in some other user's machine.

We chose a somewhat radical approach to reach these goals. The main idea behind MEX is based on an *extremely flat hierararchy model*, *open application interface* and *services*.

The flat hierarchy allows us to keep the system both flexible and efficient; the hierarchy encourages the application designers to split the applications into several modules (for instance, some functional modules and a user interface module). Since all of these modules are distinct services under MEX, they can be easily replaced. The openness of the system allows a variety of applications (including existing applications) to connect to MEX through an extremely simple programming interface.

The most important aspect, however, is that of *services*. We rejected the conventional client-server model often used in distributed architectures; actually, in MEX any application can provide any number of services to the other applications. These applications can be further divided into modules as described above. Even MEXes in different computers can act as clients or servers to each other depending on the case.

It could be said that even the concept of an "application" in its traditional meaning is somewhat blurred in MEX; an application can be thought as a collection of services it offers, and a collection of services it requests through MEX.

As can be seen from the description above the MEX architecture is, in fact, close to traditional event based architectures (also known as implicit invocation, or selective broadcast) with the same advantages and disadvantages [4].

2. Related work

The area of software architectures for wearable computing is still rather young, as is the whole wearable computing paradigm itself. There has been some previous research on such architectures, most notable of which is with no doubt the software organization for Netman [1, 3].

MEX is comparable to Netman software architecture in many respects; actually, we found amazingly similar solutions for several problems independently, including e.g.

the environment-directed computing concept and dynamic software reconfiguration. There are some crucial differences, though. While Netman relies on a middleware solution and that services are provided by the middlelayer, MEX goes even further by allowing any application to provide any service: thus, no middleware layer is needed. The same holds true for the different system architectures for environment-directed computing; with MEX, any of the three methods can be used. The intelligent environment registers with MEX and informs it about the services available. MEX does not care about the actual implementation of those services.

There has also been some research on application design for wireless computing [7]. Watson discusses the dividing of the application functionality between the mobile device and the network. In Watson's work, the interface boundary between network and the mobile device can be changed dynamically. Watson's idea of partitioning applications is useful also in MEX, though for different reasons – while Watson wants to make effective use of the network, we want to partition applications by the nature of their usage environments and conditions.

At one point we considered using Sun's Jini architecture because their goals are similar to ours. The Jini system is "based on the idea of federating groups of users and the resources required by those users" and "the goal is to turn the network into a flexible, easily-administered tool" [5]. Even though this is almost exactly the goal we have in mind we were not ready to pay the price of switching to this solution. Especially the computational resource requirements would have been too high for a wearable computer.

As MEX and Jini are similar on the architectural level it is quite straightforward to "port" a MEX service to Jini service and vice versa. Normally it is not even necessary to port services because these two systems can coexist easily. For example, a MEX service that acts as a MEX interface to Jini services is quite easy to implement and (again) vice versa. By not adopting Jini totally we were able to use large amounts of ready-made code without too much trouble and did not have to care about the expensive migration costs.

3. System design

The NetWalk research method is based on application requirement analysis, user interface analysis and extensive field testing with different prototypes and demonstrations. To support these methods, we have built a demo platform to allow testing of both hardware and software components.

With its dynamic nature, MEX supports perfectly this kind of "trial-and-error" approach.

3.1. Hardware

The wearable information system designed to the research platform of MEX and applications utilizing MEX architecture is built from commercial off-the-self hardware. The system as a whole is body-worn; the computer with the accessories is integrated to a vest made especially for this purpose (Figure 2).

Figure 2. Wearable information system.

To avoid the possible transfer of electric charge between bodies of different electrostatic potential in proximity or through direct contact the vest is fabricated from special conducting ESD textiles. The pockets of the vest are designed to keep the hardware firmly in place. Some Velcro tape is added for the wires. The design of the vest assures that the loading of the system is equally distributed throughout the user's upper body.

The MEX architecture does not require any specific features for the computer used. This means that the only requirements set to the computer used are the small size and the number of applicable ports for input and output devices needed for the applications. We ended up using a PC approximately 3.5x13x21 cm in size - a bit bigger than a VHS tape. Because the PC is one of the biggest components of the system, weighing some 1200 grams, it was decided to place to a pocket locating near the small of user's back. The form factor of the PC chosen works well under the user strain caused by activities such as sitting and resting against the backrest.

The PC is equipped with one serial port, one parallel port, a keyboard/mouse interface, two PCI card slots, a VGA connector, and a headset connection. It has a 166 MHz Pentium MMX processor, 32 MB RAM and 1.94 GB hard disk space. Instead of a keyboard a wireless mouse was used for user comfort.

The display of the PC is normally left unused. Instead, we run applications using a Sony Glasstron. This color display device has SVGA resolution of 600x800 pixels and a diagonal field of view of 18 degrees, and it is switchable between a see-through mode and an immersive mode. In the future we hope to upgrade this to a better display solution.

We selected the following peripheral devices for our system to meet the specific needs of the WalkMap application:

The WalkMap application needs to know the position and the orientation of the user. For position information a *Trimble Nav-Guide GPS system with differential correction* service is used. The orientation information is also important, and for this purpose a *gyro from InterSense Inc.* was selected. This gyro has an angular resolution of 0.02 degrees (relative) and a latency of 38 ms ±2 ms. The maximum angular rate of the device is 400 deg/second (Yaw) and 360 deg/second (Pitch and Roll). A special software driver was developed to allow flexible use of the angular information given by the gyro.

GSM Card Phone. The Nokia Card Phone is a PC card with a built-in GSM phone [2]. It was chosen for this project because it allows us to turn our wearable computer into a wireless communication system without additional interface adapters or cables. The Nokia Card Phone works with basic Windows and communication applications and the user is able to send and receive Short Messages, faxes and e-mail, access the Internet, connect to databases and download files over digital GSM networks. The Short Message capabilities are used with our WalkMap application described later.

3.2. MEX architecture

Our software architecture has to be able to adapt to varying needs as smoothly as possible. That is why we constructed the system from very loosely coupled services, which together form a MEX environment.

A MEX environment consists of one MEX server and a number of services associated with the server (Figure 3). The server is just a "post office" keeping track of available services and transferring events to the services. Each service registers itself to the MEX environment by connecting to the environment server and specifying the service name and the events it is interested in.

Normal services connect to just one environment but in some cases it is necessary for the service to be able to connect to (at least) two different environments. For example, the WalkMap service has to be connected to both the local MEX (UI, GPS etc.) and the actual map database, which might be somewhere else in the network. These kind of services are called MEX proxies as they mediate between different MEX environments.

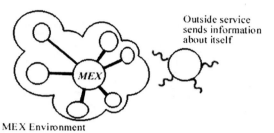

Figure 3. MEX environment.

The local MEX environment can be described as a personal bubble around the user. This bubble can, if need be, "engulf" nearby services provided by devices which are not within the user's MEX environment. A solitary service which is not in any MEX environment is normally in the discovery mode, actively trying to get connected to a MEX environment. For example, the user walks into a room containing a colour printer. The service discovery proxy in the user's MEX environment discovers the printer service and engulfs it (Figure 4). The printer service is now inside the user's local MEX environment and the user can print nice holiday photos from his/her digital camera. When the service discovery proxy loses the connection to the printer the service is automatically unregistered from the user's MEX environment.

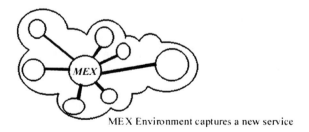

Figure 4. Service Discovery.

There can be several service discovery proxies in the MEX environment, one for each different method of service discovery.

Service discovery methods can be categorized into two distinct groups: autonomous and infrastructure dependent. In autonomous service discovery the device providing the service is communicating autonomously with the service discovery proxy (IrDA/BlueTooth). Infrastructure dependent discovery uses external information to locate needed services (service look-up directories, Service Location Protocol) [8].

Two MEX environments use the same external service

Figure 5. Personal bubbles overlap.

As one of our goals is to enhance communication and cooperation of the users of the wearable systems the service location proxies are able to locate other similar proxies. In this scenario the user may configure some of their services to expose their interfaces to external users (Figure 5). This would allow, for example, the user to upload those nice holiday pictures to another user's digital imaging service.

The possibility of accessing other user's personal bubble raises issues of access control and security/privacy. Apart from the possibility of configuring the external service interfaces we have not put much effort to this issue yet.

In the current implementation we are using TCP/IP for the connection between the service and the server, but it does not require much effort to switch to any other reliable point-to-point protocol. In fact, some of the service discovery proxies use different point-to-point protocols by nature (IrDA, serial cable).

4.   Application scenario: WalkMap

Among the applications currently under development for NetWalk, an outstanding example is the map. Our WalkMap is conceived in the modular software structure typical of MEX and fully integrated with the NetWalk system services that will be described below.

Particular research and testing in WalkMap is focused on its user interface: it has to be freely customizable and its parts must be easily modified and replaced for extensive testing. In our flat and modular software architecture, we are currently designing a component-based audio-enhanced spatial user interface with 3D icons where different input methods generate the same MEX activation commands: the user can then interact with the system through the channels s/he prefer. Other wearable input devices and paradigms, such as eye and hand tracking, may be seamlessly added without any additional structural effort.

From the architectural point of view, WalkMap is split into several components that register as MEX services. They are semantically grouped as follows:

1.   User interface components.

2.   The map navigation abstraction layer, which transparently manages input devices for browsing and zooming within the map.

3.   Graphical outputs, which both visualize the map in different modes and allow the user to interact with it, for example by defining places with a click.

4.   Location dependent services, which are utilized once they first connect to MEX and after that define themselves in the user interface. They can be eventually called from any other NetWalk application.

The interaction between these independent modules happens entirely through MEX events. WalkMap components have access to several system services in the NetWalk platform, such as unified database access and a position-aware device management system.

WalkMap accesses the database by registering to a secondary dedicated MEX server, which can be in the local MEX environment or in the network, where multiple resources are managed transparently as independent services (as in Figure 5, where WalkMap acts as a proxy between two different MEX environments).

In the local NetWalk environment coordinates coming from DGPS and other devices (such as from IR-beacons) are retrieved through the *WearAmI* service, which responds to GetPos and SetPos requests (the latter command allowing the user to manually specify his/her position when information from DGPS is missing or inaccurate). *WearAmI* calculates the accuracy of the signal in a time-dependent way and determines the most reliable value from the instruments. Any NetWalk module can instruct *WearAmI* to feed it with coordinate information at regular intervals or only when triggered by proximity to defined locations. The latter allows us to define tasks to execute when in the vicinity of a certain location. That allows us to create applications such as a context-aware to-do task list.

Several map services are under construction. *Query* can answer simple questions in a position-aware mode (for example "where is the nearest bookstore") by accessing DGPS information and the geographical database. *WayFinder* interactively guides the user through the streets of a city suggesting the fastest way based on the information available, for example utilizing public transportation timetables and recommending that the user should head for the proper bus stop. By means of the Nokia Card Phone, the *Connect* plugin can interrogate another user through a Short Message message about position and visualize it on the map as an icon, and eventually open a data or voice connection with him/her with a click.

5. Future work

Our research on NetWalk actively continues as does the development and further research on MEX. Our next goals for MEX include security issues and testing connectivity with different ubiquitous devices. We will also examine quality of service issues, e.g. performance and reliability.

On a more abstract research level, we are exploring a scripting feature for NetWalk. MEX messages can be easily translated into text commands, and the whole software system can be seen as a set of components interacting with each other via MEX asynchronous command queue. With little effort a *Macro* service can be implemented to put a predefined set of messages in the queue as a single macro event. It would even be possible to define these macros manually, so that the system can be customized to a very fine granularity scale with the maximum number of degrees of freedom.

On a concept level, we're investigating the possibility of installing an agent based on some kind of neural network, which monitors the queue and infers recurring patterns from the user behavior. In this way, the system may be able to forecast the intentions of the user and taking action, such as activating a macro as soon as some activity begins. The user would be presented with a confirmation message for the complete action – an affirmative response would skip all the intervening steps of the procedure. We are moving towards the direction of a user interface for wearable computers that unobtrusively filters the man-environment interaction and helps the user in a seamless and invisible way by augmenting his power, memory and reality.

6. Acknowledgements

We wish to thank Hannu Nieminen, Juha Kaario, Stephan Meyers and Jouka Mattila from Nokia Research Center and Atte Kinnula from Nokia Mobile Phones.

This project is partly funded by Tekes Technology Development Centre, Finland.

7. References

[1] M. Bauer, T. Heiber, G. Kortuem, and Z. Segall, "A Collaborative Wearable System with Remote Sensing", *Proceedings of the Second International Symposium on Wearable Computers (ISWC) 1998*, IEEE Computer Society Press, 1998, pp. 10-17.

[2] Nokia Card Phone Support, Available at http://www.forum.nokia.com/support/cardphone/cpsupport.html.

[3] S. Fickas, G. Kortuem, and Z. Segall, "Software Organization for Dynamic and Adaptable Wearable Systems", *Proceedings of the First International Symposium on Wearable Computers (ISWC) 1997*, IEEE Computer Society Press, 1997, pp. 56-63.

[4] D. Garlan, M. Shaw, "An Introduction to Software Architectures", in *Advances in Software Engineering and Knowledge Engineering, Volume I,* edited by V.Ambriola and G.Tortora, World Scientific Publishing Company, New Jersey, 1993.

[5] Jini Architecture Specification. Available at http://www.sun.com/jini/specs/

[6] S. Mann, "An historical account of the 'WearComp' and 'WearCam' inventions developed for applications in 'Personal Imaging'", *Proceedings of the First International Symposium on Wearable Computers (ISWC) 1997*, IEEE Computer Society Press, 1997, pp. 66-73.

[7] T. Watson, "Application Design for Wireless Computing", in Proceedings of the Workshop on Mobile Computing Systems and Applications, 1994.

[8] J. Veizades, E. Guttman, C. Perkins, S. Kaplan, "Service Location Protocol, RFC2165"

Wearing Bike Components

Jo Herstad[1], Do Van Thanh[2]
[1] University of Oslo, P.O. Box 1080, N - 0316 Oslo, Norway
jo@herstad.com
[2] Ericsson, P.O Box 34, N- 1361 Billingstad, Norway
van.thanh.do@ericsson.no

Abstract

This paper addresses the requirement to support component mobility. Field studies of bike messenger operations in Oslo and New York City has been conducted to inform design. We have investigated how component mobility is critical for enabling tailoring of personal mobility in general, and on-body off-body mobility specifically. We suggest that taking mobility seriously may not only contribute to our understanding of current support for mobility, but also raise more general issues concerning requirements and design of mobile technologies. Instead of building a terminal by integrating several terminals into one, our approach suggest, first, a dissolution of the current terminals into pieces called "basic components", and then reassemble the selected basic components to form a customized terminal.

1 Introduction

The bicycle is a fairly new invention. The wheel has been around since about 3.500 BC, but until 150 years ago, nobody had made it possible to on top of only two wheels. Some scholars date the bicycle back to the quintessential Renaissance man, Leonardo da Vinci or one of his student's mechanical drawings known as "Codex Atlanticus". However, investigating the copies of the drawings today tells us that the bike could not have worked if it was implemented [1].

Electronic telecommunication is also a fairly new invention. The telegraph, the telephone and the radio were all invented and developed around the same time period as the bicycle [2]. Today, electronic telecommunication is used almost everywhere, from homes, from offices – and from other places and in transit. Electronic telecommunication has become ubiquitous [3].

There are very few bikers that use electronic communication appliances, but some do indeed depend on the possibility to communicate over distance while biking. Bike messengers and police bike inspectors are two such groups. There are also a growing number of bike commuters that use electronic telecommunication solutions. In Scandinavia, where a part of this research has been conducted, the penetration of cellular phones is approximately 50 % of the population.

The bike messengers investigated in this paper use terminals for electronic communication, like pagers, cellular phones, PDAs and private mobile radio terminals. The terminals in use for the bike messengers are different from the wearable computers with head mounted display such as reported in [4], [5]. The terminals are however worn at all times, always on and it has various types of network connectivity.

The term "terminal", strictly speaking, means a device to terminate some activity or an end point. In communications, a terminal is a device that terminates the telecommunications systems. It is obvious that such a definition is net-centric or operator-centric. The network or operator has the main focus in this definition. However, if the focus is reversed i.e. if the user has the main role then the "terminal" is actually the start of every activity. It is through the terminal that the user comes into contact with the technology, the networks and other people. The terminal hence plays a crucial role in the adaptation of the technology to the user. The less effort the users have to make in accessing services and applications, the more functionality must be integrated in the terminal. The terminal must show both high level of flexibility and high capabilities i.e. offering multiple functions. Ideally, the terminal must be capable of adoption to the user's customs, habits, communication patterns, etc. and melt away or become transparent. It should be transparent to the user in the sense that he can just communicate or use any service without having to be concerned about the presence of the terminal.

Another issue originates from the composition of the terminal. In the early days of telecommunications, there was only the telegraph instrument and the telephone instrument [3]. There have emerged multiple types of communication terminals, such as: pager, laptop PC, PDA, dealer board terminals, cellular phones etc. When talking about terminals, it is unclear whether it is the telephone alone, or the connected PDA alone or the combination of both. Quite often a user has the need of multiple terminals for different services, e.g. PDAs, cellular phone, pager, radio etc. but wishes to view them as an integrated terminal. In other words, all the terminals although still as separate physical devices, are able to collaborate and act consistently in order to provide the user with a coherent interface.

Instead of building a terminal by integrating several terminals into "one", our approach suggests, first, a dissolution of the current terminals into pieces called "basic components", and then reassemble the selected "basic components" to form a customized terminal. In the assemblage of components, the connections and communications between components are, however, not necessarily realized by wire or electronic circuits e.g. I/O bus, but also by wireless link. Examples of such wireless links are BlueTooth [6] or IEEE 802.11. By this way, the assembled components do not form a rigid physical device but constitute a virtual distributed terminal. Such a virtual distributed terminal can become transparent, i.e. unnoticeable and unobtrusive to the user, if each basic component fits well to the human user and they are able to cooperate and synchronize in the delivery of the services.
In order to fit well to the human user, a "basic component" can be small, light and worn by the user but it can also be large and placed at fixed location. The most important requirement is that it does not obstruct the sensory apparatus of the human user, and that the user feels comfortable when interacting with it. Such a "basic component" can also be moved easily.

The borderline issues introduced in [7] have been used as an analytic device to investigate the use of mobile electronic communication terminals. The latent border resources, which lie beyond what is normally recognized as the canonical artifact as for example a phone, are explored. These, often unnoticed, resources are often developed over time, as an artifact is integrated into an ongoing practice and stable connections or genres grow up around them (ibid.). An example may illustrate this. The cable is today used to interconnect various parts of an electronic communication setup. When the cables are removed from the user and replaced by wireless connections, some of the borderline issues that needs to be understood to inform design is shown, such as security, visibility of connection, mechanical pulling out the plug etc.

Before going into the description of the component based terminal in detail, the field study that has informed the design of the component based terminal is presented.

2 Field study of bike messenger operations

This field study is part of a suit of field studies conducted to investigate highly communication intensive activities, and highly mobile activities. The other field studies are Bike Police operations and field engineer work [8] and Sports Activities [9].

The study has been conducted between 1997 and 1999, and the main method used for the study has been contextual inquiry [10] and interviews. Since the operations in question are conducted in varying contexts, it was necessary to employ a method that enabled the capturing of contextual information. In addition, unstructured interviews have been used to elicit further information pertaining to some of the issues found using the contextual inquiry method. Elements from the Delta method [11] have been used for the usability engineering phases of the research. There have been four researchers involved in this study, and 20 contextual inquiry sessions have been conducted. Four different bike messenger companies are investigated, two in Oslo, Norway and two in New York City, USA.

The main operations of the bike messenger is to pick up packages at given customer site, transport the package to another customer site, and deliver the package to the customer. In order to do this; there is a complex web of communication networks and terminals to support the bike messengers. The bike messengers are equipped with communication terminals such as: cellular phones for voice communication and messaging by Short Message Services (SMS), Private Mobile Radio (PMR) terminals for access to private radio networks, pagers for messaging between the dispatching center and the messengers, paper based workflow system on clipboard with pen. In addition to the above mentioned communication terminals, some of the users are confined to use fixed terminals, such as public pay phones or the desktop phones at customer sites. The contextual inquiry has shed light into the use of the existing communication terminals for this highly mobile activity. The terminals are at all times mounted on the body of the messengers, both during biking through the city, during walking inside office building, at the pavement etc. The bike messengers are engaged in highly mobile, and highly communication intensive activities. There have been attempts to describe the type of mobility that the users are engaged in, and we find the framework of Heath and Luff [12] to be of use, to view the different types of mobility such as micro mobility.

There are five findings from the field study that will be highlighted in the following sections, and that are relevant for the component-based terminal. These findings all have implications for the design of the platform for the component based terminal. These findings are grouped into the following areas of concern:

- component selection and choice
- differentiation of communication media
- direct communication and communication at a distance
- task at hand
- context variation.

Each of these findings is described in more detail in the following sections, and the implications for the component-based terminal is outlined.

2.1 Component selection and choice

The user have different preferences when it comes to mounting and wearing the communication equipment on the body, much in the same way as they have different preferences when it comes to type of bike, type of shoes, type of tires etc. There are identified a set of problems with respect to the wearing aspects of the basic components such as microphones, loudspeakers, displays and so forth. This has implications for the component placement.

A common situation observed is when the PMR radio is mounted on the bike messenger bag and the cellular phone is mounted on the bike messengers belt. The bike messenger is engaged in a telephone conversation with one of his colleagues using his cellular phone in a handsfree fashion while on his bike. To engage in the activities that biking implies, such as navigating through the traffic, breaking etc. the bike messengers need to place the radio equipment in a way that is not obstructing their primary tasks.

The users are tailoring the existing communication equipment to fit their use situation and their individual preferences. During the contextual inquiry we have observed that the bike messengers are tinkering [13], [14] with cables, devices and accessories so as to make the communication terminal fit. The users define their own subjective definition of what does indeed fit. One bike messenger may be happy with a solution that someone else of the same overall shape and size would reject. The history of fashion and the difference between cultures make it clear that "fitting" is an interpretation within a particular horizon [15].

During peak hours, the user has to use the communication terminals both during biking in the streets, and when the user is inside the customer's premises. The mounting of parts of the terminal on the bike is therefore not done, since the need for communication is present also when the user is not with his bike. This points to the need for a flexible choice and placement of on body components, and also the roaming between on body components that the bike messenger is wearing, and components that are stationary in the environment of the user.

2.2 Differentiation of communication media

The users have miscellaneous preferences when it comes to differentiating the various communication media and communication channels. The main channels for electronic communication is:

- internal communication between the bike messengers and the dispatch operation users at a distance
- external communication with customers, suppliers etc. at a distance.

Internal communication points to the communication that takes place within the Messenger Company, whereas external communication is the communication between the messenger companies and customers outside the company.

Priority between electronic communication channels is done manually and often in an *ad hoc* manner. This is pointing towards requirements when it comes to component configuration. Today, identifying different physical components does this differentiation of communication media. The bike messenger is using the physical PMR radio, the physical pager device or the cellular phone device, and know which media is used by which communicating parties. For example, when there is a call on the PMR radio, the bike messenger knows that the call is from the dispatch center, whereas if the call is on the cellular phone, he will interpret this as being from a customer.

2.3 Direct communication and communication at a distance

The bike messengers operate in their own region. A region may be defined as any place that is bounded to some degree by barriers to perception. Regions vary, of course, in the degree to which they are bounded and according to the media of communication in which the barriers to perception occur. Thus thick glass panels, such as are found in broadcasting control rooms, can isolate a region aurally but not visually, while an office bounded by beaverboard partitions is closed in the opposite ways [16]. At the same time as operating in their region, the bike messengers are engaged in electronic teleconversations outside their region.

The switch between "distance communication" and "direct communication" is experienced as challenging for the bike messengers. The mechanism to signal to the environment, which is now consisting of both the region of operation and the distant party, what kind of communication is at hand differs between the users. This is pointing towards requirements for component placement, component configuration - in addition to new services. The bike messenger is often talking directly with a customer when he is picking up or delivering a packet, to negotiate delivery address, changes and so forth. At the same time the messenger is often receiving incoming calls from the dispatch center at a distance. This is a highly situated action [17], where the calls from the dispatch center may arrive while the bike messenger is engaged in a conversation with a customer. In this situation, the bike messenger has no standard way to indicate to the people in his region that he is engaged in electronic communication over distance.

2.4 Task at hand

The task at hand when interacting with the communication terminals while biking is observed as:

- reading signs and symbols in the environment like street signs, traffic lights, movement of traffic flow etc. used for navigational purposes
- planning collection and delivery routes
- communication with the dispatch center for updating the job log
- communication with other messengers for sharing stories and planning activities.

This indicates that the users main attention is not directed towards the terminal in use, but to the objects that appear in the environment as a result of the movement of the users. This is pointing towards the usability of the components itself.

The bike messengers share stories or narratives of their work. The stories are about the customers, the dispatch center and the equipment they are using. This sharing of stories is mostly done face to face during lunch breaks and during informal meetings, but also via electronic telecommunication while on the road. As described in [18], the narratives that bike messengers share in the triangle of equipment, customers and bike messengers is mainly done by talking. The task of communicating with

distant parties, sharing stories, is done simultaneously with operating in their region, with real objects such as cars and people. In the case of a user navigating through the traffic, the basic components have to be unobtrusive, and draw minimal attention from the users. Handsfree operation is a basic requirement, since both hands are used for biking. During periods when there is little activity, the user is usually stopping while communicating with the dispatch center. This so as to only do one task, that is to receive updates on new delivery missions. However, during high activity periods, it is seen that the messenger does not stop while communicating with the dispatch center. The messenger is then receiving new commissions while biking.

2.5 Context variations

The users are operating in varying contexts; like on the road, on the pavement, inside office buildings, in basements, during varying climate, traffic patterns, light conditions, temperature conditions etc.
The observations with respect to the use in different contexts has shown the following situations about the person using the communication terminals:

- person cannot see very well (or at all), e.g. delivery is done in the evening
- person cannot hear very well (or at all), e.g. found in noisy traffic situation
- person cannot read very well (or at all), e.g. while biking from a pick up site to a delivery site
- person cannot move their heads or arms very well (or at all), e.g. while biking from a pick up site to a delivery site
- person cannot speak very well (or at all), e.g. while at he premises of a customer
- person cannot feel with their fingers very well (or at all), e.g. while it is too cold
- person cannot remember well (or at all), e.g. while there are more than five pick up and delivery addresses

This is not a result of the communication solution or technology *per se*, but a direct result of varying context that the bike messengers are operating in. This is pointing towards requirements for component selection, component placement and component configuration. The fact that the bike messengers are operating in a dynamically changing environment does indeed have implications for the components in use. It is also natural for the user to use different types of bike uniforms or bike clothes depending on the context he is working in.
The findings reported above are all related to the bike messenger operations. During the other field studies that

are conducted, we have seen similar findings, that all point towards the design of a component based terminal. We are here addressing three main areas of concern: the assemblage of terminal components to fit the user, the placement of terminal components to fit the user and the configuration and reconfiguration of terminal components to fit the user. In the next section we will describe the proposed component-based terminal.

3 The Component based terminal

The component-based terminal consists of a set of basic components. These basic components are of two types, that is:

- effectors
- sensors.

The effector term is used as a generic term for the component that is giving output to the user. The sensor term is used as a generic term for components that is receiving input from the user. The classification is done according to the human senses, and not according to the network or services. Note that this classification is not restricting for human users only. The user of the component-based terminal may also be non-human. Examples of effectors are:

- loudspeaker
- diodes
- display
- buzzer.

Examples of sensors are:

- microphone
- camera
- keyboard
- touch sensitive display overlay
- sensors for contextual information such as GPS, temperature, blood pressure, etc.

For each basic component, there is a corresponding "component agent". The "component agent" is the name of the program and related data that has responsibility in the system for the basic component. The information that the "component agent" holds is related to the basic component, such as:

- identity for identification
- capabilities
- state
- owner
- network Access Points (NAP).

For each user, there is a "terminal agent". The "terminal agent" is the name of the program and the corresponding data that has the responsibility in the system for the assemblage and configuration of the different basic components that the user may use, and for the communication to the corresponding network(s). The information that the "terminal agent" holds is related to the basic component, such as:

- user identity
- user preferences/profile
- network Access Points (NAP)
- list of component agents.

The hardware for the terminal is a number of basic components and transmission links between the basic components, and between the basic components and the network. The question if the physical transmission medium is of wireline or wireless type is transparent to the component-based terminal.

The two software blocks are the "component agent" and the "terminal agent". These basic software blocks are represented at the terminal side, and in the network itself. The distribution of which functions that are placed at the terminal side, and which is placed at the network side, and which are placed both is transparent to the component-based terminal, and is an issue of implementation concern. Functions like user control, authentication, fault correction, security and so forth are handled by the software entities in question.

The component-based terminal is solving the three basic problems of:

- the assemblage of terminal components to fit the user
- the placement of terminal components to fit the user
- the configuration and reconfiguration of terminal components to fit the user.

By solving these three problems, there are a number of advantages as seen from the user.

Flexibility: Higher degree of mobility and flexibility for the user changing on sensors/effector level instead of terminal level according to: availability, location, context and user preferences. The flexibility achieved is an extension of the terminal mobility described in [19]. Person mobility is achieved by introducing component mobility into the framework of the other mobility concerns, such as terminal mobility, application mobility, session mobility, and service mobility.

User attention: The user need not to make effort or notice the terminal when accessing the service or application because he may need to devote full attention to other task such as driving, biking, working at physical objects at hand etc. This is achieved by giving the user freedom to assemble the components and place the components according to the requirements from the situation at hand.

Tailoring: Customization/tailoring to fit individual user preferences when it comes to ergonomics, aesthetics and functionality. The possibility to assemble a personal terminal as a composite of basic components is giving necessary condition for the user to tailor the terminal to the situation at hand.

Upgrading and introduction of new media: When new media are introduced, this can be done in a flexible and modular way. Instead of replacing the traditional terminal when new media is introduced, this may be done by adding separate new components or upgrade individual components.

Media selection and change: The user can at own preference select the appropriate media.

Translation between media formats: The user may select and change the type of media at hand according to his own preferences.

4 Conclusion

This paper has introduced a new way of viewing a terminal. The field study has informed us about the tinkering that the bike messengers are doing with the on body terminals. The tinkering is done so as to make the various terminals fit the individual user and the use situation. We have discussed the bike messenger field study in this paper, and let the field study inform the design of the component-based terminal. The component-based terminal is not fully implemented and tested outside the laboratory.

Acknowledgment
Thanks to Egil Ofstad at Ericsson, Øystein Olsen, Hans Skjerpen, Torgeir Fritsvold, Steinar Kristoffersen and Ole Smørdal at the University of Oslo and Odd-Wiking Rahlff and Rolf K. Rolfsen at Sintef for biking with us.

References

1. Pridmore, J and Hurd, J., *The American Bicycle*, Motorbooks International 1995.

2. Pasachoff, N. (1996). *Alexander Graham Bell, Making Connections*, Oxford University Press, 1996.

3. Fisher, C. S., *America Calling: A social History of the Telephone to 1940*, University of California Press, 1992.

4. Bauer, M., Heiber, T., Kortuem, G., Seagall, Z., *A Collaborative Wearable System with remote sensing*, The second international symposium on wearable computers, Pittsburg Pennsylania, October 1998.

5. Mann, S., *WearCam (The Wearable Camera)*, The second international symposium on wearable computers, Pittsburg Pennsylania, October 1998.

6. Haartsen, J., Bluetooth - *the universal radio interface for ad hoc, wireless connectivity*, Ericsson Review, No 3, Stockholm, 1998.

7. Brown, J., S., Duguid, P., *Borderline Issue Social and material aspects of design*, Human Computer Interaction 1994, Volume 9, pp. 3/36.

8. Herstad, J., Olsen, J.O., Koht-Tøfte. E., *Important Aspects of Person Oriented Mobility*, Information systems Research Seminar In Scandinavia, Sæby, Denmark, 1998.

9. Redin, M. S., *Marathon Man*, Thesis for the master of engineering in electrical engineering and computer science at Massachusetts Institute of Technology, USA 1998.

10. Beyer, H., Holzblatt, K., *Contextual Design: Defining customer centered systems*. Morgan Kaufman, 1998.

11. Carlshamre, P., *A Collaborative Approach to Usability Engineering*, Linkoping Studies in Science and Technology, Thesis No. 455, 1994.

12. Luff, P., Heath, C., *Mobility in Collaboration*, CSCW conference, Seattle Washington USA, 1998.

13. Ciborra, C., *Groupware and Teamwork, what does groupware mean for the organisation hosting it?* John Wiley and Sons, 1996.

14. Strauss, L., *The savage mind*, The University of Chigago Press, 1962.

15. Winograd, T. and Flores, F., *Understanding Computers and Cognition: A New Foundation for Design*, Addison-Wesley, 1986.

16. Goffman, E, *The presentation of self in everyday life*, Penguin books, 1971.

17. Suchman, L, *Plans and situated action*, Cambridge University Press, 1987.

18. Orr, J., E., *Talking about machines, an ethnography of a modern job*, Cornell University Press, 1996.

19. Thanh, D. v., *Mobility as an Open Distributed Processing Transparency*, thesis for the Doctor Scientiarum degree, Department of Informatics, University of Oslo, 1997.

MoCCA: A Mobile Communication and Computing Architecture

Asim Smailagic, Dan Siewiorek, Len Bass,
Bob Iannucci*, Anton Dahbura*, Steve Eddleston*, Bob Hanson*, Ed Chang*
{asim, dps, ljb}@cs.cmu.edu;   {bob, atd, seddleston, hanson, changed}@crl.dec.com

Institute for Complex Engineered Systems
Carnegie Mellon University, Pittsburgh, PA 15213

*Compaq, Cambridge Research Lab, Cambridge, MA 02139

Abstract

In this paper we present an integrated computing system designed to help increase the efficiency of mobile workers, specifically field service engineers. Our solution, a Mobile Communications and Computing Architecture (MoCCA), consists of both a futuristic award-winning concept design and a first-generation working prototype. The prototype has support for collaborative multimedia: on-the-move networking for high-tech equipment maintenance using voice, video clips, and access to maintenance databases. We describe the user interface, software, and hardware architectures of our prototype. The hardware architecture uses a multi-tier networking scheme to trade off a small lightweight client and high computation power and battery life. Finally, we present lessons learned from user tests in applying a novel mobile computing architecture to a complex real-world task.

1. Introduction

The use of current mobile computing hardware has grown at a rate of about 15% per year, with no signs of slowdown in the near future [1]. A large fraction of those devices are used in vertical applications such as sales, healthcare, and field service. In those applications, standard mobile computing devices such as laptops are customized with software to become useful industry-specific tools. For example, some systems integration companies advertise total solutions for vertical markets without displaying much innovation in mobile devices. Other companies introduce cycles of innovative end-user products for the horizontal market, e.g. the Palm and WinCE devices. There is, however, significantly less work done on a systems level that combines multiple devices and functions synergistically. Thus there is a gap in the mobile computing space: total connectivity solutions for vertical applications that include customized novel end-user devices and applications.

To explore this area further, we designed the Mobile Communication and Computing Architecture (MoCCA). The vision of MoCCA was to create a very portable integrated system supporting a group of geographically distributed mobile workers. We chose field service as our specific test application because of our ties to Digital/Compaq's field service organization. Our goal was to design a system that would increase the productivity of the field service engineer (FSE) and to replace many of the gadgets currently carried or worn.

2. Field Evaluations

After settling on the specific task of FSE, we began field evaluations to formally rethink how communications and computing should be designed for mobile workers. Our goal was to create a workflow model that would formulate a basis for the MoCCA device requirements. To begin this process, we interviewed and shadowed FSEs through various actual work scenarios. We then condensed our experience into the following four-stage model as shown in **Figure 1** below.

We found the following complexities in the FSE work environment delineatead by this model. For the first stage of accepting a new call, the FSE would often be required to balance multiple calls and go through a complex negotiating process with the customers and main office in order to set a ordered schedule of call processing. Since the FSE could not see the overall workload, there was a large degree of unpredictability in the call response times. In addition, many problem reports were incomplete, hampering the FSE's ability to effectively prepare for calls in the second stage.

Upon arriving at the customer site (stage 3), the FSE is limited to voice communication via phone or two-way radio. Some customer sites will provide landline telephone, but others cannot. In either case,

FSE's would prefer to be self-sufficient for their communications needs to appear more in control of the situations. As for the current cell phones and two-way radios, the wireless technology is not yet fully mature and has trouble reaching into some buildings.

Finally, the fourth stage of closing the call has difficulties both in entering and disseminating the information. Often the full experience is not able to be captured in a form that can be transmitted to the other FSEs in the organization. The existing databases, like much of the documentation in the computer industry, is often full of unhelpful or outdated information. As a result, when an FSE encounters an unfamiliar situation, he turns to an informal network of other FSE's to find someone who has experience with this particular problem. A better system of recording experience would aid the next FSE in handling the same problem without resorting to human intervention.

Thus we found the following three key conditions that drive the work practice:

- Planning: The FSE wants to work on the right thing and have a better outlook on the upcoming schedule. This requires a better means of coordination with the other FSEs and the dispatch office.
- Preparation: The FSE wants better information to know more about a call request before arriving at the customer site.
- Professional Image: The FSE wants to appear proficient and capable of handling the problem. The FSE does not want to rely on the customer's phone, computer system, or documentation. Furthermore, the FSE wants to look like the other employees at

the customer site. Early inquiries into novel wearable computing solutions with head-mounted displays were met with strong resistance.

From these conditions we were able to arrive at a set of design requirements. The design had to support existing practices and positive changes in those practices. In addition, the device was to be used in multiple settings. We found that the FSE is at the dispatch office about 30% of the time, on the road another 30%, and the remainder of the time at customer sites. Ideally the device would have different modes of entering and retrieving information that would account for all three of those locales.

Thus the fundamental challenge was to provide a system that allows the FSEs to access information and advice from other FSEs while on customer sites and while commuting between sites. The final design wish list was as follows:

- The system should have all of the functionality of a laptop computer including a large color display and an operational cycle of at least eight hours.
- The system should be very light, preferably less than one pound in weight.
- The system should provide both synchronous and asynchronous communication. The former is used to maintain contact with other FSE team members, using the telephone metaphor. The latter is more of the computer or web browser model, in which information can be stored and retrieved at the FSE's convenience.
- The system should have access to several legacy databases across different corporate computing systems. The most frequently used databases are textual-oriented. On rare occasions, access to graphical databases is required.

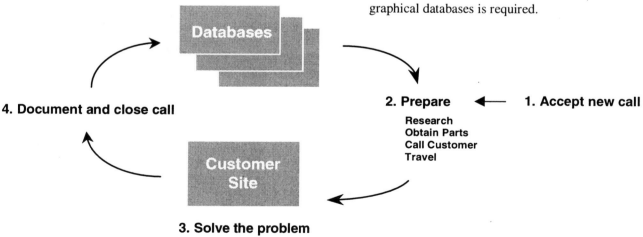

Figure 1: FSE Work Process Model

3. Research Issues

Given the design constraints and considerations of FSE work, we chose to address three primary research issues in MoCCA:

- **Wearable, multi-tier design**
  The main design issue was to tradeoff between high functionality (wireless access, large screen, long battery) and low obtrusiveness (size and weight). We addressed this with a multi-tier design that split the core functionality between a small wearable client and a larger, more powerful base unit included in the FSE toolkit.

- **Voice as primary medium**
  One of the primary design requirements was to keep the current ability of contacting other team members via phone or two-way radio. MoCCA was allowed to augment but not replace this existing feature. In addition, we wished to explore the use of voice as a control system to leave the users hands free.

- **Hybrid multi-modal interaction**
  The final issue was to explore the space of using a combination of voice, text, and graphics to provide a richer mobile interaction and more functionality.

Previous work at CMU on wearable computers [2-5] provided background for this project. Collaboration using portable computers has been reported in [6-8].

4. Concept Design

Our team worked with Compaq's Industrial Design department and Fitch Inc. to create a concept design that could be produced three to five years in the future. The end result is the 4-inch wearable computer shown in **Figure 2**. It has an ergonomic folding handle and a pair of folding Organic LED (OLED) touchscreens; this provides a large display size in a small package. The integrated camera, microphone, and speaker allow video-conferencing or capturing pictures or video clips. Finally, wireless access provides phone connectivity, data transmission, and location awareness.

Because of the folding handle and screens, the MoCCA concept design could be used in a number of different positions. In addition to being held like a standard palmtop computer, it could be stood on a flat surface like a picture frame or worn around the neck to free one's hands, as shown in **Figure 3**. This concept design was chosen for the 1998 Business Week Design Exploration award [9].

This MoCCA concept design showed how harnessing a powerful, wearable communications processor to high-speed voice and data networks could provide the following functions for the FSE of the future. First, MoCCA could connect the user to one or more team members or customers via voice and video. Second, the device provided voice or touch-activated mailbox management for voicemails, e-mail, and video mail. Third, back-end servers could handle information and data queries to remote databases. And finally, the MoCCA device could replace the scheduling and phone list functions of a standard PDA.

Figure 2: MoCCA Concept Design

Figure 3: Handsfree usage

5. Overview of System Components, Use and Design

Although the concept design was compelling, it was also not feasible to build in 1996. **Figure 4** depicts the components of the prototype MoCCA system we actually built, with a field service engineer shown in the center of the figure:

1. A base unit, about the size of a small laptop computer which is connected to a remote server (located at the home office) wirelessly through a CDPD connection.

2. A cellular phone associated with the base unit and tethered to it through a PCMCIA port. The cellular phone communicates wirelessly with the local cellular provider and thus has access to the telephone network.

3. The FSE holds a smaller satellite unit that is connected to the base unit. This link allows the satellite to show the contents of the base unit screen and to link its keyboard input directly to the base unit keyboard.

4. The FSE wears a microphone and headset that are wirelessly linked to the cellular phone.

Figure 5 is a view of the functional system architecture. The software architecture uses a thin client approach to minimize the amount of software on the system by exploiting web-browsing technology and wireless CDPD Internet connection to communicate with a server. The satellite unit is not running the browser; it is merely displaying whatever is currently on the base unit display.

There are six buttons defined for the user interface. The Bboard button provides access to a phone-based voice bulletin board where FSEs may asynchronously collaborate to solve problems. The Calls button accesses the summary of active field service calls for the engineer. The phone button invokes an auto-dialer keypad. The FSE button brings up a directory of FSEs, and the Availability button shows their current status. The Pager button accesses the list of current Pager messages. The FSE directory, Pager message list, Calls list, and Availability form are all web pages, generated automatically from various field service databases.

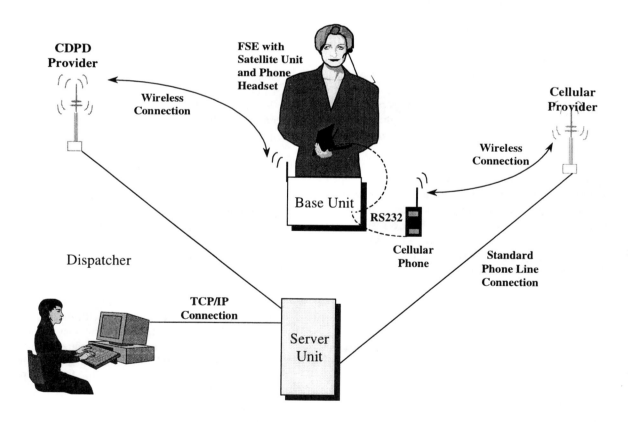

Figure 4: MoCCA Prototype System Architecture

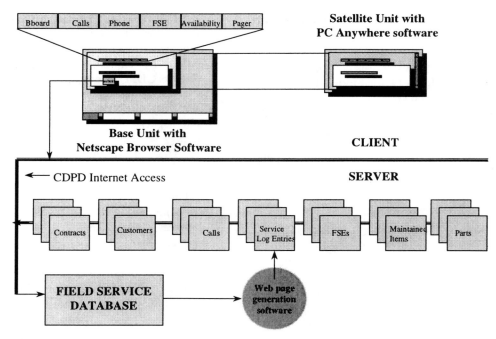

| Bboard | Calls | Phone | FSE | Availability | Pager |

**Satellite Unit with
PC Anywhere software**

**Base Unit with
Netscape Browser Software**

CLIENT

← CDPD Internet Access

SERVER

| Contracts | Customers | Calls | Service Log Entries | FSEs | Maintained Items | Parts |

FIELD SERVICE DATABASE

Web page generation software

Figure 5: Data Architecture

The legacy databases and access software reside on the server machine located at the home office. It contains a database of field service information that was designed and customized to the specific needs of Field Service Engineers. When the FSE presses one of the user interface buttons or link on one of the browser web pages, a request is sent to software developed for the MoCCA unit to initiate a query on the Field Service Database. The results from the query are dynamically formatted into a web page. Then all the appropriate links are made to enable related queries and the page is passed across the CDPD network to the client machine that displays the web page.

This approach is more flexible than having a set of pre-made web pages. The web pages are up-to-date with the data in the database and allow very precise queries to be performed. In addition, monitor software residing on the server can watch certain directories and when data changes, notify the FSEs browser to change the color of one of the user interface buttons to alert them to re-run the query.

6. User Interface

A summary of the integrated user interface software is presented in **Figure 6**. The Field Service Engineer Call List is the central screen and all other screens can be accessed following hypertext links or the screen buttons. From the Call List screen, the user can select a primary function to be performed, such as database query (Call List) or messages via a pager. Depending on the primary

function selected, subsequent secondary screens will display more detailed information. In the case of pager messages, the secondary screens allow the user to enter new information.

Consider the following typical usage scenario of MoCCA. The FSE checks the current status and the status of other FSEs by clicking on the "FSE Information" button. This leads to a web page (**Figure 7a**), generated from the MoCCA database, listing the names of all the FSEs, their cell phone numbers, their e-mail addresses, and their current status. The FSE changes his status from "Off Duty" to "Available" to let others know that he can be reached by cell phone. This is done by clicking on the "Availability" button at the top of the screen, leading to the Availability Selection page, Figure 6. Clicking on the "Available" button leads back to the FSE Information page. To check the list of calls assigned to the FSE, he clicks on the "Calls" button at the top of the screen, and brings up the "Call List" screen, **Figure 7b**. The page is assembled from a database query of the calls assigned to the FSE. It filters the list of all calls to only display those with an "Open" status. The table lists each call with the customer name, the time the call was received, the service contract, the contact person, their phone number, and a short description of the problem. Each underlined entry leads to further information about that field. If the FSE wants to review the assigned calls, and the previous problems at a site, he clicks on the "Call Query" button, which brings up the "Call List Queries" page. To get more

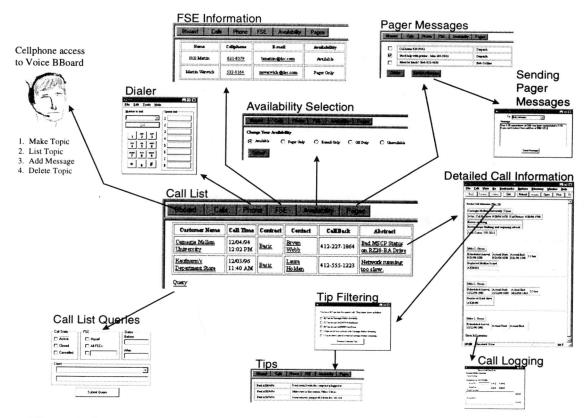

Figure 6: Summary of the integrated user interface software

details on a particular call, the FSE clicks on the description of the problem, showing the "Detailed Call List" screen, **Figure 7b**. The page is assembled from a database query of the calls assigned to the FSE. It filters the list of all calls to only display those with an "Open" status. The table lists each call with the customer name, the time the call was received, the service contract, the contact person, their phone number, and a short description of the problem. Each underlined entry leads to further information about that field. If the FSE wants to review the assigned calls, and the previous problems at a site, he clicks on the "Call Query" button, which brings up the "Call List Queries" page. To get more details on a particular call, the FSE clicks on the description of the problem, showing the "Detailed Call Information" list. By clicking on the "Service Log" button, the FSE can review the Service Log entries associated with that call, leading to the "Call Logging" list. If there is a "Tip" recorded with information, the FSE can examine its contents. After reviewing the call history, he can look at the current "Call List" again.

The inclusion of a small satellite unit into the system made an impact on the user interface design. This effectively reduced the amount of information that could be displayed to the user and meant that two separate

interfaces would have to be developed, resulting in a simpler user interface for the satellite. Earlier simplifications had been driven more by the cost of downloading screens over CDPD than by the size. The Cassiopeia has a screen size of 2.5" x 4.75". The Cassiopeia measures 480 x 240 pixels to the base unit's 640 x 480 pixels. This difference between the two screen resolutions is significant because the software used to send information from the base unit display to the satellite unit (PC Anywhere under Windows CE) works merely as a static viewing port. The smaller screen does not show the entire contents of the base unit screen, but rather, a section of it equal to the size of the smaller screen.

Also note that the Windows CE software and the Netscape browser windows use screen real estate, leaving a very tiny area for user screen interface controls and information. As the PC Anywhere software provides a scroll bar, the satellite viewing port can be moved to other locations on the base unit screen. However, having to scroll the screen up and down can be annoying to users. Thus the first screens are developed in a manner that made it possible to avoid scrolling.

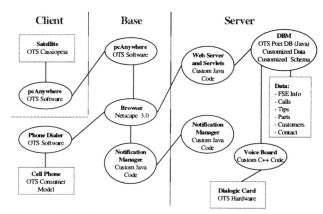

Figure 7a. Sample Screen Image for FSE Information

Figure 7b. Sample Screen Image for Call List Pages

7. Software and Hardware Architecture

The architecture of the MoCCA software is depicted in **Figure 8**. The architecture can be broken into three different subsystems: Client, Base and Server. The communication among the subsystems employs different mechanisms. The Client communicates with the Base unit using a serial connection. The Base communicates with the server by TCP/IP over variety of media. The software was divided into functions to facilitate parallel development. The Client appears as a window into the Base. This functionality was achieved by using an off the shelf product called PC Anywhere. Netscape Navigator browser runs on the Base unit and can view the web pages generated by the Server. The browser retrieves the information from the Notification Manager, and displays it as the first page. The Notification Manager informs the FSE of a newly arrived event and is represented by a button. The Server contains two data types, the first contains FSE and customer data, the second contains the voice bulletin board data. The Server contains a database manager and a voice database manager, which are accessed via servlet calls. A Java database called Poet was chosen. Poet is a "cross-platform" database supporting both C and Java schemas, and allows for easy integration of different software components. The Notification Manager server informs the Notification Manager on the Base of changes to the databases. Both

Notification Managers are implemented as custom Java applets. The server also contains a hardware component, the Dialogic board, with associated software that controls the voice bulletin board system and dialing in.

Figures 9 and 10 depict the base unit components and the satellite unit hardware. The base unit includes a 586 133MHz processor, running the Windows 95 operating system. There are two PCMCIA slots on the base unit: one is occupied by the AirCard CDPD/Modem, and another by the modem dialing to the cell phone. Finally, an RF transceiver links cell phone and the headset.

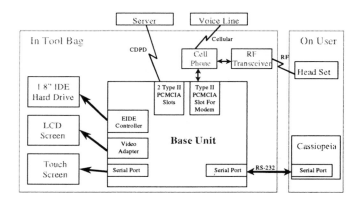

Figure 8: Software Architecture

Figure 9: System Architecture

8. Conclusions

In this paper we posed the research problem of designing an integrated computing system that would help increase the efficiency of mobile workers, specifically field service engineers. Our solution, a

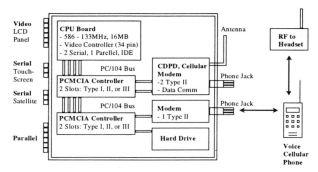

Figure 10: Base Unit Hardware

Mobile Communications and Computing Architecture (MoCCA), consisted of both a futuristic award-winning concept design and a first-generation working prototype. The prototype had support for collaborative multimedia: on-the-move networking for high-tech equipment maintenance using voice, video clips, and access to maintenance databases.

One of the first lessons we learned that was the appearance of a wearable computer is a primary consideration for its acceptance in a mainstream application. Small devices that make the transition from tool to accessory or clothing are judged much more strictly on aesthetic grounds. Furthermore, there was strong resistance to the cyborg or robotic look. Since the MoCCA prototype was built in 1996, there have been many advancements in display technology [10]. But there is still a long way to go before production and social acceptance of unobtrusive wearable displays.

Through user tests, we found that the combination of voice and data resulted in a richer interaction useful for field service engineers. The ability to choose the data type of interaction was critical in providing flexibility of usage situations. Finally, our prototype multi-tier network architecture demonstrated a viable method of trading off a small lightweight client with high processing power and battery life.

9. Acknowledgements

The research reported in this paper is supported by Compaq Computer Corporation, the DARPA, and the Institute for Complex Engineered Systems at Carnegie Mellon University. Fitch Inc. design studio also contributed to the final appearance of the MoCCA prototype. Finally, we would like to thank Chuck Kukla for designing and conducting the user field studies, and Jane Siegel for her help and insight. The field tests were conducted at Compaq's facilities in Forest Hills near Pittsburgh, PA, and San Jose, CA.

10. References

[1] P. Redman, "The Mobile Enterprise", *Mobile Computing and Communications 1999 Annual Deployment Guide*, January, 1999

[2] A. Smailagic, D. P. Siewiorek, "The CMU Mobile Computers: A New Generation of Computer Systems", *Proc. IEEE COMPCON 94*, IEEE Computer Society Press, pp. 467-473, February 1994

[3] A. Smailagic, "ISAAC: A Voice Activated Speech Response System for Wearable Computers", *Proc. IEEE International Conference on Wearable Computers*, Cambridge MA, October 1997

[4] A. Smailagic, "An Evaluation of CMU Audio-Centric Wearable Computers", *Journal on Mobile Networks and Applications, ACM and Baltzer Science Publishers*, 1999

[5] D. P. Siewiorek, A. Smailagic, et. al., "Adtranz: A Mobile Computing System for Maintenance and Collaboration", *IEEE International Conference on Wearable Computers*, Pittsburgh, PA, October, 1998

[6] M. Billinghurst, S. Weghorst, T. Furness III, "Wearable Computer for Three Dimensional CSCW", *First International Symposium on Wearable Computers*, Cambridge, MA, October 1997

[7] J. Rekimoto, "Transvision: A Hand-held Augmented Reality System for Collaborative Design.", *Proceeding of Virtual Systems and Multimedia - 1996*, Gifu, Japan, September, 1996

[8] M. Bauer, T. Heiber, G. Kortuem, Z. Segall, "A Collaborative Wearable System with Remote Sensing", *Second International Symposium on Wearable Computers*, Pittsburgh, PA October 1998

[9] "Annual Design Awards: Cell Phone Meets Laptop", *Business Week*, May 25, 1998

[10] Wearable Computing Displays list at MIT: http://lcs.www.media.mit.edu/projects/wearables/display.html

Smart Sight: A Tourist Assistant System

Jie Yang, Weiyi Yang, Matthias Denecke, Alex Waibel

Interactive Systems Laboratories
Carnegie Mellon University
Pittsburgh, PA 15213
{yang+, wyyang, denecke, waibel}@cs.cmu.edu

Abstract

In this paper, we present our efforts towards developing an intelligent tourist system. The system is equipped with a unique combination of sensors and software. The hardware includes two computers, a GPS receiver, a lapel microphone plus an earphone, a video camera and a head-mounted display. This combination enables a multimodal interface to take advantage of speech and gesture input to provide assistance for a tourist. The software supports natural language processing, speech recognition, machine translation, handwriting recognition and multimodal fusion. A vision module is trained to locate and read written language, is able to adapt to to new environments, and is able to interpret intentions offered by the user, such as a spoken clarification or pointing gesture. We illustrate the applications of the system using two examples.

1 Introduction

A tourist faces many challenges in unfamiliar territory. Unfamiliar geography makes it difficult to navigate streets and identify landmarks. Unfamiliar language makes it difficult to read signs, take a taxi, order food, and understand the comments of passers by. Recent technological advances have made wearable computers available which could be used to ease the plight of tourists. Wearable computers can "see" as the tourist sees, "hear" as the tourist hears, and travel along with the tourist. With accessing local database and the Internet, the system might be able to have better knowledge of the environment than the tourist. This makes them excellent platforms for tourist applications. Furthermore, the mobile computing technology has made it possible for wearable computers to access information from any location.

In this paper, we present our efforts towards developing Smart Sight, an intelligent tourist assistant system. The research is to employ mobile computers to alleviate the language barrier, provide navigation assistance, and to handle queries posed and answered in natural language. The system is equipped with a unique combination of sensors and software. The tourist location is derived from a GPS (Global Positioning System) receiver. A lapel microphone plus an earphone allows for speech input and output. A video camera provides visual capabilities. This combination enables a multimodal interface to take advantage of speech and gesture input to provide assistance. For example, a tourist in a foreign land may stand in front of an information sign, circle the text and ask "what does this mean?" - for which the language translation module can then offer an informative interpretation. If there is relevant information in an online database, the information can be retrieved and be presented to the user.

This work is related to augmented reality and multimodal human computer interaction. The term augmented reality has been used to refer to enrichment of the real world with a complementary virtual world [10; 5; 4; 11]. The augmented reality systems use a see-through head-mounted display that overlays graphics and sound on a user's real vision and audition. These systems provide users with visual information that is tied to the physical, and enhance the real world by superposing additional information onto it. Multimodal signal interpretation provides a natural and flexible way for human computer interaction in a mobile environment. Multimodal interfaces consider all available human communication signals and cues rather than one alone, to better and more flexibly interpret and process human intent in communication. The multimodal signals include speech, handwriting, gesture, pointing, spelling, eye-gaze, face-location and head pose, etc.. The effectiveness of multimodal human-computer interaction has been investigated by many researchers [8; 1; 7; 9]. Over the last few years, we have focused on developing sensible and useful user interfaces to support multimodal human-computer interaction [13; 14; 16].

The remainder of this paper is organized as follows. Section 2 describes system architecture. Section 3 introduces adaptive multimodal server. Section 4 addresses problem of natural language understanding. Section 5 discusses applications of the system using two examples. Section 6 summarizes the paper.

Figure 1: The system setup

2 System Architecture

A challenge for tourist applications is how to minimize system weight and bulkiness. As a suitable compromise between basic requirements of a tourist and mobility, we have employed a combination of a laptop and a wearable computer. Figure 2 shows both front view and side view of a tourist with the Smart Sight system. The system uses two computers, the Thinkpad 600 (Pentium II 333MHz) and the Xybernaut MAIV (Pentium 233Mhz), to support different tasks. The Thinkpad handles language translation task, and supports multimodal server as well map server. The Xybernaut MAIV handles the microphone input, the head mounted display, and the miniature camera input. The Thinkpad is in the backpack and the Xybernaut MAIV is on the waist belt. Two computers are connected via Ethernet using 3Com Ethernet PCMCIA cards. The hardware architecture is shown Figure 2. The reason of using two computers is partially because insufficient computing power and hardware/software support from a single computer. It is expected that we could use only one computer to accomplish the same task in the future.

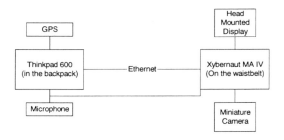

Figure 2: The hardware architecture

Figure 3 shows the software configuration of the system. The multimodal server running on the Thinkpad controls the GPS server, the Map server, the Dialogue Server and the Speech Translation System. The following components are on the Xybernaut: the speech recognizer, the gesture recognizer, the OCR module and image processing module. The results from both the

Thinkpad and Xybernaut MAIV are displayed on the head mounted display.

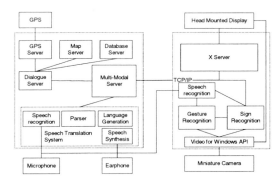

Figure 3: The software configuration

3 Adaptive Multimodal Server

The multimodal input signals are processed and interpreted by a multimodal server. The multimodal server is to provide multimodal interpretation of speech, handwriting and gestures to its clients. We have demonstrated the feasibility of the multimodal server in both web [15] and wearable [17] applications. In a wearable computer application, wearable computers can be weakly interconnected by low-speed wireless networks, or disconnected for some reasons. When the computer is connected to network, it can share a variety of resources via network. When the computer is disconnected from network, it should be able to perform it's task at least at a minimum level. It is desirable that the system has the ability to dynamically select its network service based on cost and performance requirements. This can be achieved by a dual server structure as shown in Figure 4. The multimodal inputs can be processed locally, or remotely, or partially local and partially remote.

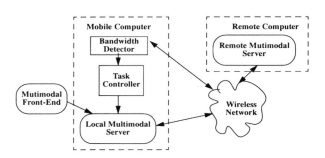

Figure 4: The dual server structure

Each server has a similar architecture as shown in Figure 5. The server can perform recognition for the modalities of speech, handwriting, and pen gesture, and interpret the recognition results. From the communication

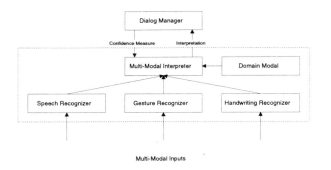

Figure 5: The multimodal server architecture

point of view, we only need to handle speech and pen inputs for modalities of speech, handwriting and gesture. In the next section we will propose a way of balancing the use of available bandwidth and computing resources.

The multimodal server is supported by the Multimodal Toolkit [12], which includes a library of software components that can be assembled to create multimodal applications. This library contains speech and pen input recorders and recognizers, multimodal event handlers, interprocess communication facilities, and a user interface in the form of a Java applet. The user interface includes ready-made objects that handle input capture and synchronization, communicate with speech and pen input recognizers, and direct the control flow of the multimodal interpretation process. This modularity permits multimodal application developers to customize each system component separately or even replace certain modules if the need arises. The distributed nature of the framework serves to spread the computational load among multiple machines, improve the responsiveness of the system, and allow resource sharing using a client/server architecture. Each major component of the system runs as a separate process which can be hosted on a different machine if necessary. The Multimodal Toolkit includes a communication layer that presents an abstract interface for interprocess communication, hiding all the details of network protocols and synchronization.

4 Natural Language Understanding Component

The system is based on a client server architecture. Currently implemented servers include a map server used for calculation and display of paths and sights, a database server using an SQL server accessing any domain-related information, and a date and time server which is also used to resolve and generate deictic time expressions such as `tomorrow` and `three hours from now`, and a GPS server.

In addition to the client/server communication scheme, there is a message passing communication mechanism that allows components to generate information. This avoids constantly polling information providing modules such as the GPS server.

4.1 The Parser

The spoken language input is analyzed by the MISO parser [6] using semantic grammars for robust speech analysis and interpretation. Although the generated parse tree contains the semantic information associated with the interpretation of the sentence, its form is not independent of the syntactic structure of the sentence. For this reason, a semantic construction algorithm converts the parse tree into a normalized partial representation, or more specifically, in a set of typed feature structure [2]. Each feature structure represents either an object in the domain (as might be expressed by a noun phrase) or a unary, binary or ternary relation between objects (as might be expressed by verbal or adjectival phrases).

4.2 The Dialogue Manager

The dialogue manager combines functionality to control and access the different servers with the original dialogue control. In addition to the server modules, the dialogue manager has control over a four layered dialogue history. The four layers contain the input representations (such as text, or gesture hypothesis), the parse trees as generated by MISO, the normalized semantic representations as generated by the semantic construction, and objects referring expressions might refer to, respectively. The dialogue history is constructed during the dialogue and may contain hierarchical structure to correctly model clarification and subdialogues. A declarative knowledge base called *type hierarchy* (figure 6) holds information on the domain in form of IS-A and IS-PART-OF relations. This knowledge base provides a typing discipline for the typed representations used in the dialogue history. The only representations used are based on typed feature structures and their generalizations.

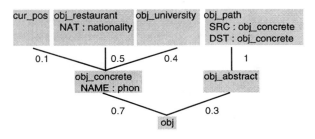

Figure 6: A part of the type hierarchy and its appropriateness conditions used in the map application. The least specific type is at the bottom of the tree.

The dialogue manager is programmable by a set of expert-system style rules. Rules may contain typed variables that range over the currently active representations in the dialogue history [3]. These rules are the only instance that defines the behavior of the system. This allows for easy adaptation to new input modalities or fast deployment of the system in new situations. In addition, since our representations are theoretically well-founded and typed, off-line type checking can be used to

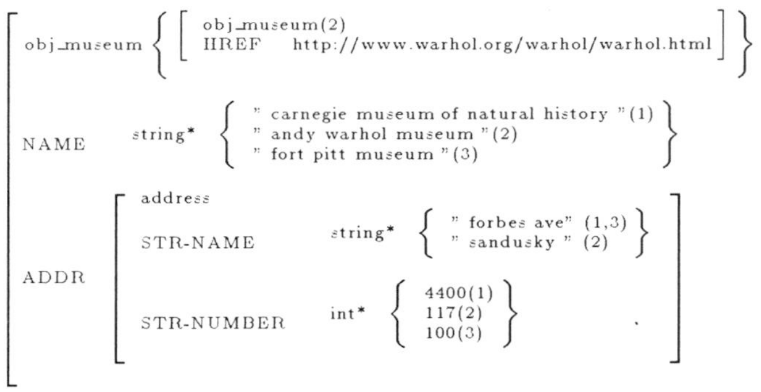

$$
\begin{bmatrix}
\text{obj\_museum} & \left\{ \begin{bmatrix} \text{obj\_museum(2)} \\ \text{HREF} \quad \text{http://www.warhol.org/warhol/warhol.html} \end{bmatrix} \right\} \\
\text{NAME} \quad \text{string}^* & \left\{ \begin{array}{l} \text{" carnegie museum of natural history "(1)} \\ \text{" andy warhol museum "(2)} \\ \text{" fort pitt museum "(3)} \end{array} \right\} \\
\text{ADDR} \begin{bmatrix} \text{address} & & \\ \text{STR-NAME} & \text{string}^* & \left\{ \begin{array}{l} \text{" forbes ave" (1,3)} \\ \text{" sandusky " (2)} \end{array} \right\} \\ \text{STR-NUMBER} & \text{int}^* & \left\{ \begin{array}{l} 4400(1) \\ 117(2) \\ 100(3) \end{array} \right\} \end{bmatrix}
\end{bmatrix}
$$

Figure 7: Three underspecified feature structures representing the objects referred to by the NPs "the museum", "the Beehive" and "Primanti Brothers". There are two objects called "Beehive" in our data base, one being a cinema, the other one a cafe. Moreover, we find three different museums and three restaurants called "Primanti Brothers".

detect errors in the specification of the rules, a mechanism that is not available to systems such as GALAXY which are based on simpler representation formalisms such as frames, slots and fillers.

The rules are used to act as constraints to determine the relationship between simultaneously occurring input events (such as deictic references accompanied by a gesture) and sequential input events (such as answers to questions). The dialogue manager tries to relate the active discourse information with a set of predefined dialogue goals. Dialogue goals are equally expressed in typed feature structures and serve as informational lower bounds. If the available information is not sufficient to uniquely determine a dialogue goal, the dialogue manager generates discriminating information of the goals which is served as a basis for a clarification question. Additional information will then be used to disambiguate the dialogue goal. In a second step, the information that is required by the dialogue goal is sought by the dialogue system. This can be compared with a form filling approach with the important difference that over- and underspecified information also may be incorporated in the goal representation in order to allow for more flexible question and answering. An example for such an underspecified representation that serves as the basis for generating clarification questions is shown in figure 7.

Another advantage of using rules as constraints to relate different dialogue acts is the simple integration of gestures as answers in dialogue. Note that discriminating information can be generated over a set of goals as well as a set of representations of objects or actions, since in each case the representations are typed feature structures. Once the information related to the dialogue has been established, a procedure call associated with the dialogue goal is executed and the goal related information is passed on to the procedure.

The reasoning in the dialogue system is considerably fast. If no database access or other input/output operation is involved, a question can be generated as fast as half a second after receiving the input event. This time measure includes parsing, semantic construction, dialogue processing and generation. Since the input is event-based and time-stamped, no information is lost in times natural language and dialogue processing take over system control.

5 Application Examples

The Smart Sight system can help a tourist in many ways. Two applications are currently under development.

5.1 Tourist Diary

When people go vacations, they are excited about what they have seen. They take pictures to help them to remember their experience and share it with their family members or friends. However, not all the people are good at organizing their memories. Figure 8 shows a fact that among the people who take photos on vacation, 40% rarely or never put those photos into an album. It is desirable to have a system help people to organize their memories before their enthusiasm disappears.

Figure 8: Disorganized memories (Opinion Research for Globus & Cosmos tour operator)

"Tourist Diary" is to help a tourist to organize his/her trip experience by multimodal interaction. The system is activated by voice commands. A tourist can request to take a picture or a video clip. He/she can add a caption to the picture and/or dictate his/her diary. Figure 9 shows the software flow chart of the system. When the tourist arrives at a point of interest, the system will log the position and time retrieved from the GPS and system clock. The tourist can ask the system to take a picture or digital video clip, and dictate the description or comments during his/her visit at the point of interest. When a local database is available, the system could also retrieve background information based on the position. After the tourist finished the site or the day, he/she could ask the system to generate an HTML document based on the stored information. He/she could then easily publish it on the web or send it to other people via email. Figure 10 shows screen shoots of the system.

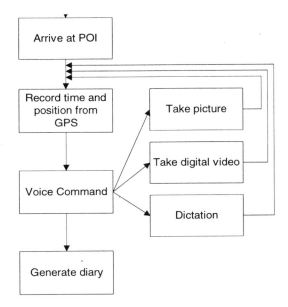

Figure 9: The software flow chart of tourist diary

5.2 "Is This an Interesting Tourist Area"

One of the most common problems in both navigation and sightseeing, typical activities of the tourist, is the identification of landmarks. How often does the average tourist point to a building and ask its name or purpose, only to have the question go unanswered? This problem could be solved by locating the tourist location and database search. If there is a sign for the landmark, the landmark can be identified by sign recognition instead of database search.

Although OCR technology has been widely used in many applications, sign identification is not a trivial problem. Challenges include difficulty in segmentation and low resolution of video image. Automatic segmentation of signs is, in principle, impossible to accomplish because they are embedded in the graphics. Fortunately, we can solve this problem by multimodal interaction in this particular application. Since a human is in the loop, the user can tell the system where he/she is interested by combination of speech and gesture. The tourist can input the sign to the system using the camera. Then he/she could ask the system "Is this an interesting tourist area?" or "Does this sign warn of a hazardous area?" with the gesture circling the location where the sign is.

The low resolution image can be enhanced by the super resolution method before the system performs the OCR. The basic idea is to take advantage of a sequence of images. The basic theory behind our approach is that of inverse graphics. That is, given a sequence of images, we want to find the ground truth (surface) that would have generated them. The most difficult part of this process is recovering the motion for each image. To do this, we will register all the images with respect to a reference image to an accuracy of a small fraction of a pixel; this

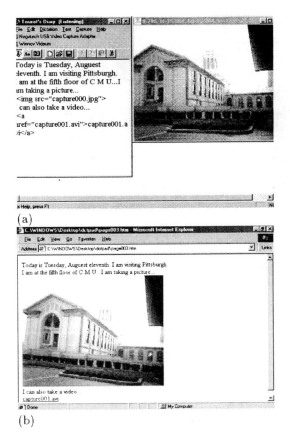

(a)

(b)

Figure 10: Screen shoots of "Tourist Diary": (a) working process (b) html format result.

registration will tell the system how an image maps onto a higher resolution image that is needed.

The system inputs the enhanced image into the OCR module and displays the result in the head mounted display. Figure 11 shows an example of recognizing a door label.

6 Conclusion

We have presented our efforts towards developing an intelligent tourist system. The system takes advantages of multimodal interaction and wireless communication. The system is equipped with a unique combination of sensors and software. The hardware includes computers, a GPS receiver, a microphone and an earphone, a video camera and a head-mounted display. The software supports natural language processing, speech recognition, machine translation, handwriting recognition and multimodal fusion. This combination enables a multimodal interface to take advantage of speech and gesture input to provide assistance for a tourist. We are currently working on system integration and developing various new applications.

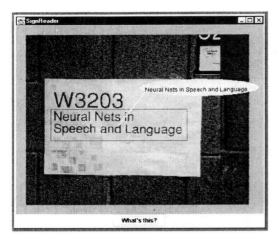

Figure 11: An example of sign recognition

Acknowledgements

We would like to thank Daniel Kiecza and Edmund Wong for their support to this project. We would also like to thank some colleagues in Interactive Systems Lab for technical support and discussions.

References

[1] Ando, H., Kitahara, Y., and Hataoka. N., "Evaluation of multimodal interface using spoken language and pointing gesture on interior design system," *Proc. ICSLP'94*, Vol. 2, pp. 567-570, Yokohama, Japan.

[2] Carpenter, B. *The Logic of Typed Feature Structures*. Cambridge University Press, 1992.

[3] Denecke, M., *A Programmable Multi-Blackboard Architecture for Dialogue Processing Systems*. Proceedings of the Workshop on Spoken Dialogue Processing, ACL/EACL, Madrid, Spain, 1997.

[4] Bajura, M. and Neumann, U. "Dynamic Registration and Correction in Augmented Reality Systems." Proc. VRAIS '95 (Virtual Reality Annual International Symp.), IEEE Computer Society Press. Los Alamitos, CA, 189-196.

[5] Caudell, T. and Mizell, D. (1992). "Augmented Reality: An Application of Heads-Up Display Technology to Manual Manufacturing Processes." Proc. Hawaii International Conf. on Systems Science, Vol. 2, 659-669.

[6] Marsal Gavalda and A. Waibel. *Grwoing Semantic Grammars* Proceedings of ACL/ Coling 1998, Montreal, Canada.

[7] Nakagawa, S. and Zhang, J.X., "An input interface with speech and touch screen," *Trans. Inst. Elec. Eng. Jpn. C (Japan)*, Vol. 114-C, No. 10, pp. 1009-1017, 1994.

[8] Nishimoto, T., Shida, N., Kobayashi, T., and Shirai, K., "Multimodal drawing tool using speech, mouse and keyboard," *Proc. ICSLP'94*, Vol. 3, pp. 1287-1290, Yokohama, Japan.

[9] Oviatt, S.L., Cohen, P.R., and Wang, M., "Toward interface design for human language technology: modality and structure as determinants of linguistic complexity," *Speech Communication (Netherlands)*, Vol. 15, Nos. 3-4, pp. 283-300, 1994.

[10] Robinett, W. "Synthetic Experience: A Taxonomy." Presence: Teleoperators and Virtual Environments, 1(2), Summer 1992.

[11] Starner, T., Mann, S., Rhodes, B., Levine, J., Healey, J., Kirsch, D., Picard, R. and Pentland, A. "Augmented Reality Through Wearable Computing." Presence 6(4), 1997.

[12] Vo. T.M., "A Framework and Toolkit for the Construction of Multimodal Learning Interfaces," Ph.D. Dissertation CMU-CS-98-129, Carnegie Mellon University (April 1998).

[13] Waibel, A., Vo, M.T., Duchnowski, P., and Manke, S., "Multimodal Interfaces," Artificial Intelligence Review, Special Volume on Integration of Natural Language and Vision Processing, McKevitt, P. (Ed.), Vol. 10, Nos. 3-4, 1995.

[14] Waibel, A., Suhm, B.. Vo, M.T. and Yang, J., "Multimodal Interfaces for Multimedia Information Agents," Proceedings of 1997 ICASSP.

[15] Jing, X., Yang, J., Vo, M. and Waibel, A., "Java Front-end for Web-based Multimodal Human-computer Interaction," Proceedings of Workshop on Perceptual User Interfaces , pp. 78-81.

[16] Yang, J., Stiefelhagen, R., Meier, U. and Waibel, A.,"Visual Tracking for Multimodal Human Computer Interaction," Proceedings of CHI 98, pp. 40-147.

[17] Yang, J., Holtz, W., Yang, W. and Vo, M., "An Adaptive Multimodal Interface for Wireless Applications," Proceedings of International Symposium on Wearable Computers , Pittsburgh, PA, Oct. 19-20, 1998.

Situated Documentaries:
Embedding Multimedia Presentations in the Real World

Tobias Höllerer
Steven Feiner
Dept. of Computer Science
Columbia University
New York, NY 10027
{htobias,feiner}@cs.columbia.edu

John Pavlik
Center for New Media
Graduate School of Journalism
Columbia University
New York, NY 10027
jp35@columbia.edu

Abstract

We describe an experimental wearable augmented reality system that enables users to experience hypermedia presentations that are integrated with the actual outdoor locations to which they are are relevant. Our mobile prototype uses a tracked see-through head-worn display to overlay 3D graphics, imagery, and sound on top of the real world, and presents additional, coordinated material on a hand-held pen computer. We have used these facilities to create several situated documentaries *that tell the stories of events that took place on our campus. We describe the software and hardware that underly our prototype system and explain the user interface that we have developed for it.*

1. Introduction

Mobile and wearable computing systems provide users access to computational resources even when they are away from the static infrastructure of their offices or homes. One of the most important aspects of these devices is their potential to support *location-aware* or *location-based* computing, offering services and information that are relevant to the user's current locale [1]. Research and commercial location-aware systems have explored the utility of a variety of coarse position-tracking approaches, ranging from monitoring infrared signals emitted by "active badges" [23], to relying on wireless paging cell size to provide local weather and traffic updates [18].

Augmented reality, which demands far more accurate position tracking combined with accurate orientation tracking, can provide an especially powerful user interface for location-aware mobile computing. By supplementing the real world with virtual information, augmented reality can substantially enrich the user's experience of her environ-

ment and present her with an integrated user interface for interacting with the surrounding augmented material.

We have been experimenting with using a mobile augmented reality system (MARS) testbed to create location-aware multimedia presentations for outdoor users. Building on our earlier work on a MARS campus tour guide [7], we introduce the concept of a *situated documentary* that embeds a narrated multimedia documentary within the same physical environment as the events and sites that the documentary describes. One of the most important principles of journalism is to locate a story in a physical space. We accomplish this by situating the news consumer literally at the story's location, and layering a multimedia documentary over that space.

As depicted in Figure 1, the user wears an experimental backpack-based system, based on commercial hardware that we have chosen for programmability and power at the expense of comfort and wearability. Graphics and imagery are overlaid on the surrounding world by a see-through head-worn display. Head tracking is accomplished using a centimeter-level real-time kinematic GPS position tracker and an inertial/magnetometer orientation tracker. Audio is presented through the head-worn display's earphones, and coordinated video and other multimedia material are presented on a companion hand-held display. Interaction occurs through a set of selection mechanisms based on positional proximity and gaze orientation, a trackpad that is used with the head-worn display, and a pen-based user interface on the hand-held display.

In this paper, we first discuss how our work relates to previous research in Section 2. Next, in Section 3, we introduce our main application scenario and its user interface techniques: a multimedia documentary of highlights in the history of Columbia's campus. We then briefly describe the hardware and software used for our current testbed in Sec-

Figure 1. Situated documentaries. a) Our backpack-based testbed, with tracked see-through head-worn display and pen-based hand-held computer. b) An image photographed by a video camera that wears our testbed's see-through head-worn display. The labels and virtual flags are part of the user interface, described in Section 3. c) Related information displayed on our hand-held computer.

tion 4. Finally, Section 5 provides our conclusions and a discussion of ongoing and future work.

2. Related Work

As computers continue to shrink in size, researchers have begun to address the development of outdoor location-aware mobile and wearable systems. Some have relied on modifying the environment being explored; for example, Smailagic and Martin [19] label campus information signs with bar codes to provide location-specific information on a hand-held computer equipped with a bar code scanner. In contrast, others have combined GPS and orientation trackers to produce map-based contextual displays [11], to provide audio navigation assistance to blind users [12], and to annotate the world with overlaid textual labels [7, 22, 9].

Situated documentaries rely in part on the idea of creating hypertextual links between physical and virtual objects or locations. In earlier indoor work, using short-range, magnetic and ultrasonic tracking systems, we developed a hypermedia system that supports linking arbitrary X11 windows, displayed on a tracked see-through head-worn dis-

play, to a variety of targets, including 3D world locations and tracked objects [6]. Wearable systems by Rekimoto et al. [17] and Starner et al. [21] allow people to register digital data with visually-coded or infrared-tagged objects. Billinghurst et al. [2] use similar visual fiducials to position texture-mapped representations of participants in an augmented reality teleconference. Mann [15] and Jebara et al. [10] associate information with untagged objects using visual recognition algorithms. Pascoe [16] uses a hand-held display and GPS to allow an ecologist to link observation notes to the locations at which they are written. All these projects can be seen as leading towards the goal articulated in Spohrer's proposal for a "WorldBoard" [20]: the creation of a world-wide spatial hypertext of information anchored to physical locations and objects.

Our work is built on top of a new version of the backpack-based wearable MARS testbed that we developed for our earlier "Touring Machine" [7]. This system uses a campus database to overlay labels on buildings seen through a tracked head-worn display. Users can request additional overlaid information, such as the names of a building's departments, and can view related information, such as a de-

Figure 2. Virtual flags denoting points of interest, photographed from the top of a campus building.

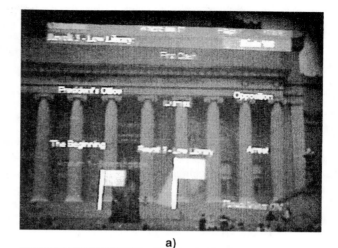

a)

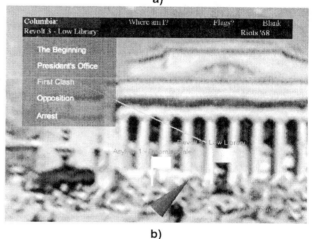

b)

Figure 3. Two different menu designs for listing multimedia snippets about the student revolt. a) World-stabilized circular menu around Low Library (photographed through an earlier, low-resolution, see-through, head-worn display). b) Head-stabilized list with anchor to its flag (screen dump of the system running in indoor test mode, with an omnidirectional image as a backdrop).

partment's web page, on a hand-held display. The situated documentaries that we describe here extend this previous work in several ways:

- Rather than linking individual labels or web pages to locations, we support context-dependent, narrated multimedia presentations that combine audio, still images, video, 3D graphics, and omnidirectional camera imagery.

- We make extensive use of overlaid 3D graphics for both the user interface (e.g., 3D widgets for user guidance) and the presentation content (e.g., *in situ* reconstructions of buildings that no longer exist and views of visually obstructed infrastructure).

- We embed the informational elements in an early version of a new *physical hypermedia* user interface that guides users through a presentation, while giving them the freedom to follow their own trails through the material.

3. User Interface

Our user stands in the middle of Columbia's campus, wearing our experimental backpack computer system and a see-through head-worn display, and holding a tablet computer (Figure 1a). As the user moves about, their position and head orientation are tracked, and through the head-worn display they see the campus environment overlaid with virtual material, such as that shown in Figures 1(b) and 2.

The user can interact with the surrounding environment in different ways. On the hand-held computer, which is networked to the backpack computer that drives the head-worn display, the user can view and interact with information, and input data with a stylus. All information on the hand-held display is presented using a standard web browser. Items seen on the head-worn display can be selected with an approximation to gaze-oriented selection described below. A menu on the head-worn display can be manipulated using a two-button trackpad mounted on the back of the hand-held computer for easy "reach-around" selection.

The head-worn user interface consists of a screen-stabilized part and a world-stabilized part. The menu bars on top of the screen and the cone-shaped pointer at the bottom (shown most clearly in Figure 3b) are screen-stabilized and therefore always visible. World-stabilized material is visually registered with specific locations on campus. World-stabilized 3D elements are displayed in the correct perspective for the user's viewpoint, so the user can walk up to these elements just as they can to physical objects

3.1 Application Scenario

Our situated documentary begins with a narrated introduction, explaining that the user will be able to learn about events related to the campus, and referring the user to the hand-held display for an overview. Before turning to the hand-held computer, the user looks around and sees virtual flags with textual labels denoting points of interest, positioned around the campus (see Figures 1b and 2). The virtual flags are world-stabilized user-interface elements that are iconic representations of the topmost *group nodes* in a hierarchical presentation.

The hand-held display provides an overview of the material embedded in the surrounding environment. Three main topics are currently available: a description of the Bloomingdale Asylum for the Insane, which once occupied the current campus before Columbia's move in the late 19th century, a documentary on the Columbia student revolt of 1968, and a tour of Columbia's extensive underground tunnel system. Looking at the surrounding flags, the user can see how the different stories are distributed over the campus area. The labeled flags come in three different colors: red for the student revolt, blue for the tunnel system, and green for the Bloomingdale Asylum.

The user can select a flag in several different ways. One method, which works when the user is in the system's *VisualSelect* mode, is to look in the flag's direction, orienting one's head so the desired flag's projection is closer than any other to the center of the head-worn display and within a fixed target area. When these criteria are met, the flag's label changes color to yellow. If the criteria hold for a half second, then the flag is selected and its label changes color to green. (This approximation of gaze selection was originally developed for selection of building tags in [7].) Flags are selectable from any distance. Although the flags scale with distance, their textual labels do not, so there is always a visible anchor that is selectable.

A second selection method is based on positional proximity. A menu item allows the user to ask the system to select the flag to which they are currently closest (or to select another flag by name), and the cone-shaped pointer on the head-worn display will point towards that flag, guiding the user to it. Finally, a flag can be selected automatically by following a link in the presentation.

When a flag is selected, it starts to wave gently, and all flags of a different color are dimmed (reduced in intensity). Therefore, when a user looks around while a flag is selected, the other flags in its category stand out. The cone-shaped pointer always points toward the selected flag, so that the user can be guided back to it should they look away.

Selecting a flag causes the second menu bar (the green *context* menu below the blue top-level menu) to display that flag's label plus additional entries that are available for its group node (e.g., links to other group nodes). All these entries can be selected using the trackpad. The group nodes (and their corresponding flags) have a default numbering corresponding to an order set forth in the presentation description. A button click on the trackpad directs the user to the next node in this order; however, at all times the user can choose to select a different flag using any of the methods mentioned above.

In our case, the user selects the entry for the student revolt from the overview menu on the hand-held computer. The cone-shaped arrow on the head-worn display points to a red flag, which starts waving, in front of Low Library, which is about 150 yards away. This flag is the starting point for information on the student revolt.

Once a flag is selected, the user can display an overlaid *in-place* menu (see Figure 3), which lists the parts of the presentation associated with the flag's group node. (Section 3.3 discusses the in-place menus further.) The in-place menu for Low Library's revolt flag provides access to background information on how the student revolt started, grouped into five segments.

Selecting an entry in this menu using the trackpad starts that entry's part of the multimedia presentation, each of which ranges in length from seconds to minutes in our current material. Here, the user selects the entry labeled *First Clash*. This results in a narrated description of how the students and the police clashed for the first time on the steps of Low Library, where the user is now looking. The presentation includes coordinated still images that are overlaid on the scene (Figure 4a) and videos that are played on the hand-held computer (Figure 4b).

The head-worn display's menu bar allows the user to display an overview of the student revolt on the hand-held computer or to follow links to other places directly by selecting them with the trackpad to learn more about about the revolt and what happened at other campus buildings.

At this point, the user has found a description of how the students used Columbia's tunnel system to occupy buildings guarded aboveground by the police. The user decides to follow a link to learn more about the tunnels by exploring the blue flags. Since the real tunnels are difficult (and illegal) to enter, the user can vicariously explore portions of them through a set of 360° omnidirectional camera photo-

a)

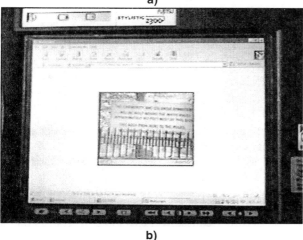

b)

Figure 4. Imagery documenting the student revolt in 1968: a) Still image, overlaid on top of Low Library, b) video material displayed on the hand-held computer

a)

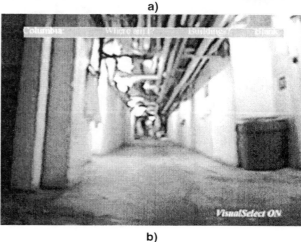

b)

Figure 5. Exploring Columbia's tunnel system: a) Schematic view of how a user experiences an omnidirectional camera image. b) The omnidirectional camera image seen from a user's perspective.

graphic images (Figure 5) that temporarily teleport the user underground, supplemented by maps and blueprints.

The presentation mentions that the oldest parts of the tunnel system preceded Columbia's move to the area and were originally built for the Bloomingdale Asylum. Intrigued, our user turns to the green flags to find out where the main asylum buildings were situated, and is shown a 3D model of the buildings overlaid in place on the campus, in conjunction with historical images (see Figure 6). The documentary mentions that one building built for the asylum is still standing and is now known as Buell Hall, and points the user toward it.

3.2. Multimedia Presentations

The multimedia material in each presentation node is a coordinated media stream (see Section 4.2) that typically, but not necessarily, makes use of both the hand-held display and the head-worn display, and which includes an audio track. The different media that can be freely combined to create a multimedia presentation are:

- *Audio material on the head-worn display.* Audio is played over the head-worn display's earphones, and includes both narration and non-speech audio (e.g., recordings of the 1968 revolt).

- *Images on the head-worn display.* Images (e.g., Figure 4a) are displayed as world- or head-stabilized 3D textured polygons that can make use of simple ani-

a)

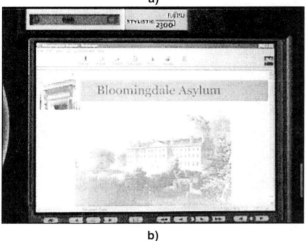

b)

Figure 6. a) A simplified 3D model of the main Bloomingdale asylum building overlaid on Columbia's campus by the see-through head-worn display. b) Documentary material displayed on the hand-held computer.

mated effects. For example, we often "flip up" head-stabilized images from a horizontal position until they fill the screen.

- *Web pages that include static images, video material, and applets on the hand-held display.* Figures 4(b) and 6(b) show examples of images and video, created by calling up related material on the hand-held browser using our communication infrastructure (see Section 4.2).

- *3D models.* Figure 6(a) shows a simple example. Models are shown full-size and world-stabilized in their actual location.

- 360° *omnidirectional camera surround views.* These allow us to immerse the user in an environment that is not physically available. We use a commercial omnidirectional camera [5]: a digital camera pointing at a parabolic mirror that captures a 360° hemispherical surround view in a single image. Each of these anamorphic images is texture-mapped onto a hemisphere displayed around the user, as depicted schematically in Figure 5(a), so that the user can look around (Figure 5b). The see-through head-worn display's opacity is controlled by a dial, allowing us to make the display opaque when viewing these images. (Unfortunately, the display's opacity cannot be set in software.)

3.3. Exploratory UI Design

We also use omnidirectional images as backdrops for indoor demonstrations of our system and for exploratory development of new user interface elements and variants. Figure 3 demonstrates this approach. Part (a) shows our original version of an in-place menu, shot outdoors through a low-resolution see-through head-worn display; part (b) shows our current version of the same menu, captured as a screen dump of the system running indoors, using an omnidirectional image of the campus as a backdrop. In the latter design, the menu is a head-stabilized element, rather than the world-stabilized circular menu of part (a). A leader line links the menu to its associated flag, allowing it to be followed back if the user turns away from the flag, an approach that we used to direct users to objects that were not within their field of view in an earlier indoor augmented reality system for maintenance and repair [8].

4. System Design

4.1. Hardware

Our current backpack is an updated version of our first outdoor MARS testbed [7], with the following changes:

Head-worn Display: We use a Sony LDI-100B color display with 800 × 600 triad resolution. It has a dial to adjust its opacity from nearly totally opaque to about 20% transparent. In our experience, under a bright cloudy sky the preferred setting is close to the most opaque. We have just begun to experiment with a stereo version of this display, the Sony LDI-D100B.

The images in this paper were shot directly through the LDI-100B display worn by a dummy head containing an embedded NTSC camera. Images 3a) and 4a) stem from earlier footage, shot through a Virtual I/O i-glasses display with 263 × 230 triad resolution.

Hand-held Computer: The hand-held computer shown in Figures 1, 4(b), and 6(b) is a Fujitsu Stylistic 2300 with a 233 MHz Pentium MMX CPU and a transflective 800×600 color display, designed to be readable in bright sunlight. The Fujitsu's performance is adequate for playing MPEG movies of up to VGA resolution at reasonable frame rates, but it is heavier than we would like (3.9 pounds). We have just switched to a 2.2 pound Mitsubishi AmITY CP pen-based computer with a 166 MHz Pentium MMX CPU and 640×480 color display.

Orientation Tracker: We use an Intersense IS-300Pro inertial/magnetometer orientation tracker with a single sensor mounted rigidly on a head band that we attached to the head-worn display's temple pieces, as shown in Figure 1(a).

Position Tracker: Position tracking is done with an Ashtech GG24 Surveyor real-time kinematic differential GPS system, which uses both US GPS and Russian Glonass satellite constellations to increase the number of visible satellites. We have installed a base station on campus, from which we broadcast correction signals via radio modem. This system provides centimeter-level accuracy in open areas, such as those depicted in the figures, where we have line-of-sight to more than six satellites. However, tracking degradation and loss remain a problem when we pass too close to tall buildings or beneath trees.

4.2. Software

We extended the software architecture of our previous prototype [7], which is based on our COTERIE distributed virtual environment infrastructure [13, 14]. We run a custom-built HTTP server on the hand-held computer, allowing it to communicate with the backpack computer and accept user input from any web-based interface, including Java applets.

The multimedia information to be conveyed through the augmented reality interface has to be arranged and locally distributed over the target region. For this purpose we designed several authoring tools.

To create the multimedia presentations, we developed a simple extension to the interpreted language *Repo*, our extended variant of the lexically scoped interpreted language *Obliq* [4]. Each multimedia presentation is stored as a *Repo* script, referencing by filename the multimedia "chunks" (images, video segments, audio snippets, 3D animations, omnidirectional views) it uses. Each chunk is stored on the computer (backpack or hand-held) on which it is to be played; additional material to be presented on the hand-held computer can be obtained from the web using a wireless network interface.

Students in a graduate Journalism class taught by the third author used our multimedia prototyping environment to break the footage they had collected into chunks and wrote scripts to create our multimedia presentations. Synchronization takes place purely at the level of these relatively coarse-grain media chunks by exchanging *Repo* messages between the main server on the backpack computer and the HTTP server on the hand-held computer.

All location-based information is stored in a campus database on the backpack computer. This database contains the complete structure of the situated documentaries, including the contents of all context-menus and links to the multimedia presentation scripts.

We used an early version of a map-based tool we are developing to place 3D objects at any specified latitude–longitude. For this project, we scanned in a high-resolution map of Columbia's campus that provides a placement resolution of about 6 inches in latitude or longitude.

5. Conclusions and Future Work

Although most of our user experience has been limited to the authors of this paper and to the students who helped construct the presentations, our system has been demonstrated informally in several Journalism classes, to visitors to our lab, and to attendees of a Department of Defense seminar who tried the indoor version. While feedback has been encouraging, users understandably cite the current prototype's form factor, weight (about forty pounds), and appearance as drawbacks. We are confident, however, that these issues will be addressed by the commercial development of sufficiently small wearable devices.

For the near term, we note that much of our backpack's weight is due to its computer, which together with its external battery weighs about twenty-two pounds. We selected this machine (Fieldworks 7600) for the programming comfort of the system's developers, rather than the physical comfort of its wearers. Its flexibility and extensibility (expansion ports for six PCI and ISA cards, and the ability to run a desktop operating system and programming environment) have been invaluable during development and testing. We are investigating options for replacing it with a lighter, more powerful laptop, but require high-performance support for the OpenGL 3D graphics API that we use, which is not yet offered by current laptops. To provide a lighter hand-held display, we are beginning to experiment with the Casio Cassiopeia E-100 running Windows CE, a palm-top computer with a 240×320 16-bit color display.

There are many directions that we are currently exploring to further develop our software. For example, our system currently provides no reasonable facilities for end-user authoring. We are especially interested in developing this kind of support, with emphasis on how such a system might be used by journalists in the field to develop stories. We are also working on an interface between our backpack system and an indoor multi-user augmented reality system [3] to make possible collaboration among indoor and outdoor users. Using a 3D model of the environment, indoor users create virtual objects and highlight real objects for outdoor users to see, and maintain histories of outdoor users' activities. In turn, outdoor users point out interesting objects and events for indoor users to view.

6. Acknowledgements

We thank Blair MacIntyre for developing Coterie, for his work on the first generation MARS testbed on which this work builds, and for his advice on Coterie programming issues. Gus Rashid developed the map-based tool mentioned in Section 4.2, and Elias Gagas helped write the GPS drivers and assisted in testing and improving the system. Students in John Pavlik's Journalism courses in the Center for New Media collected multimedia material, turned it into coherent presentations, and participated in helpful discussions on the user interface. In particular we would like to thank Aklilu Hailemariam, Tali Dayan, Dave Westreich, Stephen Newman, Dave Terraso, Dave Derryck, and Sheryl LeDuc.

This work was supported in part by Office of Naval Research Contracts N00014-97-1-0838, N00014-99-1-0249, and N00014-99-1-0394; and gifts from IBM, Intel, Microsoft, and Mitsubishi.

References

[1] H. Beadle, B. Harper, G. Maguire Jr., and J. Judge. Location aware mobile computing. In *Proc. ICT '97 (IEEE/IEE Int. Conf. on Telecomm.)*, Melbourne, Australia, 1997.

[2] M. Billinghurst, J. Bowskill, M. Jessop, and J. Morphett. A wearable spatial conferencing space. In *Proc. ISWC '98 (Second Int. Symposium on Wearable Computers)*, pages 76–83, 1998.

[3] A. Butz, T. Höllerer, S. Feiner, B. MacIntyre, and C. Beshers. Enveloping users and computers in a collaborative 3D augmented reality. In *Proc. IWAR '99 (Int. Workshop on Augmented Reality)*, San Francisco, CA, October 20–21 1999.

[4] L. Cardelli. A language with distributed scope. *Computing Systems*, 8(1):27–59, Jan 1995.

[5] Cyclovision Technologies, Inc. ParaShot—One Shot 360 Degree Surround View Images. http://www.cyclovision.com, 1998.

[6] S. Feiner, B. MacIntyre, M. Haupt, and E. Solomon. Windows on the world: 2D windows for 3D augmented reality. In *Proc. UIST '93*, pages 145–155, 1993.

[7] S. Feiner, B. MacIntyre, T. Höllerer, and A. Webster. A touring machine: Prototyping 3D mobile augmented reality systems for exploring the urban environment. In *Proc. ISWC '97 (First Int. Symp. on Wearable Computers)*, pages 74–81, Cambridge, MA, October 13–14 1997.

[8] S. Feiner, B. MacIntyre, and D. Seligmann. Knowledge-based augmented reality. *Communications of the ACM*, 36(7):52–62, July 1993.

[9] B. Jang, J. Kim, H. Kim, and D. Kim. An outdoor augmented reality system for GIS applications. In Y. Ohta and H. Tamura, editors, *Mixed Reality, Merging Real and Virtual Worlds*, pages 391–399. Ohmsha/Springer, Tokyo/New York, 1999.

[10] T. Jebara, B. Schiele, N. Oliver, and A. Pentland. DyPERS: Dynamic personal enhanced reality system. In *Proc. 1998 Image Understanding Workshop*, Monterey, CA, November 1998.

[11] S. Long, D. Aust, G. Abowd, and C. Atkenson. Cyberguide: Prototyping context-aware mobile applications. In *CHI '96 Conference Companion*, pages 293–294, April 1996.

[12] J. Loomis, R. Golledge, and R. Klatzky. Personal guidance system for the visually impaired using GPS, GIS, and VR technologies. In *Proc. Conf. on Virtual Reality and Persons with Disabilities*, Millbrae, CA, June 17–18 1993.

[13] B. MacIntyre and S. Feiner. Language-level support for exploratory programming of distributed virtual environments. In *Proc. UIST '96*, pages 83–94, Seattle, WA, November 6–8 1996.

[14] B. MacIntyre and S. Feiner. A distributed 3D graphics library. In *Computer Graphics (Proc. ACM SIGGRAPH '98)*, Annual Conference Series, pages 361–370, Orlando, FL, July 19–24 1998.

[15] S. Mann. Wearable computing: A first step toward personal imaging. *IEEE Computer*, 30(2), February 1997.

[16] J. Pascoe. Adding generic contextual capabilities to wearable computers. In *Proc. ISWC '98 (Second Int. Symp. on Wearable Computers)*, pages 92–99, Cambridge, MA, October 19–20 1998.

[17] J. Rekimoto, Y. Ayatsuka, and K. Hayashi. Augment-able reality: Situated communication through physical and digital spaces. In *Proc. ISWC '98 (Second Int. Symp. on Wearable Computers)*, pages 68–75, Cambridge, MA, October 19–20 1998.

[18] Seiko Communications. Seiko message watch documentation. http://www.messagewatch.com, 1998.

[19] A. Smailagic and R. Martin. Metronaut: A wearable computer with sensing and global communication capabilities. In *Proc. ISWC '97 (First Int. Symp. on Wearable Computers)*, pages 116–122, Cambridge, MA, October 13–14 1997.

[20] J. Spohrer. WorldBoard—What Comes After the WWW? http://www.worldboard.org/pub/spohrer/wbconcept/default.html, 1997.

[21] T. Starner, S. Mann, B. Rhodes, J. Levine, J. Healey, D. Kirsch, R. Picard, and A. Pentland. Augmented reality through wearable computing. *Presence*, 6(4):386–398, August 1997.

[22] B. Thomas, V. Demczuk, W. Piekarski, D. Hepworth, and B. Gunther. A wearable computer system with augmented reality to support terrestrial navigation. In *Proc. ISWC '98 (Second Int. Symp. on Wearable Computers)*, pages 168–171, Pittsburgh, PA, October 19–20 1998.

[23] R. Want, A. Hopper, V. Falcao, and J. Gibbons. The active badge location system. *ACM Trans. on Information Systems*, 10(1):91–102, January 1992.

A Run on Sterling – Personal Finance on the Move

Lee Cooper

Industrial Ergonomics Group
University of Birmingham
l.cooper@bham.ac.uk

Graham Johnson

NCR Knowledge Lab
g.john@exchange.ncr.
scotland.com

Chris Baber

Industrial Ergonomics Group
University of Birmingham
c.baber@bham.ac.uk

Abstract

A number of organizations are currently engaged in the creation of electronic wallets as platforms for electronic commerce and banking. Significantly the wallet developed by Swatch is wearable. The Swatch 'Access' thus represents one of the few applications of truly wearable technology within the financial service sector. This paper summarizes research intent upon exploring and highlighting the non-technical requirements associated with electronic wallets such as the Swatch Access. To achieve this goal the research adopted an ethnographic approach. A series of interviews and observations was carried out, addressing the content of the people's existing wallets and how the wallet and its contents are used in everyday life. The 'findings' are subsequently discussed in terms of their implications for the development of future wearable electronic wallets.

1. Introduction

A number of organizations are currently engaged in the creation of electronic wallets, which typically combine the traditional wallet with computer and, in some instances, communication technology. Their rationale is that the wallet is inherently associated with personal finance and will therefore provide a natural platform for electronic commerce and banking.

The electronic wallet developed by AT&T, for example, is intended to replace the traditional wallet within the Mondex smart card system. Smart cards are similar to conventional credit cards but contain an embedded computer chip. Some smart cards, such as the Mondex card, are designed to store monetary value. In combination with the Mondex smart cards, AT&T's 'Mondex Wallet' (see Figure 1) allows users to perform on-line transactions and view balance and transaction information stored on their card.

Figure 1. AT&T's 'Mondex Wallet'

The electronic wallet developed by Swatch, however, differs from those that are traditionally inspired. The Swatch Access (see Figure 2) is a wristwatch featuring a miniature antenna and a computer chip, similar to those used in conventional smart card payment systems. This allows users to perform transactions using money stored on the chip [1].

Figure 2. Swatch's 'Access'

87

In Finland, for example, 'Access' users can pay a given amount of money to the public transport authority, which is stored on the watch's chip. The cost of a ride is then automatically deducted from the chip when a user passes near a ticketing terminal when they board [2].

Significantly the Swatch 'Access' exhibits the five characteristics of a wearable computer suggested by Bass [3]:

(i.)   It may be used while one or both hands are free, or occupied with other tasks;

(ii.)   It exists within the corporeal envelope of the user, i.e., it should be not merely attached to the body but becomes an integral part of the person's clothing;

(iii.)   It must allow the user to maintain control;

(iv.)   It must exhibit constancy in the sense that it should be constantly available.

The 'Access', therefore, represents one of the few applications of truly wearable technology within the financial service sector of industry.

Although the development of the wearable electronic wallet may be motivated more by technological innovation than consumer desire, the history of the wallet has shown that it has always been influenced by technology. As a "container of the necessities of everyday life" both the wallet's content *and* form have evolved to accommodate a society's technological development's [4]. Be it the introduction of paper money or the development of the credit card, the wallet has adapted. Therefore in an age of wearable technology and electronic commerce and banking it is hardly surprising that the wallet is currently 'Being Digital' [5] and body mounted.

In acknowledging the technological requirements that have motivated the wallet to change, however, we should not neglect consumers' non-technical needs that are more closely allied to the 'user experience' than the technology *per se*. For example, whilst the debut of cash demanded flatter more robust containers (a technical requirement) the compartmentalization of notes according to value, common to many wallets, was motivated solely by convenience (a non-technical requirement).

In order to develop an acceptable wearable electronic wallet it is essential that an understanding of consumers' technical and non-technical requirements are gained.

This paper summarizes research intent upon exploring and highlighting the non-technical consumer requirements associated with electronic wallets. To achieve this goal the research adopted an ethnographic approach.

There is currently growing recognition that a detailed understanding of consumers' current practices is essential in determining their requirements of new technologies. As such ethnography is increasingly being linked with the technology development process. "The term ethnography refers both to the process of conducting field research and to the written text produced as a result" [6].

Ethnography was originally developed within anthropology as a way of gaining an insight into the cultural practices of societies. As employed by the technology development community, the technique is a way of gaining an insight into more everyday practices. Central to ethnography, however, is an emphasis on understanding implicit activities [7].

Due to their familiarity, many important activities are often taken for granted by those who perform them. Subsequently it is not enough to simply ask people about their practices. Furthermore, people generally find it difficult to articulate their knowledge of how they do things [8]. Therefore, in addition to interviews, ethnography relies on observation.

With regard to this research it is hoped that by interviewing consumers and observing how they currently use wallets, the non-technical requirements associated with future wearable wallets can be determined.

2. Method

Participants in the research were 55 adults, aged 17-75 years, from various social and economic backgrounds. A series of semi-structured interviews was carried out, addressing the content of the people's wallets and how the wallet and its contents are used in everyday life.

The interviews were augmented with observations of how wallets were used. Specifically, numerous photographs were taken, recording the contents of participant's wallets.

As well as providing a record of exactly how participants used their wallets, the process of emptying the wallet's contents for documentation served as a prompt for discussion itself.

3. Results

The participants in this study perceived the wallet primarily as a financial artifact. This was despite the fact that the participants were observed to store a multitude of non-financial objects such as membership cards, photographs and business cards. In fact many of the wallets in this study were found to contain rather unusual items including plasters, textile samples, teeth, and pocket battleships! So when asked why they carried a wallet the vast majority replied that it was "to keep my cards and money in", despite their actual use being much broader and varied.

Figure 3. Electronic commerce and banking acceptor

The amount of financial 'stuff' that participants carried around in their wallets was clearly related to their general attitude towards electronic banking and electronic commerce. Those wallet users who actively accepted and made use of electronic transactions as a primary means, subsequently found themselves loaded down with multiple bankcards, credit cards, debit cards, store cards and loyalty cards (see Figure 3). Furthermore, the enormous number of receipts which are frequently a by-product of electronic transactions, were packed into the

wallet along with the cash (and coins) necessary for 'micro-transactions'. Micro-transactions are those transactions under five pounds sterling which typically include the purchase of "bus tickets", "newspapers" and "sandwiches". In contrast, those participants who chose to reject electronic banking and commerce were far less encumbered with respect to their wallet content (see Figure 4). Table 1 summarizes the financial content of the participants' wallets.

Figure 4. Electronic commerce and banking rejecter

Financial objects carried in wallets	Proportion of consumers carrying object (%)
Receipts	81.0
Money	70.7
Cash	29.3
Coins	26.8
Cash & coins	14.6
Loyalty cards	65.9
Debit cards	53.7
Bankcards	48.8
Credit cards	46.4
Charge (smart) cards	17.1
Cheques	12.2

Table 1. The financial content of participants wallets

Interestingly, although many of the participants carried a similar combination of bankcard, debit card and loyalty card, the participants' specific affiliations with various card suppliers were distinct. Whilst, one participant carried a Nat West bankcard, a Switch debit card and a Tesco loyalty card, another carried a TSB bankcard, a Delta debit card and a Safeway loyalty card. The ease by which participants were able modify their wallets contents was not only reflected in their ability to 'mix-and-match' their particular financial alliances. The day-to-day constituent of individual wallets was also adjusted.

A number of participants constantly transferred money and cards between their wallet, Filofax, pockets and spare wallets depending on what was needed and when. Indeed, 21% of those who took part in the study used more than one wallet simultaneously. One female participant commented:

"I carry a purse and a wallet because I can't fit all my cards and money into just one thing ... but I don't usually carry both at the same time, it depends on where I'm going and what I'm doing. If I'm just going to the shop for a paper, I'll just take my purse with some money. But if I'm going into town shopping I'll probably just take my cards [in my wallet] and leave my purse at home".

Figure 5. Multi-wallet users

The wallet and its contents thus afforded a great deal of flexibility. As noted, in many situations the entire wallet contents just weren't required. In those instances, when only certain items were needed, they could be carried more adaptively in coat pockets, bags or other containers. Furthermore, the process of transferring objects around was perceived by several participants as a means of "keeping on

top of things", in other words organizing and managing their affairs. Receipts were stored for a given number of days then transferred to a spare wallet, stuffed in a kitchen draw, then checked against statements at the end of the month.

Table 2 lists the most common non-financial stuff found in the participants' wallets. Less prevalent content included; keys, jewelry, bills, birth certificates, nail files, toys, safety pins, plasters, insurance details, train timetables, pencils, teeth and donor cards.

Given that those who actively accepted electronic commerce and banking were often loaded down with financial stuff, participants that made less use of these electronic means subsequently had far more room in their wallets to fill with non-financial objects. Hence it was often those rejecters of electronic transactions whose wallets contained excessive amounts of non-financial stuff.

Non-financial objects carried in wallets	Proportion of consumers carrying object (%)
Membership cards	73.2
Business cards	43.2
Driving licenses	36.6
Telephone numbers	34.2
ID cards	29.3
Postage stamps	27.3
Lottery tickets	22.0
Coupons	19.5
Photographs	19.5
National insurance card	17.1
Medical prescriptions	17.0
Train tickets	12.2
Calendar	9.8

Table 2. The non-financial contents of participants wallets

Typically, "anything that's card-shaped" was stuck into the wallet, at least on a temporary basis. Most notably this included membership cards, and business cards. However, in addition to these cards which may be used on a day-to-day basis, National Insurance cards, for example, which are needed once in blue moon were also packed into the wallet solely on the basis of its shape. "I know that *all* my cards are in my wallet" commented one participant. In contrast to the financial stuff much of the wallets non-financial content seemed tucked away and forgotten about, to be used only occasionally or in an "emergency".

Although the exact non-financial content of the participants' wallets varied greatly, what was common to almost all wallets, however, was the presence of some form of emotive object. Indeed, even in the most sparsely populated wallet, there could be found an old football match ticket or a picture of a son or daughter. Indeed, the wallet itself often held great sentimental value. As much as the wallet is a financial artifact it is equally an emotional one.

Finally, with regard to the form of the wallets carried by participants. Due to excessive filling a number of the participants considered their wallets unsightly. The immense bulk of many of the wallets drove some of their owners to despair. One of the male participants commented:

> "Carrying around something like that [pointing at his hugely overflowing wallet] ruins the line of a suit, and then if you have to carry a mobile phone around with you!"

Several of the female participants made similar complaints and added that they were regularly forced to carry their purses around in their hands because they had no pockets. Indeed, the minority of those interviewed who did not carry any form of wallet (9.1%) argued that it was because wallets *per se* were so unsightly that they didn't bother with them. Of this minority of non-wallet carriers, all were males aged 19-26 years old.

Notably a number of participants had used a wearable wallet. On holiday, for example, 'money belts' and 'bum bags' were used. This use was predominantly motivated by the belief that wearing a wallet was somehow more secure than just carrying it. However, the need to be unencumbered encouraged one participant to use a wrist wallet whilst jogging to store "emergency cash".

4. Discussion

'The Splendid Shilling' mocks the pow'r of time,
And glows through ages in Miltonic verse,
But never poet, or in blank or rhyme,
Paid cheerful homage to an empty purse.

The Lady's Magazine, 1799

Ford and Wood [9] describe well the added problems faced by ethnographers in comparison to researchers who use more structured research methods:

> *The time needed to conduct a thorough ethnographic study is greater than that needed for survey or experimental methods. This can make an ethnographic study difficult to justify to research sponsors. The extended and in-depth nature of study necessarily means that fewer individuals are studied than is the case with other methods. This means that conclusions are based on data from fewer individuals and may be seen as less reliable or generalizable to larger populations. Finally, because much of the resulting data is unstructured description rather than tightly defined quantitative measurement, ethnographic research is sometimes suspect because it seems superficially less "scientific" than other approaches.*

Despite, suffering many of these problems the ethnographic approach adopted here, nevertheless, revealed many hidden facets to the wallet, its contents and use.

With regard to the development of electronic wallets it is particularly significant that the very consumers who are most likely to want to use them, typically carry the most stuff around with them. Future electronic wallets, be they wearable or not, must be able to deal with the large amount of financial objects. Electronic wallets must provide as effective a storage facility as traditional wallets.

The modifiability, of existing wallets must also be taken into consideration in the design of future wallets. The flexibility afforded by the traditional wallet must be mimicked in electronic wallets. It is necessary that the contents of future wallets can be swapped around as easily as taking a bankcard from a current wallet and placing it an alternative cardholder. Likewise it is necessary to cater for the corporate affiliations of consumers.

Electronic wallets must form as basic a platform as traditional wallets.

Perhaps the least obvious yet most challenging of these non-technical requirements, however, is the storage of emotions in the form sentimental content. A critical role of the wallet, although one that is that often taken for granted, is the storage of happy memories. Future electronic wallets must achieve the status of 'emotional artifact'.

Whilst these requirements may be equally matched by wearable or traditionally inspired electronic wallets, the former come into their own in terms of portability. Electronic wallets must be at least as portable as traditional wallets.

Generally consumers are inconvenienced by having to carry their wallets around with them. Indeed, many rely on the inherent flexibility of the wallet to make their life easier, 'editing' the contents of the wallet depending on where they are going or what they are doing. Whilst the use of smart cards in traditionally inspired electronic wallets, may partly lighten the load, consumers are still forced to carry the wallet about their person. As a result fashion may favor a wearable solution.

Advances in textile manufacture since the 1950s have encouraged slimmer and better fitting clothing in which bulky pockets look unsightly. While this has not deterred the majority of Englishmen from filling their pockets with ever-larger wallets, the more fashion-conscious Italians adopted shoulder and wrist wallets in the 1950s. Only recently have the English begun to look for alternatives to the traditional wallet. Figure 6, for example, depicts a wearable shoulder wallet recently featured in a British fashion magazine.

Changing trends in the clothing industry may thus offer limitless potential for wearable consumer technology. However, it seems ironic that a wearable revolution may be stimulated by the non-technical requirement to "look good", a need which has often been overlooked by the wearable computer community at large. This finding underlines the value of the ethnographic approach in highlighting issues which would probably not have emerged from a standard research approach.

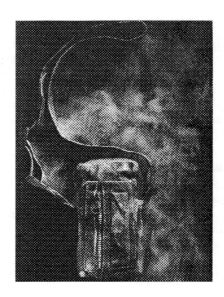

Figure 7. Shoulder wallet, 1998

References

[1] S. Taggart, "Smart watches buy more than time", *TechWeb*, http://www.techweb.com/wire/news/aug/0811watches.html

[2] J. Sanchez-Klein, "Smart card watch carries your carfare", *Computerworld*, http://computerworld.com/home/news.nsf/all/n812174bus

[3] L. Bass, *Conveners Report of CHI '97 Workshop on Wearable Computers*, Personal communication to attendees, 1997

[4] V. Foster, *Bags and Purses*, Batsford, London, 1982

[5] N. Negroponte, *Being Digital*, Coronet, London, 1995

[6] J. Blomberg, "Ethnography", in: *Perspectives on HCI*, A. Monk (Ed), Academic Press, London, 1995

[7] J. Hughes, I. Somerville, R. Bentley & D. Randall, "Designing with ethnography: making work visible", *Interacting with Computers*, **5**, pp. 239-253, 1993

[8] J. Hughes, D. Randall & D. Shapiro, "From ethnographic record to system design: some experiences from the field", *Computer Supported Cooperative Work*, **1**, pp. 123-141, 1993

[9] J. Ford & L. Wood, "An overview of ethnography and system design", in *Field Methods Casebook for Software Design*,

D. Wixon (Ed), John Wiley & Sons, New
York, 1996, pp. 268-282

A Small Planar Inverted-F Antenna for Wearable Applications

Pekka Salonen, Lauri Sydänheimo, Mikko Keskilammi, Markku Kivikoski

Tampere University of Technology
Institute of Electronics
P.O.Box 692, 33101 Tampere, Finland
psalonen@ele.tut.fi

Abstract

Small printed antennas will replace the commonly used normal-mode helical antennas of mobile handsets and systems in the future. This paper presents a novel small planar inverted-F antenna (PIFA) which is a common PIFA in which a U-shaped slot is etched to form a dual band operation for wearable and ubiquitous computing equipment. Health issues are considered in selecting suitable antenna topology and the placement of the antenna. Various applications are presented while the paper mainly discusses about the GSM applications.
Index Terms—Wearable Systems, PIFA, Dual-Band Antennas

1. Introduction

The development of wearable computer systems has been rapid. They are coming more and more lightweight and quite soon we will see a wide range of unobtrusive wearable and ubiquitous computing equipment integrated to into our everyday wear. To reaching this featherweight level requires optimization of every single part and subpart of wearable system. The main parts of a typical wearable system are presented in figure 1.

As we can see both the short range and long range wireless communication plays an important role in mobile wearable system. However these communication systems contain several subparts and antennas are essential subpart of wireless communication systems. This paper will present how antennas for long range data transmission system, i.e. GSM900 (Global System for Mobile communications) in this case, can be integrated to the garment. If the same antenna has dual-band characteristics, it can be used to operate also e.g. wireless short range data transmission such as Bluetooth. This integration will help to reach the goal of unobtrusive wearable equipment.

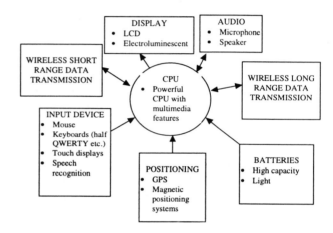

Figure 1. Block diagram of typical wearable system.

The effect of radiation on human body has been also considered in order to design such an antenna structure which has less radiation power in that direction. The ground plane of planar antennas have this kind of property while a commonly used normal-mode helical antennas have omnidirectional radiation pattern, i.e. they radiate all directions normal to the antenna axis.

The application of the proposed antenna is GSM standard, which is the dominant digital access technique in mobile communications in Europe. However this is easily applied for other standards and systems used e.g. in USA such as PCS.

This proposed system can reduce required GSM transmission power and thus increase the operating hours of batteries. This is achieved by a good impedance matching of the antenna feed when the power loss due to reflected waves is minimized. Multi-band antennas for combining antennas for both short and long range systems are discussed as well.

2. Antenna Design

Resonant antennas are a class of antennas in which their size is comparable of the wavelength of operation. The antennas of this class operate well at single frequency or selected narrow frequency band. These are popular when simple structure, light weight and real input impedance is needed. A good example is half-wavelength dipole, which is the initial structure to be modified in this paper.

Most cellular mobile phones use a resonant antenna. The main goal of this paper is to present a dual-band antenna which operates at GSM frequency (900MHz) and Bluetooth frequency (2.4GHz) and is suitable for wearable systems. Bluetooth is the code name for a technology specification for small form factor, low-cost, short range radio links between mobile PCs, mobile phones and other portable devices. It will enable users to connect a wide range of computing and telecommunications devices easily and simply, without the need to buy, carry, or connect cables. It delivers opportunities for rapid ad hoc connections, and the possibility of automatic, unconscious, connections between devices. Because Bluetooth can be used for a variety of purposes, it will also potentially replace multiple cable connections via a single radio link. It creates the possibility of using mobile data in a different way, for different applications such as "Surfing in the sofa", "The instant postcard", "Three in one phone" and many others. It will allow them to think about what they are working on, rather than how to make their technology work.

The half-wave dipole antenna consists of two wire arms of which are bent 90 degrees, figure 2, in which the current distribution is also shown along dipole arms. If the lower arm is replaced by a ground plane the dipole antenna reduces to a monopole antenna of a length of quarter-wavelength, figure 3. This idea of reducing the size of the dipole is based on the image theory [1,2]. This reduction of the size does not affect the radiation characteristics because the current is maximum at middle of the half-wave dipole. Thus the ground plane can be placed at the same location where the current has maximum. It is worth of mentioning that the input impedance of the antenna is now a half of that of the half-wave dipole.

The effect of the ground plane is that an antenna does not radiate in the direction of the ground plane. Thus, it forms a kind of a shield for human not to radiate towards the organs. However, this shield is as large as the ground plane is. The function of the ground plane is to be a reflector for radiation. The directivity is also doubled to that of the half-wave dipole which now 5.16dB. The directivity is the ratio of the power density in the direction of the radiation pattern maximum to the average power density at the same distance from the antenna [3].

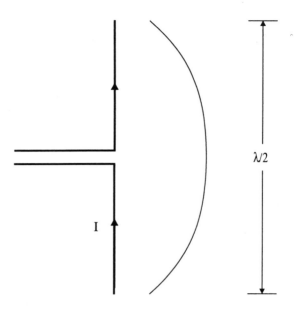

Figure 2. Half-wave dipole antenna with current distribution shown.

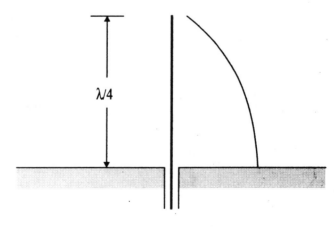

Figure 3. Quarter-wave monopole antenna. The current distribution is shown (solid line), which is compared to the current distribution of the half-wave dipole antenna (dashed line).

2.1 Proposed Antenna

Many antennas interact with objects that are placed close to them and must therefore be mounted at a sufficient distance from walls or at the top of masts. Also, many antennas tend to be perturbed when placed in the close vicinity of another antenna. In rather sharp contrast, microstrip antennas are somewhat shielded by the presence of the ground plane, so whatever is located in the back of them does not significantly affect their operation. This means, in particular, that microstrip antennas can be mounted directly on the walls of buildings or on the clothing and are thus less conspicuous than other antennas.

Microstrip antennas are planar and thus these can be manufactured on printed circuit board. This makes them as an attractive type of antenna due to their low cost, conformability, and ease of manufacture. The planar structure is very suitable for wearable systems because of the planar antennas are thin.

The proposed planar microstrip antenna type is PIFA (Planar Inverted-F Antenna). The side profile looks like an inverted F figure. Inverted-F antennas are like quarter-wave monopole antennas, which are folded coplanar with the ground plane as shown in figure 4. The original quarter-wave monopole is stretched to form a plane. This also increases the radiation resistance. The impedance bandwidth can be controlled by the height of the PIFA from the ground plane but to make it thin enough the height should be less than 10mm. This is well enough needed for GSM operation [4,5].

The matching of the antenna can be controlled by the feed line distance from the shorted edge of the PIFA. For wearable systems the antenna is separated from other electronics thus a cable is needed. The standard coaxial cables have characteristic impedance of 50Ω or 70Ω. Thus, the matching must be designed for the cable to be used. A good match is an important feature of the antenna. A parameter, which describes impedance match is called voltage standing wave ratio (VSWR) and it

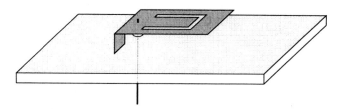

Figure 5. A standard PIFA in which a U-shaped slot is etched to form a dual-band antenna. The physical length of the antenna is remained the same as needed for the lower frequency operation.

should be less than 2 in the operation frequency band. If VSWR is less than 2, 90% of the input power of the antenna will radiate.

The geometry of dual-band PIFA is shown in figure 5 for U-shaped slot. The length l and width w of the PIFA determines the lower resonant frequency, which can be approximated by the formula [6]

$$f_{l0} = \frac{c}{4(w+l)} \qquad (1)$$

Where c is the velocity of light, l and w are the length and width of the radiating element, and f_{l0} is the lower operating frequency. The upper resonant frequency can be determined by the same formula where the outer dimension length l and width w is replaced by the inner length l_2 and width w_2 respectively. This dual-band antenna has almost the same size as a single-band planar inverted-F antenna operating at the lower frequency band.

2.2 Health Concerns and the Placement of the Antenna

Public concern about the health hazards of electromagnetic fields from radiotelephones has increased. Specifically, there is concern that, as the antennas deployed in the new generation of personal telecommunications systems are brought close to the head, there may be either a thermal insult produced by power deposition in tissue (acute effects) or other (long-term) effects.

Microwave radiation absorption occurs at the molecular, cellular, tissue and whole-body levels. The dominant factor for net energy absorption by an entire organism is related to the dielectric properties of bulk water, which ultimately causes transduction of electromagnetic energy into heat [7]. The dominant digital access techniques available in Europe and USA use low level electromagnetic radiation, which is probably safe.

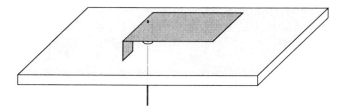

Figure 4. Basic geometry of a planar inverted-F antenna. A monopole antenna is folded coplanar to the ground plane and stretched to form a plate. The impedance match can be controlled by the feed distance from the shorted end of the PIFA.

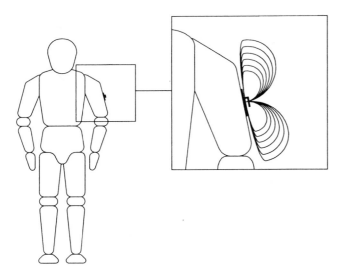

Figure 6. One possible placement of the antenna in which the radiation towards the head is tried to keep as low as possible. The effect of the antenna's ground plane to the direction of the strongest radiation is also shown.

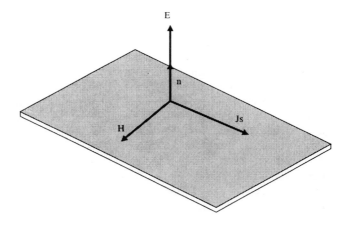

Figure 7. Electromagnetic field in the vicinity of a perfect conductor.

Since the major concern about the effects of radiation at low levels on the head is unknown the placement of the antenna is proposed to be inserted on the sleeve as shown in figure 6. This has an effect of reducing the radiation on the head as compared to an antenna in the close vicinity of the head. The ground plane has the effect of reducing the back radiation to other organs while the normal-mode helical or dipole antennas do not have. This property is common for all planar antennas, which have a ground plane. Since the ground plane is made of conducting medium its effects on electromagnetic fields can be obtained from the following boundary conditions.

In a conducting medium the electric field **E** creates a current density **J** related to **E** by Ohm's law **J** = σ**E**. A perfect conductor has by definition an infinite conductivity σ. Taking into account the finite nature of the current density, this implies that the electric field **E** should be zero in a perfect conductor. According Maxwell's equations [8], **H** (magnetic field), **J** (volume current density) and ρ (volume charge density) must be zero too. There are no currents or charges inside a perfect conductor, only on its surface. The conditions of continuity allow us to determine the **E** and **H** fields in the vicinity of some point on the surface of a perfect conductor, in a dielectric of permittivity ε, in terms of current surface densities **J**$_s$ and charges ρ$_s$ in the vicinity of the same point, figure 7. Thus the following properties for a perfect conductor can be obtained: [9]

- The electromagnetic field is zero inside the conductor.

- There are neither currents nor volume charges.

- The electric field is normal to the surface. It is related to surface charge density by

$$\mathbf{E} = \frac{\rho_s}{\varepsilon}\mathbf{n} \qquad (2)$$

- The magnetic field is tangential to the surface. It is related to surface current density by

$$\mathbf{H} = \mathbf{J}_s \times \mathbf{n} \qquad (3)$$

These fundamental laws show that conducting medium such as metal ground plane prevents the propagation of the electromagnetic radiation through it. The radiation generates surface charge and current densities on the surface of the conducting medium that cancel the original electromagnetic field.

3. Numerical Simulation and Experimental Validation

Given the complexity of the structure, the effects of different physical parameters of the antenna were studied quantitatively using Method of Moments that solves electromagnetic field integral equation in the harmonic domain. The complex integral equations are reduced to a system of simpler linear equations in which the field quantities are related to circuit quantities via Green's functions for a specific geometry under consideration [10]. The Method of Moments expands field and circuit quantities, like electric current density **J** in a linear space and transforms integral equations into linear equations. The equations are derived from the Maxwell's equations. The code requires all the conducting parts of the geometry to be divided into triangular or rectangular cells. When the electric and magnetic current densities are known on all surfaces of the antenna, electric and magnetic fields can be calculated anywhere else. In this way, the input impedance and the resonant frequencies can all be determined. Moreover, the thickness of the metal layers can also be taken into account.

Based on the simulations the dual-band antenna prototype have been designed using new U-shaped slot topology and built with air dielectric as described in section 2.1. In order to characterize the antennas a HP8722D network analyzer was used to measure the input return loss of the antennas as a function of frequency. The values for the input impedance were specified as the frequency bandwidth in which the voltage standing wave ratio (VSWR) is less than 2:1. A 2:1 VSWR is equivalent to a 10-dB return loss, the level at which 10% of the incident power is reflected back to the source.

The dual-band antenna was fabricated by etching the slot figure on the top plate, which is 0.2mm thick copper and soldered on the copper groundplane of dimensions: length 180mm, width 95mm. The shorting strip was made of 0.2mm thick copper and the dimensions used: height 9mm and width 3mm. The outer dimensions of the PIFA were: length 53.5mm and width 33.5mm. The resonant frequency for the lower band given by equation (1) agrees well with measured results. The inner radiating element dimensions surrounded by U-shaped slot were: length 24mm and width 11mm. The resonant frequency for the upper band given by equation (1) is slightly less than compared to measured results. It should be emphasized here that the etching process was not accurate which caused errors to the dimensions of the antennas and thus, the 0.2mm change in dimensions had an effect of moving the upper resonant frequency quite a lot at this frequency band. Also, the bandwidths of the antenna depend on the size and the shape of the groundplane, which is not optimized for these frequencies.

The measured and simulated return loss of the U-shaped slot PIFA is shown in figures 8 and 9, respectively. The bandwidth of the lower resonant frequency is 90MHz (10%) which agrees well with the simulations. However the simulated null depth is much less compared to measured results. The upper resonant

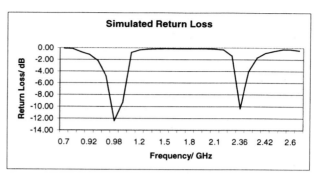

Figure 8. Simulated return loss as a function of frequency. A 2:1 VSWR is equivalent to a 10-dB return loss, the level at which 10% of the incident power is reflected back to the source.

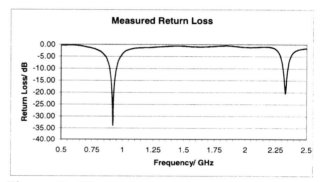

Figure 9. Measured return loss as a function of frequency. A good agreement with the simulations is obtained.

frequency is slightly shifted down because of the manufacturing inaccuracies. The null depth and the bandwidth 80MHz (5%) agrees well with the simulations. This slot configuration is versatile for most wireless communication applications because of bandwidths. The lower frequency bandwidth is enough e.g. for GSM or PCS and the upper band is enough e.g. for Bluetooth, which requires only approximately 80MHz band.

4. Conclusion and Future Work

The proposed antenna geometry is low profile PIFA, of which basic geometry is modified in order to make it operate at two different frequency bands. The new geometry is actually a combination of monopole antenna and PIFA. This paper mainly discusses about the GSM antenna, a digital access system used in Europe, but the antenna can be also designed for PCS applications very easily.

The advantages of planar inverted-F antennas are the reduction of size comparable to e.g. patch antenna of which resonant length must be half-wavelengths. The PIFA radiates only in one half space, thus increasing the directivity and gain in comparison of commonly used normal-mode helical antennas. The increase in gain and directivity makes the proposed antenna more sensitive to weak signals. The third advantage is that the radiation to the body of human is reduced because of the ground plane needed by the antenna.

This proposed antenna can be designed for future wireless network applications in order to operate at two or more different frequency bands e.g. at GSM and ISM (Industrial, Scientific and Medical) frequencies. This possibility reduces the number of different antennas needed and it is also cost effective, because only one antenna is needed. Comfortability of the wearable systems can be increased if the new flexible PCB materials are used in the fabrication of the antenna. To make the antenna 'invisible' it can be designed so that it has two functions: an antenna and a tie pin. This is possible because the geometry of the antenna and the tie pin is similar.

The future work will continue in designing more sophisticated antenna systems. The next research goal is to design a multi-band antenna which operates at the frequency bands of GSM, GSM-1800 and Bluetooth (2.4GHz) and PCS and Bluetooth frequencies. This kind of antenna can handle both the short range and long range data communications. This is a very ideal situation when one antenna can operate at different radio systems.

5. References

[1] R. F. Harrington, *Time-Harmonic Electromagnetic fields*, McGraw Hill, UK.

[2] C. A. Balanis, *Advanced Engineering Electromagnetics*, Ingram International , UK, 1989.

[3] W. L. Stutzman, G. A. Thiele: *Antenna Theory and Design*, 2nd Edition, New York, John Wiley & Sons, 1998.

[4] H. Nakano, N. Ikeda, Y.-Y. Wu, R. Suzuki, H. Mimaki, J. Yamauchi, "Realization of Dual-Frequency and Wide-Band VSWR Performances Using Normal-Mode Helical and Inverted-F Antennas", *IEEE Trans. Antennas Propagat.*, vol. 46, pp. 788 - 793, June 1998.

[5] C. R. Rowell, R. D. Murch, "A Capacitively Loaded PIFA for Compact Mobile Telephone Handsets", *IEEE Trans. Antennas Propagat.*, vol. 45, pp.837 – 841, May 1997.

[6] Z. D. Liu, P. S. Hall, D. Wake, "Dual-Frequency Planar Inverted-F Antenna", *IEEE Trans. Antennas Propagat.*, vol. 45, pp. 1451 – 1458, Oct. 1997.

[7] A. D. Olver, *Microwave and Optical Transmission*, Wiley, UK, 1992.

[8] J. A. Stratton, *Electromagnetic Theory*, McGraw-Hill Inc. New York, 1941.

[9] S. Drabowitch, A. Papiernik, H. Griffiths, J. Encinas, B. L. Smith, *Modern Antennas*, Chapman & Hall, UK, 1998.

[10] A. F. Peterson, S. L. Ray, R. Mittra, *Computational Methods for Electromagnetics*, IEEE Press, New York, 1998.

Non-ideal Battery Properties and Low Power Operation in Wearable Computing

Thomas L. Martin, Daniel P. Siewiorek

Institute for Complex Engineered Systems, Carnegie Mellon University, Pittsburgh, PA 15213

[tlm,dps]@cs.cmu.edu

Abstract

This paper describes non-ideal properties of batteries and how these properties may impact power-performance trade-offs in wearable computing. The first part of the paper details the characteristics of an ideal battery and how these characteristics are used in sizing batteries and estimating discharge times. Typical non-ideal characteristics and the regions of operation where they occur are described. The paper then covers results from a first-principles, variable-load battery model, showing likely areas for exploiting battery behavior in mobile computing. The major result is that when battery behavior is non-ideal, lowering the average power or the energy per operation may not increase the amount of computation that can be completed in a battery life.

1. Introduction

Two of the major constraints on mobile and wearable computing are size and weight, of which the battery is a large portion. Reducing the battery is thus a key to reducing the overall system bulk. The usual approach to achieving this is to decrease the power consumption of the hardware, either by power management, putting unused systems into low power modes; or by a power-performance trade-off, completing a computation at a slower speed for less power. While power management and power-performance trade-offs are important for all mobile computers, they are more so for wearable computers because of their performance intensive user interfaces and their tighter constraints on size and weight. Previous work in power-performance trade-offs attempted to minimize the energy-delay product [4] or the energy per operation [9]. When the system is battery-powered, however, minimizing either measure may not maximize the computations per battery life. Non-ideal battery properties may come into play, as will be shown using both simulation results from a first-principles battery model. These properties must be considered during wearable computer design and for software control of power management and power-performance trade-offs.

The paper begins by describing the ideal characteristics of batteries in Section 2. Then Section 3 covers the non-ideal characteristics of batteries and the regions of operation where the characteristics are exhibited. Section 4 presents simulation results from a first-principles, variable-load model of Li-ion cells. Finally, Section 5 summarizes ways in which the non-ideal battery properties can be exploited.

2. Ideal battery properties and discharge time estimates

The two most important properties of batteries from the viewpoint of someone using them are voltage and capacity. An ideal battery has a constant voltage throughout a discharge, which drops instantaneously to zero when the battery is fully discharged, and has constant capacity for all values of the load, as shown in Figure 1.

For sizing batteries, the battery voltage should be in the allowable range of the power supply of the device in question. The battery voltage is considered to be the rated voltage of the battery, e.g. 1.2V per cell for NiCd batteries and 3.6V per cell for most Li-ion batteries. The charge capacity of the battery is typically given in terms of Amp-hours or milliAmp-hours and is called the battery's "C" rating. The C rating is used in the battery industry to normalize the load current to the battery's capacity [6]. The advantage of C ratings is that it allows battery manufacturers to present one graph of discharge curves for batteries of similar construction but different capacities. Loads are then measured relative to the C rating, e.g. a 10 mA load on a battery with a rated capacity of 100 mAh is a load of 0.1C.

For mobile systems, the discharge time T is usually estimated to be the battery's rated voltage V multiplied by the charge capacity C, divided by the average power P of the system, or $T = (C \times V)/P$. The rated voltage multiplied by the charge capacity is the battery's nominal energy capacity, typically given in Watt-hours (1 Wh = 3600 J). As Section 4 will show, this method will overestimate the battery life if the load has a large peak value.

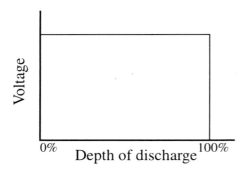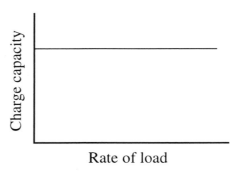

Figure 1. Characteristics of an ideal battery: Constant voltage and constant capacity

3. Non-ideal battery properties

While ideally a battery has constant voltage and capacity, in practice both vary widely. Figure 2a shows the battery voltage as a function of discharge time for two different loads. Load 1 is smaller than load 2. Because of resistance and other losses, the voltage throughout the discharge is lower for load 2 than load 1. The voltage for each load also drops over the course of the discharge due to changes in the battery's active materials and reactant concentrations.

The capacity also varies with the value of the load. The two major ways in which it varies are loss of capacity with increasing load, and an effect called recovery where an intermittent load may have a larger capacity than a continuous load. Figure 2b shows the loss of capacity with increasing load current for a typical NiCd battery. The capacity decreases by about 40% over a range of discharge rates of 0.1C to 10C. (Note that the capacity in Figure 2b exceeds 100% at low rates because the C rating is specified as the capacity for a given time of discharge. The capacity in Figure 2b was measured at the 2 hour rate, since 100% capacity occurs at 0.5C. If the capacity had been measured at the 10 hour rate, 100% would have occurred at 0.1C.)

The second non-ideal capacity property, recovery, is shown in Figure 2c. A reduction of the load for periods of time results in an increase in battery capacity. The voltage rises while the load is reduced, and the overall time of discharge increases. This phenomena occurs because, during the time when load is reduced, reactants in the battery diffuse to the reaction location, allowing more of them to be used during the life of the battery. The degree to which the battery recovers depends on the discharge rate and the length of time the load is reduced, as well as the details of the battery construction.

It is widely known that the battery voltage varies during discharge. For example, power supplies are usually rated over a range of input voltages. When a power supply is used with a battery, it is necessary to ensure that the range of the supply's input voltage includes the range of the battery voltage during discharge. Since the voltage variation is widely known, this paper will not focus on it. The non-ideal capacity properties, on the other hand, are not widely known, and so will be the main subject of the remainder of this work. Given that a battery's discharge time is typically estimated using ideal values of voltage and capacity, the loss of capacity can lead to an overestimate of the discharge time for large loads. While a chart such as Figure 2b or a model such as Peukert's equation [6] allows one to account for the loss of capacity for loads that are constant and continuously on, in general loads are intermittent and variable. If recovery occurs, then the duration of the off times of the load must be considered in addition to the duration of its on times and its value while on. Models that account for both capacity loss and recovery are needed to determine if recovery occurs for the loads encountered in mobile computing, and if so, to properly estimate battery lives for intermittent loads.

4. Results with Doyle's variable load model

The typical load of a mobile computer system is not constant, but variable. A model is needed, then, to estimate the discharge time with variable loads. A variable-load model would ideally possess the following characteristics:

- Accurate relative capacity information (i.e. if several loads are simulated, then the model should correctly predict the relative difference in discharge times,

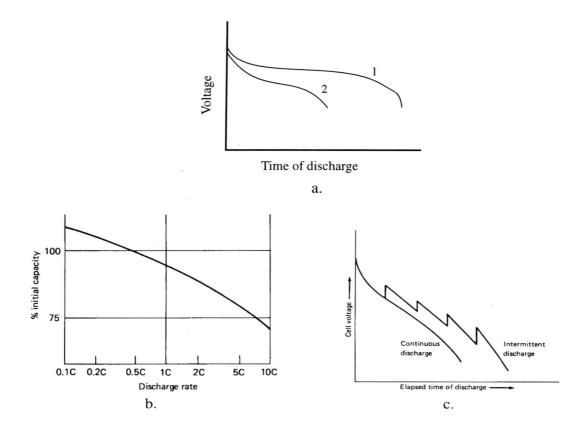

Figure 2. Non-ideal battery properties: (a) voltage change, (b) loss of capacity, and (c) recovery (after [6])

even if the actual differences are inaccurate.)

- Applicable to a variety of battery types
- Intuitive parameters and behavior
- Ease of correlation to actual cells

Of these four criteria, the first is the most important for this paper. The last three will become more important when battery models are more widely used in mobile system design. A number of battery models were investigated [1][3][5][7], but Doyle's model inspired the most confidence due to its having been created solely for Li-ion cells and due to its use in industry [2]. The other models had not been created for use with Li-ion cells and hence results with them would have required lengthy correlation with actual cells before their predictions could have been trusted.

Doyle's model was used to study the effect of intermittent discharges on the capacity. It was found that peak power predicts battery capacity better than average power.

Figure 3 shows the model results for battery capacity versus average power for continuous discharges over a range of loads, and for intermittent discharges for several combinations of peak power and duty cycle. The intermittent discharges were square waves with an off power of 0 W/kg. The two major features of the results are that the capacity decreases as the load power increases for continuous loads, and that there is a range where the peak power of an intermittent load rather than the average power is a stronger indicator of the battery's capacity. For example, the 300 W/kg continuous load results in a battery capacity of 90 Wh/kg (point A in the figure) and the 75 W/kg continuous load results in a battery capacity of 140 Wh/kg (point B), while the intermittent load with a peak power of 300 W/kg and duty cycle of 25% (i.e. an average power of 75 W/kg, point C) results in a capacity of approximately 100 Wh/kg. Thus using the average power of this intermittent load would over-estimate the battery capacity by about 40% (i.e., point B's 140 Wh/kg would be expected), while using the peak power would under-estimate it by only about 10% (i.e., point A's 90 Wh/kg

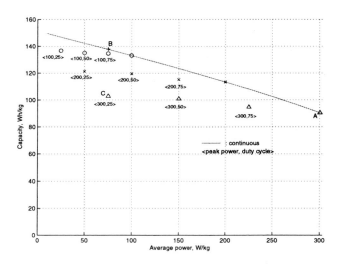

Figure 3. Doyle's Li-ion model results for capacity versus average power, showing difference between continuous and intermittent loads of same average value.

would be expected). To put these results in more common terms, the 75 W/kg continuous load B would have a battery life of about 1.9 hours, while the intermittent load C, with the same average power, 75 W/kg, would have a battery life of about 1.3 hours. Only when the peak power is below about 50 W/kg (about a 3 hour discharge when continuously on) would the peak and average power give about the same estimate of battery life.

The characteristics displayed in Figure 3 mean that minimizing energy per operation may not maximize computations per battery life. For example, suppose a mobile system has a dynamic power profile that is cyclic, having periods of activity with a high peak power followed by idle periods of low power. If one has a choice between a 20% reduction in the energy per cycle by reducing the idle power and a 20% reduction in the energy per cycle by reducing the active power, the average power is reduced by 20% in both cases. If the battery capacity were constant as is commonly assumed, one would expect that the battery life would increase by a factor of $1/(1-20\%) = 1.25$ for both cases. But because the capacity is determined by the peak power, the battery life will be increased more by reducing the active power than by reducing idle power. Not only will the average power be reduced but the capacity available will be increased. Hence, once all the subsystems that can be put into idle mode are put into idle mode, one should focus on reducing the power during the active time rather than focus on reducing the power during the idle time.

A second example is if the designer has a choice between reducing the active time and the active power by some factor. Both will result in the same decrease in the average power. But again, reducing the active power will result in a bigger increase in battery life when the active power is large. This means that the focus should be on reducing peak power rather than reducing duty cycle.

For a more concrete example of each method of reducing average power, consider the dynamic power profile as shown in Figure 4. The average power, P_{ave}, is equal to $(P_{active} \times t_{active} + P_{idle} \times t_{idle})/t_{cycle}$. To reduce the average power P_{ave}, the active power can be reduced (A), the idle power can be reduced (B), or the active duty cycle can be reduced (C). Table 1 shows the results from Doyle's model for the waveform of Figure 4. The waveform was simulated for three different values of initial average power, and the desired reduction in average power for each case was 20%. As expected, reducing active power (A) results in the greatest increase in battery life when the peak power is large. Reducing idle power (B) always results in the least increase in battery life. Reducing the duty cycle (C) always does better than reducing the idle power and does as well as reducing peak power only for the lowest value of peak power. But when the peak power is larger, reducing the duty cycle does not increase the battery life by as much as reducing the active power.

The column labeled "% difference from expected" refers to difference between the simulated battery life of the modification and what would be expected given the initial battery life and the factor by which the power was reduced. For example, the initial battery life of the waveform with the 300 W/kg peak power is 51 minutes. Because the average power for each of the modifications is 80% of the initial waveform, one would expect the battery

Table 1. Doyle's model results for waveform of Figure 4.

Waveform modification	Duty Cycle, t_{active}/t_{cycle}, %	Peak power, W/kg	Idle power, W/kg	Average power, W/kg	Battery life, minutes	% difference from expected
none	20	300	75	120	51	--
A	20	180	75	96	83	+30
B	20	300	45	96	67	+5
C	9.3	300	75	96	68	+7
none	20	200	50	80	87	--
A	20	120	50	64	132	+21
B	20	200	30	64	117	+8
C	9.3	200	50	64	118	+9
none	20	100	25	40	202	--
A	20	60	25	32	268	+6
B	20	100	15	32	253	0
C	9.3	100	25	32	268	+6

life for them to be 51/0.8 = 64 minutes. But this ignores the non-ideal capacity behavior. As the results show, the non-ideal capacity behavior can cause two loads with the same average power to have greatly different battery lives. The dynamic power must be considered as well as the average power.

The results of Figure 3 may explain why the advertised battery life of the typical notebook computer is greater than what users realize in practice: Suppose the notebook manu-facture is advertising an estimated battery life rather than a measured one. If the manufacturer estimates the battery life by using the battery's rated capacity and the average power of the system, then the estimate will be too large because of the loss of capacity of the battery at higher rates. While the notebook computer manufacturers reap an advantage by

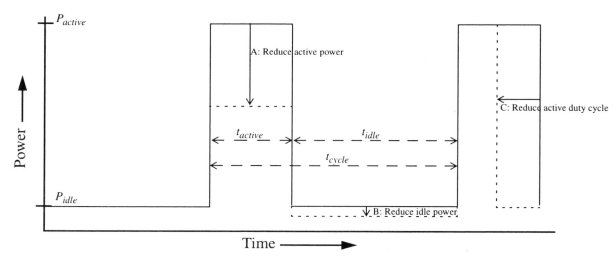

Figure 4. Dynamic power profile example. Modifications A, B, and C reduce the average power.

advertising a longer battery life than is achievable in practice, obviously a motive to be considered, they may simply be using the rated battery capacity rather than the capacity available at the notebook's peak power.

The results shown in Figure 3 and from other simulations with Doyle's model (not shown due to space limitations) show that recovery is a much smaller effect than loss of capacity for loads that would be typical of mobile computing. This has two consequences. First, models of battery behavior under continuous loads can be used to estimate battery life. Second, continuous discharges are sufficient for measuring the effect of a change to lower power so long as the energy consumed while the system is idle is accounted for.

5. Conclusions

Because the battery is a key factor in the overall system weight and volume, its characteristics must be carefully considered. Non-ideal battery properties can lead to misestimates of battery life. Models that capture the non-ideal behavior are necessary both for wearable computer design and for software control of power management and power-performance trade-offs [8].

In summary, this paper has shown the following:

- Battery capacity will vary with load power.

- Peak power is a better indicator of battery capacity than average power. Estimating battery life using average power can be overly optimistic if peak power is large.

- Total system power must be considered. Power-performance trade-offs made by examining a subsystem in isolation may not lead to an increase in the computations per battery life because total peak power is ignored.

- Peak power should be reduced wherever possible, which means background operations should be performed serially rather than concurrently. Serial operation is better than concurrent operation when each consumes roughly the same energy.

- Reducing active energy is more important than reducing idle energy.

- Continuous behavior can be used to estimate intermittent behavior.

Because of non-ideal battery behavior, reducing average power or energy per operation may not increase the amount of computation completed in a battery life. Battery behavior must be considered to properly make decisions about low power operation in wearable computing.

Acknowledgments

The authors are affiliated with the Wearable Computing Laboratory at the Institute for Complex Engineered Systems at Carnegie Mellon University. The Wearable Computing Lab receives funding from the National Science Foundation and DARPA. The authors are grateful to Marc Doyle for allowing access to his battery model.

References

[1] M. Doyle and J. Newman, "The Use of Mathematical Modeling in the Design of Lithium/Polymer Battery Systems," Electrochimica Acta, vol. 40, no. 13-14; 1995; pp. 2191-2196.

[2] M. Doyle, J. Newman, and J. Reimers, "A quick method for measuring the capacity versus the discharge rate for a dual lithium-ion insertion cell undergoing cycling," Journal of Power Sources; vol. 52, no. 2; December 1994; pp. 211-216.

[3] S. Hageman, "Simple PSpice models let you simulate common battery types," EDN, October 28, 1993; pp. 117-132.

[4] M. Horowitz, T. Indermaur, and R. Gonzalalez, "Low-Power Digital Design," Proceedings of the 1994 Symposium on Low Power Electronics, October 1994, pp. 8-11.

[5] E. Hyman, W. C. Spindeler, and J. F. Fatula, "Phenomenological Discharge Voltage Model for Lead-Acid Batteries," Proceedings of the AIChE Meeting, November 1986, pp. 78-86.

[6] D. Linden, *Handbook of Batteries*, 2nd ed. New York: McGraw-Hill, Inc. 1995.

[7] J. Manwell and J. McGowan, "Lead Acid Battery Storage Model for Hybrid Energy Systems," Solar Energy Vol. 50, No. 5, pp. 399-405.

[8] T. Martin and D. Siewiorek, "The Impact of Battery Capacity and Memory Bandwidth on CPU Speed-Setting: A Case Study," Proceedings of the 1999 International Symposium on Low Power Electronics and Design, to appear.

[9] M. Weiser, B. Welch, A. Demers, and S. Shenker, "Scheduling for Reduced CPU Energy," Proceedings of the 1st USENIX Symposium on Operating Systems Design and Implementation, November 1994, pp. 13-23.

Wearable Sensor Badge & Sensor Jacket for Context Awareness

Jonny Farringdon$^\alpha$, Andrew J. Moore$^\alpha$, Nancy Tilbury$^\beta$, James Church$^\beta$ & Pieter D. Biemond$^\alpha$

Philips Research Laboratories
Cross Oak Lane, Redhill, Surrey, RH1 5HA, UK.
$^\alpha$*Software Engineering & Applications Group,* $^\beta$*Philips Design*
farringdon@bcs.org.uk   Andrew.Moore, Nancy.Tilbury @philips.com
james.church@btinternet.com   pieterb@acm.org

Abstract

The addition of sensors to wearable computers allows them to adapt their functions to more suit the activities and situation of their wearers. Here a wearable sensor badge is described constructed from (hard) electronic components, which can sense perambulatory activities for context-awareness. A wearable sensor jacket is described that uses advanced knitting techniques to form (soft) fabric stretch sensors positioned to measure upper limb and body movement. Worn on-the-hip, or worn as clothing, these unobtrusive sensors supply abstract information about your current activity to your other wearable computers.

Keywords— *accelerometers, context-aware computing, gesture recognition, mobile computing, soft sensors, smart clothing, smart fabrics, technical textiles, wearables.*

1. Introduction

Wearable computers and devices are becoming increasingly aware of their wearer's current activities. Current personal and mobile devices, such as personal digital assistants (PDA's) and mobile phones have little or no knowledge of their owner's situation. They execute their functions with no regard for appropriateness, and thus ring, vibrate, and bleep when they think they should, no matter what.

The addition of sensors to a wearable device allows for the wearable's behaviour to be related to the wearer's current activity or situation, [9]. Two sensors commonly used with wearable computers are small cameras and chorded keyboards. The idea of a sensor unit able to derive a person's activity is established as a useful

addition to other wearable devices. Van de Velde's Technology for Enabling Awareness (TEA) project underway at Starlab with Nokia is constructing such a device for use with a mobile phone [12]. The first TEA prototype contains the following sensors, "light, temperature, CO gas, microphone, two accelerometers for movement, a pressure sensor, and an infrared (IR) sensor for motion detection."

The use of biometric sensors with wearable computers is discussed by Picard and Healey [7]. Such sensors allow for new interactions between the wearable and the wearer based upon affect detection, prediction, and synthesis [6]. Biometric monitoring for personal health in a wearable is described by Mann, using commercial sensors and algorithms such as signalling danger when the ratio of heart rate and walking speed goes outside a certain range, [3].

Here we describe wearable hard and soft sensors. Other wearable devices can exploit sensing information in order to mediate their behaviour, making them somewhat aware of, and thus behave more appropriately to, their user's current activities. Using commercially available electronic components and custom software a sensor badge detecting six perambulatory activities has been developed. Using bespoke knitwear and garment design a sports top detecting eleven degrees of limb and upper body movement is described. The relative merits of each sensor system are also discussed. In addition, the benefit to the user of wearing sensors is the improved behaviour of their wearable computer now related to their current activity.

2. The Sensor Badge

The sensor badge uses stock electronics components housed in a belt worn unit. Novel software to derive high level meaning from the sensor data runs on a microcontroller chip, and the current activity of the wearer is displayed on the front of the badge as well as

107

output to any wearable device via an RS-232 serial connection.

2.1. Sensor Selection

Determining a person's activity within the sensor badge is achieved by measuring the accelerations, constant and varying, exerted on the badge by the movements of the user. The sensor chosen to measure acceleration was the Analogue Devices ADXL05, an accelerometer that can measure up to 5g accelerations in the direction of one axis. It was chosen due to its measurement of constant and varying accelerations and its relative low cost, around 20 US$ in small quantities. Two directions of acceleration were chosen as the most fruitful, forward horizontal and vertical acceleration, relative to the wearer of the badge. This made necessary the use of two ADXL05 accelerometers. The two accelerometers were calibrated to a full scale of +/- 2g.

2.2. Sitting, Standing & Lying

Identifying when a wearer of the sensor badge was sitting, standing or lying was a simple exercise. These are states where the wearer of the sensor badge is not subjecting it to any varying accelerations, therefore determining the state of the user is simply a matter of examining the magnitude of the voltages produced by the accelerometers. Figure 1 shows the different orientations of the sensor badge in standing, sitting and lying positions. These all result in different voltage levels from the horizontal and vertical accelerometers that reflect the g-force and direction of the users current state.

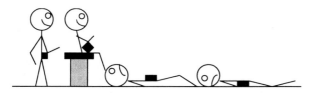

Figure 1. Orientation of the sensor badge in standing, sitting and lying positions

To reliably detect one of the four states above, both accelerometer output voltages were sampled 20 times per second, the average for each was calculated together with the difference between the maximum and minimum values. If this difference was small enough as to suggest that the wearer of the badge was stationary, the average values were examined to determine the users current state.

2.3. Walking & Running

A slightly more complicated algorithm was employed for detection of walking and running. The sampling rate of 20 samples per second was found to be satisfactory for representation of the walking and running accelerometer traces as shown below in Figure 2 and Figure 3. These traces were captured during an initial data collection period using a Xybernaut wearable computer connected to a Pico Technology ADC11 parallel port analogue-to-digital converter, [10], connected to two similarly aligned accelerometers.

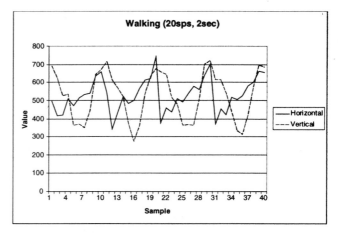

Figure 2. Horizontal and vertical accelerometer walking traces

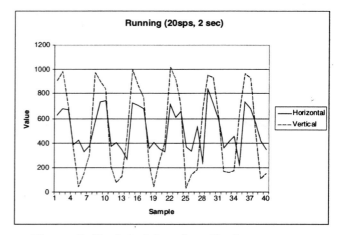

Figure 3. Horizontal and vertical accelerometer running traces

The difference between maximum and minimum, i.e. the heights of the traces are used as characteristics to detect walking and running. The horizontal heights of the walking and running traces can be seen as similar, while the running vertical height is much larger than the walking vertical height. These magnitudes are used as a first indicator of either walking or running. The average values of the above traces are similar to the average values obtained when the wearer of the badge is standing still. This information is used as a second indicator.

The frequency of the traces is also important to identify whether the user is walking or running or neither. As the sensor badge uses a PIC microcontroller with limited memory, a crude measure of frequency was used. By counting the number of times each trace crossed the average value, an approximate measure of frequency was obtained. Using this information together with the two measures described above, the detection of walking and running was achieved.

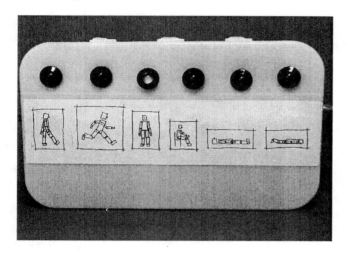

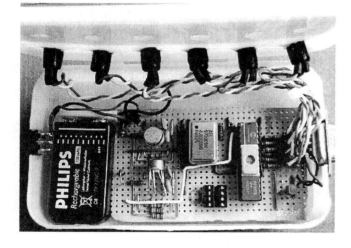

Figure 4. Front and inside views of the sensor badge

2.4. The Sensor Badge

The prototype "Sensor Badge" as shown in Figure 4 is the first physical implementation of the above algorithms. It uses six LED's to show the users current state from walking, running, standing, sitting, lying face up and lying face down. The serial port is designed to make the sensor badge a source of context information. Another wearable device may be able to use the context data supplied by the sensor badge to modify its own behaviour in a manner more befitting the user.

3. The Sensor Jacket

The aim of the "Sensor Jacket" is to detect the posture and movements of the user by using knitted stretch sensors and knitted conductive *tracking* (described later). Designing technical textiles into a jacket has resulted in a unique completely fabric worn sensor. This new unobtrusive sensor can be connected to a wearable computer. Indeed it becomes part of the sensory apparatus of the wearable computers.

Most current systems for the analysis of human motion cannot be used for wearable applications because they use external devices mainly suitable for research labs or other "Smart Rooms", [5]. Cheap and wearable soft sensors can be used as an alternative to expensive and often very obtrusive sensors and trackers. If the sensors are integrated in everyday clothing then the gesture recognition isn't bound to a specific location and can be used at any place at any time.

3.1. Technical Textiles & Smart Clothing

Using the electrical properties of soft materials and advanced knitting techniques new fabric sensors and tracking have been created. These technical textiles can be seamlessly integrated in clothes, making them 'smart' or 'intelligent'. Smart clothing is considered as empowering the wearer with smart devices for their personal use. Mann [2, 3] addresses other forms of smart clothes and smart uniforms. Post and Orth [8] discuss the use of smart fabric switches and circuits by using conductive yarn. Smart fibres are currently of particular interest in the textile trade who consider "anti-stress, calm-inducing properties, or pamper with fibres impregnated with fragrant oils or vitamins, or even being able to electronically monitor the wearer's health or state of mind through interactive wearable computers." [13].

Additional benefits of fabric sensors are that they:

- can be integrated into smart clothes in a non-obtrusive way
- can be manufactured using standard garment industry production techniques
- are washable and ironable, unlike some hardware-enhanced clothing.

3.2. Knitted Stretch Sensors

The sensors used measure stretch from resistive changes in knitted strips. Strips 10mm wide are prepared, typically a 10 meter length. The sensor gives a linearly increasing asymptotic resistance with stretch, up to almost maximum stretch. Stretches of over 50% are possible with these strips. This curve is shown in Figure 5.

Resistance with stretch

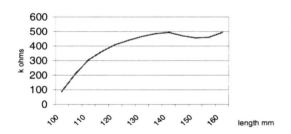

Figure 5. Resistance of a 10mm wide 100mm long knitted sensor strip as it is stretched from its 100mm length

3.3. Knitted Conductive Tracking

A knit containing a conductive fibre for the purpose of transmitting an electrical signal we refer to as tracking. Knitted tracking is used in place of wiring to the terminals of the sensors. Conductive threads chosen for their stable properties are introduced to this knit. The tracking used is 10 mm wide and exhibits a 3 ohms resistance over 100 mm. This particular knit can be stretched by approximately 5%. When the sensor and tracking materials are slack the sensors exhibit a resistance 25 times greater than that of the tracking, and when stretched this ratio increases to 100 times. The sensor and tracking material is shown in Figure 6.

Figure 6. A strip of stretch sensor knitwear and a 10 meter roll of knitted conductive tracking

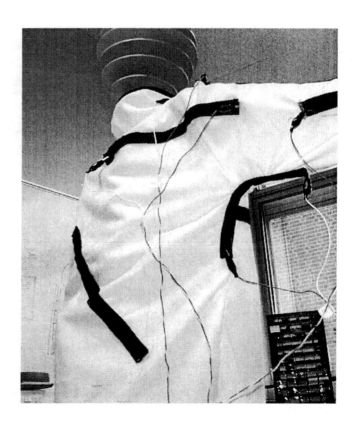

Figure 7. The initial toile – sensor jacket prototype made from toiling fabric. Sensor strips are sewn onto toiling fabric and connected by wires

3.4. Jacket Design

A jacket has been designed that positions 11 knitted sensor strips over the elbow and shoulder joints. In the initial toile (the first cut of our garment using toiling fabric), six sensors are distributed about the right side. Right elbow movement is measured by one sensor along the joint. Three sensors measure the position and movements of the right upper arm. Two of them are used for measuring (upper) arm-movements in the frontal (vertical) plane. They are positioned on top of the shoulder and at the armpit. A sensor strip on the upper back and shoulder measures position and movements of the upper arm in the transverse (horizontal) plane. A sensor positioned diagonally across the centre of the back detects bending forward, with an additional sensor positioned horizontally across the right breast, as shown in Figure 7.

During development only the sensor strips are designed into the jacket, with wires and crocodile clips taking the place of the knitted tracking. The tracking has similar stable properties to the wires and this plays little part in the positioning of the sensors themselves.

After a second toiling, positioning the sensors and tracking on left and right sides, a bespoke sensor jacket was manufactured to commercial standards (pattern cutting, manufacture and materials). When gesture and arm position recognition was shown to be successful the pattern was graded up to a size large (chest 47.25 inch, 120 cm), Figure 8.

3.5. Signal Processing

A wire umbilical attaches the sensor jacket to a analogue to digital converter and a PC. A Picotech ADC11 analogue to digital converter is used, giving 11 channels, 11-bit precision and a sample rate of up to 10kHz [10]. The sensor signals are used as an input to a kinematic geometry model. This mathematical model represents the mobility of the user's arms and neglects all other aspects (e.g. mass distribution, force), [14]. Each arm is simplified as being a two-link kinematic chain and the shoulders are considered fixed in space. This model is capable of detecting the position of the elbows and wrists of the wearer.

Each time the jacket is worn, it has to be calibrated by the wearer because the users under clothing (shirt, t-shirt, etc.) and body shape (e.g. shoulder and chest breadth, length of the arms) influence the sensor readings. During the calibration process the user is asked to put his arms down, outstretched, forward and then up. The software can detect these states automatically regardless of the users body shape by using pre-calibrated ranges. These

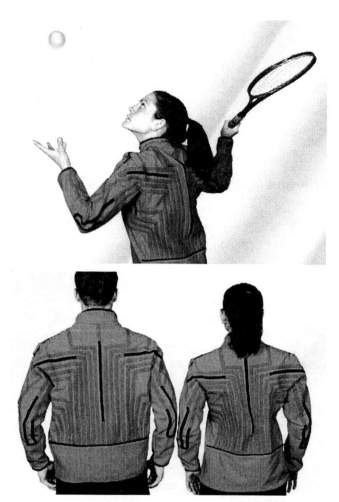

Figure 8. The final sensor jackets. Sensors are shown in black, and are connected at each end by covered conductive tracking

poses make the various sensors stretch and the information about the minima and maxima of each sensor are used in the algorithms for detecting the angles of the joints.

After the calibration process, demonstration software on the PC illustrates the positioning of the arms. Motions and gestures are recognised and displayed in real-time, sampled at 50 Hz.

4. Hard & Soft Sensors

It may be possible to have a sensor garment that detects limb and upper body motion using only hard accelerometers positioned throughout the garment. A body suit using soft sensor fabric may also be able to detect perambulatory activities such as walking and running. The merits of electronic and fabric sensors are highly dependent upon their application, with the availability and cost of the components highly significant for current applications. Particular benefits of the sensor badge are its small size and its suitability to be worn with any other clothing. The sensor jacket has the particular benefits of being both socially acceptable and comfortable to wear.

5. Future Work

Work continues on identifying additional activities from the sensor badge. For example distinguishing travelling in a car or by train.

Two potential applications of the sensor badge can be applied to mobile phones as well as wearable computers. The first application is for using the sensor badge to detect whether you are driving in your car. If you are, your devices can detect this automatically and go to a hands-free mode. A second application is for people who want to instruct their devices not to bother them when it's not convenient. For example, you might want to instruct your devices not to bother you with unimportant messages when you are active (e.g. running for a bus or a train), or lying down (resting, sleeping). As soon as the system thinks you are ready, it will give you the messages it has saved.

To complement the sensor-jacket, trousers and shorts are being considered to allow for full-body sensing. A wireless to PC link and on-jacket data recording are also being investigated.

Future interfaces are to be expected to combine several modalities (e.g. gesture and speech) in order to provide more natural ways of communicating without the use of a keyboard or a mouse, [4]. Context-aware devices like the sensor badge and smart clothing like the sensor jacket can be used for future multimodal human-computer interfaces, [4, 11], which can be used at any time and at any place.

6. Conclusions

A variety of sensing technologies have been developed for wearable devices to enable limited awareness of a user's ongoing activities and context. One sensor solution is composed of hard electronics, the other soft fabrics.

Commercially available electronics can be readily assembled into a belt wearable sensing device. However the development of software (or other means) for interpreting the sensor data into high level abstractions is not trivial. The sensor badge described here uses two accelerometers and software running on a PIC

microcontroller, outputting identified activities to other wearable devices through an RS-232 port.

The sensor jacket includes knitted fabrics which have electrical properties suited for either sensing stretch or for use as non-sensing conductive tracking. The first toile of this jacket measures movement through six sensors on the right hand side and back and the final jackets uses 11 sensors over both sides. A connections port on the jacket can be connected to other wearable devices supplying data regarding the current limb movement and body position of the wearer.

Both the belt worn sensor badge and the sensor jacket are suitable for continuous wearing. The benefit for the user of wearing such sensors is in the situational awareness their wearable computer gains. The interface between wearable computer and wearer can be sympathetic to the user's activities, which can also mediate wearable software applications.

Acknowledgements

With particular thanks to Dr. Frances Geesin, senior research fellow at the London College of Fashion, for her continuing support and original work initiated at the Royal College of Art, London, on the technical use of industrial and conductive fibres and cloth.

Thanks also to Philippa Wagner MA RCA (textile designer), Juliette Allen (pattern cutting, machining) and Canan Geyik (production assistant) for the production of the sensor jackets.

References

[1] F. Geesin, "Interactive Fabrics Show Potential", *Technical Textiles International*, Elsevier Science Ltd., October 1996.

[2] S. Mann, "Smart Clothing: The Shift to Wearable Computing", *Communications of the ACM*, Vol. 39, No. 8, August 1996, pp. 23–24.

[3] S. Mann, "Smart Clothing: The Wearable Computer and WearCam.", <http://www.wearcam.org/personaltechnologies/>. Last visited: Aug. 4, 1999. Also appeared in *Personal Technologies*, Vol. 1, No. 1, Springer, 1997, March 1997.

[4] J. Nielsen, *Noncommand user interfaces*, <http://www.useit.com/papers/noncommand.html>. Last visited: Aug. 4, 1999. Revised version of the paper that appeared in *Communications of the ACM*, Vol. 36, No. 4, April 1993, pp. 83–99.

[5] A. Pentland, "Smart Rooms, Smart Clothes", *Proceedings Fourteenth International Conference on Pattern Recognition*, pp. 949–953, 1998.

[6] R.W. Picard, *Affective Computing*, MIT Press, Cambridge, MA, 1997.

[7] RW. Picard and J. Healey, "Affective Wearables", *Proceedings of the First International Symposium on Wearable Computers, IEEE*, pp. 90–97. October 13–14, 1997.

[8] R.E. Post and M. Orth, "Smart Fabric, or Washable Computing.", <http://www.media.mit.edu/physics/people/rehmi/cloth/>. Last visited: Aug. 4, 1999. Appears abridged as "Smart Fabric, or "Wearable Clothing"", *Proceedings of the First IEEE International Symposium on Wearable Computers*, Cambridge, MA, October 13–14, 1997, pp. 167–168 (abridged).

[9] B. Rhodes, Context-Aware Computing (or, why context needs wearables and wearables need context), <http://wearable.www.media.mit.edu/projects/wearables/context.html>. Last visited: Aug. 4, 1999.

[10] Pico Technology Limited, <http://www.picotech.com>, Cambridge, UK.

[11] R. Sharma, V.I. Pavlovic, T.S. Huang, "Toward Multimodal Human-Computer Interface", *Proceedings of the IEEE*, Vol. 86, No. 5, pp. 853–869, May 1998.

[12] W. van de Velde, *TEA: Technology for Enabling Awareness*, <http://www.starlab.org/bits/smartdevices/tea.html>. Official TEA-site: <http://www.omega.it/tea/>. Last visited: Aug. 4, 1999.

[13] P. Watkins, "Get Smart.", *Drapers Record Textiles*, pp. 33–34, September 1998.

[14] V.M. Zatsiorsky, *Kinematics of Human Motion*, Human Kinetics, 1997.

Electric Suspenders: A Fabric Power Bus and Data Network for Wearable Digital Devices

Michael M. Gorlick

The Aerospace Corporation
El Segundo, California
gorlick@aero.org

Abstract

One goal of wearable computing is to create digital devices that are as easy to don and as comfortable to wear as common articles of clothing such as blouses, pants, and belts. New forms of woven materials such as conductive webbings, which incorporate durable electrical conductors directly into the matrix of the weave, offer exciting possibilites for closely integrating digital electronics with conventional clothing. However, many practical obstacles hinder the adoption of these materials, not the least being a lack of reliable electrical connectors for the interconnection of conventional electronics with conductive fabrics. We present a simple and workable design for just such connectors and demonstrate how a commonplace article of clothing — suspenders — can be transformed into an effective power bus and data network for wearable digital devices. Both the power bus and the data network are described in detail, including the mechanics of attachment and an outline of the network protocols. The techniques illustrated here can be readily applied to other articles of clothing and accessories.

1 Introduction

It is a mistake to think of wearing just one computer. Instead, we will wear a multitude of digital devices, some general-purpose and some specialized. All of these devices will require power and their utility is greatly amplified if they can intercommunicate. Novel power sources have been proposed for portable devices — parasitic power harvesting [1] and miniature fuel cells [2] to name only two. Possible mechanisms for interdevice communication include near-field radio [3], human skin as a transmission medium [4], and low intensity infrared [5]. We offer a more prosaic alternative — a battery-driven, wired power bus and data network embedded within the fabric of ordinary, everyday clothing.

A common power bus and data network, shared by two or more wearable devices, offers several advantages. A single, centralized power source shared in common:

- Allows one battery to do the work of many. Battery efficiency tends to increase with size. Furthermore, the weight or volume of a single large battery may easily be less than the combined total weight or volume of the separate, smaller batteries of a set of individual devices

- Reduces the risk of battery failure. It is a simple matter to increase the number of batteries in a shared common pool or to add an additional battery of equal or lesser capacity as an emergency backup

- Permits battery "hot swapping" without powering down. When a battery in the common pool discharges it can be replaced without loss of power if there is sufficient reserve in the pool as a whole. Continuous operation is more than a convenience; it may be vital in some circumstances

- Permits the use of rechargeable batteries for all devices. The frequent, ongoing, daily use of wearables dictates the use of rechargeable batteries as a matter of economy and ecology

- Reduces the volume, weight, and complexity of individual devices, which no longer must make provisions for their own batteries

- Tolerates higher discharge rates for a longer period of time than the smaller, individual batteries of separate devices

A single data network shared in common:

- Permits devices to share information to the benefit of all

- Reduces the volume, weight, and complexity of individual devices, since common services can be provided by a single shared device rather than replicating the service within each individual device

- Eases the upgrade or replacement of devices, since a new device with equivalent or improved capabilities can be substituted for an older or less capable comparable device on the network

- Speeds the introduction of new services, since additional devices can be attached to the network

- Encourages extensive task-specific customization, since the network may be populated with specialized devices suited for a limited domain

To ensure its adoption a wearable power bus and data network should be compatible with the manner in which we now wear clothing and carry small objects; robust and error-free in a broad range of environments from the office to the battlefield; and machine washable without special precautions. The design of wearable computers is as much a problem of technology as it is one of ergonomics, appearance, and fashion. If our goal is unobtrusive augmentation these desiderata suggest that the power bus and network accomodate devices that vary in size, shape, and weight; maximize individual preferences for the placement and distribution of devices; ease the addition, removal and substitution of devices; and be itself an article of clothing or be embedded in one.

Wearable devices must adapt themselves to the human form. For example, one of the reasons for the popularity of the Palm Pilot, a personal digital device, is that it fits into a shirt or pants pocket. Cellular telephones, such as the Motorola StarTAC, are so small that they can be comfortably worn on a decorative chain around the neck like jewelry. Digital devices will be carried in pockets, purses, and waist packs, hung on belts and straps, worn as pins, brooches, and rings[6], or attached to arms, wrists, and ankles as bracelets or with straps as we now do with a wristwatch.

Many of these placements and accomodations rely on existing garments and their appurtenances — belts, shirt pockets, and purses existed long before the arrival of the digiterati. We present a technology and a point design that can deliver power and communications to those locations and that also offers a whole new set of placements for wearable digital devices of many forms. In short, our goal is to transform clothing into a digital infrastructure that provides power and communications to other wearable devices. Our design relies upon a new generation of fabrics in which durable, low-resistance conductors are woven into the fabric itself.

In Section 2 we briefly describe one such fabric. Section 3 presents a design for electrical connectors for these fabrics and illustrates their use to implement a wearable, fabric power bus. Section 4 proposes a network architecture for wearable digital devices and outlines one possible implementation using the fabric previously introduced. Section 5 briefly surveys related work, while Section 6 outlines further lines of investigation and development.

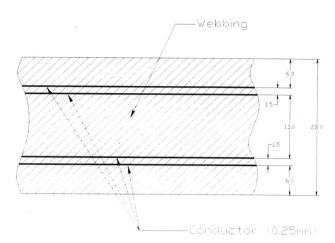

Figure 1: Top view of webbing (dimensions in mm)

2 Conductive Webbing

Webbing woven in various widths is used for belts, carrying straps, and harnesses. Common materials include cotton, Kevlar, Nomex, nylon, polyester, and various mixes of these materials. Webbings can, by varying the yarns, the weave, the thickness, and the width, be engineered to precise specifications including strength, durability, and flexibility.

We use a webbing made of Nomex with two pairs of stainless steel conductors woven directly into the webbing. A schematic of the webbing appears in Figure 1. The webbing is surprisingly flexible and its degree of stiffness is due more to the thickness of the weave and the yarn diameters than the conductors. Each conductor is a bundle of twenty strands of stainless steel wire. The webbing lies flat with the conductors neatly sandwiched between the two major planes of the webbing. The four conductors are uninsulated; the Nomex yarn is itself the insulator. We bond each conductor pair together at the ends of each webbing segment to produce two single conductors, one on either side of the webbing.

The webbing and its conductors withstand all of the rigors of industrial washing. However, it is not waterproof and, if wet, the conductors woven into the webbing will short. Consequently the webbing, as presently constituted, is unsuitable for use outdoors or in humid or damp environments. Nonetheless, with suitable precautions, it can be used indoors in many circumstances and settings such as offices, homes, and schools. We will briefly return to this issue again in Section 6.

3 Electrical Connectors

Electrical connectors for materials like the conductive webbing must: endure repeated machine washings without loss of conductivity or mechanical deterioration; permit the easy and repeated connection and disconnection of devices; resist extremes of temperature and humidity; be compatible with common manufacturing techniques for clothing and accessories; and provide a sound and reliable electrical and mechanical connection. Two forms of connectors are desirable — end connectors and surface connectors. End connectors are attached to the ends of the webbing to couple segments together or terminate it at end devices. Surface connectors are placed on the surface of the webbing. Of the two, surface connectors are the most versatile since they can be placed anywhere on the webbing surface, allowing devices to be attached at any point along the length of the webbing.

Our surface connectors are an adaptation of conventional ball and socket sew-on snaps. They are widely available in sizes ranging from approximately 5–8 mm in diameter. The materials vary, though brass and nickel-plated brass are common. They are widely used as closures in clothing of all sorts, are extremely durable, and are excellent electrical conductors.

To the ball we add a short length of stiff and sharpened stainless steel wire as illustrated in the mechanical drawing of Figure 2. The length of wire is bent into an "L" shape with the short leg of the "L" inserted into the interior of the ball where it is secured with solder. This wire, called a "stinger," penetrates the webbing and is inserted parallel to, and inside of, the conductor bundle. Figures 3 and 4 illustrate schematically the alignment of the connector with the conductor of the webbing. The short gap between the long leg of the stinger and the base of the ball allows the ball to lie flat on the webbing with the stinger in place. Once the stinger is inserted the ball is secured to the webbing with common cotton/polyester thread. As a precaution, to prevent the stinger from shifting or working through the opposite side of the webbing, stiching is applied along the length of the stinger.

Adapting the mating connector, the socket, for use as an electrical connector is more complicated since the socket does not lie flat on the material nor does it offer a convenient location for the attachment of a stinger. These problems are resolved by resting the socket on a small conductive washer that both provides an attachment point for the stinger and permits the socket to rest flat on the surface of the fabric. The socket is secured to the conductive washer and to the fabric below with ordinary sewing thread, which brings the socket in electrical contact with the washer and mechanically secures it to the fabric. A schematic of a socket and a conductive washer appears in Figure 5.

The primary advantage of these connectors, aside from their simplicity and ease of attachment, is that they may be applied anywhere along the length of the webbing. Not only can new connectors can be inserted wherever needed, but old connectors can be quickly removed without disturbing the integrity of the conducter embedded within the webbing.

To illustrate the utility of conductive webbing and the con-

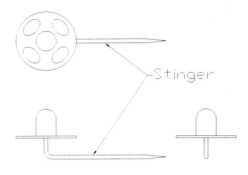

Figure 2: Top and side views of ball connector

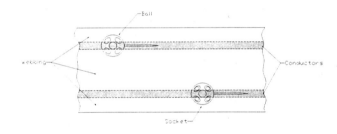

Figure 3: Top view of snaps attached to webbing

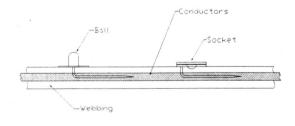

Figure 4: Side view of snaps attached to webbing

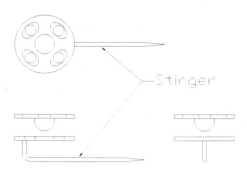

Figure 5: Top and side views of socket connector

Figure 6: Front view of electric suspenders with two batteries and an ad-hoc wireless network router attached

nectors just described we have transformed a simple article of clothing — suspenders — into a shared, low voltage, DC power bus for digital wearable devices. The matching conductors of the left and right straps are bonded together electrically at the vee of the suspenders where they cross using two matched sets of ball and socket sew-on connectors. The voltage of the power bus varies with the type, form, and chemistry of the batteries attached to it; 6–12 volts is common. Unfortunately different devices attached to the bus require different voltages (3.3 and 5.0 volts predominate today) so each device attached to the suspenders provides its own DC-DC converter(s) that converts the bus voltage to that required by the device (numerous small, efficient converters are available that accomodate inputs of 6–12 volts and, depending upon their output voltage and current capacity, vary in size from tens of square millimeters to 25 square centimeters).

Figure 6 is a front view of the "electric suspenders." The two small "pockets" attached to the suspenders are battery holders (described in Section 3.1). The large pocket is an experimental wireless ad-hoc networking node that provides wireless connectivity to the local wired intranet (and from there to the Internet at large). The wearer can choose any one of a dozen placements for these and other devices, can attach multiple devices as easily as one, and can rearrange them in accordance with need, circumstances, and personal preference.

3.1 Battery Holder

To illustrate the attachment of devices to the power bus we briefly describe a battery holder that can, quickly and easily, be attached to, or detached from, the suspenders.

The battery holder is designed for the Sony InfoLithium battery, a 7.2 volt, 1.3 ampere-hour rechargeable battery that is roughly 7 × 4 × 2 (cm). Unlike many other batteries the

negative and positive electrodes are deeply recessed in one end of the battery. A schematic of the battery holder is shown in Figure 7.

The entire battery holder is designed to fit into a small cloth "pocket." The plastic plate forming the base of the battery holder is drilled and grooved, permitting the plate to be firmly sewn The lower holes on each arm allow the back side of the bag to be sewn to each arm, thereby increasing their mechanical rigidity. The "star" pattern of holes at the end of each arm accomodates either a ball or socket sew-on snap. The dimple of the socket snap nestles within the center hole of the star. Each snap is sewn to the fabric of the bag and is electrically and mechanically secured to an arm with fine stainless steel wire that loops through the perimeter holes of the star. A battery can be inserted into, or removed from, the pocket in a matter of seconds.

4 Network

A wearable personal network must support:

- A broad range of network devices that includes everything from simple sensors with little or no computational capability to sophisticated processing elements with substantial computing resources

- Hot swapping of devices along with network plug-and-

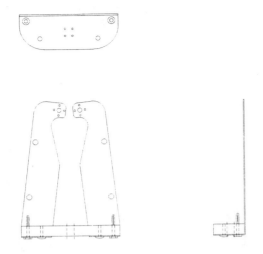

Figure 7: Top, front, and side views of battery holder

play. One may attach devices without concern for their placement or their order of attachment. Once attached a device is configured and integrated into the network. Similarly, when a device is detached the network and the remaining attached devices gracefully adapt

- Extensive error-correction and fault-tolerance to ensure reliable operation in inhospitable environs

- Inexpensive, low-power, small network transceivers

- Modest bandwidths on the order of hundreds of kilobits per second (kbs)

- Hundreds of individual devices

- Direct device-to-device communication; in other words, it must be possible for any two devices to directly intercommunicate without the repeated assistance of an intermediary device such as a bus or network master

- Comprehensive customization by the wearer, including the choice of devices, device configuration and behavior, specification of device interaction, and the assignment of quality of service to devices and device groups

Ensemble, the data network of the electric suspenders, is designed with these requirements in mind. We briefly outline it here; a fuller presentation is given in [7]. Section 4.1 describes the data link layer of the network. Section 4.2 presents the rationale and role of the Ensemble *bus master*, which manages the network on the behalf of the other network devices. Finally, Section 4.3 sketches the lower level network services that help support dynamic attachment and detachment and direct interdevice communication.

4.1 Data Link Layer

The physical and link layer of the network is CAN (Controller Area Network) [8], a robust, industrial-strength, serial bus network orginally defined by Robert Bosch GmbH, a German manufacturer of automotive components, for use as a sensor and control network in automobiles. CAN networks are capable of transmission rates of 1000 kbs and will communicate reliably in the presence of severe network faults, albeit at a greatly reduced transmission rate. CAN's flexibility and reliability led to its adoption in a variety of other industries, including medical instrumentation, process control, and textile manufacturing. Inexpensive CAN transceivers, and microcontrollers with CAN interfaces, are available from numerous semiconductor manufacturers including Intel [9, 10], Philips [11], and Motorola [12].

The CAN serial bus employs Carrier Sense, Multiple Access with Collision Detect. Ignoring the details of error correction and framing, a Standard CAN message frame consists of an 11-bit arbitration field, a 4-bit data length code, and a data field 0–8 bytes long. Unlike other popular networks such as Ethernet, the message frames transmitted on the CAN bus do not contain the addresses of either the sending node or of any intended destination node. Instead each message is labelled with an 11-bit arbitration field (the Extended CAN format, introduced in 1991, specifies a 29-bit arbitration field and is upwardly compatible with the 11-bit arbitration field of the Standard CAN format) that determines the priority of the message on the bus. The lower the numerical value of the arbitration field the higher the message's priority.

Potential bus conflicts are resolved by the network using non-destructive bitwise arbitration. The end result is as if the higher priority message was the only message being transmitted. The instant any lower priority transmitter loses control of the bus via the arbitration mechanism it becomes a receiver of the highest priority message and will not attempt to retransmit until the bus is free again.

CAN employs several error-detection mechanisms to guarantee that either all network nodes receive the message error-free or that no node receives the message.

4.2 Bus Master

Ensemble assumes the presence of a *bus master*, a distinguished network device responsible for the administration of the network and the implementation of fundamental network services. The bus master is a repository for the personal preferences of the wearer, and contains:

- Configuration and operational parameters for the individual devices that one attaches to the network

- Rules of operation and interaction for both groups of cooperating devices and pairs of devices attached to the network

- Specifications and constraints on quality of service for both network services and the services of individual devices or cooperating groups of devices

- Recovery procedures in case of device failure or degradations in network service

The bus master also implements many of the basic Ensemble services, including dynamic join when a device is attached to the network bus, the setup and teardown of interdevice connections, and detecting when a device has been detached from the network. When a device is physically attached to the network it is automatically customized and configured by the bus master in a manner consistent with the dictates and preferences of the user.

Placing these and other services within a single device enhances the stability of the network and simplifies the implementation of other network devices, thereby reducing their cost. A simple Ensemble-compatible sensor node can contain as little as a miniature voltage converter, a single-chip CAN transceiver, the sensor itself, and a small amount of dedicated memory and logic. Shifting the burden of configuration and integration to the bus master reduces the parts count, size, and power requirements of network devices.

4.3 Network Services

Because the CAN use of an arbitration field in place of a destination address is a slightly foreign notion we shall, from this point forward, refer to the arbitration field as a *channel*, noting that each of the 2048 distinct arbitration ids $0, \ldots, 2047$, denotes a distinct channel in order of decreasing transmission priority. Channel 0 is, by Ensemble convention, a distinguished broadcast channel on which only the bus master may transmit and to which all devices listen. We assume that each network device (also known as an accessory) attached to Ensemble contains a permanent globally unique identifier of 56 bits or less (the assignment and administration of these identifiers are topics outside the scope of this paper).

To provide a flavor of the Ensemble protocols and their use of CAN we highlight three of the low level network services. Section 4.3.1 covers network join, the process by which a newly attached device is integrated into the network; Section 4.3.2 outlines how two devices can directly intercommunicate; and Section 4.3.3 describes how the network detects the detachment of a device.

4.3.1 Network Join

When an accessory is first attached to Ensemble it issues a *join* message containing its global identifier on a well-known, fixed "join channel." Because several accessories may be joining simultaneously, their transmissions on this single shared channel may collide, resulting in repeated bus errors with no join message from any accessory getting through. In the event of collisions each individual accessory performs exponential backoff; the base period of the backoff (anywhere from microseconds to about 500 milliseconds) is a random value generated from the unique global identifier (the base period can be computed and "burned into" the accessory at the time that it is assigned its global unique identifier). If the accessory fails to join after repeated attempts it remains dormant until detached from the network and reattached again, at which point it begins anew.

When the bus master receives a join message on the join channel it assigns the accessory an 8-bit *network identifier*. A network identifier either denotes an individual accessory or a *group* of accessories. There are two distinguished identifiers: the bus master always has network identifier 0, and the broadcast group containing every accessory attached to the network has network identifier 1. The remaining identifiers $2, \ldots, 255$, are assigned to accessories and other groups, consequently an Ensemble network may have a combined maximum of 254 attached accessories and groups at any one time.

The bus master replies to a join message on a well-known, fixed "enrollment channel" with an enrollment message that contains the network identifier assigned to the accessory along with the accessory's global unique identifier. Each accessory, following a successful transmission of a join message, listens to the enrollment channel for an enrollment message containing its unique global identifier and extracts the assigned network identifier. From this point forward the accessory is known by its network identifier, which the accessory retains until it is detached from the network.

The join process requires one more step — the allocation of a channel pair to the joining accessory dedicated to bus master/accessory communication. The bus master issues a duplex channel assignment message on the enrollment channel that contains three items: the network identifier of the bus master (always zero), the just-assigned network identifier i of the joining accessory, and a single channel number n. Until told otherwise accessory i can expect to receive messages from the bus master on channel n and may send messages to the bus master on channel $n + 1$. This channel pair remains in place until the accessory withdraws from the network.

4.3.2 Interdevice Communications

When an accessory i wishes to directly communicate with another accessory j it petitions the bus master for a duplex channel assignment dedicated to i and j. i petitions the bus master by sending a message on the channel assigned to it at join time for accessory to bus master communications. If the petition is granted both i and j will receive a duplex channel assignment message (on their respective channels for bus master to accessory communications) containing (i, j, n) signifying to both that i may transmit to j on channel n and that j may transmit to i on channel $n + 1$. The channel assignments are withdrawn whenever either accessory, i or j requests the bus master to do so.

4.3.3 Network Leave

An accessory may depart the network at any time without forewarning. To accomodate such leavetaking the bus master periodically polls each and every accessory on the network (the polling period for any one device is on the order of seconds).

An accessory i that does not respond in a timely manner is presumed gone, at which point its network identifier i, channel assignments, and group memberships are retracted, and a notice is broadcast by the bus master on broadcast channel 0 to all remaining accessories that i is no longer attached.

5 Related Work

The Sensate Liner [13] is a T-shirt like garment in which is woven an unbroken plastic optical fiber. The front panel of the garment contains a 14×18 matrix of conductive fibers designed to interconnect to the data bus of a small wearable computer. Designed for military use, its initial application is the monitoring of vital signs in combat personnel and the detection, location, and characterization of bullet and shrapnel wounds on the upper torso. A variety of sensors and computing elements may be connected to, or directly embedded within, the sensate liner. The focus of the research includes the development of: insulated conductive threads, interfiber electrical connections, and connectors for power and data interconnects to and from the garment.

In a similar vein Post and Orth [14] reported on the use of commercial metallic yarns for conductors and simple data buses. They demonstrated prototype devices in which both active and passive electronic components were directly attached to conductive fabrics using combinations of soldering and sewing. They also employed "gripper snaps," a common sewing closure, as interconnects between conductive fabrics and conventional electronics.

The work of Gemperle et al [15] explores an important, but oft ignored, aspect of wearable digital devices, namely their size, shape, and appropriate placement on the body. It was this work that inspired the investigations reported here as a fabric power bus and data network greatly expands the range of placements available to the designers of wearable digital devices.

There is an increasing body of work on *wireless* personal area networks (WPANs). The network of [4] relies on the human body as a transmission medium and can achieve half-duplex transfer rates as high as 9600 bps. However, [4] describes only the physical layer — no higher-level protocols are mentioned. Bluetooth [3] is a comprehensive specification for near-field ($\leq$ 10 meters) wireless communications that includes physical, link, transport, and service discovery protocols. Finally, the IEEE P802.115 Working Group [16] is pursuing physical and media access standards for WPANs with a 0–10 meter range and data rates of less than 1 Mbs for small (2 cm^3 or less), low power, inexpensive transceivers.

6 Future Work

We are pursuing several distinct avenues of investigation. First, we will be experimenting with webbings containing four equidistant individual conductors. With four conductors two can be devoted to power and two to the network, allowing us to increase network bandwidth from 125–250 kbs to 500-1000 kbs.

We are also developing other forms of surface connectors for conductive webbings. A reliable, inexpensive connector capable of maintaining its electrical integrity when wet or when the surrounding fiber matrix is saturated is a substantive engineering challenge. Human perspiration is both highly conductive and surprisingly corrosive; its presence complicates matters further. In a similar vein we are experimenting with incorporating conductive webbings into common articles of clothing such as shirts and belts, and specialized garments such as tactical vests.

With respect to Ensemble we are designing and prototyping high level protocols suitable for the unique demands of wearable devices and personal networks. The presence of a personal, embedded, digital network greatly broadens the range of design choices for wearable devices. Devices that previously were tightly integrated can now be broken apart into separate, distinct networked (sub)devices whose services and functions can be exploited by other wearable network appliances.

Finally, we are exploring a wide range of wearable digital devices suited to a fabric power and network bus. These include chemical and environmental sensors, cameras, computing and storage modules, display devices, inertial navigation devices, and wireless, ad-hoc network routers for interperson and Internet communications.

7 Summary

Webbings of the form described here can be manufactured in an endless variety of widths, weights, colors, and patterns. Conductive webbing can be concealed in the seams of shirts, blouses, pants, and skirts, applied as decoration to garments, worn as belts or suspenders, incorporated into waist packs, knapsacks, or tactical vests, and used as straps for luggage or purses, or as carrying handles for bags of all sizes and descriptions. Using the connectors described here these separate articles of clothing and accessories can be easily interconnected to form a personal wearable power bus and digital network to which a large number of digital devices may be conveniently attached. Most importantly, these devices attach in a natural manner according to personal taste and need — they can be placed in pockets, attached to garments, and carried in purses and knapsacks — all while drawing power from a common bus and intercommunicating over a network that is literally run by the seat of the pants.

8 Acknowledgements

I am indebted to W. Horowitz of C. M. Offray and Sons who generously provided numerous conductive fabrics and webbings, both commercial and experimental, and has, with patience and humor, gently broadened my appeciation of the art, craft, and engineering of textiles.

This investigation was supported by the internal research and development program of The Aerospace Corporation. My grateful thanks to: P. E. Hanson and S. W. Hansen for their technical assistance in fabricating the "electric suspenders" and its precursor; B. Scott Michel for playing devil's advocate as I thrashed out the details of the Ensemble protocol; C. DeMatteis and C. Raghavendra for reviewing this paper; and W. Y. Kim for drafting the mechanical drawings appearing in Figures 1–5 and Figure 7.

References

[1] J. Kymissis, C. Kendall, J. Paradiso, and N. Gershenfeld, "Parasitic Power Harvesting in Shoes,' *Proceedings of the Second International Symposium on Wearable Computers*, October 1998, Pittsburgh, Pennsylvania, pp. 132–139.

[2] R. G. Hockaday, "Surface replica fuel cell for micro fuel cell electrical power pack," United States Patent #5759712, June 2, 1998.

[3] Bluetooth System Specification, Volume 1, Version 1.0A, July 26, 1999, Bluetooth Special Interest Group (available from www.bluetooth.com).

[4] E. R. Post et al, "Intrabody Buses for Data and Power," *Proceedings of the First International Symposium on Wearable Computers*, October 1997, Cambridge, Massachusetts, pp. 52–55.

[5] IrDA Serial Infrared Physical Layer Specification, Version 1.3, Infrared Data Association, October 15, 1998.

[6] Java Ring, Dallas Semiconductor Corporation, http://www.ibutton.com/java.html.

[7] M. Gorlick, "Ensemble: A Wearable Network That You Accessorize," (in preparation).

[8] CAN Specification, Version 2.0, Robert Bosch GmbH, Stuttgart, Germany, September 1991.

[9] 82527 Serial Communications Controller Architectural Overview, Intel Corporation, Document #272410-003, January 1996.

[10] 87C196CA/87C196CB 16 MHz Advanced 16-Bit CHMOS Microcontroller with Integrated CAN 2.0, Intel Corporation, Document #273151-001, January 1998.

[11] TJA1053 Fault-tolerant CAN Transceiver, Philips Semiconductors, Document #9397-750-02465, October 1997.

[12] MC68HC05X4/MC68HC705X4 HCMOS Microcontroller Unit, Revision 1.0, Motorola, Inc., Document #MC68HC05X4/D, 1998.

[13] E. J. Lind et al, "A Sensate Liner for Personnel Monitoring Applications," *Proceedings of the First International Symposium on Wearable Computers*, October 1997, Cambridge, Massachusetts.

[14] E. R. Post and M. Orth, "Smart Fabric or 'Wearable Clothing'," *Proceedings of the First International Symposium on Wearable Computers*, October 1997, Cambridge, Massachusetts.

[15] F. Gemperle et al, "Design for Wearability," *Proceedings of the Second International Symposium on Wearable Computers*, October 1998, Pittsburgh, Pennsylvania, pp. 116–122

[16] B. Heile, I. Gifford and T. Siep, "The IEEE P802.15 Working Group for Wireless Personal Area Networks," IEEE Network, 13(4), July/August 1999, pp. 4–5.

Usability Evaluation for Mobile and Wearable Systems

Juha Kaario, Nokia Research Center
Satu Ruuska, Nokia
Jane Siegel, Carnegie Mellon University
Sarah Zuberac, Microsoft

When Cyborgs Meet:
Building Communities of Cooperating Wearable Agents

Gerd Kortuem, Jay Schneider, Jim Suruda, Steve Fickas, Zary Segall

University of Oregon, Deschutes Hall

Eugene, OR 97403 USA

{kortuem,jay,jfs,fickas,zs}@cs.uoregon.edu

Abstract

This paper introduces the notion of a Wearable Community *as a group of wearable users who cooperate for their mutual benefit. In such a community, wearable computers act as personal agents on behalf of and in the interest of their 'owners'. These agents are goal-directed and will perform a broad array of tasks for the user, ranging from personal scheduling to task planning. We describe how personal wearable agents can be used to enable goal directed cooperation during physical encounters of people with selfish and conflicting goals, such that cooperation leads to mutually beneficial results. We discuss negotiation protocols, and describe the design and implementation of a wearable agent system, as well as a simulator for large-scale wearable communities.*

1 Introduction

In our modern world, the use of communication technologies like phone, fax and email has become commonplace. Despite this fact, most human interactions still occur when we meet people face-to-face. Frequently, we use such encounters to cooperate with other people and to pursue and advance our own goals. For example, we purchase items from a salesperson, coordinate schedules with co-workers during a meeting, or make travel arrangements with friends at home.

While the idea of using wearable computers for cooperation and collaboration has been around at least as long as wearable computers have become feasible, today's wearable computers are mostly used in isolation, as advanced personal assistant. A prototypical example for this situation is the Remembrance Agent [11], an augmented-memory application that continuously searches for documents with content relevant to the user's current situation.

A number of wearable systems have been designed with the explicit goal to support collaboration of remote and co-located users. Most of them are wearable videoconference systems [1,2,3,4,8,10,12,17], while others aim at establishing personal relationships between users [5]. For example, our own Proem system [9]

enables two or more users to exchange personal user profiles in real-time during face-to-face encounters with the goal to identify shared interests.

All these system have one point in common: they assume that users share common goals and want to cooperate for the mutual benefit of all participants. The shared goal is usually defined by the broader context in which people meet or collaborate, for example by the fact that both users are employees of the same company: two technicians who collaborate using a wearable maintenance assistant share the goal to find and repair an equipment failure. In our daily life, however, we are often faced with the necessity to cooperate with people with different or even contradicting goals. For example, when buying a car from a dealer our own goal might be to purchase a car that fits our lifestyle at a price we can afford, while the car salesperson's goal might be to sell a car from the lot that maximizes his commission. This type of goal-directed cooperation between users with differing or even antagonistic goals is not supported in any wearable system.

In this paper we address the question how wearable devices can be used during physical encounters of individuals to support cooperation. In particular and in contrast to most previous research, we are looking at how this technology can be used to enable *goal-directed cooperation during encounters of people with selfish and conflicting goals, such that cooperation leads to mutually beneficial results.*

We believe that wearable computers provide a unique platform to support this kind of cooperation: they are highly personal, proactive, and context-sensitive. Our emphasis in this research is on large-scale communities of wearable users where people interact and cooperate in many ways and for a variety of reasons.

This paper is organized as follows. In the next section, we start by presenting a theoretical framework of cooperation in wearable communities. In Section 3, we give an example of a negotiation protocol and discuss its properties. In Section 4, we describe the design and implementation of a wearable agent system. In Section 5, we present WALID, an interactive simulator for evaluating the behavior of agents in large-scale wearable communities.

2 Wearable Communities

We define a *Wearable Community* as a collection of wearable users who cooperate for their mutual benefit. Our notion of a community is based on three fundamental concepts:

Personal Agents: Each wearable computer acts as a personal agent on behalf of its user.

Physical Encounters: Wearable users encounter each other as they move around in space.

Agent Cooperation: Agents cooperate through negotiation that take place during encounters.

We will now discuss these concepts in more detail.

2.1 Wearable Agents

We call any wearable computer that exhibits autonomous behavior and acts on behalf and in the interest of its user a *wearable agent* (agent for short).

Agents have several important properties:

Goal-oriented: Agents are goal-directed and will perform a broad array of tasks for the user, ranging from personal scheduling and task planning, to providing hardware services in foreign locales.

Opportunistic: Wearable agents are designed to benefit their users and to act in their best interest. We do not require nor do we assume that agents will *a priori* be cooperative, share information, or negotiate for a single global goal. In particular, we do not make any assumptions about agents being "benevolent" [21].

Predictable: Agents are predictable. They act according to rules defined by their users and can be fully controlled and monitored.

Rational: Agents make rational decisions based on the utility of alternative choices.

The more complex the considerations that a wearable computer takes into account in order to advance its user's goals, the more justified it is to consider this computer an agent.

2.2 Encounters

The second fundamental concept of a wearable community is a physical encounter between individuals. We define an *encounter* as a situation where

- two or more individuals are in close physical proximity to each other;

- the wearable computers of these individuals have discovered each other's presence; and

- these computers are able to communicate.

This definition does not say anything about how wearable computers discover each other, or how close they have to be in order to do so. Many different and equally suitable technologies have been used in the past for proximity sensing, including infrared transmitters and near-field radios. Similarly, this definition does not say whether discovery and communication are independent functions or can be combined into one. The latter would be possible with Personal Area Networks [18] or future short-range wireless networks like Bluetooth [22].

Encounters have several important properties:

- Encounters can occur between two, three or more individuals.

- Encounters are reflexive: if user A encounters user B, then user B encounters user A.

- Encounters are situations with a time duration, not momentary events: encounters can be short and last only a few seconds, or they can be long-lasting going on for hours. For example, the encounter between two individuals passing each other in a hallway might last just a few seconds. On the other hand, two or more people in a lengthy meeting encounter each other for the full duration of that meeting.

- Encounters are non-transitive: if user A encounters user B, and user B encounters user C, then user A does not necessarily encounter user C.

2.3 Agent Negotiation

The third and final key concept of wearable communities is that of *agent negotiation*. An encounter between individuals is a chance for an automated interaction of their respective agents in form of negotiation.

Following Rosenschein and Zlotkin [16], negotiations are defined by *protocols* and *strategies*.

Protocols. A negotiation protocol is the set of rules governing the inter-agent communication among agents – offers and counter-offers, threats, promises, concessions, etc. In particular, negotiation protocols deal not with the mechanism of communication but with its content. A protocol specifies the kinds of deals agents can make, as well as sequences of offers and counter-offers that are allowed.

Strategies. A strategy is the way an agent behaves in an interaction. The protocol specifies the rules of the interaction, but the exact deals that an agent proposes are the result of a strategy that his designer has set. Strategies may involve the relaxation of initial goals, concessions, or even lies.

3 Negotiation Protocols and Strategies

In the preceding section we have introduced our idea of wearable agents and wearable communities in theory. We now discuss concrete negotiation protocols and strategies for wearable communities.

3.1 An Example: Delivering Packages

It may be useful here to look at an example. Suppose that two drivers working for independent delivery services meet each other at several stops along their routes, because they have to deliver packages to essentially the same destinations. Instead of following each other around, they realize that they could trade packages between them in a way that minimizes their respective routes. Let's suppose that both are members of a "Task Trading Community" whose members have agreed to use their personal agents to negotiate with other members about trading tasks – in this case delivering packages – during chance encounters.

We can formulate this scenario as a variation of the Postman domain [16] as follows:

"Agents have to deliver sets of packages to destinations, which are arranged on a graph $G = G(V,E)$. The set V of vertices represents all possible destinations while the set E of edges represents routes along which agents can travel. Agents can exchange packages at no cost during encounters at any vertex.

Task Set: The set of all destinations in the graph, namely V. If destination x is in an agent's task set, it means that he has at least one package to deliver to x.

Cost Function: The cost of a subset of destination X $\subseteq$ V, i.e., c(X), is the length of the minimal path that starts at the current vertex and visits all members of X."

We use a negotiation protocol called *Product Maximizing Mechanism* (PMM) that was developed by Nash [13]. The PMM protocol is a three-step protocol. In the first step both agents disclose their task sets; in the second step each agent proposes a deal (division of tasks) that is *pareto-optimal[1]*; in the third step agents select the deal that offers both of them the most benefits. The deal that is selected and agreed upon is the deal that has the highest utility (cost savings) when the utility to agent 1 and agent 2 are multiplied.

---

[1] Pareto-optimal: No agent could derive more from a different agreement, without some other agent deriving less from that alternate agreement.

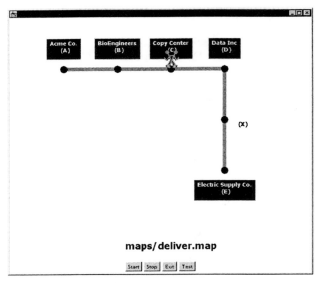

Figure 1. Graph representation of task trading domain

Let's assume two agents are negotiating at point C of the graph shown in Figure 1. Agent 1 must deliver packages to points A and D. Agent 2 must deliver a package to point A. Using the PMM system agent 1 would propose a deal that agent 1 would deliver agent 1's package to point D and agent 2 would deliver agent 1's and agent 2's packages to point A. Agent 2 would propose the deal that agent 1 would deliver agent 1's and agent 2's packages to point A and agent 2 would deliver agent 1's package to point D. The whole negotiation process looks like follows:

Initial task sets:
- Agent 1: {A, D}, cost without swapping = 4
- Agent 2: {A}, cost without swapping = 2

Proposed deals:
- Deal 1: [{D}, {A}]
- Deal 2: [{A}, {D}]

Utilities under Deal 1:
- Cost of agent 1's tasks under deal 1 = 1
- Cost of agent 2's tasks under deal 1 = 2
- Utility of deal 1 to agent 1 = 3
- Utility of deal 1 to agent 2 = 0
- Product of utilities of deal 1 = 0

Utilities under Deal 2:
- Cost of agent 1's tasks under deal 2 = 2
- Cost of agent 2's tasks under deal 2 = 1
- Utility of deal 2 to agent 1 = 2
- Utility of deal 2 to agent 2 = 1

- Product of expected utilities of deal 1 = 2

Winning deal:
- Deal 2: [{A}, {D}]

As the *Product Maximizing Mechanism* says the winning deal is the deal with the highest product of the two expected utility, deal 2 will be the winning deal. As the result, delivery driver 1 with agent 1 would deliver two packages to destination A, while driver 2 would deliver one package to destination D. An arrangement like this could save both of them a lot of time, while the end result remains the same.

Our package delivery example is an illustration of a *Task Oriented Domain* [16]: tasks can be carried out without concern about interference from other agents and each agent can accomplish his tasks without the help of other agents. On the other hand, it is possible that agents can reach agreements where they redistribute some tasks, to everyone's benefit. Negotiation is aimed at discovering mutually beneficial task distribution. The key issue here is the notion of *task*, an indivisible job that needs to be carried out.

The tasks that are negotiated can take a wide variety of forms, both physical and virtual. A trade could be "if you take my books back to the library, I'll pick up your copies from the printers" or "I'll handle all outgoing communications through my currently unused T-1 line if you process the data received." Although it is beyond the range of the initial work in this field, trades such as "I'll handle all visual data analysis if you pick up my dry cleaning" could also be useful.

In our example, we obviously made a number of simplifying assumptions that might not hold for other real-life scenarios: tasks are independent and can be carried out without interference from other agents; agents can accomplish their tasks without the help of other agents; all tasks are interchangeable and easily tradable; the cost of carrying out a task can easily be determined by both agents. This last assumption can be a problem, as determining the cost of a deal requires to compute the shortest path between a set of destinations – a process which can be computationally very expensive.

3.2 Using Deception During Negotiation

In a wearable community, the agents involved in task sharing and trading are designed and implemented by independent individuals. Maximizing personal goals is assumed to be an agent's sole motivation. It is thus possible and likely that these agents can and will use strategies in which they will lie, cheat or steal to maximize their 'owners' benefits. For example, an agent could use deception by misrepresenting its tasks or not executing

tasks it agreed upon during a negotiation.

Let's consider another example in which an agent will be less than truthful about what tasks it must perform. As this is hidden information and not verifiable by outside sources this is one easy way of cheating. Let's assume that agent 1 creates a *Phantom Task* claiming tasks of {A, D, E} as opposed to the true task set of {A, D}. We then have the following situation:

Initial task sets:
- Agent 1: {A, D, E}, cost = 7
- Agent 2: {A}, cost = 2

Proposed deals:
- Deal 1: [{D, E}, {A}]
- Deal 2: [{ }, {A, D, E}]

Utilities under Deal 1:
- Cost of agent 1's tasks under deal 1 = 3
- Cost of agent 2's tasks under deal 1 = 2
- Utility of deal 1 to agent 1 = 4
- Utility of deal 1 to agent 2 = 0
- Product of utilities of deal 1 = 0
- Sum of utilities of deal 1 = 4

Utilities under Deal 2:
- Cost of agent 1's tasks under deal 2 = 0
- Cost of agent 2's tasks under deal 2 = 7
- Utility of deal 2 to agent 1 = 2
- Utility of deal 2 to agent 2 = 0
- Product of utilities of deal 2 = 0
- Sum of utilities of deal 2 = 2

Winning deal:
- Deal 1: [{D, E}, {A}].

In this case the products of the expected utility will be equal. The first tie-breaking system used by PMM is the sum of the expected utility to all parties in the negotiations. This will mean deal 1 is the winning deal, with the higher sum of utility. Since E is a phantom task (information known by agent 1, but not by agent 2) the task set that will actually be performed is: [{D}, {A}].[2] By misrepresenting its initial task set, agent 1 has a true utility of 3 as opposed to a utility of 2 in the truthful example.

This example makes clear how agents can benefit from being untruthful. As protocol designers it is in our best interest to protect the honest agent. We expect that members of a wearable community will want to find a set

---

[2] Agent 1 must reject any deal that would pass a phantom task to the other agent.

of rules for the negotiation environment where the honest agent will perform as well as the dishonest one as this is the surest way to generate an atmosphere of trust among members – trust in the community is the single most important issue in building an effective wearable community. Without good reason to trust other members and their agents it is doubtful that people would want to join a community and cooperate with members they might not even know personally.

Rosenschein and Zlotkin [16] have shown that for some simple agent domains it is possible to define negotiations protocols in a way that 'forces' members of an agent community to adopt certain strategies, simply because they become the best strategies to advance their own goals. In particular, one can define protocols in a way that virtually prohibits agents from using deception in negotiations, because the outcome of such a lie is provably suboptimal for the lying agent (because it has to pay a higher cost or has to perform more tasks than when telling the truth.)

3.3 Building Communities

We can now rephrase our initial definition of a wearable community as a group of wearable users who a) are willing to cooperate through automated negotiation of their respective agents; b) have agreed upon a negotiation protocol for their agents; and c) have defined their own private negotiation strategies for their respective agents. A wearable community is one, in which members share a negotiation protocol. A single wearable user can belong to more than one community.

The key idea of protocols is that wearable system designers agree upon the rules of interaction, in the same way that they agree on any kind of standardization. Yet within a strategy, every wearable user can chose whatever private strategy he decides to. Members of a community do not need to know each other personally in order to engage in automated negotiation. All that is required to become a member is to implement the community protocol. These protocols could be described on special community web sites where sample agent implementations could be made available to everyone.

Good negotiation protocols create more than just fair or envy-free results. Negotiation protocols should be simple and efficient to implement, stable (so that no agent has an incentive to deviate from the protocol), and symmetric (not biased against any agent).

Two wearable agents may be expected to spend initial communication determining if they are in a common community. If they are in more than one community, i.e., they share more than one negotiation protocol, then a meta process may take place to determine the protocol that will be used. Given that different protocols support different properties, this meta-negotiation process can be key.

3.4 Additional Usage Scenarios

Automated negotiation between wearable agents does not necessarily involve trading of tasks. Negotiation is the process of several agents searching for an agreement. Agreements can be about price, meeting place, joint actions, or joint objectives.

For example, automated negotiation could take place during a swap meet, a flea market-like event where people come together in order to buy and sell rare and unusual items. One of the difficulties of swap meets is to find the person who sells the item that one is interested in. A wearable agent could identify possible trades and bid in automated auctions in competition with other agents (similar to web-based agents for online auctions [25]).

4   A Wearable Agent System

In the previous sections we discussed our idea of wearable agents and wearable communities. We now describe the design and implementation of an actual system that we use in our lab to evaluate our ideas.

As base wearable hardware platform we alternatively use a commercial Via I wearable computer with handheld monitor or a self-built wearable computer with a head-mounted display. Wireless connectivity is achieved through a Metricom wireless modem or a Lucent WaveLAN adapter. The hardware is described in more detail in [1,2,9,10].

In order to function as a wearable agent, a device must implement the following functions:

Device Discovery: A wearable agent must be able to detect the presence of other nearby agents.

Communication: A wearable agent must be able to establish a communication link with nearby devices.

Negotiation: A wearable agent must be able to perform automated negotiations.

We implemented these functions in our wearable agent system through a hierarchy of communication protocols. The architecture of the wearable system with its major software and hardware components is shown in Figure 2.

4.1 Device Discovery

We have equipped our wearable computers with near-field radio transmitters that have a maximum range of about 6-10 feet. These transmitters are connected to the parallel port and allow low bandwidth communication (14.4 baud) between devices. A beacon process that runs on each computer repeatedly sends out a unique bacon signal that can be received by near-by device. By

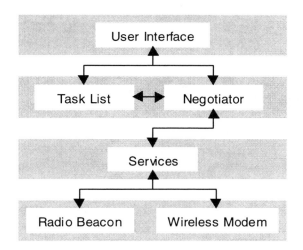

Figure 2. Wearable agent system architecture

listening for incoming signals, a device can determine which other devices are in its immediate vicinity.

We constructed the radio transmitters from radio packet controllers from Radiomatrix [20]. Figure 3 shows an early prototype without casing. The final design is much smaller, fitting comfortably in a pager case including 9V battery.

4.2 Communication

The main function of the service layer shown in Figure 1 is to establish a communication link between devices, and to give them mutual access to each other's functionality. Our solution for connecting two wearable computers devices is based on Jini, Sun's network plug-and-play architecture [19]. Jini provides simple mechanisms to plug devices together to form an impromptu community – a community put together without any planning, installation, or human intervention.

Each wearable computer implements one Jini service, which provides access to the negotiator component. Using standard Jini procedures, each device publishes its capabilities (its services) by registering them with a local *lookup service*. A lookup service is Jini's version of a service trader object. The service advertisement contains a *service handle* and an *offer descriptor*.

A device (the client) that wants to gain access to services of co-located device (the servers) has to follow a two-step procedure. The first step consists of locating the lookup services of all co-located devices. In Jini, this is accomplished by broadcasting a multicast request throughout a network. In turn, lookup services of all devices, which receive such a request answer back to let the client know that they are able and willing to provide information about services that have registered with them. The client then queries each device lookup service by

supplying a *service template*. In response, it receives a collection of matching *service proxies*.[3] These service proxies, which are moved dynamically across the network, are then used to call the remote services.

Since users and their devices constantly move around in space, devices do not form long-lasting stable configurations. Thus, having discovered a service and having gained access to it through its service proxy is not a guarantee that a service is *usable*. In between the time a service was discovered and the attempt by a client to access it, the distance between both devices might be large enough so that they are out of range. If this is the case and the service cannot be reached, the service proxy is simply discarded.

The role of client and server as described above is not fixed. Each wearable device is at the same time client and server. Upon request, each device makes its service available to other devices, and each device requests access to other device's remote services.

4.3 Agent Negotiation

The wearable system has been designed for the task-trading scenario as described above. It thus contains a task list and a negotiator component. Negotiation takes place whenever two or more agents discover each other presence. Agents keep separate lists of tradable and untradable tasks. An example of a tradable task in the implemented domain is to return a book to the library. An untradable task would be to return home after a user has finished all tasks.

At the start of the negotiation, each agent dynamically determines the path to accomplish its tasks. This is currently done using a brute force iterative deepening algorithm. When agents negotiate they use their respective strategy in order to determine how they should negotiate. The expected utility of each task-swap is determined by recalculating the costs to all parties involved in the negotiations. When an agreement has been reached between agents, they ask their respective

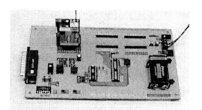

Figure 3. Radio beacon for device discovery

---

[3] The client filters out responses from devices that are not in the immediate vicinity using the information from the radio transmitter. This step would not be necessary if we used a Body-LAN or short-range wireless network.

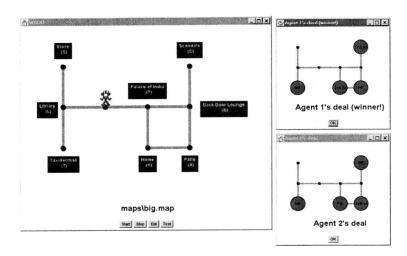

Figure 4. WALID simulator

users to approve the deal by popping up a dialog box. If both agents receive their users' ok, agents swap tasks and replace their old task-list with the new negotiated one.

5 WALID: A Simulator for Modeling Large Scale Wearable Communities

For building useful wearable communities we need to find negotiation protocols that a) are suitable for real life scenarios and b) have beneficial properties like efficiency, simplicity, stability, symmetry and fairness.

We can develop such protocols in at least two ways: On the one hand, we can use an analytic approach as Rosenschein and Zlotkin have done in [16], that is by formalizing agent domains and proving theorems about their properties. On the other hand, we could use an experimental approach. Both approaches have their own problems:

The analytic approach has the problem that it requires formal models that might not be able to capture the kind of interactions we need for real-life scenarios. On the other hand, we realized fairly quickly that it is next to impossible to design negotiation protocols from real-world experiences with wearable agents alone. First of all, since we are still in the midst of our development, there exist at best a few prototypical devices that can act as wearable agents. Second, even with a large number of functioning wearable agents, it will be difficult to get the feedback necessary to evaluate negotiation protocols and strategies.

We thus decided to build a simulator for wearable communities, called WALID. WALID is an interactive system for studying the behavior of a large number of cooperative wearable agents in a wearable community. The current version of WALID is limited, but powerful enough to simulate the task-trading scenario; other domains will be added in the future.

With WALID we can easily vary the number of agents in a wearable community, the negotiation protocol, and the private negotiation strategy of each agent. Similarly, we can define initial task lists and initial location for each agent. A simulation consists of agents moving around in space according to their tasks, and engaging in negotiation when two or more of them meet. As a result of the simulation we obtain a record of performed negotiations and the values achieved by each individual agent in these negotiation.

Agents in the WALID world operate in a customizable map space. Maps are graphs with edges and vertices and define possible movements of agents. WALID restricts the edges follow the cardinal directions (North, South, East and West.) All edges in WALID maps are of uniform length 1. The length requirement does not restrict what graphs are possible, as dummy vertices may be used to create edges of any dimension.

Figure 4 shows two agents during an encounter in WALID. Both agents have a set of destination goals that define the locations they have to visit. The large window (left) shows the current map they are operating under with their respective location. The two smaller windows (upper & lower right) show the deals proposed by each agent in the negotiation. The upper right window in Figure 4 shows the new set of tasks after the negotiation has concluded.

WALID maps and task-lists are created using XML as file format. This allows for easy creation and human readability, and leaves open the potential for expansion. The WALID simulator is written in Java for cross platform use and ease of modification. The source code is available at: http://www.cs.uoregon.edu/research/wearables/walid/source/.

130

As the agents in this task are wearable users we have also implemented a *Cost of Negotiation* (CoN). CoN is a constant value subtracted from the utility of a new task set in step 2 of PMM. This value relates to the human cost of changing the wearable users task set. In our package deliver example, tasks relate to traveling to physical locations. By adding a CoN value we prevent the wearable user from pointlessly trading tasks and spinning in place.

There are several areas for future work on WALID. We want to implement and test other protocols (for example Sum Maximizer), and compare them to PMM, as PMM assures an efficient solution but not a globally optimal one. The WALID simulation values must be compared to the values determined in real world wearable testing. Finally we hope to extend the simulator to other domains, both task-oriented and non-task-oriented.

6   Related Work

The idea of using wearable computers for cooperation and collaboration has been around at least as long as wearable computers have become feasible. In the recent past, systems have been developed both for co-located and remote collaboration. Among the first systems were several designed at Carnegie-Mellon University [8,12,17]. Similar systems have been built and evaluated at the University of Washington [3,4] and by our own research group [1,2,10]. While [3] is one of the few systems designed for co-located collaboration, it is still a sophisticated, yet traditional videoconference system intended for visual and audio communication.

Quite different from these applications is the GroupWear system designed at MIT [5]. GroupWear is a computationally augmented nametag capable of providing information about relationships between two people in a face-to-face conversation. GroupWear uses infrared transmitters to exchange personal profile information during face-to-face conversations. In contrast to our work, however, the interaction between nametags is rigid and does not involve negotiation.

Proem [9], a system developed at our lab, is the precursor to the work described in this paper. Proem is based on the notion of *personal profiles*, which are exchanged whenever two or more wearable users encounter each other. It is very similar to the system we described here, in that it supports cooperation during face-to-face encounters. However, it lacks the concept of negotiation, and instead only supports the simple exchange of personal information. It is then up to the individual user to decide how to make use of this information.

Our research on communities is related to the notion of *community computing,* a concept that was coined by Toru Ishida [6,7] at Kyoto University. Community computing deals with the creation, maintenance, and evolution of social interaction in communities. Community computing is intended to support more diverse and amorphous groups of people than traditional groupware, and supports the process of organizing people who are willing to share some mutual understanding and experiences. In other words, community computing focuses on the group formation stage. In a similar approach, Hattori et al [26] describe a multiagent system for supporting network communities.

Many of the theoretical foundations of game theory and cooperation have been formulated by John Von Neumann and Oskar Morgenstern [15], and John F. Nash in the late 40th [13,14]. For most of our treatment of agent cooperation, we follow Jeffrey S. Rosenschein and Giliad Zlotkin [16]. Their approach is somewhat unique in that they apply analytical techniques and modeling methods from the world of game theory and decision analysis to the dynamic organization of autonomous intelligent agents. Their rigorous analysis of agent systems provides a formal basis for research in agent interaction. However, they are solely concerned with the interaction between machines without interference of human intervention. The domains they analyze are necessarily simple compared to interactions that we would like to create in a wearable agent community.

7   Conclusion and Outlook

The notion of Cyborgs, communities of Cyborgs, and Collective Intelligence has been around at least as long as wearable computers have become feasible. Yet, today's wearable users largely live a lonely and disconnected life. Other than email, interaction with fellow Cyborgs is limited to the old fashioned way – through unmediated and un-augmented face-to-face conversation. We are working on the creation of communities of wearable users where opportunistic personal agents embedded in wearable computers cooperate on behalf of and in the interest of their 'owners'. We are particularly interested in how this technology can be used to enable goal-directed cooperation during encounters of people with selfish and conflicting goals, such that cooperation leads to mutually beneficial results.

In the preceding sections, we have done three things: first, we put forward a theoretical framework for building communities of cooperating wearable agents. Second, we described the initial implementation of a wearable agent device; finally we described a simulator that we use to develop and analyze negotiation protocols and strategies.

There are many areas for future work. The first step towards building cooperating wearable communities is the creation of the actual hardware and software systems that are able to establish communication with other wearable device in an ad-hoc manner. Future development in wireless networking (short-range wireless networks and body-LANs) will certainly contribute to this.

Much more unclear is how to set up a network of rules that guides the interaction of these agents. We believe we made a first step towards this goal by defining properties and characteristics of agents and their interaction. This includes notions like goal-directed and opportunistic behavior and the distinction between negotiation protocols and strategies (which we borrowed from [16]).

The development and evaluation of such protocols is made difficult by the highly distributed nature of a wearable community and the fact that agent negotiation becomes part of the social environment of its owner. We thus believe that simulating large-scale wearable communities on the computer is the only feasible way to derive agent protocols for wearable communities.

Finally, it is important to note that with the work described herein we do not propose replacing human interaction with agent interaction. The task of personal agents in a wearable community is to identify opportunities for possible cooperation and to propose them to their users. Whether or not two individuals ultimately want to cooperate depends on a careful consideration of potential benefits and risks based on their own personal judgment.

We are now pursuing continued research in the directions opened up in this paper, including the development of new negotiation protocols and the improvement of the WALID simulator.

References

[1] Bauer, Martin; Heiber, Timo; Kortuem, Gerd; Segall, Zary. *A Collaborative Wearable System with Remote Sensing.* Proceedings Second International Symposium on Wearable Computers, Oct 19-20, 1998, Pittsburgh, PA

[2] Bauer, Martin; Kortuem, Gerd; Segall, Zary. *"Where Are You Pointing At?" A Study of Remote Collaboration in a Wearable Videoconference System.* Proceedings Third International Symposium on Wearable Computers (poster), Oct 18-19, 1999, San Francisco, CA.

[3] Billinghurst, M.; Weghorst, S., and Furness, T. *A. Wearable Computers for Three-Dimensional CSCW.* First International Symposium on Wearable Computing; 1997; Boston, MA.

[4] Billinghurst, M; Bowskill, M.; Jessop, M., and Morphett, J. *A Wearable Spatial Conferencing Space.* Proceedings of the Second International Symposium on Wearable Computers; 1998 Oct; Pittsburgh, PA.

[5] Borovoy, R., Martin, F., Vemuri, S., Resnick, M., Silverman, B. and Hancock, C. (1998b) Meme Tags and Community Mirrors: Moving from Conferences to Collaboration. In *Proceedings of CSCW '98*, ACM Press.

[6] Ishida, Toru, "Towards Communityware," *International Conference and Exhibition on the Practical Application of Intelligent Agents and Multi-Agent Technology (PAAM-97)*, Invited Talk, pp. 7-21, 1997.

[7] Ishida, Toru Ed., *Community Computing: Collaboration over Global Information Networks*, John Wiley and Sons, 1998.

[8] Kraut, Robert E.; Miller, Mark D., and Siegel, Jane: *Collaboration in Performance of Physical Tasks: Effects on Outcomes and Communication.* Computer Supported Cooperative Work '96 Cambridge, MA, USA: ACM; 1996.

[9] Kortuem, Gerd; Segall; Zary; Cowan Thompson, Thaddeus G. *Close Encounters: Supporting Mobile Cooperation Through Interchange of User Profiles* . 1st International Conference on Handheld and Ubiquitous Computing (HUC), September 1999, Karlsruhe, Germany.

[10] Kortuem, Gerd; Bauer, Martin; Heiber, Timo; Segall, Zary. *Netman: The Design of a Collaborative Wearable Computer System.* ACM/Baltzer Journal on Mobile Networks and Applications (MONET), 1999.

[11] Rhodes, B. *The Wearable Remembrance Agent: A System for Augmented Memory.* Proceedings of the First International Symposium on Wearable Computers (ISWC'97), Cambridge, MA, October 1997.

[12] Siegel, J., Kraut, R.E.., John, B.E., Carley, K.M. *An Empirical Study of Collaborative Wearable Systems*, CHI Companion 1995, Denver, Colorado, 312-313.

[13] Nash, John F.. The Bargaining Problem. *Econometricia*, 28:155-162, 1950.

[14] Nash, John F. Two-person cooperative games. *Econometricia*, 21:128-140, 1953.

[15] Von Neumann, John; Morgenstern, Oskar. *Theory of Games and Economic Behavior.* Princeton University Press, Princeton, 1947.

[16] Rosenschein, Jeffrey S.; Zlotkin, Giliad. *Rules of Encounter, Designing Conventions for Automated Negotiation among Computers.* MIT Press, Cambridge Massachusetts, 1994

[17] Siewiorek, D.; Smailagic, A.; Bass, L. ; Siegel, J.; Martin, R. and Bennington, B. *Adtranz: A Mobile Computing System for Maintenance and Collaboration.* Proc. of the 2nd International Symposium on Wearable Computers; 1998 Oct; Pittsburgh, PA

[18] Zimmerman, T. G. *Personal Area Networks: Near-field Intrabody Communication*, IBM Systems Journal, Vol. 35, No. 3&4, 1996

[19] Sun Microsystems. http://www.javasoft.com/products/jini

[20] Radiomatrix Inc. http://www.radiomatrix.co.uk

[21] Huhn , Michael N.; Mohame, Abdulla; *Benevolent Agents.* IEEE Internet Computing, March-April 1999, p.96-98.

[22] *Bluetooth* Consortium web site, http://www.bluetooth.org.

[24] Schneider, Jay; Suruda, Jim; Fickas, Steve. *Modeling Agent Negotiation in a Task Oriented Domain.* Proceedings Third International Symposium on Wearable Computers (poster), Oct 18-19, 1999, San Francisco, CA.

[25] P. Maes, R. Guttman and A. Moukas. *Agents that Buy and Sell: Transforming Commerce as we Know It. Communications of the ACM*, March 1999 Issue.

[26] Hattori, Fumio; Ohguro, Takeshi; Yokoo, Makoto; Matsubara, Shigeo; Yoshida, Sen. *Socialware: Multiagent Systems for Supporting Network Communities. Communications of the ACM*, March 1999 Issue.

Asymmetries in Collaborative Wearable Interfaces

M. Billinghurst[α], S. Bee[β], J. Bowskill[β], H. Kato[α]

[α]Human Interface Technology Laboratory
University of Washington
Box 352-142
Seattle, WA 98195
USA

[β]Advanced Communications Research
BT Laboratories
Martlesham Heath
Ipswich, IP5 3RE
United Kingdom

{grof,kato}@hitl.washington.edu {jerry.bowskill, simon.bee}@bt.com

Abstract

Communication asymmetries are inherent in collaborative dialogues between wearable computer and desktop users. This paper gives a definition and overview of what communication asymmetries are and their potential impact on the design of collaborative wearable interfaces. We also review results from collaborations with two asymmetric interfaces and present a set of implications for developers of collaborative wearable interfaces.

1. Introduction

Wearable computers provide new opportunities for communication and collaboration, particularly in mobile applications. Several applications using wearable computers have already demonstrated the benefit of collaborative wearable interfaces. For example, Siegel et al. [11] found that the presence of a remote expert collaborating with a wearable user enabled subjects to work more effectively than working alone. Similarly, Kraut et. al. [7] examined subjects performing a bicycle repair task with a wearable display, head mounted camera and wireless link to a computer with a help manual. They found that subjects completed repairs twice as fast and with fewer errors with the assistance of a remote expert compared to using the help manual alone. Garner et. al. [3] and Steve Mann [9], among others, have developed similar examples of collaborative wearable systems that use shared video, audio and text.

In all these settings, the collaboration has been between a pair of participants, one with a wearable computer, the other at a desktop workstation. Indeed, one of the natural applications for wearable computers is to provide just in time assistance between a deskbound expert and a mobile fieldworker with wearable computer.

However, collaboration in this setting is very different from engaging in traditional video conferencing; the use of disparate technology by each participant results in the introduction of asymmetries in the communication. For example, in Kraut's task the user with the wearable display broadcast images of the task space back to the remote expert, while the remote expert sent back either video of their face or no video at all.

Although there has been considerable study of mediated communication outside of the field of wearable computing, this has generally been with the tacit assumption that all the participants are using the same interface. This is often not the case in collaboration between desktop and wearable computer users. In this paper we elaborate on the concept of asymmetries in collaborative interfaces and present preliminary results from several pilot studies. We are initially focussed on collaboration between two geographically remote users, one with a wearable computer, one with a desktop. However the concepts presented in the paper should be more widely applicable.

2. Communication Asymmetries

We define communication asymmetries as an imbalance in communication introduced by the interface used for communication, the expertise or roles of the people communicating, or the task undertaken.

Using this broad definition it is obvious that there are many possible types of communication asymmetries in collaborative wearable applications. In order to more fully understand the possibilities that could arise we present a simple example of a typical collaborative wearable system. Figure 1 shows a schematic of a wearable user with a head mounted display, microphone and camera collaborating with a desktop user with a monitor, microphone and camera.

133

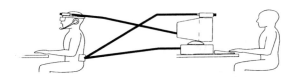

Fig 1. Wearable and desktop collaboration

If both users have the same ability to share audio, video and desktop applications then (using Bauer's definition [1]) there is symmetry in collaborative functions they can perform, i.e. *functional symmetry*. However one or more capabilities could be removed from either user to introduce *functional asymmetries*; the wearable user may be able to send video/images, but the desktop user may not have a camera to send images back. Similarly, even though the users may have the same functional capabilities they may have different physical interface properties; the resolution of the head-mounted display may be different from the desktop users monitor. We call this an *implementation asymmetry*.

If both users converse using only audio then they can share the same conversational cues. We call this *social symmetry*. However if the desktop user sends video of his face, while the wearable user sends video of the real world only one person can respond to facial non-verbal signals so *social asymmetries* are introduced.

If both users are trying to collaborate on the same task (such as collaborative sketching), and they have an equal role as collaborators and have access to the same information, then there are *task* and *information symmetries*. However if the wearable user is trying to complete a real world task and the desktop user trying to help then *task asymmetries* are introduced. The wearable user is trying to focus on the real world, while the desktop user is trying to build a mental model of the real world using the sensor data provided by the wearable user's computer. Similarly if the desktop user is an expert providing remote technical assistance to the novice wearable user, *information asymmetries* occur.

We believe that because of the disparate hardware used it is impossible to design interfaces for collaboration between a desktop and wearable computer without introducing communication asymmetries. However, by understanding these asymmetries then any damaging effect they may have on communication can be minimized.

3. Background

The majority of previous teleconferencing research has assumed that users have access to the same conferencing hardware, implying functional and implementation symmetries. Even in this case the technology introduces communicative asymmetries. Gaver discusses the affordances of media spaces describing among other things how video conferencing systems restrict peripheral vision [4]. As Heath and Luff point out, the lack of peripheral vision causes certain actions to lose their communicative impact when performed through video [5]. Thus looks, glances and gestures pass unnoticed by their intended recipients. Similar effects are seen in immersive virtual environments [6]. These effects cause Sellen to conclude that mediated collaboration will always be different from face to face collaboration [10].

Given this conclusion we can also explore how wearable systems introduce further asymmetries. In Kuzuoka's Shared View project [8] a remote instructor taught a technician how to operate a numerically controlled milling machine. The student wore a head-mounted camera and display that was used to overlay the instructor's gestures over video of what the student was seeing. They found that collaboration was most effective when instructor and student could share a common viewpoint and both the instructor and student could use gestures with speech, suggesting that functionally symmetric interfaces improve collaboration.

However, in the bicycle repair project of Kraut et. al. [7], they found there was no performance difference between the condition where both participants could use audio to communicate, or the functionally asymmetric condition where only the remote expert could use audio. They also found that varying the visual and auditory affordances did affect communication measures, such as how proactive the expert was in giving help. In both this case and Kuzuoka's the expert has more information and expertise available than the technicians with the wearable interface.

The experiments of Steed et. al. [12] compared collaboration between three subjects in a multi-user virtual environment and face to face meeting. In the virtual environment only one of these users were immersed using a head mounted display, while the others used a desktop interface, but they all had the same capability to navigate and interact with the virtual environment. They found that the immersed subject tended to emerge as leader in the virtual group, but the same person wasn't necessarily the leader in the face to face meeting. Thus, the implementation asymmetry may have effected the roles played out by group members in that experiment.

These results suggest that asymmetries can be introduced even when the physical interfaces and the roles of the collaborators are the same. In some cases these asymmetries may affect the nature of collaboration and task performance, while in others they have little effect. Obviously more research is needed to gain an understanding of the effect of communication asymmetries inherent in wearable interfaces. In the next section we present results from two pilot studies examining the effects of common asymmetries in collaborative wearable systems.

4. Preliminary Pilot Studies

In our research we have developed a number of interfaces that explore two types of collaboration:

- A wearable and desktop user collaborating on the same task with access to the same information.
- A wearable user engaged in a real world task getting help from a remote desktop expert.

In the first case, both users have equal roles and access to the same information. Thus the information flowing between the users should be symmetric and both interfaces should maximize data display and ease of collaboration.

In the second case the users are effectively engaged in two separate tasks; the wearable user in the real world task, the remote expert in creating a mental model of the real world task and providing effective assistance. The wearable user is largely responsible for data collection and sensing while the remote expert is responsible for providing expertise and higher level knowledge. Thus information flows between the users are different and there are different minimum interface requirements. The remote expert's interface should maximize the amount of data displayed from the wearable, while the wearable interface should maximize the ease of collaboration.

Considering this we have two hypotheses:

- When both the wearable and desktop users have the same task requirements and information access, then asymmetries may hurt collaboration.
- A wearable user will be able to collaborate effectively with a remote expert provided the functional, and implementation asymmetries match the task and information asymmetries.

In the remainder of this section we describe two pilot studies which explore these hypotheses further.

4.1. Asymmetric Mismatch

In this first experiment we introduced a number of asymmetries into a collaborative interface and examined the effect on user behavior. This was accomplished by comparing asymmetric conferencing between an augmented reality (AR) and desktop interface, with more traditional symmetric audio and video conferencing.

Augmented Reality Interface

The user with the AR interface wears a pair of the Virtual i-O iglasses head mounted display (HMD) and a small color camera. The iglasses are full color, see-through and have a resolution of 263x234 pixels. The camera output is connected to an SGI O2 computer and the video out of the SGI connected back into the HMD. The O2 is used for image processing of video from the camera and generating virtual images at 10-15 fps.

Fig 2. Using the AR Interface

They also have a set of small marked user ID cards, one for each remote collaborator with their name written on it (figure 2). To initiate communication, the user looks at the card representing the remote collaborator. Computer vision techniques are then used to identify specific users (using the user name on the card) and display a life-sized video view or a 3D virtual avatar of the remote user. Vision techniques are used to calculate head position and orientation relative to the cards so the virtual images are precisely registered [9] (figure 3).

Fig 3. Remote user in the AR interface.

They also have a virtual shared whiteboard (figure 3), shown on a larger card with six registration markings. Virtual annotations written by remote participants and 2D images are displayed on it, exactly aligned with the plane of the physical card. Users can pick up the card for a closer look at the images, and can position it freely within their real workspace.

Desktop Interface

The wearable user collaborates with a user at a desktop interface. This interface has a video window of the image that the desktop camera is sending, the remote video from the AR user's head mounted camera and a shared white board application (figure 4). The video view from the AR user's head mounted camera enables the desktop user to collaborate on real world tasks. Users can also talk to each other using VAT, a program which enables audio communication between remote machines.

The shared white board application consisted of small views of five pictures as well as a large view of the currently active picture (figure 4). Clicking with the left mouse button on a picture changed the active picture to that picture. In the AR interface the selected picture was shown on the virtual whiteboard. The currently active picture could be drawn on by holding down the left mouse button, while the right mouse button erased the user's annotations. Either user could change the pictures or make annotations.

Fig 4. Desktop User Interface

Asymmetry Experiment

We compared collaboration with the AR and desktop interfaces to more traditional audio and video conferencing in three conditions:

Audio Only (AO): Subjects were able to speak and hear each other using headphones and wireless microphones, and collaboratively view and annotate pictures on a simple desktop application (figure 4).

Video Conferencing (VC): In addition to the conditions above, a desktop video conferencing application was used to show live video of the remote collaborator.

Augmented Reality (AR): One of the subjects was using the AR interface described above. The other subject was using the desktop interface of figure 4. The desktop user could also see video from the AR user's head-mounted camera, giving them a remote view of the AR users desktop.

Referring to our original classification, in the audio and video conferencing conditions both users have the same interface and so have symmetric communication conditions. However, in the AR condition we introduce three clear types of asymmetry:

- *Functional Asymmetries:* The AR user can see a virtual video window of the desktop user's face, but the desktop user sees the AR user's workspace, not their face.
- *Implementation Asymmetries:* The AR user sees images on a HMD, while the desktop user sees them on a monitor.
- *Social Asymmetries:* The AR user can see and respond to their partners non-verbal facial and gestural cues, while the desktop user primarily relies on voice.

If our first hypothesis is valid then we should expect these asymmetries to affect collaboration.

Procedure

There were 12 pairs of subjects from 19 to 45 years old; six pairs of males, three of females and three mixed pairs. They did not know each other and were unfamiliar with the application and collaborative task. After each condition subjects were given a communication survey, and after all the conditions they were asked to fill out an overall ease of communication survey.

A within subjects design was used. Each of the subject pairs experienced all three conditions. Subjects were told that they were to act as art buyers for a large art gallery. For each of the conditions they had to decide together which three pictures out of a set of five that the gallery should buy and the reasons why. Each subject was also give a paper copy of the five pictures they were considering in each condition, enabling them to see a higher resolution version of the images.

Before the experiment began subjects received training on how to use the desktop interface and also spent a few minutes in each condition with a sample set of pictures. In the AR condition, both subjects tried the HMD and desktop interface for a few minutes so they could gain an understanding of what the other user was experiencing during the actual experiment. For each condition subjects were given 10 minutes to complete the task, although in some cases they finished ahead of time. The order of conditions and the images used in each condition were varied to reduce order effects.

Survey Results

We differentiated each subject of the pair according to whether they were at the desktop for all conditions (No-HMD), or if they wore the HMD in the AR condition (HMD). In general the survey scores given by the HMD and No-HMD subjects for each condition were very similar, but varied across condition.

Overall, subjects felt that the AR condition was more difficult to communicate in than the audio only (AO) and videoconferencing conditions (VC). Figure 5 shows a graph of average subject responses to the question on overall communication; *Rate each communication mode according to how much effort you felt it was to converse effectively (0=Very Hard, 14=Very Easy).*

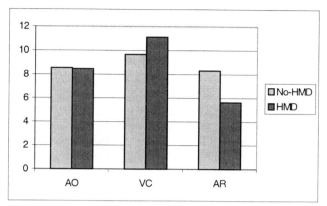

Fig 5: Communication Effort Across Conditions

Using a two factor (subject, condition) repeated measures ANOVA, we find a significant difference in scores between conditions ($F_{(2,47)}=4.19$, $P<0.05$), but not between subjects ($F_{(1,47)}=0.20$, $P=0.65$).

A similar result is found in the communication survey given at the end of every condition. Table 1 shows the average response to the statement *"I was very aware of the presence of my conversational partner" (0=Disagree, 14=Agree)*. The AR condition is given a co-presence rating between that of the audio and video conferencing conditions. Using a two factor repeated measures ANOVA, we find a significant difference in scores between conditions ($F_{(2,47)}=4.99$, $P<0.05$), but not between subjects ($F_{(1,47)}=0.01$, $P=0.90$).

	AO	VC	AR
No-HMD	8.06	11.93	10.06
HMD	9.99	11.58	8.78

Table 1: Average Co-Presence Score

Subjects also felt that the visual cues provided by the AR condition were not as useful as the cues provided by the video conferencing condition for determining if their collaborator was busy. Table 2 shows the average scores in response to the question; *"I could readily tell when my partner was occupied and not looking at me"*. Using a two factor repeated measures ANOVA, we find a significant difference in scores between conditions ($F_{(2,47)}=15.70$, $P<0.01$), but not between subjects ($F_{(1,47)}=0.40$, $P=0.70$). Both the video and AR conditions were rated significantly higher than the audio.

	AO	VC	AR
No-HMD	3.18	11.56	6.13
HMD	2.27	9.04	8.29

Table 2: Average Awareness Scores

Finally, figure 6 shows the average response to the statement *"The mode of communication aided work"*. As can be seen the AR condition is again rated less helpful than both the audio and video conferencing conditions. A two factor repeated measures ANOVA finds a near significant difference in scores both between conditions ($F_{(2,47)}=3.17$, $P=0.054$), but not between subjects ($F_{(1,47)}=0.04$, $P=0.80$).

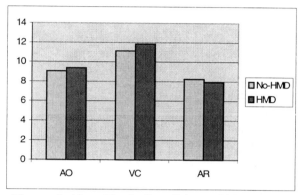

Figure 6: How Much Conditions Aided Work

Subject Comments

Several subjects commented on the asymmetries introduced by the AR interface. Most of these comments were about the functional asymmetry of the interface. Some desktop users found it disconcerting that the AR user could see them, but they couldn't see the AR user. They also felt uncomfortable seeing their own face in the task space video sent back by the AR user and said that set up an "unequal relationship". The virtual image of the remote person was also seen as distracting by some people, especially when it flickered in and out of sight due to the narrow field of view of the head mounted display.

Discussion

In this experiment subjects were given the same task and access to the same information. However in the AR condition functional, implementation and social asymmetries were present. As these results show these significantly impacted how well the subjects felt they could collaborate together, in some cases causing the subject to feel the AR condition was even less useful than audio alone. These results seem to support our theory that if the roles of the collaborators are the same then combinations of functional, implementation and social asymmetries may impede the collaboration.

4.2. Asymmetric Matching

The second study explored asymmetries in interfaces designed for collaboration between a desktop expert and wearable user. As previously discussed, this situation already introduces task and information asymmetries. However we hypothesized that if the functional and implementation asymmetries matched these asymmetries then collaboration would not be affected.

Experimental Task

The goal of the wearable user was to construct plastic models out of an Erector set with the help of a remote desk-bound expert. The wearable user wore a Virtual i-O head mounted display modified by removing one eyepiece to be monocular, and a small video camera. The remote expert used a desktop computer (an SGI O2) on which was shown the video from the head-mounted camera and a shared image browser application (figure 7). The shared image browser was developed using the TeamWave toolkit [13] and enabled images to be uploaded and drawn on. The expert could also annotate on the live video. Video output from the O2 was fed back into the head mounted display via a video switching box. This enabled the wearable user to switch between either views of the annotated camera image, or the image browser application. A full duplex audio connection between users was also provided.

Fig 7. Expert and Wearable User Collaborating

Using this interface we wanted to explore further the effect of asymmetries on collaboration by varying the video frame rates that each user saw. If our second hypothesis is correct then performing a task with varying video frame rates should more severely affect the remote expert who is focussing on the wearable users task space through the desktop interface than the wearable user who is focussing on the real world itself.

Procedure

The task was for the wearable user to build an Erector set model with expert guidance from the remote user under the following four video frame rates; 0 frames per second (FPS) (audio only communication), ¼ FPS, 1

FPS, and 30 FPS. For each of these four conditions the wearable user would initially begin building the model with no help and using incomplete instructions from the Erector set instruction booklet. After 5 minutes, communication with the remote expert would be allowed and then the expert would assist the wearable user for the next 10 minutes using the complete instruction book. This was to simulate a real-world remote technical assistance call. The expert was able to aid the wearable user by annotating their video of the task space and by uploading images from the model instruction booklet into the shared image browser.

Eight pairs of subjects took part in the pilot study, 14 men and 2 women, aged 18 to 28. Each group went through each of the four frame rate conditions with four different Erector set models. The order or sequence of the three video-present conditions was randomized to minimize the effect of learning on our results. Before the experiment began they were trained on a separate model until they felt comfortable with erector set construction.

The outcome of the collaboration was measured by the completeness of the models (number of steps finished), and a questionnaire asking for opinions about how easy it was to collaborate in each condition and other interface aspects.

Performance

There was no significant difference in performance across conditions. Table 3 summarizes the number of steps completed on each model for each of the frame rates. Using a single factor ANOVA, we found no significant difference between the number of steps completed across frame rate conditions (Single Factor ANOVA, $F_{(3,20)} = 2.50$, P value = 0.065).

	0 fps	1/4 fps	1 fps	30 fps
Steps	5.75	3.50	4.75	4.67

Table 3: Average Number of Steps Completed.

Subjective

The expert and wearable user had different subjective experiences with the collaborative interface. After each condition they were asked to rate the answers to a number of questions on a scale of 1 to 10, where 1 was Ineffective and 10 Very Effective. The first three questions on the user questionnaire were:

(Q1) *Did the interface enable you to effectively understand the wearable user situation/be understood by the expert?*

(Q2) *Did the interface enable you to effectively understand questions/ communicate questions?*

(Q3) *Did the interface provide an effective means to give/get guidance?*

A single factor ANOVA was used to compare between the average subject scores for each question. Table 4 shows the average answers for each of these questions across the different frame rates, the ANOVA F statistic (F(3,28)) and resulting P significance value.

	0	¼	1	30	F stat.	P Value
Q1*	4.88	6.16	6.76	8.38	2.95	P<0.01
Q2*	4.17	5.67	6.25	8.38	8.05	P<0.01
Q3*	4.29	6.33	7.38	8.46	8.93	P<0.01

Table 4a: Average Expert Response

	0	¼	1	30	F stat.	P Value
Q1*	6.08	6.35	7.92	8.21	3.22	P<0.05
Q2*	6.50	5.75	7.29	8.0	3.49	P<0.05
Q3*	4.90	5.83	7.67	7.83	4.87	P<0.05

Table 4b: Average Wearable User Response

As can be seen from these tables all the responses are significantly different. Subjects felt that as the frame rate increased they could understand the situation better (Q1), communicate more effectively (Q3) and give and get guidance more effectively (Q2). In the wearable users case there was little difference between ranking on these questions between 1 and 30 fps, while the expert always ranked the 30 fps case much higher than the 1 fps case.

This difference is particularly noticeable in the answers to question 5; *What degree of co-presence did you feel with the expert/wearable user (1=None, 10=Very Present)?* Figure 8 shows the average scores for the expert and wearable user across the different frame rates. A single factor ANOVA gives a significant difference between the experts' co-present ratings (F(3,28) = 9.38, P< 0.05), but not for the wearable user (F(3,28) = 2.95, P = 0.35).

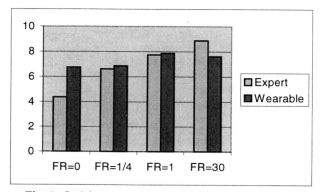

Fig 8. Subject ratings of Co-Presence (Q5).

Interface Components:

Subjects were also asked to rank how helpful the individual interface components were on a scale of 1 to 10 (1 = little help, 10 = very helpful). For the expert the interface components were audio (A), video of the task

space (TS), shared graphics images (SG), the ability to annotate on the graphics images (AG), and the ability to annotate on the video image (AV). While the wearable user considered the following components; audio (A), the expert view of task space (EV), and the shared graphics image (SG). Table 3a shows the expert users' average ratings for each of the components, the ANOVA F statistic (F(3,28)) and the resulting P significance values. Table 5b shows the wearable users' component ratings.

	0	¼	1	30	F stat	P values
A	8.50	8.88	9.34	9.50	2.94	0.22
TS*	NA	4.38	7.38	8.63	8.38	< 0.01
SG	5.57	5.00	6.14	5.71	3.01	0.87
AG	4.71	4.00	5.14	6.00	3.01	0.44
AV*	NA	4.42	6.57	8.43	8.50	< 0.01

Table 5a: Expert Ratings of Interface

	0	¼	1	30	F stat	P values
A	9.00	8.75	9.00	9.25	2.95	0.88
EV	NA	7.13	8.13	8.38	3.47	0.25
SG	7.87	6.00	6.42	6.14	3.01	0.29

Table 5b: Wearable User Interface Ratings

As can be seen there are no significant differences between wearable user ratings for interface components across different frame rates. However the remote expert found the video of the task space and the ability to annotate on the video significantly more useful as the frame rate increased.

Both the wearable user and expert rated audio as the most helpful interface component. Using a two factor (frame rate, interface component) repeated measures ANOVA we can compare ratings for the different interface components. Doing this for the wearable user we find no significant difference between frame rates (F(2,63)=0.32, P = 0.74), but a highly significant difference in results between interface components (F(2,63)=21.64, P<0.001). Similarly, for the expert user we find a highly significant difference both between frame rates (F(2,90)=15.15, P <0.001), and between interface components (F(4,90)=16.69, P<0.001).

Discussion

These results agree with our second hypothesis. The wearable users felt they could collaborate equally well with 1 fps video as with 30 fps video, while the experts felt they needed high video frame rates for more effective collaboration. Similarly the experts rated the video view of the task space and the ability to draw on the video significantly more useful as the frame rate increased, while the wearable user thought the usefulness of the experts view didn't change as the frame rate increased. This implies that the expert and wearable user should be able to collaborate together effectively if there is the functional asymmetry of low frame rate video (1 fps) from the expert to the wearable user and high frame rate (30 fps) the other way. Thus if the functional asymmetries in the wearable interface match the task and information asymmetries collaboration may not necessarily be affected.

5. Conclusions

Computer mediated communication is fundamentally different from face to face communication and collaboration between a wearable computer user and a desktop user introduces a wide range of inherent asymmetries into the communication. In this paper we have described some of the possible asymmetries that may occur and presented results from pilot studies exploring various asymmetries.

Although our results are very tentative, it seems that the effect of communication asymmetries depends largely on the roles of the collaborators and nature of the task that they're engaged in. In the first study, when users both had equal roles, they felt that the differences between the interfaces impeded their ability to communicate, compared to traditional teleconferencing systems. In the second study, the asymmetries matched the differences in roles and so had less of an impact.

One implication from this is that designers of collaborative wearable interfaces need to match the interface capabilities to the roles of the users. For example, in supporting collaboration between a wearable user and remote desktop expert in a technical assistance role, half duplex high bandwidth video may be sufficient. Secondly, interface designers need to evaluate carefully the impact of providing additional communication cues. For example, in the first experiment adding visual communication cues in the AR condition did not improve performance over the audio only case. Finally, interface designers need to use a multifaceted approach to measure the impact of communication asymmetries. In our experiments, the interface differences affected measures of co-presence, awareness, communication effort and communication effectiveness.

In the future we plan to carry out more controlled studies to further characterize the effect of communication asymmetries. We will be particularly focussing on wearable interfaces that facilitate optimal collaboration between a worker in the field and a deskbound expert.

6. References

[1] Bauer, M., Heiber, T., Kortuem, G., Segall, Z. A Collaborative Wearable System with Remote Sensing. In proceedings of ISWC 1998, pp. 10-17.

[2] Billinghurst, M., Kato, H., Weghorst, S., Furness, T. *A Mixed Reality 3D Conferencing Application.* Technical Report R-99-1, 1999, Human Interface Technology Laboratory, University of Washington.

[3] Garner, P., Collins, M., Webster, S., and Rose, D. "The application of telepresence in medicine," *BT Technology Journal,* Vol. 15, No 4, October 1997, pp.181-187.

[4] Gaver, W. The affordances of media spaces for collaboration. CSCW '92. Sharing Perspectives. Proceedings of the Conference on Computer-Supported Cooperative Work. Toronto, Ont., Canada. pp. 17-24. ACM. 31 Oct.-4 Nov. 1992.

[5] Heath, C., Luff, P. Disembodied Conduct: Communication Through Video in a Multi-Media Office Environment. In proceedings of CHI 91, 1991, pp. 99-103.

[6] Hindmarsh, J., Fraser, M., Heath, C., Benford, S., Greenhalgh, C. Fragmented Interaction: Establishing mutual orientation in virtual environments. In Proceedings of CSCW 98, 1998, pp. 217-226.

[7] Kraut, R., Miller, M., Siegal, J. Collaboration in Performance of Physical Tasks: Effects on Outcomes and Communication. In *Proceedings of CSCW '96*, Nov. 16th-20th, Cambridge MA, 1996, New York, NY: ACM Press.

[8] Kuzuoka, H. Spatial Workspace Collaboration: A Sharedview Video Support System for Remote Collaboration Capability. In Proceedings of CHI 92, May 3-7, 1992, pp. 533-540.

[9] Mann, S., "`Smart Clothing': Wearable Multimedia Computing and `Personal Imaging' to Restore the Technological Balance Between People and Their Environments". <http://wearcam.org/acm-mm96/>

[10] Sellen, A. Remote Conversations: The effects of mediating talk with technology. *Human Computer Interaction*, 1995, Vol. 10, No. 4, pp. 401-444.

[11] Siegal, J., Kraut, R., John, B., Carley, K. An Empirical Study of Collaborative Wearable Computer Systems,. In *Proceedings of CHI 95 Conference Companion,* May 7-11, Denver Colorado, 1995, ACM: New York, pp. 312-313.

[12] Steed, A., Slater, M., Sadagic, A., Bullock, A., Tromp. J. Leadership and Collaboration in Shared Virtual Environments. In Proceedings of VR 99, 1999, pp. 112-115. IEEE Press.

[13] TeamWave Web Site http://www.teamwave.com

Wearable Computing Meets Ubiquitous Computing: Reaping the best of both worlds

Bradley J. Rhodes, Nelson Minar and Josh Weaver

MIT Media Lab

20 Ames St., Cambridge MA 02139

{rhodes | nelson | joshw}@media.mit.edu

Abstract

This paper describes what we see as fundamental difficulties in both the pure ubiquitous computing and pure wearable computing paradigms when applied to context-aware applications. In particular, ubiquitous computing and smart room systems tend to have difficulties with privacy and personalization, while wearable systems have trouble with localized information, localized resource control, and resource management between multiple people. These difficulties are discussed, and a peer-to-peer network of wearable and ubiquitous computing components is proposed as a solution. This solution is demonstrated through several implemented applications.

1 Introduction

Ubiquitous computing and wearable computing have been posed as polar opposites even though they are often applied in very similar applications. Here we first outline the advantages and disadvantages of each and propose that the two perspectives have complementary problems. We then attempt to demonstrate that the failing of both ubiquitous and wearable computing can be alleviated by the development of systems that properly mix the two. This concept is demonstrated by the description of several applications that have been developed using Hive, a distributed agent architecture that supports peer-to-peer messaging for creating decentralized systems

1.1 Ubiquitous Computing

When Mark Weiser coined the phrase "ubiquitous computing" in 1988 he envisioned computers embedded in walls, in tabletops, and in everyday objects. In ubiquitous computing, a person might interact with hundreds of computers at a time, each invisibly embedded in the environment and wirelessly communicating with each other [1]. Closely related to the ubiquitous computing vision is the more centralized idea of smart rooms, where a room might contain multiple sensors that keep track of the comings and goings of the people around [2].

Many applications have been demonstrated in ubiquitous computing and smart rooms. Some of these have concentrated on intelligent configuration of an environment based on who is in the room. For example, air conditioners and lights might automatically turn off when no one is in the room, or blinds may open and close depending on natural light levels in the room [3]. Other applications have implemented what is called *proximate selection* interfaces, where objects that are nearby are automatically easier to select. For example, a print command might automatically default to the nearest printer [4]. In a similar vein is the presentation of contextual information, where information or annotations about a particular location or object are automatically displayed to a person when she enters an area. Finally, systems have been created that watch a user's location and actions and store that information in an automatic diary [5].

1.2 Problems with ubiquitous computing

In the purest form of ubiquitous computing, all computation is contained in the environment rather than on the person. This extreme has several problems.

- **Privacy issues**: Probably the most important problem is that ubiquitous computing environments pose serious privacy risks. By watching everything a user does these systems have the potential to leak all our actions, preferences, and locations to others unknown to us, now or in the future. Unfortunately it seems to be a truism

141

that the most useful information is also the most personal. For example, several experiments at Xerox PARC, EuroPARC, and the Olivetti Research Center used active badge systems to support location-based information and collaboration. In these systems, participants wear badges that broadcast their location to sensors positioned in each room [6]. The researchers suggested a combination of both technical and social mechanisms to help address this problem. However, as Foner points out [7], sometimes good security and a strong corporate privacy policy is not enough to protect a person's privacy. Central databases are a prime target for subpoena, and the more places that sensitive information resides the more potential places there are to compromise that information. Finally, there are always situations where someone should not trust the environment to keep her information secure. One case is in the customer-provider relationship, where we already have seen a large interest in logging customer profiles and buying habits to increase sales. Another case is when entering a hostile environment. For example, if a businessman is entering a competitors company to negotiate a contract, he probably would not like all his personal profile information to automatically be uploaded to their system where it might be viewed to gain an unfair advantage.

- **Difficulty with personalized information**: The second problem is that it is often difficult to maintain personalization of ubiquitous computing system. In the worst case, every time a new person joins a work-group or community her personal profile needs to be added to every device. Even if all the devices and environments on a campus share a personal profile database, profiles need to be updated every time she moves to a new site.

1.3 Wearable computing to the rescue (?)

The wearable perspective suggests that instead of putting sensors and cameras in the room, put them on the person. In the purest form, the wearable user would do all detection and sensing on her body, requiring no environmental infrastructure at all.

Wearables offer a solution to most of the problems mentioned above. Because the wearable always travels with the wearer, personal profiles never need to be transfered to a new environment. And because a wearable might stay with a user for many years her profile can automatically evolve over time. Further-

more, wearable computers are an inherently more private location for sensitive data because it never needs to leave the person. If the data is never transmitted it becomes much harder to intercept, and the distribution of personal profiles across several wearables (possibly owned by many entities, each with a vested interest in keeping his own data private) makes them a less convenient target for compromise, subpoena, or strong-arm tactics.

Of course, one might still infer a person's location by the fact that a room's resources are being controlled by a particular network address. Traffic analysis is a serious threat to privacy, and the TCP/IP protocols have no features for anonymity. At the application level, a possible solution is bunching together many requests in a scheme such as Crowds [8]. At the network level, Chaum Mixes such as the Onion Routing system [9] show promise. Of course, the physicality of wearable applications may make traffic analysis unnecessary if an eavesdropper is at the end resource itself. For example, if my office light receives a request to light up, it is not hard to surmise that I am at work no matter how anonymous the request was. However, since this requires an eavesdropper at the end resource (i.e. at my office light) there is still no central point of attack. Finally, sometimes privacy leaks are inherent in the application itself. For example, an application that shows where a person is on a map has no choice but to reveal that information; that's its job. Our goal is not to maintain total privacy, but rather to design a system whereby personal data is distributed on a need-to-know basis.

Many wearable systems have been demonstrated that act very similar to smart rooms and ubiquitous computing. For example, wearables have been used to create proximate selection interfaces for room control [10] as well as personalized room controllers for the disabled [11]. Wearable systems have also been used to help create automatic diaries of a user's state over time, both for health monitoring applications and video diaries [12][13]. Finally, many applications exist that present context-based information such as tour-guides [14][15] and general notes related to a user's context [16] [17]. In these systems location is sensed on the wearable either by GPS (for outdoors) or indoors by location beacons. The location beacons are essentially the same as the active badges used in ubiquitous computing, except that instead of being worn by a person to broadcast his identity they are placed in rooms to broadcast locations [18][10]. Similar systems have used paper labels that are recognized through machine vision to recognize a location or object [19]

Table 1: Features provided by Ubicomp vs. Wearables

Feature	Ubicomp	Wearables
Privacy		X
Personalization		X
Localized information	X	
Localized control	X	
Resource Management	X	

[20], while still others recognize objects or locations without any tagging or infrastructure at all [21][22].

1.4 Problems with wearable computing

Wearable systems are well suited to providing privacy and personalizations, but they tend to lack in other areas:

- **Localized information**: Just as smart rooms are ill-suited for personalized information, wearable computer systems have trouble maintaining localized information. For example, if information about a single location gets updated then every wearable needs to be given the new information. Furthermore, is it often difficult for a wearable system to sense information beyond the user's local area.

- **Localized control**: If a wearable is used to control a resource off the persons body, such as a stereo, big screen display, or air conditioner, it is often much easier to design the system with the resource-specific drivers in the device itself. When low-level control is left to the wearable it tends to produce higher demands on the wearable's CPU and wireless network and necessitates that the wearable have code to control each kind of device that might be discovered.

- **Resource management**: Wearables are also not well suited to managing resources among several people. When more than one wearable user wants to use the same stereo, for example, often it is desirable to have a more intelligent system than simply allowing the last request to take precedence.

1.5 Having your cake and eating it too

In this paper we argue that by properly combining wearable computing and ubiquitous computing, a system can have the advantages of both. This synthesis is demonstrated by several applications that have been developed using Hive, a distributed agent architecture that links programs running on wearable computers, desktop computers, and "things that think" [23]. While the details of Hive are beyond the scope of this paper, a brief description is in order. For a more thorough discussion, see the citation [24].

2 Hive

Hive is a distributed agents platform, a decentralized system for building applications by networking local resources. The key abstraction in Hive is the software agent: applications are built out of an ecology of multiple agents interacting over the network.

From a programmer's perspective, each Hive agent is a distributed Java object and an execution thread. However, Hive agents also implement the following properties:

- **Agents are autonomous**: Agents can be sent into a system and entrusted to carry out goals without direct human micro-management.

- **Agents are proactive**: Because agents have their own threads, they can act independent of other running agents. They encapsulate computational activity.

- **Agents are self-describing**: an ontology of agent capabilities can be used to describe and discover available services. Hive agent descriptions consist of both a syntactic description (represented by the Java class of the agent) and a semantic description written in the Resource Description Format (RDF). RDF is in turn encoded in the eXtensible Markup Language (XML).

- **Agents can interact**: Agents can work together to complete a task. Hive agents can communicate both through an asynchronous event / subscriber mode and through Java RMI (Remote Method Invocation). Agent communication is completely peer-to-peer, so an agent might both send and receive at different times.

- **Agents can be mobile**: Agents can move from one physical device to another.

Along with agents, the Hive architecture defines "shadows." Shadows are the low-level drivers for the physical resources of a particular object. For security, only local agents can access a particular shadow.

All remote agents that wish to access local resources must go through local agents. Finally, Hive defines the concept of a "cell" which encapsulates a group of agents. The cell is essentially a Java process that implements an environment within which the agents operate. Generally there will be one cell per local object or wearable computer, though this is not a hard and fast rule. Agents are free to communicate and move between cells. Hive also provides a graphical interface to view and manipulate agent interactions. The interface is itself just one more Hive agent that receives and displays agent events.

2.1 Agent Discovery

In mobile applications such as those described above it is particularly useful to be able to identify what resources are available in a given area, or with a given set of criteria. Hive supports the discovery of new agents through two kinds of lookups. Agents can be queried both based on their syntactic description and on their semantic description. Semantic descriptions include information such as a resource's owner or the room it lives in.

Using this infrastructure, several agents have been created to make resource finding simple for wearable computer users. For example, a "resource finder agent" has been created that receives location events and produces sets of agents whose semantic description matches that location. These agent sets can then be winnowed further by other resource finder agents that are looking for specific services like stereo equipment or large-screen monitors. For more information on agent discovery in Hive, see the cited thesis [25]. To bootstrap the initial list of cells, a resource finder agent contacts a known master cell-listing agent. The creation of new agents are announced to subscribing agents in the form of events, or a special cell-managing agent can be queried.

2.2 Hive with wearables

In our system, each wearable computer is simply another Hive cell in a decentralized Hive network. The peer-to-peer relationships of Hive are a primary difference between our model and the client-server model used by Hodes [10] and by Kortuem [26]. We have found this more symmetric architecture especially useful when implementing applications such as the "Where's Brad?" agent described below, where the wearable user is not the primary recipient or user of information. Sometimes the wearable is the interface to an external service, sometimes the wearable

is a service provider for an agent in the environment (or on another wearable), and sometimes the wearable and environment are interacting.

Hive itself is a Java program. For the wearable side, it runs on the Lizzy wearable computers developed by Thad Starner [27], with the Digital Roamabout wireless system for network connectivity. To gather location information, several rooms in the media lab have been equipped with the "locust" location beacons [28]. These beacons are based on a 4MHz PIC 16C84 micro-controller and measure about 1" by 3". The original locusts communicated via infrared, but our current ones have been modified by Alex Loffler of British Telecom to broadcast via RF. This makes it possible to cover an area with fewer beacons, and obviates the need to place them in line-of-site of a wearable. The range varies depending on other equipment in a room, but one or two beacons will usually cover a small room adequately.

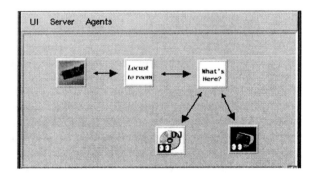

Figure 1: A screen-shot of the Hive user interface, showing connections between several agents. In this configuration, events flow from the locust shadow (far left), to an agent that converts the beacon to a location, to a resource finder agent. Resources for a given location are then passed to a DJ-finder agent and a display-finder agent.

3 Applications

The applications listed below have been implemented and are currently running on the Lizzy wearable and in the lab. The applications range from the useful to the whimsical, and have been chosen to display a range of requirements, including privacy, personalization, localized resources, and scarce resource management. The applications are listed starting with those that emphasize the wearable. The list continues through applications that use both wearable and the environment, and ends with those that primarily emphasize the environment. Next to the name of each application, the salient features demonstrated are listed in parentheses.

3.1 Automatic diary (privacy)

One of the simplest applications is an automatic event logger. As a user walks between rooms, the shadow in charge of receiving RF locust beacons automatically sends the new location to its subscribers on the wearable's Hive cell. One of these agents simply writes the current location to disk. Whenever the wearable user types in a note or idea, that note is automatically timestamped and tagged with the location in which that note took place [16]. Unlike ubiquitous computing automatic diaries (e.g. [5]), the user's location never leaves the wearable.

In this agent, all computation occurs on the wearable. No computation occurs in the environment, except in the transmitting location beacons.

3.2 Proximate selection of a big-screen display (privacy, localized resources)

Sometimes a wearable user wants to project a display on a large screen for others to view. With this application, typing a single chord on the chording keyboard automatically puts the current Emacs buffer onto the nearest screen, where it can be edited by multiple people.

When the user enters a new room a resource finder agent automatically looks for any display agents within the room. If one is found, the display agent is queried for its X-windows screen name, which is then written to a file. The screen name is then used by XEmacs to display the file.

In this application most computation still occurs on the wearable. However, the screens that are available for a given location are maintained in that physical location. If a display name changes or a new one is added, the only information that needs to be updated is in the room itself.

3.3 Theme music (privacy, personalization, localized resources)

One of the original inspirations for this work was that the primary author wanted to have theme music played whenever he entered his office. We have therefore implemented a room automation system in the form of a theme-music agent. Whenever a wearable user enters a room, this agent tries to find a DJ agent that runs on a computer hooked up to a stereo for that room. If it finds one, and if the DJ isn't currently playing music, it sends the URL of a an MP3 file containing the user's personal theme music (for example, the "Inspector Gadget" theme). This music is then played, usually to the annoyance of everyone else in the room.

This is the first agent described that actually performs negotiation with a localized resource. The wearable keeps track of private information (the user's location) and personalized information (the theme music). At the same time, the DJ agent maintains resource information like whether music is already being played. It also maintains final control over the local hardware (the stereo), as will be seen in the next agent description.

3.4 DJ (privacy, personalization, localized resources, resource management)

As is implied by the theme-music agent, people might not want their DJ agent to play music whenever someone enters the room, or only want certain kinds of music played, or want to make sure that no one hogs the DJ with his own taste in music. For this reason, the DJ agent implements resource management policies to insure fairness. In the default case, a DJ takes requests sequentially and plays one request for each agent that has a song. Thus people's requests will be played in a round-robin fashion, one request per person.

It is difficult to do resource management in a completely decentralized, wearable-only system, and so it is extremely convenient to let the DJ itself do the management with the resource it controls. At the same time, the DJ needn't know who is in the room, nor need it keep profiles of favorite songs for people who might visit the room. This information is kept on individual wearables. When a DJ-finder agent finds a DJ agent it automatically sends a play-list of song URLs.

3.5 Remembrance Agent (privacy, personalization, localized information)

An earlier version of an entirely wearable-based remembrance agent (RA) has been described in previous publications [16]. In the old version a user's location and other contextual information was used as a query into her personal note files to proactively bring up information that may be useful in her current environment. This version worked well for making suggestions from personal data because all the database was stored on the wearable itself, where it was easily personalized and kept private. However, for the reasons discussed earlier it was difficult to maintain information about the environment in the database. In the combination ubiquitous / wearable computing system, users can integrate personal and localized data seamlessly. An early version of this combined system was used with an augmented reality system for the Media Lab's 10th anniversary open house in 1995 [19].

As an example, imagine a wearable that acts as a tour guide at a museum. As the visitor moves through various exhibits, extra information about each site is presented on her wearable. Because this information is location specific, it is more easily maintained if it resides in the museum databases and is only sent to a visitor's wearable she enter the exhibit area. However, other information is personal: the fourth-grader would like to know how this exhibit is related to the worksheets he did last week, while the anthropologist would like to know how an exhibit relates to her dissertation. In the new system, resource agents associated with an exhibit provide varying levels of detailed description to the RA. These descriptions can be presented to the visitor as exhibit-specific information, but can also be used as more info for the query into the personal remembrance agent. In this way, the museum can update exhibit information in its database, while visitors can keep personal data locally on their own wearable computers, and both can be presented in a context-sensitive manner.

In this application, information and computation are shared equally between the wearable and the environment. Personal information is still kept private on on the wearable, as is the visitor's location. Localized information is kept in the environment where it can be updated easily.

3.6 Context-aware alert filtering (privacy, personalization, localized information)

The message filtering agent receives alerts, communications, and other information that might interest a wearable user and filters based on the wearer's context and personal profile. For example, if the wearer is at the media lab, messages relating to the lab appear on his or her head-mount display. These messages include requests to play doom death-matches and automatically generated messages announcing food has been left in the lab kitchen. When outside the lab, these messages are not displayed. The agent also filters based on a personal profile. For example, announcements of incoming emails can be filtered to only show personal mail or mail mentioning certain keywords. Negative keyword lists can also be used, for example, to filter out announcements of Indian food in particular.

This application also shares computation and information between the environment and the wearable. Personal profiles are kept on the wearable where they can be updated easily, transported to new environments, and where they can be kept private. Contextual filtering is also done at the wearable so the contextual cues being used (e.g. location) can be kept private. However, triggered information like the arrival of food are processed in the environment since they are outside the sensor range of the wearable.

3.7 "Where's brad?" agent (privacy, personalization, localized resources)

While the agents described so far are services mainly for the wearable user, the architecture makes it easy for the wearable to act as a service provider as well. The "Where's brad?" agent runs on a computer anywhere at the media-lab and produces a map that shows the current location of a wearable user. This agent uses the same resource discovery tools as do the agents on the wearable, except now instead of finding agents associated with a location they find agents associated with a particular person. The amount of disclosure is controlled at the wearable end. For example, the wearable can decide to only allow certain agents to subscribe to location information, or can only reveal certain info to certain people. This privacy policy might not simply be a hierarchy of increasing access. For example, a user might want a policy where coworkers will his location if he is within the workplace, but will only see a "not here" if he is outside. Friends and family may see more detailed information outside of work, but only see an "at work" otherwise.

This agent primarily emphasizes information being displayed in the environment, for people other than the wearable user. However, because a person's location is provided by agents running on his own wearable, he can still maintain fine-grained control over sensitive information.

4 Related Work

While we have our own take on implementation, the applications described in this paper were deliberately chosen to be similar in function to common applications found in ubiquitous and wearable computing. These systems have been described earlier in the paper. In part because of the difficulties cited earlier, others have also designed hybrid wearable / ubiquitous computing systems. Of particular note are Kortuem [26] and Hodes [10] who both describe wearable systems that discover room resources and automatically download interfaces to control them. However, both of these systems follow a client-server model, which makes them less suited for applications where control rests more in the environment and less on the wearable. This work is also related to toolkits for building context-aware applications such as the context-aware toolkit developed at Georgia Tech [29].

The Hive infrastructure is also closely related to several several distributed agent architectures, the closest being Sun's Jini system [30]. Both Hive and Jini are Java-based agent architectures, both rely on RMI distributed objects and mobile code, and both systems represent devices and capabilities on the network, proxying if necessary. However, there are some design differences that make Hive more flexible than Jini for these particular kinds of applications. One is that Jini does not have the conceptual split between shadows (trusted controllers of local resources) and agents (possibly untrusted, possibly mobile code that communicates with shadows and other agents). This split gives Hive a useful abstraction barrier similar to device drivers in an operating system. Hive also has a more location-dependent model of computation. In Hive, an agent's cell can indicate where the agent is physically, what resources it has access to, etc. Jini focuses mostly on services; the actual place a service is hosted on is not a major part of the Jini model. For a more detailed comparison between Hive, Jini, and other agent architectures, see the citation [24].

5 Future Work

The interfaces to almost all the applications described are implicit rather than explicit; the user cannot choose an action other than the default action in a given environment. For many applications, a combination of explicit and implicit interfaces is necessary. For example, the user might need fine-control over a slide projector, or want to specify a different play-list for a DJ agent. Negotiating interface requirements is still an open research issue, especially when different users may have different interface hardware.

Another open research topic is making service discovery scalable. Currently agents are filtered using semantic and syntactic descriptions, but the initial set of Hive cells to query for potentially useful agents is provided by a central server. This works fine for our small-scale system, but will not scale to hundreds of cells in the world. Models include hierarchical structures as used for Domain Name Service (DNS) [31], or location beacons that include a bootstrapping address for downloading service information [10]. However, both methods constrain service discovery along a constrained and pre-determined dimension such as service name or physical location. They do not lend themselves to free-form service discovery along several potentially shifting dimensions.

6 Conclusions

We have presented what we see as fundamental difficulties in both pure ubiquitous and pure wearable computing paradigms. In particular, ubiquitous computing and smart room systems tend to have difficulties with privacy and personalization, while wearable systems have trouble with localized information, localized resource control, and resource management between multiple people. By implementing several applications that span this space of requirements we have tried to show how a peer-to-peer network of wearable and ubiquitous computing components, with proper information flow, can help solve these difficulties.

Acknowledgements

Special thanks go to the rest of the Hive team: Matthew Gray, Oliver Roup, Raffi Krikorian, and to Pattie Maes. Thanks also go to our sponsors at Merrill Lynch and British Telecom, to Thad Starner, Rob Poor, and Alex Loffler for their work on the Locust room beacons, and to Chris Wren for his food-alert system.

This paper is dedicated to the memory of Mark Weiser.

References

[1] M. Weiser, "Some computer science issues in ubiquitous computing," *Communications of the ACM*, vol. 36, no. 7, pp. 75–84, July 1993.

[2] A. Pentland, "Smart rooms," *Scientific American*, April 1996.

[3] S. Elrod, G. Hall, R. Costanza, M. Dixon, and J. Des Rivieres, "Responsive office environments," *Communications of the ACM*, vol. 36, no. 7, 1993.

[4] B. Schilit, N. Adams, and R. Want, "Context-aware computing applications," in *Workshop on Mobile Computing Systems and Applications*, Santa Cruz, CA, December 1994, pp. 85–90, IEEE Computer Society.

[5] M. Lamming, P. Brown, K. Carter, M. Eldridge, M. Flynn, and G. Louie, "The design of a human memory prosthesis," *The Computer Journal*, vol. 37, no. 3, pp. 153–163, 1994.

[6] R. Want, A. Hopper, V. Falcao, and J. Gibbons, "The active badge location system," *ACM Trans. on Info. Sys.*, vol. 10, no. 1, pp. 91–102, January 1992.

[7] L. Foner, *Political Artifacts and Personal Privacy: The Yenta Multi-Agent Distributed Matchmaking System*, Ph.D. thesis, MIT Media Laboratory, 1999.

[8] M. Reiter and A. Rubin, "Anonymous web transations with crowds," *Communications of the ACM*, vol. 42, no. 2, pp. 32–48, February 1999.

[9] D. Goldschlag, M. Reed, and P. Syverson, "Onion routing," *Communications of the ACM*, vol. 42, no. 2, pp. 39–41, February 1999.

[10] T. Hodes, R. Katz, E. Servan-Schreiber, and L. Rowe, "Composable ad-hoc mobile services for universal interaction," in *Third ACM/IEEE International Conference on Mobile Computing*, Budapest, Hangary, September 1997.

[11] D. Ross and J. Sanford, "Wearable computer as a remote interface for people with disabilities," in *First International Symposium on Wearable Computers*, Cambridge, MA, 1997, pp. 161–162, IEEE Computer Society.

[12] J. Healey and R. Picard, "Startlecam: A cybernetic wearable camera," in *Second International Symposium on Wearable Computers*, Pittsburgh, PA, October 1998, pp. 42–49, IEEE Computer Society.

[13] S. Mann, "Smart clothing: The wearable computer and wearcam," *Personal Technologies*, vol. 1, no. 1, pp. 21–27, 1997.

[14] G. Abowd, C. Atkeson, J. Hong, S. Long, R. Kooper, and M. Pinkerton, "Cyberguide: A mobile context-aware tour guide," *ACM Wireless Networks*, pp. 3:421–433, 1997.

[15] S. Feiner, B. MacIntyre, and T. Höllerer, "A touring machine: Prototyping 3D mobile augmented reality systems for exploring the urban environment," in *First International Symposium on Wearable Computers*, Cambridge, MA, October 1997, pp. 74–81, IEEE Computer Society.

[16] B. Rhodes, "The wearable remembrance agent: A system for augmented memory," *Personal Technologies Journal Special Issue on Wearable Computing*, vol. 1, no. 4, pp. 1:218–224, 1997.

[17] J. Pascoe, "Adding generic contextual capabilities to wearable computers," in *Second International Symposium on Wearable Computers*, Pittsburgh, PA, October 1998, pp. 92–99, IEEE Computer Society.

[18] J. Ioannidis, D. Duchamp, and G. Maguire, "Ip-based protocols for mobile internetworking," in *ACM SIGCOMM Symposium on Communications, Architecture, and Protocols*. 1991, pp. 235–245, ACM Press.

[19] Thad Starner, Steve Mann, Bradley Rhodes, Jeffrey Levine, Jennifer Healey, Dana Kirsch, Rosalind W. Picard, and Alex Pentland, "Augmented reality through wearable computing," *Presence*, vol. 6(4), 1997.

[20] J. Rekimoto and K. Nagao, "The world through the computer: Computer augmented interaction with real world environments," in *The 8th Annual ACM Symposium on User Interface Software and Technology*. November 1995, pp. 23–36, ACM Press.

[21] T. Jebara, B. Schiele, N. Oliver, and A. Pentland, "DyPERS: Dynamic Personal Enhanced Reality System," in *1998 Image Understanding Workshop*, Monterrey, CA, November 1998.

[22] T. Starner, B. Schiele, and A. Pentland, "Visual contextual awareness in wearable computing," in *Second International Symposium on Wearable Computers*, Pittsburgh, PA, 1998, pp. 50–57, IEEE Computer Society.

[23] Neil Gershenfeld, *When Things Start to Think*, Henry Holt & Company, 1999, ISBN: 0805058745 http://www.media.mit.edu/physics/publications/books/ba/.

[24] Nelson Minar, Matthew Gray, Oliver Roup, and and Pattie Maes Raffi Krikorian, "Hive: Distributed agents for networking things," Submitted to ASA/MA '99. http://hive.media.mit.edu/, 1999.

[25] M. Gray, "Infrastructure for an intelligent kitchen," M.S. thesis, MIT Media Lab, 20 Ames St, Cambridge MA 02139, May 1999.

[26] G. Kortuem, Z Segall, and M Bauer, "Context-aware, adaptive wearable computers as remote interfaces to 'intelligent' environments," in *Second International Symposium on Wearable Computers*, Pittsburgh, PA, October 1998, pp. 58–65, IEEE Computer Society.

[27] T. Starner, "Lizzy: MIT's wearable computer design 2.0.5," http://wearables.www. media.mit.edu/projects/wearables/lizzy/, 1997.

[28] T. Starner, D. Kircsh, and S. Assefa, "The locust swarm: An enviromentally-powered, networkless location and messaging system," in *First International Symposium on Wearable Computers*, Cambridge, MA, 1997, pp. 169–170, IEEE Computer Society, http://wearables.www.media.mit.edu/projects/wearables/locust/.

[29] Daniel Salber, Anind Dey, and Gregory Abowd, "The context toolkit: Aiding the development of context-enabled applications," in *CHI '99*. May 15-20 1999, ACM Press.

[30] Ken Arnold, Ann Wollrath, Bryan O'Sullivan, Robert Scheifler, and Jim Waldo, *The Jini Specification*, Addison-Wesley, 1999.

[31] P.V. Mockapetris and K. Dunlap, "Development of the domain name system," in *ACM SIGCOMM '88*, August 1988.

"Where Are You Pointing At?"
A Study of Remote Collaboration in a Wearable Videoconference System

Martin Bauer
University of Stuttgart
Computer Science Dept.
Breitwiesenstrasse 20 –22
70565 Stuttgart, Germany

MP.Bauer@studbox.uni-stuttgart.de

Gerd Kortuem
University of Oregon
Dept. of Computer Science
Deschutes Hall
Eugene, OR 97403 USA
+1 541 346 1381
kortuem@cs.uoregon.edu

Zary Segall
University of Oregon
Dept. of Computer Science
Deschutes Hall
Eugene, OR 97403 USA
+1 541 346 0488
zs@cs.uoregon.edu

Abstract

This paper reports on an empirical study aimed at evaluating the utility of a reality-augmenting telepointer in a wearable videoconference system. Results show that using this telepointer a remote expert can effectively guide and direct a field worker's manual activities. By analyzing verbal communication behavior and pointing gestures, we were able to determine that experts overwhelmingly preferred pointing for guiding workers through physical tasks.

Keywords

Wearable computing, CSCW, video conferencing, telepointer, augmented reality, empirical study.

1. Introduction

Remote collaboration is one of the most promising applications of wearable computing technology. Past studies of mobile collaborative systems have shown that field workers make repairs more quickly and accurately when they have a remote expert helping them [6,7,8].

From experience with desktop-based groupware systems like MMConf [2], CoLab [3] or GroupWeb [4] we know that *telepointers* are an effective means for users to establish a common understanding during computer-mediated conversation. A telepointer is a mouse pointer controlled by a remote user that allows pointing at objects in a shared window. Without telepointers, users have to rely on verbal description, since they cannot simply say 'that one'. Instead they have to give a precise description of the object they refer to, for example 'the yellow round hole in the upper right corner'.

In this paper, we report the results of an experimental study conducted at the University of Oregon that aimed at evaluating the utility of a *reality-augmenting telepointer* in a wearable videoconference system. We use the term *reality-augmenting telepointer* to describe a telepointer that is displayed on a wearable computer's head-mounted display and is used for pointing at real-world objects in the wearable user[1]'s physical space.

We conducted this experiment in order to compare remote collaboration with and without reality-augmenting telepointer. In particular, we were interested if and how users employ pointing gestures in combination with verbal explanations when guiding another user's manual activities.

Results show that by using a reality-augmenting telepointer a remote user can effectively guide and direct a wearable user's activities. By analyzing verbal communication behavior and pointing gestures, we were able to determine that experts overwhelmingly preferred pointing for guiding workers through physical tasks. In addition, we were able to determine that the majority of verbal instructions contained deictic references like 'here', 'over there', 'this', and 'that'. Because deictic references are mostly used in connection with and in support of gestures, this finding is a strong indication that participants heavily relied on a combination of pointing. gestures and verbal communication.

While there are many interesting theoretical issues related to communication behavior, our work was also motivated by practical issues. This study was carried out within the larger context of the Netman project [1,4,5], which is targeted at developing collaborative wearable systems for the support of network technicians.

---

[1] We use the term *wearable user* to describe a user wearing a wearable computer.

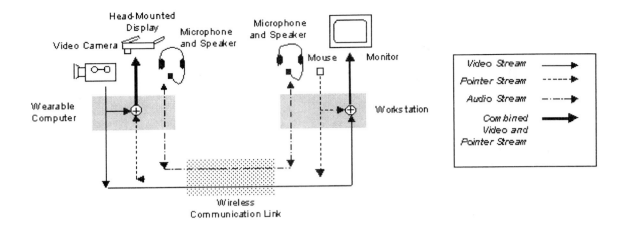

Figure 1. Implementation of Reality-Augmenting Telepointer

2. The System

We have built a wearable system for real-time video collaboration that integrates a telepointer. Because of its ability to augment a wearable user's view of the surrounding physical world, we use the term *reality-augmenting telepointer*. This system is a hybrid system enabling office-based *experts* to collaborate with highly mobile *field workers* using wearable computers. The wearable computer has a head-mounted display (HMD) to which a video camera is attached. The camera is pointing away from the user in the approximate direction of the user's gaze and captures images of the task area. The video image is displayed on the HMD as well as sent over a wireless network link to the remote expert's desktop computer. The expert, in turn, controls a telepointer the (x,y) coordinates of which are sent back to the wearable computer where they are used to display the telepointer on the wearable display (see Figure 1). In order to compensate for the wearable user's head movements, we provide the remote expert with an image-freezing feature: pressing the mouse button freezes the most current video frame on both the wearable HMD and the desktop computer. The expert can then move the telepointer without having to follow the wearable user's head movements.[2]

This arrangement is well suited for "over the shoulder" consultations. The expert can quickly provide assistance by pointing at objects in the wearable user's environment while giving verbal explanations like "connect this cable here". Similarly, the expert can guide the worker through a solution, and watch the novice attempt it himself.

---

[2] The system was implemented using Microsoft NetMeeting.

3. The Study

3.1. Overview

In order to evaluate the effectiveness of reality-augmenting telepointing, we conducted an experimental study where pairs of test users used our wearable videoconference system to perform a set of artificial tasks. Of each pair, one user played the role of an *expert* or *instructor* guiding the other user, the *worker* or *apprentice,* through a set of predefined tasks. The worker was using the wearable computer with HMD as described above, while the expert gave instructions watching and directing the worker's actions from his desktop computer.

For this study, we used a combination of controlled experiment, protocol analysis, and user questionnaires. Our data includes videotapes, notes taken by experimenters during sessions, post-experimental coding of videotapes, and questionnaires.

3.2. Experimental Hypotheses

Our primary interest in this study was to find out what effect reality-augmenting telepointing has on collaboration. In particular, our goal was to compare outcomes and communication patterns with and without telepointing. Additionally, we studied how image freezing was used by participants.

In order to clarify our expectations, we formulated several hypotheses.

H1. Pointing will be the most decisive communication element. In other words, the expert will use pointing gestures first and foremost and support them by verbal explanations, not the other way around.

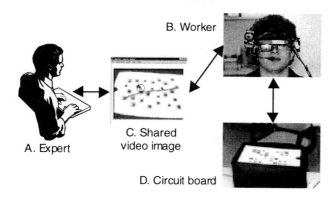

B. Worker

C. Shared video image

A. Expert

D. Circuit board

Figure 2. Experimental Setup

H2. The combination of telepointing and verbal communication is faster than verbal communication alone.

Hypotheses H1 and H2 are based on our expectation that telepointing, if implemented adequately, allows the expert to more easily and more precisely direct the worker's actions. As corollary, we put forth the next hypothesis:

H3. Language will be used in the same way as in unmediated co-located situations: In 'difficult' situations, it is used to augment pointing gestures. In less difficult situations it will be used less often.

Our believe that freezing is an effective means to cope with rapid head and camera movements is formulated in hypotheses H4:

H4. The expert will use freezing quite often to compensate for the worker's head movement.

Finally, we expect that pointing leads to a decrease in *communication errors*. We define an *error* as a situation where the worker performs an action different from the expert's instructions or where the result of an action does not match the given instruction.

H5. There will be less *communication errors* and misunderstandings when pointing is used in combination with speech compared to speech-only conditions.

3.3. Method

3.3.1. Participants. Nine pairs, or 18 people altogether, took part in our study. Seven participants were female, eleven were male. All participants were university students majoring in Computer Science or had similar computer science background. All had normal color

vision and were free of other uncorrected vision problems that could limit their ability to use a HMD.

3.3.2. Experimental Design. In this study, we used a set of artificial tasks that were derived from the network maintenance scenario of the Netman project [5]. The tasks simulate a situation where an expert or instructor remotely guides a technician through the process of wiring network equipment, such as a network closet full of routers and bridges.

In the study, participants were working in pairs in building a *mockup* circuit (see Figure 2). The "expert" using the desktop computer was given a wiring plan that had to be completed by the "worker" The mockup circuit had to be plugged together on top of a cardboard box (see Figure 2 D.). We could replace the top part of the box with different cardboard templates. The templates had square holes cut into them that were arranged in different ways. Instead of real cables, we used colored cords.

We designed six different templates representing six "difficulty levels" (see Figure 3). The templates differed in the coloring and the arrangement of the holes. One pair of templates arranged the holes as a grid; another pair used a structured arrangement, while holes of the final pair were arranged chaotically. Within each pair, one template was color-coded with yellow, red, blue and green holes, while the second template used no colors at all. The cables were color-coded as well in white, yellow, blue/red, and blue/green.

Our expectation was that the structured templates were more suited for verbal descriptions, while the unstructured ones would force the participants to use pointing gestures more often. Similarly, color-coded holes and cables made it easier for participants to refer to them using verbal descriptions.

For the controlled experiment, we used a within-groups experimental design in which we compared task performance under three conditions:

A. *No-pointing:* participants collaborated through-shared video and audio.

B. *Mainly Pointing:* participants collaborated through shared-video, audio, and pointing gestures, but were asked to use pointing as often as possible, using speech only as a last resort.

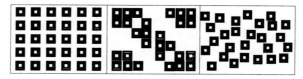

Figure 3. Three circuit templates representing different difficulty levels.

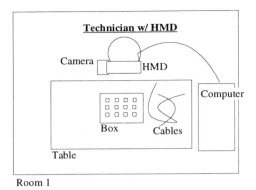 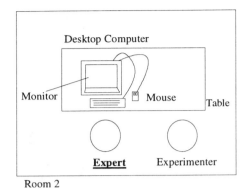

Figure 4. Experimental Setup

C. *Speech & Pointing:* participants collaborated through shared-video, audio, and pointing gestures, in any way they felt most comfortable with.

We did not run tests without image freezing, because our initial observations indicated that movements of the head-mounted camera made it very difficult to use the telepointer without image freezing.

3.3.3 Setup. Each member of a pair was working in a separate room. There was no direct communication; all communication was mediated through our prototype system. Figure 4 shows a plan of the setup in the two rooms seen from above.

The worker was standing or sitting in front of a table, whatever he/she felt was more comfortable. The box, on which the circuit was to be built, was placed on the table. The cables could be found next to it. During the test, the worker had to plug the cables into the holes guided by the expert sitting next door in front of a desktop computer. The expert was given a wiring plan for each subtask. During the test, he/she had to instruct the worker how to set up the circuit according to the wiring plan.

For practical reasons, we had the HMD and the video camera connected to a desktop computer instead of a wearable computer.

3.3.4. Procedure. Each test session, which lasted for approximately 90 minutes, was divided up into six parts:

Introduction: In each test session, both participants were first given a handout containing some information about the goals of the usability study and a short description of the tasks that they were going to perform. Then both participants were shown around both work areas and they had the opportunity to ask questions about the test. We tried to make sure that they had understood how the test was going to be conducted. We left it to each pair to decide who

wanted to work with the HMD first. We switched roles about three-fourth through the test, so that all participants had a chance to see both sides.

We had an experimenter/investigator in each room. It was their job to help the participants with the equipment, e.g. to put on the HMD, to prepare the different tasks, and to make sure that the expert had the right wiring plan. During the experiment, they filled out protocol forms that provided us with some information for the evaluation of the study. In addition to the protocols and questionnaires, we videotaped the experiment for later evaluation. We had two cameras: one was directed at a monitor showing the image of the head-mounted display; the other, recorded as picture in picture, was pointed at the wearable user and the task area.

Warm-up Task: To start out, we gave the participants a warm-up task that enabled them to familiarize themselves with the equipment. The worker looked around in the room and the expert picked an object (e.g. the telephone). He/she then froze the picture and pointed at the object while the wearable user had to identify the object. The users were asked to repeat that a couple of times until they felt comfortable enough to continue.

Section 1: In the first real section of the test, the participants were asked to collaborate under no-pointing conditions, i.e. by audio and video only, and without the telepointer[3] (Condition A). Thus, the expert had to describe verbally how the circuit was to be set up while watching the worker's actions on his screen. Two wiring templates were used: a template with a white grid, and one with a structured arrangement of color-coded holes.

---

[3] To ensure that pointing was not used, we disconnected the mouse from the expert's computer.

Section 2: For the second section of the test, the participants were asked to collaborate under Condition B (pointing-only), i.e. using telepointing as often as possible while keeping verbal communication to a minimum. The same templates were used as in the first section, but with different wiring plans.

Section 3: In the third section, the same participants were asked to accomplish a set of tasks under Condition C (speech & pointing), i.e., they could use whatever combination of verbal communication and pointing gestures they felt most comfortable with. All the templates were used that had not been used in section 1 and 2.

Section 4: After the third section, the participants changed roles. The warm-up task was repeated to familiarize them with the equipment they had to use for their new roles. In the fourth section, they repeated the third section (Condition C, speech & pointing) with switched roles. The same templates, but different wiring plans were used.

After Section 2 and 4, participants were asked to fill out a questionnaire containing questions regarding the usefulness of telepointing in general and our implementation in particular. Most importantly, participants were asked to rate their preferences of using verbal directions only, pointing only, or a combination of verbal directions and pointing gestures.

4. Findings

4.1. Terminology

In order to classify the expert's actions we introduce the following terminology:

Pointing Act: a pointing act is a situation in which the expert uses the telepointer to point at a particular hole.

Referential Speech Act: A referential speech act is an expression or utterance used by the expert to identify in which hole the worker has to plug a cable. We distinguished between three different types of referential speech acts:

- An *absolute reference* identifies a hole by its absolute location, as exemplified by the phrase 'the second hole to the left of the lower right corner'.
- A *relative reference* identifies a hole by referring to another object, i.e. hole or cable. It is

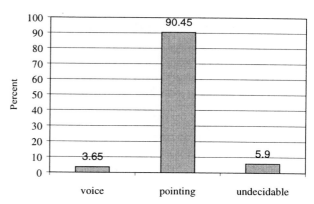

Graph 1. Importance of Communication Elements for Condition C

exemplified by the phrase 'above the yellow cable'
- A *deictic reference* identifies a hole by means of context dependent phrases like 'here', 'there', or 'this' and 'that', as used in "plug it in here" or "put it over there". Deictic references cannot stand alone, but are only used in connection with and in support of pointing gestures.

Freezing Act: A freezing act is a situation where the expert freezes the video image by pressing the mouse button.

4.2. Pointing Acts

Pointing gestures were used very often throughout the experiment. In Condition C (speech & pointing), there were a total of 576 cases in which the worker had to connect a cable to a hole. Out of this theoretical maximum, pointing acts were used in 572 (99.31%) cases.

Yet, more interesting is the question which communication element was most decisive for the worker's decision to connect a cable to a particular hole. In some cases, the expert would direct the worker by simultaneously giving a verbal command and making a pointing gesture. In other cases, however, the expert would use either speech or gestures, but not both.

We define the *decisive element* as the communicative element that first establishes the identity of the object being referred to by the expert, so that the worker can act upon this information. In order to determine the decisive element, we analyzed the information that was available at the exact moment when the worker started moving towards the target.

We found that in Condition C, that is when users were given a choice whether to use speech or pointing, in 521 (90.45%) cases, a pointing act could be determined as the

Table 1. Frequency of Pointing and Referential Speech Acts for Condition C[4]

	Absolute References	Relative References	Deictic References	Pointing
Grid Template	35.43%	5.55%	38.88%	98.61%
Struct. Template	32.64%	7.65%	36.78%	99.30%
Chaos Template	17.7%	2.07%	55.89%	99.30%
Overall	28.59%	5.09%	43.87%	99.07%

Table 2. Frequency of Pointing and Freezing Acts for Condition C

	Absolute Number	Absolute Percentage	Relative. Percentage
Pointing Acts (total)	572	99.31%	100%
Freezing Acts (total)	330	56.77%	100%
Freezing Acts (short)	21	3.67%	6.36%
Freezing Acts (long)	228	39.58%	69.09%
Freezing Acts (permanent)	79	13.71%	23.94%

decisive element; in 21 (3.65%) cases it was a speech act and in 34 (5.9%) cases it couldn't be decided (Graph 1). This is a strong indication that users overwhelmingly relied upon pointing and that they recognized the telepointer as a tool that helped them accomplish a given task more efficiently.

It is interesting to note that the different template types (grid, structured or chaotic arrangement) that were intended as difficulty levels did not have a large effect on the use of pointing (Table 1). All template types show a very high number of pointing acts around 99%.

4.3. Referential Speech Acts

Table 1 lists the frequencies with which experts used different types of speech acts. Overall, users clearly preferred deictic references, which were used in 43.87% of all cases. Since deictic references can only be used simultaneously with and in support of pointing gestures, this result again indicates the users' strong preference for pointing.

Contrary to our expectations, the template style (grid, structured or chaos) did not have a great impact on communication behavior. Although the deictic references are slightly higher for the chaos template (55.89%) than for grid (38.88%) and structured template (36.78%), the difference is not as big as expected.

4.4. Image Freezing Acts

Freezing was used in 56.77% of all cases (see Table 2). The usage of freezing differed considerably between the groups. As shown in Graph 2, there were two pairs that

practically didn't use it at all (0%-3%), two groups used it all the time (96%-98%) and the other five groups fell somewhere in between (41%-81%).

One possible explanation for this large variance in the use of image freezing may be a bug in our implementation, of which we became aware only about halfway through the experiment. Occasionally, it caused the frozen image of wearable and desktop system to be off by one frame. In such a case, when the expert pointed at a particular hole, the telepointer on the worker's display would actually point at another hole or be slightly off. Amazingly some participants were able to identify the problem and recover from it. Others, however, were visibly confused. Some users who experienced these problems may have decided to stop using freezing entirely. This is supported by the fact that one group stopped using freezing abruptly between two tasks. In total, we counted 20 out of about 576 pointing acts, in which the pointer was noticeably off.

Percentage in which freezing was used for each group

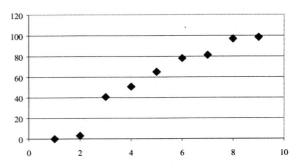

Graph 2. Image Freezing Acts per Group in Percent

---

[4] The numbers for grid and structured templates have been adjusted to account for the fact that twice as many chaos templates were used in Condition C than grid and structured templates.

Not everyone used freezing in the same way. Some participants froze the image only for a very short time: 6.36% of all freezing acts were less than two seconds. The majority of freezing acts lasted longer than 2 seconds (69.09%) There were even a few pairs that developed the 'permanent freeze' method. They froze the image once at the beginning of each subtask and kept it frozen until the last cable was plugged in. We had an amazingly high percentage (23.94%) of permanent freezing acts. Some of the users who did not use the image freezing feature at all, "implemented" their own way of freezing: the wearable user kept the head still, so the camera image would remain stable at all times.[5]

4.5. Task Completion Time

Although we got the impression during the experiment that telepointing speeds up task completion considerably, - with only nine pairs participating in the study - we couldn't hope for reliable numbers regarding a possible "speedup".

There are a lot of factors involved in human communication, which may account for the variance in completion time that we got for the pairs of participants. In addition, since we measured times by hand and task completion times were rather short (about one to two minutes for one wiring plan), systematic errors may have been introduced making our results less reliable.

Still, pairs relying almost exclusively on telepointing appeared to be the fastest. We plan additional tests to measure the influence of pointing on task performance.

4.6. Communication Errors

Owing to the simplicity of the tasks, task completion rate was 100%. However, workers sometimes made mistakes by not following or misunderstanding the experts directions. For example, occasionally the expert would instruct the worker to connect a cable to one hole, but the worker would actually plug it into a different hole. Throughout the entire experiment, experts were very effective in detecting workers' errors by watching the shared-video image. In general, errors were detected and corrected as soon as they occurred.

Apart from the problem with freezing that we discussed in 4.4, we identified the following reasons for communication errors:

- Vague language: Especially in Condition A (no-pointing) we noticed that verbal directions given by the expert were oftentimes difficult to understand. In

Condition C (pointing), the need to use complicated verbal descriptions was reduced, since users could simply point at holes instead of having to describe them. Informal observations suggest that the number of errors in Condition C was much lower than in Condition A. However, we currently do not have enough data to substantiate this claim.

- Poor audio quality: There were a number of misunderstandings that were caused by poor audio quality. We noticed especially low volume, long delays, and lost packets as contributing factors. Part of this problem was due to the audio equipment, especially the headsets; others were caused by how Microsoft NetMeeting handles sound. In the questionnaire, two participants noted audio as a severe problem.
- Poor image quality: The blue/red and blue/green cables were hard to distinguish on the video, so they were sometimes confused. We counted 12 cases in which the worker picked up and used a wrong cable. Except for one group, the participants noticed the problem and corrected the error. Similarly, the white cable is very hard to see on the white templates, especially if the holes are not color-coded. Therefore, the expert was sometimes not able to identify what the worker was doing and to verify if the worker plugged the cable into the correct hole. However, experts were in all cases aware of this problem and were able to resolve it by asking the worker for clarification.
- Low video frame rate: The video frame rate in our experiment never exceeded three frames per second. Thus, rapid head and camera movements resulted in jerky video that made it difficult for the users to collaborate. This resulted in an increase in meta-communication in which the expert instructed the worker to look at a particular object or in a particular direction.

4.7. User Feedback

The results of the questionnaire show that all participants thought the system was useful and enjoyed using it. They gave our telepointer implementation an average of 4.5 on a scale from 1=useless to 5=useful with a standard derivation of 0.6. The difficulty of both pointing (in the role of the expert) and figuring out what was being pointed at (in the role of the worker) was rated as 1.8 on a scale from 1=easy to 5=difficult. The standard derivation was 1.0 and 0.7 respectively.

---

[5] This behavior was only possible because our artificial tasks did not require the worker to walk or look around much.

5. Discussion

For the most part, the results of this study matched our expectations. The results show that by using a reality-augmenting telepointer a remote user can effectively guide and direct a wearable user's activities. The analysis of verbal communication behavior and pointing gestures clearly indicates that experts overwhelmingly used pointing for guiding workers through physical tasks. While the use of pointing reached 99%, verbal instructions were used considerably less. In more than 20% of all the cases experts did not use verbal instructions at all, but relied on pointing alone instead. Indeed, we would sometimes observe a pair rush through the tasks with hardly any verbal communication at all.

The majority of verbal instructions contained deictic references like 'here', 'over there', 'this', and 'that'. Because deictic references are mostly used in connection with and in support of gestures, this finding is a strong indication that participants naturally combined pointing gestures with verbal communication, much the same they do in face-to-face conversations.

We were not able to prove or disprove our second hypothesis, which states that the combination of pointing and verbal communication is faster than verbal communication alone. Although we saw indications during the experiment that pointing decreases task completion time, we do not have enough data at this point to back up our claim. The same is true for an expected decrease in communication errors.

At the onset of this experiment, we thought that the head movements of the wearable user might represent a severe impediment for effective telepointing. However, the image-freezing feature we implemented proved to be quite effective. The image-freezing feature was used on average in close to 60% of all cases.

We were surprised to find that two pairs used 'permanent freezing', a method in which the picture was frozen at the beginning of the task and would not be released until the entire task was completed. The reason that some participants were able to use permanent freezing was that our experiment did not call for extensive head movements. The cable box fits entirely into the camera view, so that head movements were almost unnecessary. In more realistic field situation, permanent image freezing is no longer possible.

6. Conclusion

We have shown that a reality-augmenting telepointer is an effective means for enhancing remote collaboration of wearable users. Participants of our study overwhelmingly used the telepointer to guide a wearable user through a series of physical activities. We see it as an indication of the utility of the reality-augmenting telepointer that participants in our study rarely, if ever used phrases like: "Which hole do you mean?" or "Where are you pointing at?" Such questions would have indicated serious problems in our design.

The system, the evaluation of which we presented here, is a hybrid system for collaboration of users with desktop and wearable computers. As our next goal, we are looking at modifying our system for direct collaboration of two or more wearable users.

Acknowledgments

The results presented in this paper would not have been possible without the generous support of the Human-Interface Group at the University of Oregon. In particular we would like to thank Jay Schneider, Sarah Douglas, Eck Doerry and Ted Kirkpatrick.

References

[1] Bauer, Martin; Heiber, Timo; Kortuem, Gerd, and Segall, Zary. *A Collaborative Wearable System with Remote Sensing.* Proceedings of the 2nd International Symposium on Wearable Computers; 1998 Oct; Pittsburgh, PA. pp.10-17.

[2] Crowley, Terrence; Milazzo, Paul; Baker, Ellie; Forsdick, Harry, and Tomlinson, Raymond. *MMConf: An Infrastructure for Building Shared Multimedia Applications.* Proceedings of Computer Supported Cooperative Work (CSCW) 1990.

[3] Greenberg, Saul and Roseman, Mark. *GroubWeb: A WWW Browser as Real Time Groupware.* In Companion Proceedings of the ACM SIGCHI'96 Conference on Human Factors in Computing Systems; 1996.

[4] Kortuem, Gerd. *Some Issues in the Design of User-Interfaces for Collaborative Wearable Systems* Position paper for VRAIS98 Workshop on Interfaces Wearable Computers, March 15, 1998, Altlanta, GA.

[5] Kortuem, Gerd; Segall, Zary, and Bauer, Martin. *NETMAN: The Design of a Collaborative Wearable Computer System.* MONET: Mobile Networks and Applications; 1999

[6] Kraut, Robert E.; Miller, Mark D., and Siegel, Jane. *Collaboration in Performance of Physical Tasks: Effects on Outcomes and Communication.* Computer Supported Cooperative Work '96 Cambridge, MA, USA: ACM; 1996.

[7] Siegel, J., Kraut, R.E.., John, B.E., Carley, K.M. *An Empirical Study of Collaborative Wearable Systems*, CHI Companion 1995, Denver, Colorado, 312-313.

[8] D. Siewiorek, A. Smailagic, L. Bass, J. Siegel, R. Martin and B. Bennington. *Adtranz: A Mobile Computing System for Maintenance and Collaboration.* Proc. of the 2nd International Symposium on Wearable Computers; 1998 Oct; Pittsburgh, PA

[9] Stefik, M.; Foster, G.; Bobrow, D. G.; Kahn, K.; Laning, S., and Suchman, L. *Beyond the Chalkboard: Computer Support for Collaboration and Problem Solving in Meetings.* Computer Supported Cooperative Work: A Book of Readings. Edited by Irene Greif. San Mateo, CA: Morgan Kaufmann. 1988.

Wearable Location Mediated Telecommunications; A First Step Towards Contextual Communication.

J. Bowskill[α], M. Billinghurst[β], B.Crabtree[α], N.Dyer[α], A. Loffler[α]

[α]Emerging Technologies Laboratory   [β] Human Interface Technology Laboratory

BT Laboratories   University of Washington

Martlesham Heath   Box 352-142

Ipswich, IP5 3RE, UK   Seattle, WA 98195, USA

{jerry.bowskill, barry.crabtree, nick.dyer2}@bt.com, grof@hitl.washington.edu

Abstract

Wearable computers provide constant access to computing and communications resources. In this paper we describe how the computing power of wearables can enhance computer-mediated communications, with a focus upon collaborative working. In particular we describe the idea of contextual communication, where contextual cues collected by the wearable computer are used to establish and enhance communication links. We describe the hardware and software technology we have developed to support contextual communication and two experimental contextual communication systems. The first, a wearable conferencing tool uses the user's physical location to select the on line conference which they connect to. The second, MetaPark, is a mixed reality educational experiment which explores communications, data retrieval and recording, and navigation techniques within and across real and virtual environments.

1: Introduction

Since the birth of computers, it has been a design goal of hardware manufacturers to make systems as small and compact as possible. This led on to the migration from monolithic mainframe computers to desktop workstations, and then to portable computers. In more recent years a trend has emerged for full function 'palmtop' computers, such as the Toshiba Libretto, and even 'wearable' computers [1]. The authors use the term wearable to refer to all computing devices that are designed to be mobile. While portable computers are carried to a location and used when the user is stationary, mobile computers are designed to be used whilst the user is moving around and active in other tasks.

Most applications for commercial wearable computers, have been restricted to tasks involving mobile data input or retrieval. However, body worn networked computing devices are suited to many applications and the impact on personal communications will be significant. For example, a networked wearable computer can behave as a mobile phone, audio graphic conferencing terminal, a video conference terminal or as a virtual conferencing terminal (Walker et al [2] presents an overview of such telepresence technologies). The mobile phone itself is the most widely used networked wearable on the planet. Although the physical device has a limited multi-modal interface they typically contain a 250 MIP processor and can act as a 'thin client' to network embedded services, for example allowing users to send and receive email, fax and video.

We are interested in designing and evaluating novel telecommunications applications suitable for future mobile devices and networks. Researchers such as Bauer et. al. [3] and Kraut et. al. [4] have already shown that the ability to run standard desktop conferencing applications improves remote collaboration between a user of a wearable computer and remote expert. However, there are many other telecommunication applications in which the capabilities of the wearable computer can be used to significantly enhance communication.

Fickas identifies context sensitive computing as one of the unique capabilities of wearable computers [5]. Our research has focussed on the idea of 'contextual communication' and in this paper we show how the context sensitive capability of wearable computers can be used to develop contextually aware communication applications. We then describe hardware and software technology we have developed to create contextual communication interfaces and finally several sample applications.

2: Context Sensitive Computing

As Fickas notes, wearable computers are intimately associated with their users and the surrounding environment. Sensors can be connected to the computer to detect changes in the state of the user or the environment, thus the wearable computer can be sensitive to contextual cues. We use the broad term "contextual computing" to

159

describe a computer interface that identifies and responds to changes in user or environmental contextual cues. The notion of context sensitive computing also encompasses Picard's "Affective Computing"[6], Pentland's "Perceptual Computing" [7] and other similar terms.

There have been many examples presented of context sensitive wearable applications. For example Healy and Picard use biometric sensors to detect which a user is startled and take pictures of the event that caused the fright [8], while Feiner et. al. use position sensing to display virtual cues over the real world as a navigation aid [9]. At present, much of the context must be entered manually, although the phone can respond unprompted to the in-car adapter. In the future there will be much more direct input from sensors and other networked devices.

Much of the near term research activity around context sensitive wearables is addressing "contextual information services", primarily "mobile location services". These aim to deliver timely and location specific media such as traffic reports or tourist information to either mobile phones or palmtop PC terminals. However instead of using location to just provide information it could also be used to provide context based communication services.

We define contextual communication as communication that is mediated or initiated by contextual cues arising from the user or environmental state. A simple example of a wearable contextual communication device is a heart monitor that initiates an emergency call in response to a heart attack, connecting the victim to medical staff.

Although we are interested in all the possible varieties of contextual communication, our initial research focus has been on location based communication. A specific research focus is on using wearables to allow people in a real world environment to access remote people and multimedia information held within an on-line collaborative virtual environment. In concept this is similar to the idea of "co-habited mixed realities" [10]; as "wearers" move through the real world they also move through either literal or abstract virtual environments. For example, when entering our research laboratory a wearable computer user can be connected to an augmented reality conferencing session with other team members who are working remotely.

The use of location to mediate communication has several benefits for asynchronous and synchronous conferencing, including:
- giving the user access to remote people who are familiar with their context, when they need them.
- Allow the user to communicate within their physical community even when they are remote
- promoting communications within a community

Location based contextual communication is a first step

toward a "ubiquitous telepresence" in which telecommunication is being dynamically mediated based on a "contextual awareness" of the wearer's current location, task, availability, skills and social profiles. Our vision of "ubiquitous telepresence" shares many features with Mark Weiser's [11] earlier work on "ubiquitous computing", and "ubiquitous media" by Buxton et al [12]. It is motivated by technology trends in miniaturisation and performance, which will enable an unparalleled range of hardware and services – an explosion in the technical possibilities which serves to emphasize the importance of user studies, in informing future developments. Our long-term research goal is to deliver "seamless service": a re-purposing of interface and content, which delivers appropriate functionality to the user across a range of devices and in a variety of settings. Seamless service would include transitions between different bandwidths and terminals, in an extension of the hand-over between base stations in existing mobile services.

Even in a desktop service, context may play a significant role. For example an incoming communications request could be handled differently, depending on factors such as availability, relationship with the caller, terminal characteristics, and other ongoing and scheduled activities. The same initial contact might result in a videoconference, audio connection or voicemail. Sawhney demonstrates similar availability features in his Nomadic radio wearable audio interface [13], although Nomadic radio does not support synchronous communication.

Context is even more important in a wearable setting, with many more permutations of terminal type, network connectivity, user activity and perceptual loading. In handling all the service options, there will be a role for intelligent personal agents and profiles to manage the mushrooming complexity. Personal Agents [14] adapt and learn users interests and needs to be able to perform specific tasks on the users behalf. A good example is a personal agent that learns how to manage a users incoming e-mail, and automate the filing or deleting of irrelevant messages. These agents can provide a better service by knowing not only the interests and needs of the user, but also taking advantage of the immediate context to help mediate information filtering or delivery.

3: Enabling Hardware - Location

In order to develop location aware contextual communication applications, it is necessary to use position sensing technology. In this section we describe custom RF beacon hardware which we have developed for location detection.

Previous researchers at MIT have shown how small InfraRed (IR) transmitters and receivers (so-called

"Locusts") can be used for location sensing [15]. Similar work has also been used by researchers at Georgia Tech for location aware information presentation. However there are some limitations with using IR for broadcasting location including limited range, reliance on line of sight and interference from other light sources – especially out of doors where daylight levels make a major impact. In order to overcome these limitations we have modified the original MIT Locust design to support RF signals.

We have converted the standard MIT Locust boards into either an RF transmitter (mounted in the environment as a beacon), or an RF receiver worn as part of the wearable (figure 1). Complete details of the modifications and the components used can be found on our web site [16]. The transmitter was created by adding the MPT 1340 low power low cost RF transmitter to the Locust board. The MPT 1340 is a 418MHz AM Transmitter capable of transmitting at 1200bps with a range of up to 100 meters. The receiver was created by adding a Super RX AM receiver to the Locust board. Low Power Radio Solutions produce both devices [17]. The modifications make use of unused I/O pins and as such do not affect the current IR capabilities of the Locust board.

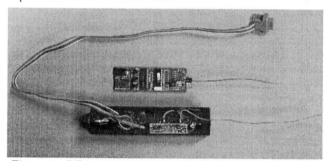

Figure 1. RF Locust Receiver (below) and Transmitter

These RF devices are inexpensive and can transmit a signal, a packet containing a unique ID, that can be received with sufficient accuracy even where physical obstructions cause radio attenuation. The major disadvantage is that these devices all transmit the same frequency and can therefore cause interference when used in close proximity with each other. To alleviate the problem, the strength of the beacon must be balanced between providing adequate coverage for each specific location, and enough attenuation to prevent interference with neighboring beacons.

4: Example Applications

In this section we describe two sample applications for wearable computers that illustrate location mediated communication. Building these systems has helped highlight some of the general issues and opportunities for contextual communications. The first, the location aware wearable communications space has been completed while the second, MetaPark, is still under development.

4.1 Location Aware Wearable Conferencing

In previous work we presented a Wearable Communication Space (WearCom) [18]. This enabled a wearable computer user to communicate with multiple remote people in a virtual environment that supported high quality audio communication, augmented reality visual representations of the collaborators and an underlying spatial metaphor. Figure 2 shows the wearable user's view of the conferencing space with the virtual avatars of the participants overlaid on the real world.

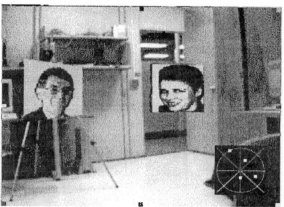

Figure 2. The WearCom wearable conferencing space.

We have developed a location aware version of the WearCom application by coupling the audio components of the WearCom interface with the RF beacon transmitters and receivers described in the last section.

The WearCom audio code creates a unique TCP/IP multicast group that allows client applications to communicate with each other through multicast sockets. The multicast protocol is an efficient mechanism for broadcasting data to multiple network nodes [19] and has been shown to scale extremely well. In our location aware application we have modified this code to allow the creation of multiple multicast audio groups. All the clients connected to a particular group receive the audio data broadcast only to that group.

For location sensing we have RF Locust beacons distributed throughout our laboratory. Each of these beacons broadcasts a specific ID which is mapped to a particular multicast audio group address. More than one ID can be mapped to the same address. The wearable user carries a RF Locust receiver attached to the serial port of their wearable computer. In initial experiments we are using modified Toshiba Libretto handheld computers with head mounted display, GPS, radio LAN, GSM, microphones and speakers (figure 3).

When the user starts the wearable audio application they are connected to a default multicast audio group. If the microphone is active any words they speak are digitized, broadcast to the multicast group and re-broadcast to all the other user connected enabling them to have full duplex continuous audio communication. However, when the wearable user is within range of a particular beacon their client code notifies the user and prompts them to see if they want to change audio spaces. If they agree, then the multicast group is changes to that corresponding to the beacon ID. Since beacons only broadcast their ID numbers intermittently the multicast audio group only changes if a new beacon is detected. All the connections to the multicast groups are bi-directional and users can connect and disconnect at will without affecting other users in the particular conferencing space.

Figure 3: Modified Toshiba Libretto Wearable

The effect is that the user can immediately be connected to audio communication spaces associated with physical locations. For example, a user in the coffee area on one floor of our laboratory can be in audio communication with all the other users in the other coffee areas throughout the building since the beacon IDs for these locations map to the same audio group.

This application demonstrates how location aware contextual communication applications fuse the real and virtual worlds. In this case the users real location is used to connect them to a virtual audio conferencing space. In the next section we discuss MetaPark, an application under development which uses contextual communication to mix real and virtual visual and auditory spaces.

4.2 MetaPark

The concept of using contextual cues to fuse real and virtual space is being explored through the development of an educational environment called 'MetaPark'. MetaPark is currently under construction and consists of a collaborative virtual environment modeled on a real park which is used by schools in central Ipswich as a learning resource. This work has evolved after a number of years research into the use of collaborative virtual learning environments, including interactive video environments and wearable augmented reality information spaces.

The central idea behind MetaPark is to create a 'co-habited mixed reality' using a literal virtual representation of a real world park which is accessible either on-line or via moving through the real world space itself. Palmtop and wearable devices are used as novel interfaces onto virtual environments and as 'portals' between virtual world content and the inhabitants within the real world park. For example we imagine field workers with wearables being able to access, gather and store information. Fellow children at school will communicate and exchange information through the real time 3D simulation of the park.

The MetaPark prototype is based on the Sony Community Place software [20], although the long term objective is to use the experimental MUON framework [21] described in the next section. A Community Place 'Bureau' multi-user server, running on a Unix workstation, hosts the online environment and maintains the consistency of the world to the many simultaneous users. Users of more conventional desktop computers run the Community Place Browser, a stand-alone application rather than a plug-in, which allows the world to be viewed and navigated. A view of the world through the browser is shown in figure 4, along with the corresponding chat window. The browser also supports communications within the world including text chat and the ability to select a number of standard avatar actions, such as smiling or waving goodbye. To maximise system speed, a concern with such a large model, each client has a local copy of the VRML model. As they select to join a world the local model is loaded and a connection made to the bureau which serves the initial world state, including the location of the other inhabitants, and subsequent state changes. As a user navigates the world so these changes are relayed to the bureau. User's accessing the virtual world using the browser are represented by standard avatars.

Figure 4. Community Place Browser.

The browser was not considered appropriate for the wearable clients for a number of reasons. As the real world environment from which the virtual world is based surrounds the wearer there is little value in seeing the

3Dmodel. Rather the wearer need only be aware of those inhabitants of the virtual world who share their current location. The browser also requires the user to move their own avatar using the mouse or cursor keys. Therefore a custom client was created for the wearable, a Java application which connects to the bureau via the Community Place application object interface. This application behaves as a browser client, allowing user's to connect to the world, receive state information and update the bureau of avatar movements and actions. However the interface is radically different. A user navigates the virtual world not through the keyboard but by making corresponding movements in their real world environment. GPS positional data from the remote wearable system is used to place a virtual representation of the remote user within the 3D park model. This will allow the class mates to follow the path of the remote users as they explore the environment. The Java application reads GPS data from a Garmin GPS-35 connected to a serial port, calculates movements in virtual world co-ordinates, and updates the bureau. User's entering the world from the application object are represented with a different avatar, signifying that they are a 'real person' in the 'real world'.

The experimental graphical interface used on the wearable computer is shown in figure 5. People from the virtual world who are within the aura of the wearable user appear on the interface as a picture icon in a dedicated area. Up to ten of these icons (two rows of five) can be shown at any one time while preserving space at the bottom of the screen for text chat messages. The size of the icon gives an indication of their proximity, the icon getting bigger as they approach and smaller as they get further away. The rate of movement of the icon indicates their speed of movement through the virtual environment.

Background colour is also used to indicate movement and more importantly requests for communications. A black/grey/white background indicates they are moving away/stationary/towards you. A chequered background indicates they want to talk to you, currently via text chat. In the future we will be supporting duplex speech either through the Community Place bureau which supports voice over IP or directly as a GSM voice call to a Nokia PCMCIA card phone in the wearable.

While the MetaPark environment is still being developed, the authors have been able to demonstrate elements of the system. For example the underlying network framework has been implemented, the Community Place based system is running and user evaluation is now possible.

From a technical viewpoint, the network architecture that supports remote communication between the real and virtual MetaPark visitors provides a technical challenge of significant complexity. When the system is functionally complete a more intensive period of evaluation will commence. In particular the authors hope to understand the relationships between the virtual and real space communities, the types of learning that occurs and the communications mechanisms used.

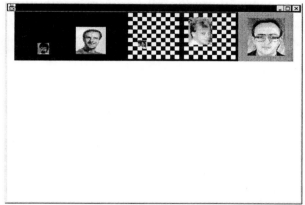

Figure5. Wearable Interface.

In terms of evaluation, longitudinal studies will provide qualitative understanding of the practical appeal of ubiquitous telepresence, but with radically new hardware there is also scope for more constrained, quantitative assessment of the options in presenting and interacting with wearable interfaces.

5: Requirements for Contextual Communications

In order to support contextual communication it is necessary to design a network architecture that allows mobile users to communicate without the need to concern themselves with the underlying technical issues which this implies. This network architecture should also transparently support the various contextual cues collected by the wearable computer. The experiments detailed above have helped us highlight the important issues.

It is worth considering the generic capabilities of contextual applications. Pascoe [22] identifies four capabilities that can be summarised as follows:

- **Sensing** – the wearable detects sensor data, perhaps processes it, then presents it to the user.

- **Adaptation** – context data is used to adapt application behavior to be in keeping with the user's environment.

- **Resource Discovery** – the wearable searches for resources that can be exploited while they remain in the same context.

- **Augmentation** – the wearable is used to augment the environment with additional information by associating data with a particular context.

We believe an additional generic capability also exists, namely the wearable *brokering* context to other people. For example a fire officer may need to be aware of the location of others within a burning building and use a wearable computer to receive this information from context sensing devices attached to computers inside the building. As our long-term focus is on producing an application framework for contextual communications, these capabilities must be accommodated. Our solution has been to specify a client / server network support system called the MUON (Mobile User Object Notification) Framework. A previous publication gives details of the proposed system architecture [21]. The specific features that a contextual communications network architecture (such as the MUON framework) must support are now discussed under the headings proposed by Pascoe.

5.1 Contextual Sensing
Context is obviously subjective and potentially based on many raw sensors both on the wearable and within the environment. Several generic cues emerge for contextual communications and, not surprisingly, location is the most obvious. To facilitate location awareness, the client requires a mechanism that determines its current position within a pre-defined mapping of physical space. This was accomplished by the use of radio location beacons mentioned previously and client receiver modules. From a software viewpoint, the server maintains a master database of each named location matched with its respective beacon code. When a client receives a beacon it passes this up to the server, which replies with the matching location name. In this manner, the server can track each client as it moves around its environment, and a user can interrogate the system to find the location of another client. The issue of privacy can be managed by allowing each user to dynamically switch between broadcasting or hiding their location as they see fit.

Sensing the availability of people is a significant goal within contextual communications. In practice this will involve physical activity sensors on the wearable in combination with system/application usage monitors. We have developed an example of such a device; a locust PCB which has been modified to include tilt switches mounted on the end of a trailing lead (figure 6). The PIC has been reprogrammed to gather location data and perform a moving average on the switch positions. If the tilt switches are worn in the user's pocket it becomes possible to detect if they are sitting, standing or walking and their cadence. We intend the Java application to use this activity data to animate the user's avatar in the

MetaPark environment.

The nature of wearable computers dictates that the user can be in many states of availability according to their current situation. It has been a design goal from the outset to allow clients to employ the features of agent technologies that provide user availability information, and allow the system to respond to this information accordingly. Gateways allow the server to connect to agent servers, allowing information to be exchanged between various applications. This allows clients to utilize these services without the need to have a predefined IP address (as some of the agent servers require this) or be continuously connected to the network, as the server (which does have a unique IP address) acts as the go-between.

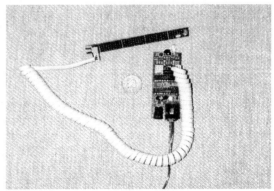
Figure 6. User activity sensor

5.2 Contextual Adaptation
The ability for an interface or application to adapt to the user's context has much potential. For example the activity sensor shown in figure 6 has been successfully used to switch between audio and visual location augmentation so the user has to stand still before information is displayed on the screen. In terms of communications a key goal will be for the interface to adapt in order to promote the most appropriate communications channel. The wearable MetaPark client exhibits a degree of adaptation, the properties of the communications icons are varied based on the location and speed of movement of remote people (or rather their avatars) in a virtual world. Given a voice channel in addition to text chat then decisions could be made about which type of communication to offer the user based on attributes such as available bandwidth, distance between people, how well the people know each other, personal preferences etc. This is unlikely to be trivial.

5.3 Contextual Resource Discovery
There are many potential examples where acquiring a resource, such as a display, may enhance a communications task on a wearable. However the fundamental resource that needs arbitrating in real time is

the network. An ability to switch between networks transparently is a major consideration. This ability to automatically switch between service providers should accommodate when the connection drops, a better bandwidth is available, or even when lower power consumption can be achieved via a different service provider e.g. switching from a wireless LAN to BlueTooth. The currently supported service providers are wired LAN, wireless radio LAN, infrared via serial, direct serial connection, and modem (including GSM mobile modem). Clients can select the best service providers available at log-on time, and monitor the availability of other services based on a pre-defined prioritized list.

5.4 Contextual Augmentation

With the ability to determine location, the network can provide location-based messaging. This is where a message can be directed to a location instead of an individual user. As users with location tracking devices move around their environment, they receive messages that have been "posted" to their current location. Conversely, they may post messages at specific locations. The location messages are sent to the server, and stored in the beacon database. When messages have expired, the server deletes them accordingly. Each message is assigned a unique ID, that is used to amend a user's database each time they read a location message, to prevent continuous notifications being sent for messages they have previously received. Previous similar work on location based messaging has been reported by reported by Pascoe [21] and Rekimoto et al [23].

The MUON Framework allows users to send text and binary (pictures, files, etc.) data to people and locations. When two (or more) users are online simultaneously, a location based dialog can be arranged between each client. This semi-synchronous communications medium is more commonly known as text-chat. To support contextual communications other forms of synchronous communications must be possible. For synchronous communications, both users must be online and have enough available bandwidth to cope with the continuous stream of data between each other. Audio and video communications channels are then possible. For example, the conferencing space described in section 4.1 establishes multiple voice connections based on location. The MUON Framework will not support synchronous communications services directly, but will support external IP-based services by negotiating the connection and disconnection processes between the users.

5.5 Context Brokering

Making user context available to other, trusted, parties is a desirable feature. For example within multiparty collaborations there may be real benefits in releasing information like location as it provides cues that allow others to appreciate the constraints which govern your conversation. This is particular true between mobile wearable users and non-mobile desk users. There is also an important role for a "context provider" to present the user with at least a degree of consistency and integration. The role of this provider would include consistency in areas such as billing and authentication, and also avoid duplication of profiles and real-time contextual data such as location and availability. The MUON framework server stores context data which may then be accessed from other services. There many security and privacy issues with this and our aim is to explore the issues, benefits, and disadvantages of local verses remote context brokering.

6: Conclusions

In this paper we have discussed the concept contextual communications and highlighted some of the current wearables research at BT Laboratories that seeks to explore this concept. The potential of developing contextual communications around wearables is significant. Firstly it will impact current mobile telephony and services. It is already clear that location aware mobile communicators will proliferate. This will certainly promote location based information services. However other sensors within the device are sure to follow, allowing information or calls to be mediated based on the availability of the user and their ability to attend to their device. For example it is easy to imagine the activity sensor board shown in figure 6 integrated into a mobile communicator allowing the device to select to play or display messages. It is also easy to imagine that the type of communication could be mediated by context, since it is already possible for a wearable computer to access any known communications channel.

Of equal importance is the ability of user devices to send contextual cues to others, such as giving people an awareness of the movement of others in MetaPark. Giving other people contextual cues has the potential to compensate for some of the asymmetries that are endemic with wearable and mobile communications, particularly when connected to others who are not mobile. For example, when calling a number that has a mobile prefix allowances are usually subconsciously made for transmission quality and the ability of the person being called to manage the call. The mismatch in expectations can be noticeable when people call a normal number but which is being diverted to a mobile device being used while walking in the street.

Beyond the evolution of current day services and devices our research into wearables has the potential to develop new forms of communication. For example the marrying of a real world community with an on-line community, within a common purpose and geographical context, via MetaPark. At the time of writing the MetaPark research has not been evaluated but the expectation is that communications will become more appropriate, richer and frequent. Time will tell. What is certain is that as wearables become more pervasive mechanisms will be needed to mediate the constant availability of the hardware in line with our variability to respond.

7: References

[1] T. Starner, S. Mann, B. Rhodes, J. Levine, J. Healey, D. Kirsch, R. Picard, and A. Pentland, 'Augmented Reality Through Wearable Computing', Presence 6(4), 1997.

[2] G.Walker and P.Sheppard, ' Telepresence – the future of telephony', BT Technology Journal, Vol. 15, No. 4, October 1997.

[3] Bauer, M., Heiber, T., Kortuem, G., Segall, Z. A Collaborative Wearable System with Remote Sensing. In proceedings of ISWC 1998, pp. 10-17.

[4] Kraut, R., Miller, M., Siegal, J. Collaboration in Performance of Physical Tasks: Effects on Outcomes and Communication. In *Proceedings of CSCW '96*, Nov. 16th-20th, Cambridge MA, 1996, New York, NY: ACM Press.

[5] Fickas, S., Kortuem, G., Segall, Z., Software Issues in Wearable Computing. Position paper for CHI Workshop on Research Issues in Wearable Computers, March 23-24, 1997, Atlanta. http://www.cs.uoregon.edu/research/wearables/Papers/

[6] Picard, R. Affective Computing. MIT Press, 1997.

[7] http://www.media.mit.edu/Projects/pentland.html

[8] Picard, R. W., & Healey, J. (1997). Affective Wearables. In Proceedings of the International Symposium on Wearable Computers, (pp. 90-97). Los Alamitos, CA, USA: IEEE Computer Society.

[9] Feiner, S., MacIntyre, B. Hollerer, T. A Touring Machine: Prototyping 3D Mobile Augmented Reality Systems for Exploring the Urban Environment. In Proc. 1st International Symposium on Wearable Computers, Cambridge, MA, October 13-14, 1997, Los Alamitos: IEEE Press, pp. 74-81.

[10] Van de Velde W., "Co-habited mixed realities", Proc. international workshop on "community ware", IJCOAI, Tokyo, Japan 1997.

[11] Weisner M., "The computer for the 21st century", Scientific American, 265(3), pp. 94-104, 1991.

[12] Buxton W., "Living in Augmented Reality: Ubiquitous Media and Reactive Environments". In K. Finn, A. Sellen & S. Wilber (Eds.). Video Mediated Communication. Hillsdale, N.J.: Erlbaum, pp. 363-384, 1997

[13] Sawhney, N. and Schmandt, C., 'Speaking and listening on the run: design for wearable audio computing', Proc. 2nd international symposium on wearable computers, pp.108-115, October 19-20, 1998.

[14] Crabtree,B., Soltysiak, S.J., and Thint, M.P., Adaptive Personal Agents, Personal Technologies, Vol. 2, pp141-151, 1998

[15] Starner, T., Kirsch, D., & Assefa, S. (1997). The Locust Swarm: An Environmentally-Powered, Networkless Location and Messaging System [poster]. In Proceedings of the International Symposium on Wearable Computers, (pp. 169-170). Los Alamitos, CA, USA: IEEE Computer Society.

[16] RF Locust Radio Beacon Details http://wearables.www.media.mit.edu/projects/wearables/locust/rf-locust/

[17] Low Power radio Solutions. http://www.lprs.co.uk/

[18] Billinghurst M., Bowskill J., Jessop M.and Morphett J., "A wearable spatial conferencing space", Proc. 2nd international symposium on wearable computers, pp.76-83, October 19-20, 1998.

[19] Kumar V. Mbone: Interactive Multimedia on the Internet. New Riders, Indianapolis, Indiana, 1995.

[20] Sony Community Place. http://www.community-place.com

[21] Dyer, N., Bowskill, J., 'Ubiquitous Communications and Media: Steps towards a Wearable Learning Tool', British Computer Society Conference on 'Digital Media Futures', 13-15 April 1999, Bradford, UK.

[22] Pascoe, J., "Adding generic contextual capabilities to wearable computers", Proc. 2nd international symposium on wearable computers, pp.92-99, October 19-20, 1998.

[23] Rekimoto, J., Ayatsuka, Y., and Hayashi, K., 'Augment-able reality: situated communication through physical and digital spaces', Proc. 2nd international symposium on wearable computers, pp.68-75, October 19-20, 1998.

Batteries and power supplies for wearable and ubiquitous computing

Robert Hahn, Herbert Reichl
Fraunhofer Institute for Reliability and Microintegration
Gustav-Meyer-Allee 25, 13355 Berlin, Germany
hahn@izm.fhg.de

Abstract

The paper discusses the energy storage requirements of wearable computer technology and identifies research topics for novel battery technologies. Three categories of devices with basically different battery requirements were defined. They comprise the wearable computer main unit, small devices which are distributed around the human body and active tags which enable situated and ubiquitous computing. There is a demand for small, high energy density rechargeable batteries which enable a flexible design and for very low cost thin primary batteries for smart label active tags. Prototypes of 120 μm thick AgO-Zn batteries have been fabricated by a screen printing process. They can be directly integrated into plastic cards, smart labels and hybrid circuits.

1. Introduction

During last years impressive examples of wearable computing have been demonstrated within the scientific community. Nevertheless wearable computers impose major challenges to microelectronic packaging and power supply technologies. Systems not only have to become much smaller in size, packages must also become mechanically flexible and water-resistant (washable computing) and they have to be fabricated at low cost. Another issue is energy supply. Batteries are a significant source of size, weight and inconvenience to present-day systems.

Although research is underway to utilize energy of the human body as a source of electrical power for wearable computers [1, 2], there is still a need to improve batteries and to optimize them for specific applications.

2. Energy Storage Requirements

The power requirements of the wearable computer main unit may be comparable to high performance notebooks. Energy can be saved since there is no large area display to operate and part of the energy consuming data processing can be done on a wireless interconnected host computer. On the other hand many energy intensive functions will be in operation on the mobile device such as natural language processing, vision processing and data storage.
A second category of power requirements is related to devices which are distributed at several points around the human body like smart glasses with a virtual display, smart watches, sensors and others. They must have their own power supply since connecting them to a central power source by running wires through ones clothing is undesirable and would reduce user acceptance greatly. The use of primary batteries which have to be replaced regularly becomes problematic for these devices as the number of carried appliances are increasing. Therefore rechargeable batteries have to be used. It would be most convenient if they receive their charging energy from power harvesting of the human body [1,2] or from wireless transmission of electrical energy compliant to the personal area network [3]. In these cases energy can be supplied fully autonomous without any user interaction.

Perhaps first implementations will use inductive charging which also avoids replacement of batteries. First systems of this kind are already on the market for hearing aids. The batteries should be small and have a high energy density. Special, application specific geometrical designs must be available, for example for smart glasses. Since the batteries are integrated into the device they must have a life time equal to the product.

A third category of power requirements is related to devices which are distributed in the users local environment which enable situated or ubiquitous computing and are based on an active tagging technology. Size and cost of most active tags are more or less dominated by the battery. The acceptable size of a tag depends on the thing it is marking. For example tags for a room or a car can be designed with existing technology. A tag carried by an individual should be no bigger than a credit card and a smart label marking a book or a bottle of milk might need to be as small as a postage stamp. For these applications small, thin batteries which can be integrated into credit cards or which are even thinner (below 100 μm) have to be developed. Depending on the application, the cost of these batteries must be very low to allow for widespread deployment. Therefore primary batteries will be used. As we might expect a tag to be essentially free of maintenance a battery life between months and several years is required.

In particular we see a demand for:

- Rechargeable batteries which are thin and mechanically flexible and available in application specific form factors. The charge/discharge cycle behavior has to be optimized for the discharge profile of the wearable components as well as for the erratic charging profile which occurs in case of power delivery from the human body, from solar cells and others.

- Primary batteries with very low self discharge to deliver energy during the whole product life time. These batteries can be integrated into the products. Therefore they have to comply with environmental regulations. Low cost fabrication techniques are imperative for widespread use in active tag systems. Many applications like smart label, smart cards and electronics integrated into clothing are demanding flat battery packages or integration of thin battery layers.

- A novel miniaturized package based on flexible circuitry, integrated passive components and thin ICs have to be developed.

3. Battery Development

A five years research project witch addresses these issues starts in 1999. It is founded with 25 million DM by the German government. The Fraunhofer Institute for Reliability and Microintegration (FhG-IZM) will lead a project team of 17 partners from industry and academia. Under the program the partner will seek to

- develop Li-polymer batteries based on a new electrolyte which will allow to reduce production cost and increase long term stability.

- develop thin primary batteries based on a polymer thickfilm technology, which can be integrated into packages and modules. For miniaturized Li-batteries humidity tight packaging is a major cost factor. Since the focus here is on very low cost products a Li-free material system will be investigated.

- develop ultra low power battery managing systems which can be implemented in a wide variety of miniaturized electronic applications. Depositable soft magnetic materials will be developed for the integration of passive components into the electronic circuitry for charging and voltage conversion.

The results of the project will be demonstrated with several applications including a new Li-polymer battery with miniaturized smart battery electronic, a credit card sized solar-battery module for charging of portable electronics, a fully encapsulated active smart label system with integrated batteries and several credit card sized sensor modules based on electrochemical sensors and primary batteries which are fabricated with compatible polymer thick film processes.

4. First Results

Small Li primary batteries can be fabricated at high productivity in button sized / coin-type format and cost below 1 US$. A long term reliable sealing is accomplished by means of two metallic terminals and a thick ring gasket. This design is no longer appropriate when very thin (<1 mm) and mechanically flexible batteries have to be used. A humidity tight sealing of thin Li batteries is a major challenge and a big cost factor.

As outlined above, very low cost thin batteries are imperative for wide spread deployment in everyday life. Therefore we have chosen a silver oxide based material system for the development of very thin batteries. Compared to Li they do not need dry room facilities for production and are compatible with more straight forward sealing methods. Although cell voltage is approximately half of Li-systems, the lower energy density can be compensated in the case of thin foil type batteries because the sealing of Li-Batteries adds remarkably to the battery volume. The silver-oxide battery is fabricated by printing of thick film pastes and can be passivated with a thin sealing layer. The comparison of a 120 µm thick printed AgO-Zn battery prototype of approximately 30 mAh [4] with coin-type cells and credit card sized Li-batteries is shown in figure 1. It demonstrates how encapsulation thickness of sheet batteries adds remarkably to the volumetric energy density.

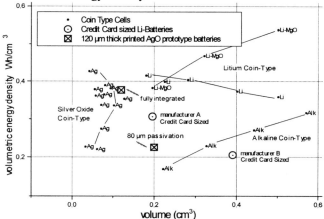

Fig. 1: Energy density comparison of prototype printable thin primary batteries with credit card sized Li-batteries and with commercially available button cells.

References

[1] T. Starner „Human powered wearable Computing", IBM Systems Journal, Vol.35, No 3&4, 1996, p.618

[2] J. Kymissis, C. Kendall, J. Paradiso, N. Gershenfeld, Parasitic Power Harvesting in Shoes, Proc. of 2. IEEE ICWC 1998

[3] E.R. Post, M. Reynolds, M. Gray, J. Paradiso, N. Gershenfeld, „Intrabody Busses for Data and Power", Proc. of First Int. Symposium on Wearable Computers, Oct. 13-14, 1997, pp.52-55.

[4] P. Otschick, C. Kretzschmar, „Projektbeschreibung Energieminimierte Systemintegration, Teil 2: Integrierbare Batterien", FhG-IKTS 1999.

Sulawesi: A Wearable Application Integration Framework

Neill J. Newman and Adrian F. Clark
VASE Laboratory, University of Essex
Colchester, Essex, CO4 3SQ, UK
{njnewm,alien}@essex.ac.uk

Abstract

This paper describes Sulawesi, a framework for developing applications for wearable computing that are capable of multi-modal interaction with the user. The design principles of the framework are described along with its main features, and some example applications that exploit the capabilities of the framework are outlined.

1 Introduction

In comparison to the desktop graphical user interface (GUI), there has been little research into the interaction between a person and a wearable computing device. It is clear from observations and research results (*e.g.,* [3]) that a desktop user interface is unsuitable. A Web questionnaire [2] showed that researchers favour some form of multi-modal user interface for interaction with a wearable, rather than the desktop interfaces in use today. The authors have attempted to address this issue by designing and constructing a multi-modal user interface framework, Sulawesi. Our aim has been to provide a system that can accommodate a wide range of interaction techniques and can be adapted through well-defined programming interfaces, making it possible to tailor the framework for any specific purpose.

2 Sulawesi: Design Principles

In the future, lower-powered processors such as the StrongARM will probably be used in wearables and hence one of the design criteria was to use a platform neutral-language. Java was chosen over C because of its binary platform independence. Sulawesi was designed as an agent-based framework, separating the agents (or services) from the interaction mechanisms; see Fig. 1. Services interact with devices through input and output managers, while the use of a service manager enables agents within the system to be

check-pointed to disk and have their progress monitored. This contributes to a further design goal of providing transparent protection against data loss, and recovery should the system lose power.

The input manager allows devices to be connected easily and configured on a running system. It also provides an *abstraction layer* between the raw data and the services. This abstraction layer extracts device-independent information from the device-specific data and sends it to a service for processing. For example, it is possible to access raw GPS coordinate data but it may be more useful to know that a particular position refers to the local supermarket.

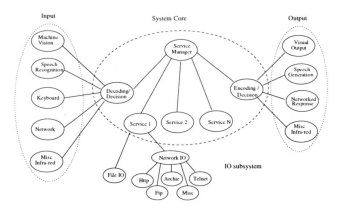

Figure 1: Sulawesi structural design

The output manager handles the rendering of information from the agents. This again provides an abstraction layer between the agents and real-world output. The output manager gathers information from the input and service managers and the agents to determine the user's current situation and can adjust the rendering of the information accordingly.

3 Framework Features

The core of the system contains a simple but effective natural language parser which converts a sentence (either spoken or typed) into a command stream [1]. Sulawesi currently performs speech recognition via Java's Speech SDK, driving IBM's ViaVoice engine under Linux and Windows. This speech module can communicate spoken words, sentences, or even just the knowledge that somebody is talking, to the system core. Two pieces of information are extracted from the sentence: the service to invoke and how the output should be rendered. The list of services is constructed dynamically by the system, while the verbs controlling the renderers are stored in a (modifiable) look-up table. This semi-natural language processing is perhaps best explained by example: *Could you show me what the time is* and *Please tell me the time* both result in the user being informed of the time, the former visually and the latter audibly.

Sulawesi also incorporates a message broadcasting system which allows the agents and the managers to communicate with each other. For example, a message can be sent from the input to the output manager telling it that the user is moving so that the output manager can decide to re-direct (where possible) visual information to the speech renderer.

4 Example Applications

To demonstrate the flexibility of Sulawesi, some example applications are outlined which illustrate different aspect of the framework's design.

The **News agent** demonstrates Sulawesi's sentence processing and automatic output re-direction mechanisms. The service receives a command in the form: *Would you tell me the sports news please*. The information is retrieved from the relevant source (*e.g.*, a website) using information stored in a configuration file and sent to the output manager. It examines all the available information from the input sensors to determine whether this would be satisfactory and, if it is, presents the information audibly.

The **Notes service** demonstrates the integration of an existing application and the use of multiple interaction techniques within a single application. It is controlled either by a simple graphical user interface tailored for wearable use or by speech. Notes are created with spoken or typed sentences such as *Would you save a note about the mail config on the web server*. Each note is stored separately, and the entire set indexed with the Remembrance Agent [4]. Queries may again be spoken or typed, such as *I would like you to query my notes about the web server*. Alternatively, the user may manipulate the GUI to save or query their notes.

The **spatial reminder service** is a truly mobile application as it monitors the user's environment through sensors and responds accordingly. It provides reminders triggered by the spatial position of the wearable. A reminder can be set using a simple spoken or typed phrase such as *When I go to the shops, remind me to buy some bread and milk*. The service monitors the user's environment using GPS and infra-red location beacons to determine position; it switches seamlessly between detectors when entering or leaving a building. (Locations are defined in a configuration file.) When the agent detects that the user is at a certain location and a reminder for that location has been set the reminder is sent to the output renderer.

5 Summary

Sulawesi has undergone preliminary testing by the authors: our experience is encouraging enough to pursue non-traditional user interfaces for wearables. Although we do not suggest that Sulawesi is *ideal* for a wearable, our experience suggests that an alternative user interface is necessary.

Further information on Sulawesi is available at `http://wearables.essex.ac.uk/sulawesi/`. You are welcome to download it and try it out.

References

[1] L.J.Najjar, J.J.Ockerman, and J.C.Thompson. User interface design guidelines for wearable computer speech recognition applications. In *IEEE VRAIS98*. Georgia Tech, 1998. `http://www.hitl.washington.edu/people/grof/VRAIS98/home.html`.

[2] Neill Newman. Wearable computing questionaire: Results, 1998. `http://wearables.essex.ac.uk/sulawesi/feedback-results.html`.

[3] Bradley Rhodes. WIMP interface considered fatal. In *VRAIS98*, 1998. `http://www.hitl.washington.edu/people/grof/VRAIS98/Rhodes.html`.

[4] Bradley J Rhodes. The wearable remebrance agent: a system for augumented memory. Technical report, Massachusetts Institute of Technology, 1997. `http://wearables.www.media.mit.edu/projects/wearables/mitres.html`.

The Matchbox PC: A Small Wearable Platform

GREG DEFOUW
Stanford University
gdefouw@cs.stanford.edu

VAUGHAN PRATT
Stanford University
pratt@cs.stanford.edu

Abstract

We describe the Matchbox PC, a fully functional PC not much larger than a box of matches yet able to run popular operating systems such as Linux and Windows and to perform most tasks commonly run on desktop PCs. Although our motivating application is wearable computing, we expect many other applications will emerge.

1 Introduction

Recent advances in VLSI and packaging technology have brought the size of general-purpose computers down into a range previously the domain of embedded computers. It is now becoming possible to use general-purpose computers to build systems that were traditionally based on custom hardware and software.

The burgeoning adoption of general-purpose computers in homes and offices is pushing their price/performance ratio down to that of embedded systems. In addition there is a remarkable volume of software available for them. Smailagic et al [1], while objecting to the high costs of off-the-shelf solutions, acknowledge a 30% reduction of software porting. For today's software systems this would seem a gross underestimate. There is much less software for special purpose computers, and it is much more expensive because each such computer has relatively few customers each of whom must shoulder a proportionately greater share of the software development costs.

This software includes tools for creating new applications. For every new embedded system that comes out, not only must software be ported to or written for these new systems but tools must be developed in order to build these new applications. This development is simpler when the target is the same platform as that on which the applications are built. In addition the motivation to provide device drivers for any given platform is greater for platforms in wider use.

This paper describes the Matchbox PC. In summary this is a general-purpose PC, having a 66 MHz 486-SX CPU, 16 megabytes of random access memory, 340 MB hard drive, 10 MB/s ethernet interface, VGA output, keyboard inter-face, two serial ports, a parallel port, and floppy interface, brought out to a miniature connector. A second connector brings out 64 ISA bus and IDE controller pins for connecting the CF socket and for further expansion such as audio. With the Microdrive installed the dimensions are 2.8" by 1.8" by .8" (4 cubic inches) with a weight of 2.5 oz. We also discuss the challenges in building the Matchbox PC and the motivations behind our design decisions.

Fig 1. The Matchbox PC

2 Design Rationale

Compressibility Matching as a Design Principle Today's laptops and PDAs package everything in the one case. This has the advantages of portability and convenience, but hinders miniaturization by putting incompressible and compressible components together in the same package. We define the "compressibility" of a component to be how much its volume decreases when "design pressure" is applied by the world's designers over say a year.

Our approach to wearable computing is to segregate components according to compressibility, allowing components in the same module only if they have a similar degree of compressibility. Our underlying philosophy here makes an analogy with the well-known impedance-matching principle for electronic components, which maximizes efficiency by connecting components of similar impedances.

The least compressible component of a portable device

172

is the battery. Battery size is shrinking much more slowly than any other component of wearable computers.

The keyboard is close behind. The limiting factor for a conventional QWERTY keyboard as used on laptops is the size of the user's hand, itself absolutely incompressible. Typing speed decreases with size of keyboard, and a user accustomed to 60 wpm on a full size keyboard will be hard pressed to achieve 30 wpm on a half-size keyboard.

The display has also resisted compression. The eye is not of itself quite as much an obstacle to display miniaturization as the hand is to keyboard miniaturization, and there has been recent promising progress in miniaturizing displays. Even here however, miniaturization of displays intended to be integrated into the unit (as opposed e.g. to head-mounted displays) has been slower than for the rest of the computer.

Connectors are also incompressible to the extent that they need to adhere not only to electrical but mechanical standards.

At the top level our design for a wearable PC matches compressibilities by moving the main incompressibles, namely power, screen, keyboard, and standard connectors, to other modules.

What remains has turned out to have compressed a lot in the last couple of years. The inclusion of incompressible components in essentially all portable computers to date has tended to obscure the extent of this shrinkage. Without them one can have a considerably smaller machine.

Choice of platform   We chose the x86 platform for three reasons. First, the platform has a wide variety of software available for it. Second, the insatiable demand for PC's of all sizes and shapes has served as a driver for many different types of design improvements over the years. Third, there are large numbers of programmers, hardware designers, and users familiar with the general layout and principles of operation of the PC.

An oft-cited drawback of the x86 is its prehistoric architecture, rooted in Intel's early-1970's 4004, 8008, and 8080 microprocessors. Its imminent demise has been predicted on this basis since the emergence in the mid-1980's of RISC processors such as SPARC and MIPS. However careful design in response to the pressure of market forces has led to impressive x86 performance gains allowing it to keep pace comfortably with the rest of the pack.

Power is at least as big a concern in the wearable industry as performance. Today the x86 does not look as good on paper as say the StrongARM, which has been carefully designed for minimal power, a factor in its adoption for Compaq's Itsy wearable computer [2]. However market forces have have been at work here too, driving down the power requirements of x86's, and it seems plausible to us that the emerging wearables marketplace will accelerate this trend and that the power/performance tradeoff for the x86 will im-

prove as dramatically in the near future as its performance has in the recent past.

3   Matchbox PC Design

The basic Matchbox PC is composed of three boards that snap together. The DIMM-PC module on top measures 2.8" by 1.8" and is a single-board computer designed by JUMPtec (www.jumptec.de). It has an AMD 486-SX 66MHz CPU [3], 16 MB of RAM and a 16 MB flash drive on board. Two serial ports, a parallel port, keyboard, a floppy drive interface, and 5 pins of an IDE interface are brought out to the pins on one side, while an ISA bus interface is brought out on the other side. The board fits into a 144-pin SO-DIMM socket intended originally for notebook memory.

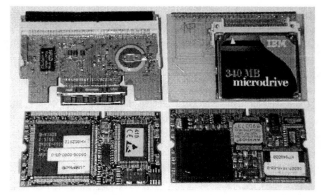

Fig 2. Main board, CF board, DIMM-IO, DIMM-PC

The JUMPtec DIMM-IO module underneath, also in SO-DIMM format, provides a VGA graphics controller with 512KB of graphics memory, a 10 Mb/s ethernet controller, and two more serial ports. The onboard VGA controller is capable of supporting CRT resolutions of 800×600 with 256 colors or 1024×768 with 16 colors. It can also support an STN or TFT flat panel display. The ethernet controller is a Crystal Lan CS8900 ISA controller capable of half- or full-duplex operations at up to 10 MB/s.

Our contribution is the interface or main board in between. It measures 2.8" by 1.8" and contains two 144-pin DIMM sockets, a 68-pin female VHDCI connector, a single-row, 32-pin receptacle, and a Compact Flash connector. The board also has some discrete components including line drivers for the serial ports, termination for the parallel port and keyboard, ethernet transformer, ethernet LEDs, and a clock battery. The VHDCI connector brings out power, ground, keyboard, VGA, ethernet, two serial ports, a parallel port, reset, and floppy. The interface board uses vias to connect the 72-pins of the ISA bus on the CPU board, mounted on one side of the board, to the respective pins on the IO board, which is mounted on the other side of the board.

The single-row connector along the back of the board receives a fourth board which contains the Compact Flash drive. The Compact Flash board contains a surface-mount Compact Flash adapter and the necessary routing of signals from the main board. The 68-pin VHDCI connector at the front of the board connects to a docking station containing standard sockets for the keyboard, serial ports, parallel port, floppy, ethernet, and power.

4 History

Web Server Our first application was to create a small web server (http://wearables.stanford.edu). This design consists of just the JUMPtec DIMM PC board described above. It weighs 20 grams and is only slightly higher and wider than a box of matches but one third as thick, measuring 2.8" by 1.8" by .2" for a volume of about a cubic inch.

The 16 MB of flash memory stores a subset of Linux, along with ssh and the Apache server daemon at first, later superseded by Boa. Connection to the internet is via PLIP, a point-to-point network protocol utilizing the Jumptec's parallel port and running at about 33 kilobytes/second.

Despite its small size, the web server has been very stable. It first went online on January 22nd, 1999, and except for four brief downtimes has been up solidly for six months, up to the time of writing. Operating system maintenance and web page revisions are made with the system remaining online.

Fig 3. Web server and matchbox.

Diskless PC Despite not being a complete PC, the web server provided a nice example of the embedded x86 technology. Our next step was to design a printed circuit board connecting the CPU and IO modules and bringing out signals for power, ground, a serial port, keyboard, VGA, and ethernet. The installation of Linux on the 16MB partition then gave us a full-functioning PC.

Complete PC While this design inched closer to what we wanted, it still was not what we considered a PC; namely, it could not run any of Windows 95 or the bulk of Linux. Therefore, our next board interfaced to a Compact Flash. We chose Compact Flash for several reasons. First, we believe the price/performance of Compact Flash cards will continue to improve as they are finding their ways into digital camera market as well as PDA market. Second, the Compact Flash standard provides a true IDE mode which allows it to act like a PC hard drive. To configure a Compact Flash unit in true IDE mode, we simply routed the appropriate signals from the IDE and ISA on the PC to the Compact Flash adapter. No extra circuitry was required. Finally, at the time of deciding what type of hard drive to add, IBM offered to lend us their Microdrive hard drive [4], providing a 340MB rotary drive in a Type II Compact Flash form.

The question then arose as to where to put the CF slot. Our first idea was to mount the DIMM-PC and DIMM-IO modules on separate boards with the CF drive in between, creating a safe haven for it. The drawback was that the ISA bus connecting the CPU and IO boards, which consisted simply of 73 vias in the one-board design, was now going to be much trickier, especially with the CF card in the way. In the end we kept the one-board approach and mounted the Compact Flash drive above the PC module board, wired to the ISA bus via a small vertical board at the back. We made this unit operational just barely in time for CeBIT'99 in Hanover, where we exhibited it courtesy of JUMPtec, who kindly made space available in their booth.

Current Design Our latest design enhances both robustness and ease of assembly. For the former we went to a 4-layer board, reducing the noise on the ground and power signals. We also replaced the delicate PCMCIA-style connector with a more sturdy, shielded VHDCI connector. And we made the Compact Flash board removable in order to simplify assembly, and also to allow those who are satisfied with just the internal 16MB hard drive to remove the Compact Flash board for reduced size. Alternatively one may replace the Compact Flash board with a board equipped with an IDE connector permitting a regular hard drive to be attached. We are currently experimenting with an ES1869-based sound card of our own design that mounts in this slot.

5 Externals

Connectors In order to keep the basic machine small we brought out all IO pins to a miniature connector. In the early prototypes we used a female 68-pin PCMCIA connector, then replaced this by two 50-pin female compactflash connectors in order to bring out LCD as well. In the latest design we have gone back to 68 pins, giving up LCD for the time being, but with a considerably more robust VHDCI connector as used with miniature SCSI equipment.

The keyboard, VGA, serial and parallel ports, ethernet, and floppy all adhere to the electrical standards for PC's at the PC's VHDCI connector. To achieve this we put all bypass and impedance components on the main board, with the expander board serving only to bring the connector pins out to standard PC connectors.

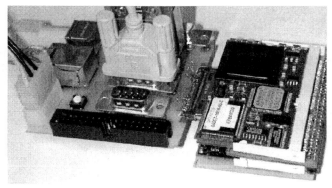

Fig 4. Full-sized port expander attached to the PC

Our goal here has been to allow more than one mode of access to the board. One mode is with a port expander, which we have built, which simply brings the wires out to physically standard connectors. As is evident from Figure 4 these dwarf the Matchbox PC, but allow it to be used like any normal PC using standard external devices and power source, and even with a video projector, which we have taken advantage of for a number of talks.

A quite different mode, one that we have not yet built but that is on our agenda of what to implement next, permits use as a wearable. In this mode a miniature display, keyboard, pointing device, etc. are wired directly to the male connector. By avoiding bulky standard connectors the devices themselves are the limiting factor for miniaturization. At the Society for Information Display's recent exhibit, Toshiba demonstrated a 120-micron pixel 4" diagonal 640×480 display which would be a good match to the size of the Matchbox PC. This mode is compatible with a battery either integral to the unit, say as a suitably sized camcorder battery, or detached and distributed say around the waist in a belt pack.

Power The system performs reliably over a range of 4.8 to 5.2 volts, dissipating 2.0 watts normally and 4.0 watts peak under Linux. (Windows draws more power than Linux, reducible with a program such as CPUIdle.) This gives users considerable flexibility in choosing their source of 5 volts. Obvious candidates are a 5 volt "wall-wart" for AC use, a 12-5 volt DC-DC converter with a car battery, etc. A simple battery would be 4 AA Nicads in series (e.g. a standard 4.8

volt "toy car battery"). NiMH or Li-Ion batteries provide longer life; for example a 7.2 volt camcorder battery (Sony offers a wide range of ampere-hour capacities) can be used with a plain 7805 voltage regulator, or with a more efficient DC-DC converter. The apocryphal suit-case battery should of course run the PC for several weeks.

Ethernet In the prototypes of the Matchbox PC we connected the ethernet module directly to twisted pair cable, which appears adequate for short runs but puts the ethernet chip on the DIMM-IO module at risk of transients or excessive DC levels. For the current version we located an ethernet transformer small enough to fit in the unit, providing the recommended isolation from stray voltages.

Acknowledgments

We would like to thank IBM for the loan of a Microdrive at a time when they were in scarce supply even within IBM. We would also like to thank Matthias Huber and Jumptec for their continued technical support and for space in their CeBIT'99 booth to exhibit the Matchbox PC.

Further photos of this and previous versions of the Matchbox PC may be found on the web at wearables.stanford.edu.

References

[1] Smailagic, A., Siewiorek, D., Martin, R., Stivoric, J., "Very Rapid Prototyping of Wearable Computers: A Case Study of VuMan 3 Custom versus Off-the-Shelf Design Methodologies", Journal on Design Automation for Embedded Systems, Vol. 3, No. 2/3, pp 217-230, 1998.

[2] Marc A. Viredaz. "The Itsy Pocket Computer Version 1.5: User's Manual", Technical note TN54, WRL, Compaq, Palo Alto, CA (USA), July 1998. On the web at gatekeeper.dec.com/pub/DEC/WRL/research-reports/WRL-TN-54.pdf

[3] "Elan SC400 and SC410 Microcontrollers Users' Manual", AMD Inc., 1997. On the web at http://www.amd.com/products/lpd/techdocs/e86/21030.pdf

[4] "IBM Family of Microdrives", IBM Inc., June 1999. On the web at www.storage.ibm.com/hardsoft/diskdrdl/micro/datasheet.pdf

A Wearable Context-Awareness Component
Finally a Good Reason to Wear a Tie

Albrecht Schmidt, Hans W. Gellersen, Michael Beigl
Telecooperation Office (TecO), University of Karlsruhe, Germany
albrecht@teco.edu

Abstract

We describe the design of a wearable context-awareness component that derives general context information from low-level sensors. Derived context information is application-independent and can be used by wearables or other personal technologies in a body network via a simple protocol. We built the context-awareness component into a tie, stressing its design as an accessory.

1. Introduction

Sensors are built into wearable computers to make them attentive for their users and usage environment, and to enable context-aware behavior. We suggest to realize sensor-based context-awareness rather as device-independent component or accessory. A wearable context-awareness component that integrates low-cost sensors is proposed. Simple methods are used to derive context information from sensor data. The derived context is application-independent and can be exploited by other wearable or personal technologies in a body network, for instance wearable computers, mobile phones, digital cameras, and personal digital assistants.

In this paper, we describe a study of wearable context-awareness. In this study we developed a wearable component that uses sensors to derive some application-independent contexts. We built this component into a tie, which is practical for placement of certain sensors, and which also stresses the component's design as accessory.

2. A Study of Wearable Context-Awareness

Context has many aspects as pointed out by [1], [2], [5]. Most reported work on context-awareness describes solutions for specific applications e.g. [3], [4], and it is evident that we lack the theoretical foundations and ontologies for general consideration of context. For a study of wearable context-awareness we chose to address a number of contexts that relate to how interruptible the user is. These contexts describe only a certain aspect of real world situations but they are general in the sense that they can be exploited by a range of applications. Such context is for instance implemented and used in the audio wearable described in [4], mimicking the human ability to recognize situations in which it is rude to interrupt, for instance when a person is engaged in a conversation or giving a talk. Context information of this kind is also useful for other applications, for instance calendars, email notification, pagers and mobile phones can make use of any context that gives an indication of whether it is a good time to interrupt a user.

The specific contexts that we chose for our study are based on aural information: user speaking, others speaking, noisy, and quiet. And based on movement of the user: walking, running, stationary. Movement context was included as it gives an indication as to whether a user can be interrupted visually.

2.1. Design of the Context-Awareness Component

Our concept of a wearable context-awareness component stresses lightweight design in every sense. A key rationale is the use of low-cost sensors and lightweight processing in contrast to for instance approaches in computer vision. Lightweight design aims at implementation as small unobtrusive wearable, and also at realization as low-cost accessory to other wearable devices such as mobile phones [2]. See Figure 1 for an image of the context-awareness tie.

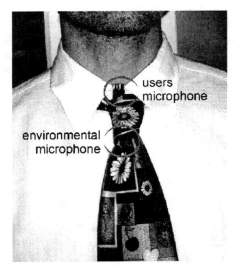

Figure 1: Context-Awareness Tie.

For recognition of aural and movement contexts, we integrated two microphones and an accelerometer in our design. One of the microphones is placed near the user's throat, the other pointing away from the user. With this configuration the distinction of speaker and environment is feasible with minimal processing cost. The acceleration sensor is used to discriminate whether a user is standing still, walking or running.

The sensor placement considerations led us to built the context-awareness component into a tie – it may be considered to build them into other accessories worn in similar ways (e.g. jewelry, neckerchief, or necklace). We also liked that a tie stresses the component's design as accessory rather than as stand-alone device.

2.2. Hardware

The hardware of our context-awareness component is build around a TINY-Tiger microcontroller, that offers four analog inputs and two serial lines. The two signals from the microphones are amplified and connected to the analog inputs. To measure the motion we used a two-axis accelerometer (Analog Devices ADXL202). The schematic of the component is depicted in Figure 2.

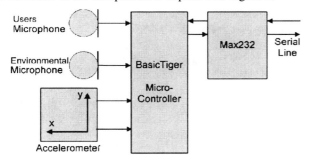

Figure 2: Schematic - Context-Awareness Device.

2.3. Software

The software is realized in Tiger-BASIC, a multitasking basic dialect for the TINY-Tiger. It reads and analyzes sensor data in a time window of about four seconds. The methods to analyze the signals are deliberately simple; they work within the time domain and are based on basic statistical measurements. Examples of methods and extracted features are:

- absolute average of signals:
  ~ volume of audio, ~ level of motion;
- distribution of distances between zero-crossings:
  ~ indication of frequency (sound and motion),
- distribution of maximum values over 20 ms: ~ low pass filter.

Based on the features calculated from sensor data the contexts are detected. This is implemented by a simple matrix multiplication on the microcontroller. The matrix is hardcoded and represents the weight set of a neural network that was trained with example data on a PC.

2.4. Protocol

The communication is based on a serial line connection using 9600 bit/s, in a simple request-reply manner. The client sends a request to the context-awareness component which sends back a reply with the current contexts, using the following protocol:

```
<request> ::= "GET\n" | "get\n".
<reply>::= "(a:" <audio_ctxt> ";m:"
              <motion_ctxt> ")\n".
<audio_ctxt>::= "n" | "q" | "s" | "l".
<motion_ctxt>::= "s" | "w" | "r".
```

The semantic of the audio contexts is:
n = **n**oisy, q = **q**uiet, s = user **s**peaking,
l = others speaking (user **l**istening).
The semantic of the motion contexts is:
s = **s**tationary, w = **w**alking, r = **r**unning.

2.5. Results

Experimentation with the context-aware tie showed that contexts were recognized in a very reliable way. Both "user speaking" vs."others speaking" and "stationary" vs. "walking" vs. "running" were discriminated correctly. A key finding is that sensor placement can be used effectively to increase reliability and to reduce required processing.

3. Conclusion and Further work

The presented study indicates the utility of a lightweight context-awareness component, that can be realized as wearable built into a tie or other clothing accessory to provide context for other personal technologies in a body network. Further work includes re-implementation of the component on a PIC microcontroller to reduce device cost and power consumption. It also includes investigation of further sensors and contexts, and integration with other devices in body networks based on short range RF.

4. References

[1] Brown, P. J., Bovey, J. D., Chen, X. Context-Aware Applications: From the Laboratory to the Marketplace. IEEE Personal Communications, October 1997.

[2] Esprit Project 26900. Technology for enabling Awareness (TEA). www.omega.it/tea/, 1998

[3] Healey, J. and Picard, R.W. StartleCam: A Cybernetic Wearable Camera. Proceedings of the Second International Symposium on Wearable Computing, Pittsburgh, PA, October 19-20, 1998.

[4] Sawhney, N., and S., Chris. "Nomadic Radio: A Spatialized Audio Environment for Wearable Computing." Proceedings of the International Symposium on Wearable Computing, Cambridge, MA, October 13-14, 1997.

[5] Schmidt, A., Beigl, M., Gellersen, H.-W. There is more to context than location. Proc. of the Intl. Workshop on Interactive Applications of Mobile Computing (IMC98), Rostock, Germany, November 1998.

Acceleration Sensing Glove (ASG)

John Kangchun Perng, Brian Fisher, Seth Hollar, Kristofer S. J. Pister

johnkcp@bsac.eecs.berkeley.edu, thorvald@uclink4.berkeley.edu,
shollar@bsac.eecs.berkeley.edu, pister@eecs.berkeley.edu

Berkeley Sensor & Actuator Center
University of California, Berkeley
497 Cory Hall
Berkeley, CA 94720
(510) 642-4571

Abstract

A glove with 2-axis accelerometers on the finger tips and back of the hand has been built using commercial-off-the-shelf components. Taking advantage of gravity induced acceleration offsets, we have been able to identify pseudo static gestures. We have also developed software that allows the glove to be used as a mouse pointing device for a Windows 95 or NT machine.

Keywords

Wearable input device, hand-gesture recognition, data glove, human computer interaction, mouse pointer, etc

Introduction

The goal of this project is to demonstrate that accelerometers can be used as sensors to detect and translate finger and hand motions into computer interpreted signals. To this end we have developed an acceleration sensing glove from commercial-off-the-shelf components. The glove contains 2-axis accelerometers on the fingers and back of the hand. Wires connect the accelerometers to a controller board that is affixed to the wrist of the user. An RF transceiver on the controller board makes it possible to transmit acceleration data wirelessly to a computer (Figure 1). Currently, we have written a simple program that allows the glove to be used as a mouse pointing device.

Hardware

The hardware consists of a wrist controller and six accelerometers, five on the fingertips and one on the back of the hand (Figure 2). Each accelerometer (1.3x1.4cm) is an Analog Devices ADXL202 with +/- 2g of range [1]. An Atmel AVR AT90LS8535 microcontroller on the forearm controller (4.4x6.6 cm) converts the analog signal

from the accelerometer to a digital signal. The wrist controller is capable of transmitting the sensor data wirelessly at 916.5 MHz (RF Monolithics). Signal processing at the computer is then used to interpret commands based on hand gestures. The overall power consumption of the glove is 45mW at 3.3 Volts.

Software

Before the accelerometer data could be analyzed it had to be calibrated, normalized, and low pass filtered. We calibrated our system by orienting our glove in particular directions and normalizing with respect to gravity. The unbuffered ADXL202 produced noise with a standard deviation of 70 mg. At 220 Hz, signals were averaged to reduce white noise. A coordinate transformation was performed which converted the Cartesian data format to polar values (R_{acc}, θ, see Figure 3).

Static Data Analysis

In static situations, the only force acting on the accelerometers is gravity (Figure 3). The resulting vector of the projection of the gravity vector, $\underline{G}$, into the plane defined by the 2 axis accelerometer is $\underline{R}_{acc}$. The orientation of the accelerometer relative to $\underline{G}$ is given as the angle, θ. The angle the acceleration plane is offset from the horizontal is given as ϕ.

By using this idea of gravity-induced accelerometer bias we were able to develop a pointing device. One 2-axis accelerometer was placed on the back of hand as a tilt motion detector for moving the pointer on the screen and three other 2-axis accelerometers were placed on the thumb, index finger, and middle finger to operate as mouse click buttons. By tilting the hand in the θ direction, the on-screen pointer will move in that direction at a rate proportional to ϕ. Curling an individual finger is

178

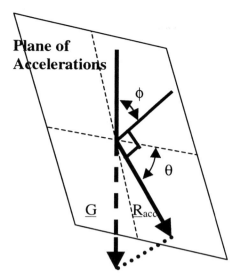

Figure 3. *Acceleration plane relative to gravity vector.*

positions. The differences in $\underline{R}_{acc}$ and θ can be seen as the fingers move up and down.

Future Potential

The finger acceleration glove is a large-scale device used to model the functionality of Smart Dust [2] on fingers. Smart Dust is a project whose 3-year goal is to integrate communications, intelligence, power, and sensors into a package that is no larger than 1 mm^3 (Figure 5). Integrating a single chip wireless solution with a MEMS accelerometer would yield an autonomous device small enough to apply to the fingernails. Because of their small size and weight, these Smart Dust devices would be less noticeable than one's own eyeglasses, providing no more discomfort than fingernail polish. People would have instantaneous input access to the digital world at all times, facilitating a paradigm shift in human-computer interaction.

Some potential applications for the Acceleration Sensing Glove are: a wireless wearable mouse pointing device, a wireless wearable keyboard, hand motion and gesture recognition tools, virtual musical instruments, computer sporting games, and work training in a simulated environment.

equivalent to clicking a mouse button. The mouse pointer currently functions in standard Windows NT or Windows 98 desktops.

Additionally, simple hand gestures can be uniquely distinguished. In Figure 4, the hand is upright while the user moves his fingers into different

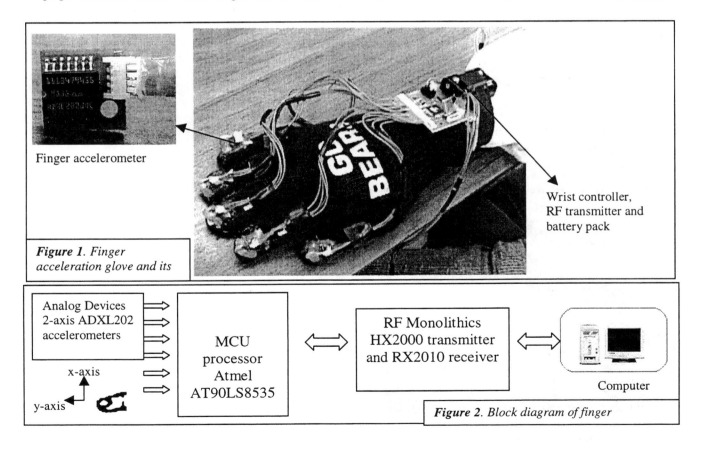

Finger accelerometer

Wrist controller, RF transmitter and battery pack

Figure 1. *Finger acceleration glove and its*

Figure 2. *Block diagram of finger*

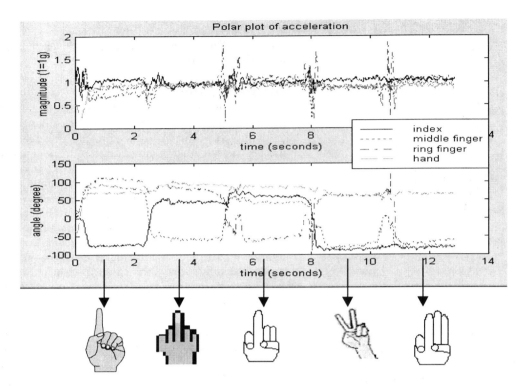

Figure 4. Plot of $\underline{R}_{acc}$ and θ over time for various hand gestures.

References

[1] Analog Devices, Norwood, MA, http://www.analog.com, September 1999.

[2] http://robotics.eecs.berkeley.edu/~pister/SmartDust, September 1999.

[3] Fukumoto, M and Tonomura, Y "Body Coupled FingeRing: Wireless Wearable Keyboard", CHI97 Conference Proceedings, pp147-154, Atlanta, March 1997.

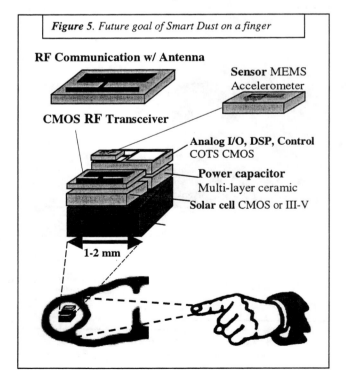

Figure 5. Future goal of Smart Dust on a finger

RF Communication w/ Antenna

Sensor MEMS Accelerometer

CMOS RF Transceiver

Analog I/O, DSP, Control COTS CMOS

Power capacitor Multi-layer ceramic

Solar cell CMOS or III-V

1-2 mm

Modeling Wearable Negotiation in an Opportunistic Task Oriented Domain

Jay Schneider, Jim Suruda
Advisor: Steve Fickas
University of Oregon, Deschutes Hall
Eugene, OR 97403 USA
{jay, jfs, fickas}@cs.uoregon.ed

Abstract

This poster details the properties involved in negotiation over a set of tasks for a wearable environment. Details relating to the specific domain as relating to wearable computing are also discussed

.

1 Ubiquitous Task Oriented Domain

Ubiquitous Wearable Computers provides a new environment for negotiating personal agents. These agents will perform a broad array of tasks for the user, ranging from personal scheduling and task planning, to providing hardware services in foreign locales. The local environment will also have its own series of tasks with agents attempting to carry them out. There is often a great deal of redundancy in the tasks being performed by the wearable and its user, other nearby wearable and their users and the local environment. Whenever redundancy occurs there is an opportunity for both parties to more efficiently accomplish their goals, through task sharing and trading.

The tasks that are being negotiated by the wearable can take a wide variety of forms, both physical and virtual. A trade could be "if you take my books back to the library, I'll pick up your copies from the printers" or "I'll handle all outgoing communications through my currently unused T-1 line if you process the data received." Although it is beyond the range of the initial work in this field trades such as "I'll handle all visual data analysis if you pick up my dry cleaning" are also possible. Task sharing and trading requires the agents involved to negotiate. Negotiation techniques developed using this system provide a solution to resolve many possible day to day conflicts by the wearable devices, for example two computer-driven cars both desiring to move into the same physical space can be resolved using negotiation techniques. Negotiations take place over a given domain, with certain expectations of behavior for those agents as expressed in [1], [2], and [3].

The domain used for the current project is limited to a subset of the Task Oriented Domain (TOD). A Task Oriented Domain is one in which agents are not required to negotiate. Each and every agent has all of the tools needed to accomplish their goals and each agent's goals are independent. However, it is possible to achieve a higher level of success (e.g. accomplishing all the goals in a shorter period of time) through negotiation. The TOD we are using is differs from the norm in that it allows for ubiquitous computing. In this Ubiquitous Task Oriented Domain (UTOD) the agents operate in an opportunistic fashion. These agents take advantage of their current context, both physical and virtual, to decide if and with whom they will negotiate. Their current context also will affect the expected worth of bargaining as per [2].

The agents involved in task sharing and trading originate from a variety of uncontrolled sources. Maximizing its personal goals is assumed to be an agent's sole motivation. These agents can and will use strategies in which they will lie, cheat or steal to maximize their benefits. A primary goal of modeling agent negotiation in a UTOD is to find a set of rules for the negotiation environment where the honest agent will perform as well as the dishonest one. These rules for the negotiating environment in games theory are referred to as the protocol. As protocol designers it is in our best interest to protect the honest agent. Honest agents are needed to accomplish the goal of the protocol designers - global optimality. [4]

Agents may engage in deceptive practices as long as the truthfulness of their actions is not independently verifiable. From this we can derive that when an agreement is made by an agent to assume responsibility for a task of another agent, that task will be properly and honestly discharged. This is because an assumed task (i.e. delivering a package) can and will draw attention if improperly executed. The party who has been acting deceptively by not fulfilling an agreed upon task will face the legal penalties for breach of contract. An underlying assumption for all agents is rationality [1], [2], [3], and as legal penalties are assumed to have a high negative utility then we can state that no agent will engage in this type of

181

deception.

A protocol is globally optimal which it can be proven that maximal efficiency will be derived by all parties negotiating under this protocol. When tasks are being assigned by a single organization or when negotiations occur between agents working towards a joint goal this is the sole issue. This is not the only concern when the parties in the negotiation are ambivalent towards each other goals or can achieve a higher goal by working towards their own ends.

In cases where the agents are concerned only with their own unshared goals, protocol design aimed at global optimality can be is restricted by the concept of *Individual Rationality*. Individual Rationality means that any deal an agent will consider must offer utility that is at least as good as the utility prior to the negotiations.

2 Negotiation Protocols

The class of TOD domain we are using for our agents is a variation on the postman domain. The traditional postman domain is described in [4] as:

"Agents have to deliver sets of letters to mailboxes, which are arranged on a weighted graph G=G(V,E). There is no limit to the number of letters that can fit in a mailbox. After delivering all letters agents must return to the starting point (the post office.) Agents can exchange letters at no cost while they are at the post office prior to delivery.

Task Set: The set of all addresses in the graph, namely V. If address x is in an agent's task set, it means that he has at least one letter to deliver to x.

Cost Function: The cost of a subset of addresses $X \subseteq V$, i.e., $c(X)$, is the length of the minimal path that starts at the post office, visits all members of X, and ends at the post office."

Our variation differs from the traditional postman domain in that it allows n postmen and m post offices ($n \geq m$), and uses the UTOD where negotiations can occur at any vertex, not just the post office. The domain also allows for negotiation to occur in a continuous fashion, allowing for opportunistic negotiations along the edges of the graph.

The model we have implemented in the modified-postman domain is described as follows:

G=G(V,E), V={v_1, v_2...v_n} with m agents. Each agent has starting vertex {v_1, v_2...v_m} and task set {s_1, s_2...s_m}

and must return to starting vertex {v_1, v_2,...v_m}. Each agent m_1 negotiates with agent m_2 when their locations are within distance d of each other.

The negotiation protocol we are using is the *Product Maximizing Mechanism* (PMM) as presented in [4]. We chose this protocol as it is satisfies all of Nash's criteria in [2]. In short, this means PMM provides a efficient solution that is in Nash equilibrium when both parties negotiating have full knowledge of the other parties task set and starting vertex.

The PMM protocol is a two-step protocol. In the first step both parties disclose their task sets. In the second step each party proposes a deal (division of tasks) that is *pareto-optimal* and *individually rational* (see [2] for more information on these terms.) The deal that is selected is the deal that has the highest utility when the utility to agent 1 and agent 2 are multiplied.

Using the WALID system described in [5] we are testing this system using n agents to compute the benefits accrued through negotiation. We can also add agents and determine average utility benefit as more agents are added to the simulation. This allows us to show a saturation point and to see what the expected utility gain is when an additional agent is added to the graph.

As the agents in this task are wearable users we have also implemented a *Cost of Negotiation* (CoN). CoN is a constant value subtracted from the utility of a new task set in step 2 of PMM. This value relates to the human cost of changing the wearable users task set. In the postman domain tasks relate to traveling to physical locations. By adding a CoN value we prevent the wearable user from pointlessly trading tasks and spinning in place.

References

[1] John Von Neumann and Oskar Morgenstern. *Theory of Games and Economic Behavior.* Princeton University Press, Princeton, 1947.

[2] John F. Nash . The Bargaining Problem. *Econometricia*, 28:155-162, 1950.

[3] John F. Nash . Two-person cooperative games. Econometricia, 21:128-140, 1953.

[4] Jeffrey S. Rosenschein and Giliad Zlotkin. *Rules of Encounter, Designing Conventions for Automated Negotiation among Computers.* MIT Press, Cambridge Massachusetts, 1994.

[5] Fickas, Kortuem, et. al. *When Cyborgs Meet: Building Communities of Cooperating Wearable Agents.* Submitted for publication International Symposium of Wearable Computing, 1999.

Force XXI Land Warrior: Implementing Spoken Commands for Soldier Wearable Systems

Gary Cleveland, Linda McNinch
Motorola, Systems Solutions Group
8201 E. McDowell Rd., Scottsdale, AZ 85257
gary.cleveland@motorola.com, P25365@email.mot.com

Abstract

Implementing effective control systems for wearable computers presents numerous design challenges, especially when the end users are soldiers who need to use their hands to control weapons rather than computers. This paper describes the work performed and the results achieved by the System Voice Control team on the Force XXI Land Warrior (FXXI LW) project at Motorola. This team integrated Motorola's CVoxCon speech recognition system into an existing soldier computer system. The successful CVoxCon implementation suggests guidance for other efforts and areas for future investigation.

1. Introduction

There are many potential design problems related to the development of a soldier-worn computer system. The soldier is on foot, carrying heavy loads, and totally exposed to sometimes harsh weather conditions. He may be depending upon his sight to find a target, or depending on his hearing to receive verbal orders or to locate potential threats. Adding a wearable computer, such as the Land Warrior Soldier System (LW), offers the benefits of integrated information sources, but also requires the soldier to interact with the computer as well as his environment. Most certainly, the infantryman faces more problems with wearable computer use than do commercial wearable computer users.

Motorola, in the Force XXI Land Warrior (FXXI LW) project, was funded to develop and demonstrate an upgrade to the LW system, the System Voice Control (SVC) spoken command capability. The goal was to provide a nearly hands-free, eyes-free computer interface. Figure 1 shows how a simple task, selecting an icon while prone, affects a soldier's performance when he also has a weapon to manage. The soldier on the left is speaking commands to his system. The soldier on the right is using the manual device on his chest to enter commands. Note that this soldier's attention and body have shifted, so that his rifle barrel is on the ground. This example typifies the

human-system performance improvement the SVC intended to achieve for the soldier.

Figure 1. Soldiers using the LW (right) mechanical interface and FXXI LW (left) speech recognition interface.

2. Design goals and constraints

Clear design requirements were defined for SVC accuracy and response time (0.25 seconds), including high accuracy (95%) in high noise environments, full functionality for near-whisper commands, and speaker independence. A major design goal was to provide an interface that was acceptable to the soldiers and compatible with their skills and environments. Soldiers participated on the SVC team to provide the end user viewpoint.

SVC implementation was subject to several stringent constraints. The SVC system could not increase LW power consumption or exceed the reserve memory. Changes to the hardware were restricted to printed wiring board areas. Changes to the LW software, including the LW user interface, were restricted to those that were absolutely necessary. The SVC needed to fit well with the existing user interface. The commands entered via the pointer mechanism and the SVC needed to seem the same to the users and to have the same effects on the interface's contexts, modes, dialogs, etc.

The SVC effort began with the selection of a speech recognition engine. A list of over 40 potential candidates was assembled, along with the parameters for trade-off analysis. Design requirements and constraints were applied, reducing the number of potential candidates. Each candidate was rated based on discrete/continuous performance, processor requirements, accuracy, speaker independence, recognition database training time, and cost. Size, weight, and power effects were also taken into account. Three recognizers were identified for full laboratory evaluation and testing. Based on laboratory test results, the Motorola CVoxCon [1] was selected.

3. Implementation Results

The SVC scored a high command recognition rate even in high noise environments. The modified LW user interface system earned a high approval rating from the soldiers. They preferred SVC interaction to the manual command input.

In environments with noise levels below 90 dB(C), recognition rates were just above 95%. (For reference, 90 dB(C) is in the range of hazardous noise). In very high noise environments outside of the specified operational range (95-105 dB(C)), recognition rates were lower, as expected.

Nearly all soldiers succeeded in successfully using the system on the first attempt, even though several soldiers exhibited strong regional accents or moderate speech impediments. Only a very few had speaker-specific problems. The soldiers definitely preferred speaking commands to entering them using the point-and-click device.

3.1. Areas for improvement

Even with the SVC, the LW system is not completely hands-free or eyes-free. Some inputs, such as target acquisition, are still best done manually. Similarly, there still exist output functions, such as changing the communications radio to another network, where audio or tactile feedback should be developed.

Three types of commands caused problems. Single syllable commands did not provide enough material for the recognition engine. Commands of five or more total syllables tended to drag off the end of the 1.5-second recording window. Phonetic similarities created recognition problems, with rhymes being especially noticeable.

The noise-canceling microphone did not perform well in a substantial wind or when placed directly in front of the mouth. The SVC was not designed for and does not work with yelling or very loud speech. Unfortunately, in battlefield situations loud speech is commonplace as a response to rising stress and noise levels.

3.2. Lessons learned

Communications to the user must be simple and immediate [2]. Although this is true throughout the user interface, it is especially true with respect to spoken commands. When the user's speech pattern is not acceptable, the system should express that feedback in plain language; for example, "Speak louder." To express it in terms of signal-to-noise ratios does not work with soldiers. Similarly, a visual indication of when the system is recording is helpful, but should be considered only as a redundant cue in order to avoid dependency on visual feedback.

Command phonetics need to be distinctly different from each other[3]. This point needs to be emphasized to avoid trouble spots such as short commands with similar vowel sounds.

4. Conclusion

There are fundamental soldier characteristics that affected the implementation of SVC. Functions that conserve energy are imperative for military applications. Soldiers may be under great physical and psychological stress when using computers; their very lives may depend on a correct computer response. A simple, efficient interface is imperative. While commercial end users rarely approach the stress levels experienced by soldiers, the approach to addressing end user implied requirements should be much the same.

5. Bibliography

[1] W.M. Campbell, K.T. Assaleh, and C.C. Broun, "Audio Sensors and Low-Complexity Recognition Technologies for Soldier Systems", Proceedings, SPIE Sensor Technology for Soldier Systems, 1998.

[2] B. Schum, B. Myers, and A. Waibel, "Interactive Recovery from Speech Recognition Errors in Speech User Interfaces", ICSLP 1996.

[3] L.J. Najjar, J.J. Ockerman, and J.C. Thompson, "User Interface Design Guidelines for Wearable Computer Speech Recognition Applications", IEEE VRAIS 98 Workshop - Interfaces for Wearable Computers, March 15, 1998.

The views expressed in this article are the views of the authors and do not reflect the position of Motorola.

Wearable Computers for the Fire Service and Police Force: Technological and Human Factors

David J. Haniff and Chris Baber
School of Electronic and Electrical Engineering
The University of Birmingham, Birmingham, B15 2TT
E-Mail: d.j.haniff@bham.ac.uk, Web site: http://www.bham.ac.uk/ManMechEng/IEG/w1.html

Abstract

Wearable computer applications can be defined broadly as situationally-aware and situationally-unaware. A situationally-aware fire-fighter application which is under development is described and a situationally-unaware police force application is presented. However, underlying these developments is the issue of the appropriateness of the user interface for these applications.

1. Introduction

Wearable computer technologies can provide information about the individual that wears the computer and the world in which this individual interacts (situationally aware). Wearable computers can also provide information that is not computationally aware of their surrounding but provide information relevant to the task a user is carrying out (situationally unaware).

This paper describes the wearable computer systems being developed at the University of Birmingham for the emergency services with a focus on the fire service and police force. In particular it examines the design of the user-interfaces for wearable technology.

2. Fire-fighter Application

Through interviews with fire-fighters at West Midlands Fire Service in the UK, various requirements for a wearable system were suggested. For example, the fire-fighters would like to know the temperature outside of the suit at various positions within their surroundings. The body temperature and blood oxygen levels would also be useful information for those outside of the building for monitoring the health of the fire-fighters. An indicator of when to leave the building was also identified as a useful feature of a wearable system. At the moment this is implemented through the use of a whistle from outside of the building. Location information about where to proceed, for example to find the fire-fighter's 'buddy' (his partner) would also be useful. Currently the whistle method can be subject to confusion in the case of large fires when other support services use the same method. In many cases it may also be difficult to hear such a signal.

The technical specifications for the situationally-aware fire-fighter application are outlined by Baber et al. [1]. A police force application has also been developed.

3. Police Force Application

For the police force an application for wearable technology has been developed to access the PNC (Police National Computer) for records relevant to an incident (see figure 2). In some cases it was pointed out that an officer might not be able to get details from a PNC query immediately due to the great demands placed on staff at the Communication Centre. The device also needs to be hands-free to enable the police officer to physically detain a suspect and access the information. A major benefit of wearable technology is that it enables hands-free operation.

The application is situationally-unaware (unaware of the surroundings). It uses speech input and output, however, unlike the 'Nomadic Radio' which also uses speech I/O [3] the application is unaware of its location and it is application specific. The speech-to-text (STT) and text-to-speech (TTS) capabilities of Dragon Dictate were used in combination with Microsoft Visual Basic and Microsoft Access for rapid software development. The application executes a PNC vehicle check. A vehicle licence plate number is spoken into the microphone, the user asks for confirmation of the number by saying 'read that', the text is output as speech, if it is correct then the number is queried with the database and details such as whether it has been reported as stolen and the name of the owner are output through speech. This small application alleviates the need to contact the Communications Centre through radio to find out such information.

Future developments of the police force application would be to add a communications link from the wearable to a remote database using a mobile communications infrastructure such as GSM or TETRA (TErrestrial Trunk Radio).

Figure 2: Device to be worn on the head by an Officer

3. Interface Design

The display whether it is visual or auditory needs to be carefully considered for the application to succeed in achieving its goal. There has not been a great deal of work on the interface design of wearable computers. Interface components can described as representations.

Peterson [2] describes representations as consisting of several dimensions: task, process (mental processing), circumstance, ontology (relevant world objects) and user (i.e. expertise levels). A particular representation will have these factors associated with it in its use.

These dimensions can be described using various notations such as predicate logic for *process* and *ontology* (commonly used in artificial intelligence), state-transition diagrams for the *circumstance* (with the user as the system), task analysis diagrams for the *task* and expert levels or cognitive abilities for the *user*.

For the fire-fighter application, for example, to indicate the direction a fire-fighter needs to go, several symbols could be used (e.g. see figure 3a). The processes for both symbols are shown in figure 3b.

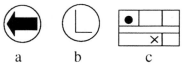

a   b   c

Figure 3a: Direction Indicators

Process:

$\forall$ a symbol(a) -> attend(a)

$\forall$ b, w symbol(b) $\land$ word(w) -> attend(b) $\land$ recall(w) $\land$ direction(w)

$\forall$ c1, c2, c3 dot_symbol (c1) $\land$ x_symbol(c2) $\land$ building_symbol(c3) -> attend(c1, c2) $\land$ match(c2,c3) $\land$ direction(c3)

Figure 3b: Internal Process

For 'a' the user needs to attend to the arrow, the meaning and direction of movement are implicit within the picture. However, for 'b' the user needs to attend to the letter L, recall the word associated with this letter (left) and then define the direction. Finally, for 'c' the user needs to attend to two indications on the map, i.e., a dot showing current location and an X showing the future location. The user has to translate direction from these two indicators.

Aspects of the ontology such as smoke and furniture are defined for the world in which the interface for the application will be used. An extremely dangerous *circumstance* within the ontology may effect the way the internal processes interpret the symbols. Therefore there should be no ambiguity between symbols.

In the case of the police force application, the auditory representations can also be examined in the same way. The process for the simple dialogue in the police application is defined in figure 4.

Process:

$\forall$ x, y LicenceNumbers(x) $\land$ LicenceLetters(y)-> speak(x) $\land$ speak(y) $\land$ listen(x,y) $\land$ clarify(x,y)

$\exists$ x, y StolenStatus(x) $\land$ OwnerDetails (y) -> listen(x) $\land$ listen(y)

Figure 4: Police application processes

For all of the licence numbers and licence letters within the number plate the user speaks them into the recogniser, the user then listens to the licence plate number and clarifies it. Also there exists a stolen status and owner details which listened to by the user.

4. Conclusion

The wearable computer applications are being developed at the University of Birmingham are situationally aware and unaware. However, in order to produce a display that is appropriate for the task the representations need to be carefully examined.

This paper has proposed an initial framework for looking at these representations that considers external factors (such as ontology) as well as psychological factors in the design of user interfaces for wearable technology.

5. References

[1] Baber, C., Haniff, D.J. and Woolley, S. (in press) Contrasting paradigms for the development of Wearable computers, *IBM Systems Journal. Vol. 38, No. 4.*

[2] Peterson, D. (1996) Introduction, In *Forms of Representation*, Intellect Books, London, pp.7-27.

[3] Sawhney, N. and Schmandt, C. (1998) Speaking and Listening on the run: Design for Wearable Audio Computing, *Proceedings of ISCW '98: International Symposium on Wearable Computing*, Pittsburgh, Pennsylvania, 19-20 October 1998, pp. 108-115.

6. Acknowledgements

This work was partially funded by EPSRC grant GR/L48508.

CMU Wearable Computers for Real - Time Speech Translation

Asim Smailagic, Dan Siewiorek, Richard Martin, Denis Reilly
Institute for Complex Engineered System, Carnegie Mellon University
Pittsburgh, PA 15213, USA
{asim, dps, martin+ }@cs.cmu.edu, dpr@andrew.cmu.edu,

Abstract

Carnegie Mellon's Wearable Computers Laboratory has built four generations of real - time speech translation wearable computers, culminating in the Speech Translator Smart Module. Smart Modules are a family of interoperable modules supporting real-time speech recognition, language translation, and speech synthesis. In this paper, we examine the effect of various design factors on performance with emphasis on modularity and scalability. A system-level approach to power / performance optimization is described that improved the metric of (performance / (weight * volume * power)) by over a factor of 300 through the four generations.

1. INTRODUCTION

The use of speech and auditory interaction on wearable computers can provide hands-free input for applications, and enhances the user's attention and awareness of events and personal messages, without the distraction of stopping current actions. The speech and wearable computer paradigms came together in a series of wearable computers built by CMU, including: Integrated Speech Activated Application Control (ISAAC), Tactical Information Assistant (TIA-P and TIA-0), Smart Modules, Adtranz, and Mobile Communication and Computing Architecture (MoCCA) [1],[2],[3],[4].

The Smart Module project adds some additional criteria to wearable computer design. The latencies involved with running the operating system and application should be kept low (close to instant response, such as a flashlight). These wearable devices must be modular, usable in different configurations, and scalable. The OS chosen was Red Hat Linux, because it is free, lightweight, scalable, and customizable.

There have been several explorations into wearable auditory displays, such as using them to enhance one's environment with timely information [5], and providing a sense of peripheral awareness [6]. Most of these prior systems have focused on speech recognition and speech synthesis. Language translation presents one additional challenge for wearable computers.

2. EVOLUTIONARY METHODOLOGY

The four generations of speech translation wearable computers span from general purpose to dedicated computers: TIA-P, TIA-0, Speech Translator Functional Prototype Smart Module, and Optimized Speech Translator Smart Module. This evolution was based on lessons learned from their field tests and deployment. These four systems were developed as two related pairs. The first member of each pair was a functional prototype that was suitable for field evaluation. The second member was optimized for power consumption, size, weight, and performance. The feedback from field tests guided the design of the next version.

2.1 SR / LT Application

The SR / LT (Speech Recognition / Language Translation) application runs on all four systems. It is a speech translation process which consists of three phases: speech to text language recognition, text to text language translation, and text to speech synthesis. The application running on TIA-P and TIA-0 is the Dragon Multilingual Interview System (MIS). It is a keyword-triggered multilingual playback system, including one-way communication, which listens to a spoken phrase in English, proceeds through a speech recognition front-end, plays back the recognized phrase in English, and after some latency synthesizes the phrase in a foreign language. The other, local person can answer with Yes and No. The domains included are medical examination, mine fields, road checkpoints, and interrogation.

The Speech Translator Smart modules run a freeform, continuous speech translation application, including two-way communication. The modules use CMU language translation and speech recognition software that was profiled to identify "hotspots" for software and hardware acceleration. We decided to proceed with a dual processor dedicated architecture (smart modules) to decrease size and response time.

2.2 Cardio Processor Subsystem

The core of all four speech translation wearable computers is the Cardio processor card, which combines the processor and many of the motherboard chips into one package, about the size of a PCMCIA card [7], Figure 1.

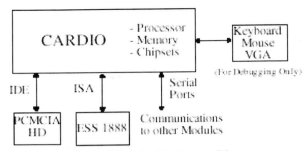

Fig. 1. Smart Module Hardware Diagram

All the necessary signals for the ISA and IDE buses come out of the Cardio card. The Cardio also supports two serial ports, which are used for communication between the modules, and a VGA interface.

2.3 System and Software Architecture

The smart modules perform two-way speech translation. Figure 2 depicts the structure of the free form, two way speech translator, from English to a foreign language, and vice versa. The speech is input into the system through a microphone. The Language Translation module includes a language model, glossary, and machine translation engine. The language model, generated from a variety of audio recordings and data, provides a knowledge source about the language properties. The Example-Based Machine Translation (EBMT) engine translates individual "chunks" of the sentence using the source language model and then combines them with a model of the target language to ensure correct syntax. The glossary is used for any final lookups of individual words that could not be translated by the EBMT engine.

The Speech Synthesis subsystem performs text to speech conversion at the output stage. To make sure that misrecognized words are corrected, a Clarification Dialog takes place on-screen. It includes the option to speak the word again, or to write it. As indicated in Figure 2, an alternative input modality could be the text from an Optical Character Recognizer.

The one way speech translator (MIS) runs on TIA-P and TIA-0. The user (interviewer) selects a domain module and target language, then selects and speaks phrases from a set of prerecorded phrases. In the next step, matching of a recognized phrase with the prerecorded phrase in a target language is preformed (phrase book lookup), and the prerecorded phrase is played back at the output stage (speakers).

3. TIA-P AND TIA-0

TIA-P is a commercially available system, developed by CMU, incorporating a 133 MHz 586 processor, 32MB DRAM, 2 GB IDE Disk, full-duplex sound chip, and spread spectrum radio (2Mbps, 2.4 GHz) in a ruggedized, hand-held, pen-based system designed to support speech translation applications.

Speech translation for one language (Croatian) requires a total of 60MB disk space. The speech recognition requires an additional 20-30 MB of disk space. Dragon loads into memory and stays memory resident. The translation uses uncompressed ~20 KB of .WAV files per phrase. There are two channels of output: the first plays in English, and second in Croatian.

TIA-P has been tested with the Dragon speech translation system in several foreign countries: Bosnia (Figure 3), Korea, and Guantanamo Bay, Cuba.

The main design goals for the TIA-0 computer were shrinking the size, reducing the weight, and incorporating the lessons learned from the TIA-P field tests. TIA-0, shown in Figure 5, is a smaller form factor system using the electronics of TIA-P. The entire system including batteries weighs less than three pounds and can be mission - configurable for sparse and no communications infrastructures. A spread-spectrum radio and small electronic disk drive provide communications and storage in the case of sparse communications infrastructure whereas a large disk drive provides self-contained stand-alone operation when there is no communication infrastructure. A full duplex sound chip supports speech recognition. TIA-0 is equivalent to a Pentium workstation in a softball sized packaging, including an embedded joypad as an alternative input device to speech.

Operational Experience: The following lessons were learned during the TIA-P field tests: wires should be kept to a minimum; handheld display was convenient for

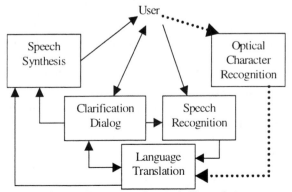

Fig. 2. Two way Speech Translator System

Fig. 3 U.S. Soldier in Bosnia Using TIA-P

checking the translated text; standard external electrical power should be available for use internationally; battery lifetime should be extended; ruggedness is important. All these lessons were used as an input into the design of the optimized version, TIA-0.

5. SMART MODULES

Smart modules are a family of wearable computers dedicated to speech processing application. A smart module provides a service almost instantaneously and is configurable for different applications. The design goals also included: reduce latency, eliminate memory context swaps, and minimize weight, volume, and power consumption. The functional prototype consists of two specialized modules, performing language translation and speech recognition. The speech recognition module uses CMU's Sphinx 2 continuous, speaker independent system [8]. The speech recognition code was profiled and tuned. Profiling identified "hot spots" for hardware and software acceleration and places to reduce computational and storage resources. Input to the module is audio and output is ASCII text. The speech recognition module also supports test to speech synthesis.

The LT module runs the PANLITE language translation software [9] and the SR module runs Sphinx II and Phonebox Speech Synthesis software. Target languages included Serbo-Croation, Korean, Creole French, and Arabic. Average language translation performance was one second per sentence.

The Smart Module system has two distinct kinds of processes: the Server-Application Group and the System Controller. A Server-Application Group consists of a UNIX background process which communicates with an application, such as PANLITE, via Inter-Process Communication within a module. The server process also communicates with the System Controller over the TCP/IP Network. The intermodule communications infrastructure is a TCP/IP based network running over serial PPP [10]. A Newton MessagePad 2000 is used as a display device.

The functional prototype of the Speech Translator Smart Module is shown in Figure 5, with one module performing language translation, and another one speech recognition and synthesis. The optimized version of the Speech Translator SM is shown in Figure 5.

Operational Experience: The lessons learned from tests and demonstrations include: the manual intervention process to correct misrecognized words incurs some delay; swapping can diminish the performance of the language translation module; the size of display can be as small as a deck of cards.

The required system resources for speech

Fig. 4. Optimized Speech Translator SM

translator software are shown in Table 1. We achieved a six times speedup over the original desktop PC system implementation of language translation, and five times smaller memory requirements.

7. PERFORMANCE EVALUATION

The performance of the family of Speech Translation modules is summarized in Figure 5. The metric for comparison in Figure 5 is proportional to the processing power (SpecInt), representing performance, and inversely proportional to the product of volume, weight, and power consumption (R), representing physical attributes. Figure 5 shows the normalized performance scaled by volume, weight, and power consumption. The diagram was constructed based on the data shown in Table 2. A TI 6030 laptop is taken as a baseline for comparison, and its associated value is one. TIA-0 is a factor of 44 better than the laptop while SR Smart Module is over 355 times better than the laptop (i.e., at least a factor of five better in each dimension). Therefore there are orders of magnitude improvement in performance as we proceed from more general purpose to more special purpose wearable computers.

8. CONCLUSIONS

Four generations of CMU wearable computers have been built for real-time speech translation applications, culminating in the Speech Translator Smart Module. Our results show that there are orders of magnitude improvement in performance as we proceed from one generation of Wearable Computers performing speech recognition to the next one. To our knowledge, Speech Translator Smart Modules are the only wearable computers capable of performing two-way speech translation (involving speech recognition and language translation).

A system-level approach to power / performance optimization improved the metric of (performance / (weight * volume * power)) by over a factor of 300 through the four generations.

	Laptop / Workstation	Functional Module SR / LT	Optimized Module SR / LT
Memory Size	195 MB	53 MB	41 MB
Disk Space	1GB	350 MB	200 MB

Table 1. Comparison of Required System Resources

Name	SpecInt	Volume (in³)	Weight (lbs)	Power (watts)	R (V*W*P)	Normalized - SpecInt/R	Log of Normalized
TI 6030	175.00	260.00	7.50	36.00	70200.00	1.00	0.00
TIA-P	55.00	88.00	3.00	6.50	1716.00	12.86	1.11
TIA-O	55.00	45.00	2.50	4.50	506.25	43.58	1.64
SR-SM	175.00	45.00	2.13	4.00	382.50	183.53	2.26
OPT-SM	175.00	33.00	1.50	4.00	198.00	354.55	2.55

Table 2. Performance Values Measured and Calculated for Wearable Computers

9. ACKNOWLEDGMENT

This work was supported by Defense Advanced Research Project Agency Contract # DABT63-95-C-0026 and Institute for Complex Engineered System at CMU.

10. REFERENCES

[1]   A. Smailagic and D. P. Siewiorek, "The CMU Mobile Computers: A New Generation of Computer Systems," Proc. of the IEEE COMPCON 94, IEEE Computer Society Press, February 1994, pp. 467-473.

[2]   A. Smailagic, "ISAAC: A Voice Activated Speech Response System for Wearable Computers," Proc. of the IEEE International Conference on Wearable Computers, Cambridge MA, October 1997.

[3]   D. Reilly, "Power Consumption and Performance of a Wearable Computing System," Masters Thesis, Carnegie Mellon University, Electrical and Computer Engineering Department, 1998.

[4]   D.P. Siewiorek, A. Smailagic, L. Bass, J. Siegel, R. Martin, B. Bennington, " Adtranz: A Mobile Computing System for Maintenance and Collaboration," Proc. 2nd IEEE Conf. on Wearable Computers, Pittsburgh, PA, 1998, pp. 25-32.

[5]   B. Bederson, "Audio Augmented Reality: A Prototype Automated Tour Guide," Proc. of CHI '95, May 1996, pp. 210-211.

[6]   E.D. Mynatt, M. Back, R. Want, and R. Frederick, "Audio Aura: Light-Weight Audio Augmented Reality," Proceedings of UIST '97 User Interface Software and Technology Symposium, Banff, Canada, October 15-17, 1997

[7]   Epson Corporation, Epson CARDIO 586-D4 Data Sheet, 1998.

[8]   M. Ravishankar, "Efficient Algorithms for Speech Recognition," Ph.D Thesis, CMU, Tech. Report. CMU-CS-96-143, May 1996.

[9]   R. E. Frederking, R. Bown, "The Pangloss-lite machine translation system. Expanding MT Horizons," Proc. 2nd Conference of the Association for MT in the Americas, 1996, pp. 268-272.

[10] J. Dorsey, "Smart Module Networking," Personal Communication, 1998.

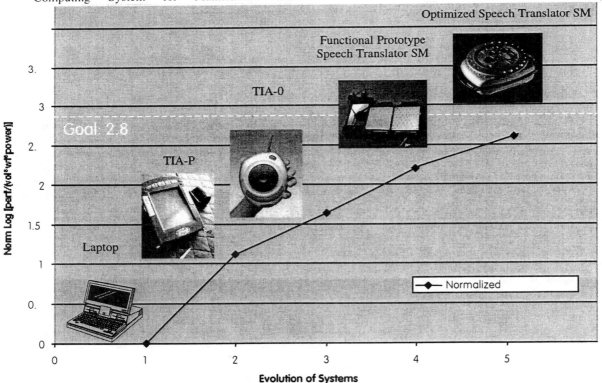

Fig. 5. Composite Performance of Speech Recognition Wearable Computers

Hummingbirds Go Skiing:
Using Wearable Computers to Support Social Interaction

Alexandra Weilenmann and Lars Erik Holmquist
Viktoria Institute
Box 620, SE-405 30 Gothenburg, Sweden
{alexandra, leh}@viktoria.informatics.gu.se
http://www.viktoria.org/

Abstract

The Hummingbird is a wearable computer that aims to support communication in co-located groups of people, by giving users a continuous awareness of the physical presence (or absence) of others. To examine the effect on group communication, we performed a study where six ski instructors used the Hummingbirds during a five-day trip. The study showed that the Hummingbirds were used more as a support for informal social interaction than for the actual work activities of the test group. In subsequent focus group sessions, we saw a clear difference between instructors who had used the devices and those who had not, in that the first group gave many enthusiastic suggestions for improvements and new usage areas, whereas the second group had great difficulties in seeing any use for the devices at all.

1. Introduction

Mobile computing and communication technology is becoming more and more common. In Scandinavia, mobile phones have entered into the fabric of daily life to such an extent that they are practically ubiquitous. With the continued evolution of the functionality of mobile phones, and the addition of wireless communication capabilities to hand-held computers, the line between communication and computing devices is starting to blur.

However, the interaction paradigm of the mobile phone has been directly inherited from the stationary phone. Receiving a call requires the user to do an explicit "context switch", thus often disrupting other activities. An alternative interaction paradigm is offered by *wearable computers*. These are always "on", continuously augmenting the user's abilities, thus requiring no context switch to use. However, most wearable computers are designed to be multi-purpose devices. By designing a wearable computer specifically for augmenting inter-personal communication, we may explore new paradigms for computer-augmented interaction.

2. The Hummingbird

Previously, we have developed the concept of inter-personal awareness devices, *IPADs* [1]. IPADs aim to support awareness between users, but not the actual communication that might result from that awareness. The *Hummingbird* is

an IPAD that enhances the *awareness of presence* between the people in a group by extending their range of "detection" even through physical obstacles and over some distance, according to the following principles:

- If two or more Hummingbirds belonging to users in the same group are close (currently roughly 100 meters apart or less) they will produce a sound – they *"hum"*.

- Additionally, a display shows the identity of the other Hummingbird users in the vicinity (since there may be more than two users in the group).

The original Hummingbirds were built from scratch using standard electronic components. For this study we developed a new generation of prototypes with a larger display and more flexibility, using a Nintendo GameBoy hand-held video game as a base. We designed a small radio transceiver, which communicated with the GameBoy through the serial port. Custom software was developed using tools freely available on the Internet [2], and transferred to commercially available blank cartridges [3]. The devices were small enough to be comfortably carried in a pocket or worn in a special case.

3. The study

To test the prototypes in a realistic environment, and to get feedback from a user group not normally exposed to wearable technology, we performed a study in the ski slopes of Oppdal, Norway. The team testing the Hummingbird was formed by six ski instructors being part of a group of sixteen instructors responsible for a trip with two hundred Swedish students. Using the qualitative framework of ethnography, the test was observed by a researcher who lived with the ski instructors during the five-day trip, thus watching how the Hummingbirds became a part of their daily life. To examine the group members' thoughts and ideas around the concept of IPADs, we performed two focus group sessions after the actual test; one focus group consisting of five users and one with four non-users.

The findings from the study are explained in terms of activities, using concepts from activity theory [4]. The framework of activity theory makes it possible to study the artifact in a context and considers the artifact as a tool to achieve a goal. The activities during the time in Oppdal can for our purposes be divided into activities related to work (skiing instruction, organizing the bus trip, etc.) or to social activities (having lunch, going to parties, etc.). These activities are then expected to occur at different times during the day and at different places. The two types of activities also differ in the need for knowing whether the others are present or not, hence we may expect difference in how the Hummingbirds will be used.

4. Findings from the study

One interesting finding was that it seemed that the ski instructors had more use of the Hummingbirds in activities that they did not consider the devices to be meant for. From the very beginning the users regarded the Hummingbird as a tool meant for work activity, more precisely teaching skiing skills. They saw the test as a way to determine how useful the Hummingbird was in helping them organizing this activity. However, it is clear that the Hummingbird was more often used in situations where the object of the activity was of a social character. It was used during the day to achieve goals such as to find other instructors in order to have lunch with them or to see who had left the cabins in the morning. During the actual skiing, the Hummingbirds were not often used, since they were considered to have a too short range; also, the sound was not sufficiently loud and it was considered cumbersome to take the device out of the pocket to look at the display. Users would look at the devices when they were in the lifts or while taking a break in the skiing session. Some of the instructors also used them when organizing the student group on the bus trip to and from the destination.

The ski instructors constantly had to negotiate with each other around the use of the artifact. These negotiations were a way for the users to reach a consensus of when, where, and for what purposes the Hummingbirds should be used. Since the instructors had not been told how and when to use the Hummingbirds, they had to establish their own roles toward the artifacts. To quote [4], the users had "an active role, using given artifacts but deciding actively how, where and when, to use them". During the test, several of these negotiations of use were noted, for instance when some people wanted to bring their Hummingbirds to the night club, and then were told by other users not to bring the devices to places that they were not meant for.

Another finding is related to the notion of privacy. During the focus group session the users expressed a fear of misuse of the Hummingbird, if designed in a way that would not give all users access to the same information. The members were afraid that such an artifact could be used for surveillance purposes and could harm the personal integrity. However, they also recognized a few contexts where such a function would be useful, such as a kindergarten. In the focus group session, the users also said the Hummingbird was different from mobile telephones and beepers, in that it *"does not demand anything from you, this is more relaxed"*.

Several improvements of the Hummingbird were suggested in order to make it more suitable for skiing; extended range, a possibility to determine direction of the others and a smaller design, for instance in form of an arm wrist watch or a badge on the sleeve.

The Hummingbird became the trip's conversation piece, a fact that the informants themselves acknowledge. They enjoyed using the Hummingbirds, and were often seen to be testing them in different ways. They expressed many creative uses for the Hummingbird. A notion that came up in the focus group session was that the Hummingbird could be seen as a means to achieve status; users appeared more important when carrying technological equipment. The ski instructors *not* using the Hummingbird differed from the users in that they could not as easily imagine potential ways to use the Hummingbird and could not understand its meaning. Considering the discussions in the two focus groups, it became clear that it is easier for a group of people to talk about a concept and imagine its possible uses, if they have been able to use the technology in practice, even if only in prototype form.

5. Conclusions and future work

Our study showed that Hummingbirds can be used to augment informal social interaction between novice users, and in the focus group sessions, users gave many suggestions on how to improve the devices to make them more useful for professional activities. The subjects who had not been using the devices, however, did not have any clear notion on what the possible use could be. We believe that by exposing potential users to new technology in realistic environments, important ideas and improvements will come up which would otherwise not have occurred, neither to the developers nor to people who have not actually tried using the technology. Future work will include studies in other types of environments, including mobile blue-collar workers, and construction of new prototypes based on these studies.

6. Acknowledgements

Thanks to Yvonne Wærn at Linköping University for help and supervision during the master's thesis on which this paper is based. This project was supported by SITI (the *Mobile Informatics* research program) and NUTEK (the *PROMODIS* research program).

7. References

[1] Holmquist, L.E., Falk, J. and Wigström, J. Supporting Group Awareness with Inter-Personal Awareness Devices. *Journal of Personal Technologies*, Vol. 3(1-2), Springer Verlag, 1999. pp.13-21

[2] *GameBoy Developer's Kit*. http://www.gbdev.org/GBDK/

[3] Bung Enterprises: *GB XChanger*. http://www.bung.com.hk/

[4] Kuutti, K. and Arvonen, T. Identifying Potential CSCW Applications by Means of Activity Theory Concepts: A Case Example. In *Proceedings of CSCW 92*, ACM Press, 1992. pp.233-240

Determination of Placement of a Body-Attached Mouse as a Pointing Input Device for Wearable Computers

Bruce Thomas[1], Karen Grimmer[2], Dan Makovec[1], Joanne Zucco[1], and Bernard Gunther[1]
School of Computer and Information Science[1]   Centre For Allied Health Research[2]
University of South Australia   University of South Australia
Mawson Lakes, SA, Australia   Adelaide, SA, Australia
[Bruce.Thomas,Karen.Grimmer,Dan.Makovec,Joanne.Zucco,Bernard.Gunther]@UniSA.Edu.Au

Abstract

We believe the notion of hands free operation is critical to the successful use of wearable computer systems. As such, we investigated possible placements of an input device, for a wearable computer, on different portions of the user's body, while the user assumed different postures (sitting, standing, kneeling, and prone).

1   Introduction

We were inspired by the paper *Design for Wearability* [4], where Gemperle *et. al.* produced 13 design guidelines to help mapped the design space for developing wearable systems [1, 3]. Current workstation input devices (such as mouse, joystick, and keyboard) would not be practical for users standing in an outdoor environment, as such devices require a level flat surface to operate. A new form of input device is required, but how would users interact with this new kind of input device? For example, how does one point or select objects displayed on a HMD? And how does one enter text or commands without a desktop keyboard?

One solution to the first question is to place a pointing device on the user's body [5]. A suitable device is the Touchpad mouse commonly found on Apple laptop computers. An example of a Touchpad mouse is shown in Figure 1. Where on one's body should such a device be placed? This study evaluates the effect of the placement of a Touchpad mouse on a user's body.

We **aimed** to determine whether there is any difference to a user operating a wearable computer with a Touchpad mouse when the following factors are varied: firstly, the position of the Touchpad mouse on the user's body – forearm, upper arm, torso, thigh front, or thigh outer side; secondly, the posture of the user – standing, sitting, kneeling, or in the prone position (laying down with the user propped up on their forearms). The study measured differences in time to complete selection tasks and the number of errors that occurred.

We reduced the number of possible combinations of mouse position and orientation from a total of twenty to seven for the final experiment, by discounting the non-preferred options[1].

2   Experimental Design

This section describes the design of the experiment, including the wearable computer system, training session, and the experimentation session. All sessions were performed in the Wearable Computer Laboratory.

The hardware portion of the computer system consists of the following components: *Toshiba Portable Personal Computer 320 Series* laptop computer, *Sony Glasstron* see-through 800 x 600 SVGA display, and *Easy Cat*[TM] Touchpad mouse [2]. The computer and power converters are stored in a small backpack.

The subjects then undergo a training session for the use of the Touchpad mouse attached to the top of a desk, while viewing the computer screen with the Sony Glasstron display in the opaque non-see-through mode.

A second experimentation session with a duration of about one and a half hours is performed individually with a supervisor. The task the subjects perform during the experiment is to use the Touchpad mouse to select

---

[1] **Acknowledgements:** Thank you to Gwen Landers for the construction the mouse attachment straps. We would also like to thank Victor Demcuzk and the Land Operations Division at the Defence Science and Technology Organisation, Salisbury, Australia for the use of the wearable computer equipment.

Figure 1: The forearm

Figure 2: The upperarm 1

Figure 3: The upperarm 2

Figure 4: The torso

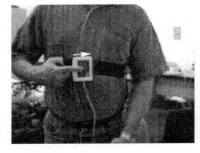

Figure 5: The torso 2

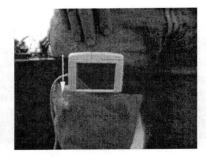

Figure 6: The front of the thigh

Figure 7: The side of the thigh

a target place in the centre of the screen. Once the target has been selected, that target is removed from the screen. A second target is placed offset of 183 pixels in one of eight directions, equally spaced around the centre of the screen. The targets are circles of 40 pixels in diameter. For each trial, the subjects perform 40 tasks in random order, the eight target positions presented five separate times.

3   Results and Discussion

This study involved 25 subjects performing selection tasks with a Touchpad mouse while wearing a wearable computer on their back and using a head mounted display. The each subject performed the tasks in 27 different combinations of four posture (sitting, kneeling, standing, and prone) and seven different placements of the Touchpad mouse on the subject's body (forearm, thigh by 2, torso by 2, and upper arm by 2). We measured the time and error rate to complete the selection of a circular target.

For posture, there are similar time effects for sitting, standing, and kneeling. These results indicate that the prone position is a posture which reduces the user's performance significantly. Further study is required to determine the cause of this poorer performance.

The effect of mouse position and orientation shows three groupings of the results for the seven different mouse positions. The front of the thigh is the best position for the mouse. The forearm, side of the thigh and

upper arm towards the user's hand are the next grouping. The least favourable mouse positions are torso (with both mouse orientations) and the upper arm with mouse buttons in the up direction.

When the posturing and mouse position conditions are combined, the results would indicate the thigh front mouse position would most appropriate for sitting kneeling, and standing postures, and the forearm mouse position is to be used for the prone position. If only one mouse position is to be used for all four postures, the forearm position would be the best choice.

References

[1] Len Bass, Chris Kasabach, Richard Martin, Dan Siewiorek, Asim Smailagic, and John Stivoric. The design of a wearable computer. In *ACM CHI 97*, pages 139–146, March 1997.

[2] CIRQUE Corporation, 433 W. Lawndale Dr., Salt Lake City, UT, USA. *Easy Cat: Touchpad mouse.*

[3] C. Esposito. Wearable computers: Field-test results and system design guidelines. In *Human-Computer Interaction IN-TERACT '97*, pages 493–500, Sydney, Australia, July 1997. Chapman and Hall.

[4] F. Gemperle, C. Kasabach, J. Stivoric, M. Bauer, and R. Martin. Design for wearability. In *2nd International Symposium on Wearable Computers*, pages 116–122, Pittsburgh, Pennsylvania, October 1998.

[5] B. H. Thomas, S. P. Tyerman, and K. Grimmer. Evaluation of text input mechanisms for wearable computers. *The Virtual Reality Journal*, 3:187–199, 1998.

The WearBoy: A Platform for Low-Cost Public Wearable Devices

Peter Ljungstrand, Staffan Björk and Jennica Falk
PLAY: Applied research on art and technology
Viktoria Institute, Box 620, SE-405 30 Gothenburg, Sweden
{peter, bjork, jennica}@viktoria.informatics.gu.se
http://www.viktoria.informatics.gu.se/play/

Abstract

We introduce the WearBoy – a wearable, modified Nintendo GameBoy – as a platform for exploring public wearable devices. We have minimized the size of a Color GameBoy circuit board to enable users to comfortably wear it, making the device not much larger than the actual screen. Technical properties of the WearBoy are discussed, along with two applications using the platform.

1. Introduction

Currently, many wearable computing prototypes are rather clumsy and heavy to wear, and often rely on several different electronic devices connected together by cables hidden in the user's clothing. This might be necessary for computationally demanding applications, but in many cases the application does not need much computational power, especially not if wireless access to more powerful resources is available. Several such low-end wearable platforms have been built and tested, e.g., the Thinking Tags [1]. These prototypes are usually custom designed around a small microcontroller with some additional features, but commonly lack a more general interface.

Most currently existing wearable computing applications act as personal companions, augmenting the individual perspective (cf. [6]). However, we believe that wearable technology could also be used to support and enrich social interaction between people to a much larger extent than is the case today. To explore these ideas, we needed a platform that would allow shared views and casual interaction between several people and/or devices.

In this paper, we present the *WearBoy*, a modified Nintendo GameBoy, as a midway alternative between using small dedicated hardware and cumbersome general-purpose hardware. By using already well-established technology, slightly modified to serve our purpose, the WearBoy allows cheap and rapid prototyping for public wearable devices.

2. The GameBoy Device

We wanted a small and versatile platform that would be self-contained, but which would also have a

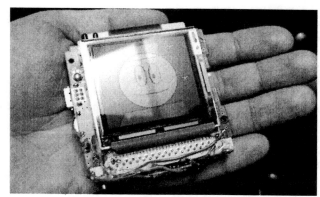

Figure 1. The WearBoy prototype

sufficiently large display to be viewed by people other than the actual wearer. The Nintendo Color GameBoy, a hand-held video game, provided these features although it was not designed to be worn. If one could redesign the device to be wearable, one could take advantage of the many features the hardware platform provided:

- Sufficient CPU. Though not as powerful as a PC-based system, the Z-80 based, 8.388 MHz MCU provides serial and IR communication. The use of exchangeable cartridges [2] makes it easy for users to change between different applications.

- Multimedia capabilities. Having a color screen (2.6", 160x144 pixels, 32K colors) and a 4-channel stereo sound output allows for quite complex information presentations.

- Small, robust, light and portable. The whole system has low power consumption (0.6W at 3V DC) and weighs only 210 grams.

- Inexpensive. At the low cost of about $70 per unit, they are expendable and allow for affordable multi-device systems. The available freeware software development tools [4] further reduce the overall cost.

One drawback of the GameBoy hardware was its limited expandability, due to the lack of sufficiently many I/O ports. This can be addressed by building an I/O expansion board that fits the GameBoy's cartridge slot

195

[7]. However, the serial port and the buttons allow digital I/O with peripheral devices with little or no hardware modifications.

3. The WearBoy Platform

Before designing the WearBoy, we had already used unmodified GameBoys fitted with radio transceivers to implement Hummingbirds – portable, personal awareness devices that convey information about what members of ones group are present in the physical vicinity [5]. During this work, we had learned that GameBoys were excellent platforms for rapid prototyping of small, wearable devices, but also that the original GameBoy was somewhat too big to be comfortably worn. However, when examining the hardware layout of the Color GameBoy, it became clear that it would be possible to reduce the circuit board size to be just slightly bigger than the screen itself, while keeping almost all the functionality intact (see Figure 1). By moving a voltage converter and some capacitors from the lower part of the circuit board to the upper part, we could remove the lower part altogether. Although this part of the circuit board contained the loudspeaker and the buttons, this loss was acceptable as new buttons and other types of I/O are easy to connect. Furthermore, it is possible to place these new buttons wherever they are feasible, i.e., where they are easy to access. Currently, the power source (2 AA size batteries) is the only external part of the device. Mounting other types of batteries directly on the board or cartridge eliminates the need for cables and reduces the weight of the device to less than 90 grams.

By arranging the GameBoy's IR port in the same direction as the screen, two WearBoys can communicate when their wearers are facing each other, similar to the Thinking Tags [1]. One potential problem is the short range (about 10 cm) of the IR port. However, amplifying the current to the IR diode and replacing the original diode with a more powerful one can extend the range. It is also possible to implement a standard IR protocol (e.g. IrDA) allowing for communication with a wealth of portable devices.

4. Applications

We are currently using the WearBoy for two projects, where the primary user of the system is not the wearer of the device but the viewers of that device. Doing this, we apply the technology to augment social interaction between people. This is in contrast to providing an information channel that is solely for the wearer, as is done in most wearable computing applications (cf. [6]).

4.1 The ActiveJewel

Merging jewelry design, graphical art and wearable technology, the ActiveJewel was designed to hold the WearBoy's display in a brooch-like frame. As the name implies, the ActiveJewel has a changing appearance with computer generated patterns constantly evolving on the display. Our aim with the ActiveJewel is to create a new kind of adornment similar to traditional jewelry, but with a visual appearance that can change over time. The ActiveJewel expands the traditional concept of jewelry, as an important aspect of self-decoration and display of symbolic values, with movement and non-repeating patterns to draw further attention to the item.

4.2 The BubbleBadge

Further exploring the design space of public, wearable applications, the BubbleBadge [3] turns the idea of a wearer's private display "inside out". The wearer's control over the information displayed is loosened, allowing the environment and viewers of the device to request information. For example, at the request of a viewer, the device can present new incoming e-mail on the wearer's display. Preliminary user tests have shown interesting new ways of interaction afforded by such devices, which require further exploration.

5. Future Work

The radio transceivers used with the Hummingbirds [5] can easily be connected to a WearBoy. This would allow for ad-hoc networking of a relatively large number of devices and experiments where many users simultaneously interacted with the devices.

As a next step, we will implement an I^2C compatible bus for the WearBoy, using the serial port. By doing this, many kinds of chips used in consumer electronics (e.g., EEPROMs, MP3 decoders, radio tuners, and programmable audio filters) can be attached to the system. This would further expand the platform's functionality while keeping the system small and affordable.

6. References

[1] Borovoy, R., McDonald, M., Martin, F. and Resnick, M. "Things that blink: Computationally augmented name tags", *IBM Systems Journal* 35, 3 & 4, 1999, pp. 488-495.

[2] *Bung Enterprises, Ltd.* Available at http://www.bung.com.hk/

[3] Falk, J. and Björk, S. "The BubbleBadge: A Wearable Public Display", in *Extended Abstracts of CHI'99*, 1999, pp. 318-319.

[4] Frohwein, J. *GameBoy Tech Page*. Available online at http://home.hiwaay.net/~jfrohwei/gameboy/

[5] Holmquist, L.E., Falk, J. and Wigström, J. "Supporting Group Awareness with Inter-Personal Awareness Devices", to appear in *Journal of Personal Technologies*, 3(1), Springer-Verlag, 1999.

[6] Mann, S. "Wearable Computing: A first step toward Personal Imaging", *IEEE Computer*, 30(3), 1997.

[7] Rawer, M. *The Gameboy Project*. Technical Report, Karlsruhe University of Technology, Department of Sensor Systems Technology, 1999. Available online at http://www.fh-karlsruhe.de/fbnw/html/Gameboy/Docs/GBProject.pdf

Context Sensing with the Twiddler Keyboard

Daniel Ashbrook
College of Computing
Georgia Institute of Technology
gt5257d@prism.gatech.edu

Abstract

Context sensitivity is an important application of wearable computers. This paper describes research on using the Twiddler one-handed keyboard for sensing motion-associated context. Two possible methods for detecting walking are described, and other types of movement context that it might be possible to sense are discussed. Results of early experiments with a preliminary Twiddler driver modification are discussed.

1. Introduction

The ability to sense context is an important component of wearable computing applications. It allows the application to automatically respond to changing situations in a way that makes the wearable even more useful. The Twiddler one-handed keyboard, manufactured by HandyKey, is very popular among users of wearable computers and is therefore the perfect device to augment with context-sensitivity.

The Twiddler's usefulness lies in the fact that it has two tilt sensors incorporated into it for use as a mouse. One sensor detects the degree of tilt in the horizontal direction, and the other in the vertical. According to HandyKey's technical information, "the tilt output is nearly linear over a ±30° range with a corresponding count range of ±50. At ±90° the count value is approximately ±200."[1]

The idea behind my research is to allow the computer to sense when the user is in various stages of motion. The first, and most basic type of motion to be detected is walking. Since walking involves a range of relatively predictable movements, it is an ideal context to attempt to sense.

Aside from the ease of sensing, context awareness of walking has several obviously useful applications. One use, suggested by Thad Starner[2] (who initially inspired this research) is to automatically pull up a to-do list, which he regularly accesses while walking from one appointment to the next. Another use, if individual steps

were detected, could be an odometer, to calculate the distance walked in a day. This could be combined with data on the usage of the computer to create yet another compelling argument for using a wearable!

Since the Twiddler's sensors only provide two degrees of freedom, positioning using only the inertial sensors is an impossibility. However, in conjunction with some fairly inexpensive (and therefore inaccurate) radio positioning tools, it might be possible to get fairly precise positional measurement.

2. Sensing walking

Looking at a graph of a simulated walk, such as the example in Figure 1 (created by bouncing the Twiddler up and down manually), two methods for detecting a walk immediately suggest themselves. One derives from the fact that the maximum hovers around 500 for about half a second for each step. This would be trivial to detect. The other possibility is to identify each individual step by some process.

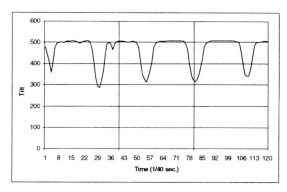

Figure 1. Manually created data set

2.1. Maximum detection

Looking at the graph in Figure 1, it is obvious that the maximum for each step floats close to 500 periodically, for about half a second at a time. During the second step, however, there is a small downspike; this is a condition that would have to be ignored in any calculations. Aside from this, watching the maximum values over a period of

---

[1] http://www.handykey.com/twiddler-data-format.gif
[2] testarne@cc.gatech.edu

several seconds, and seeing if they stay within a specific range (such as 500 ±10) would provide a very satisfactory result.

Figure 2 shows a graph of actual data collected from one of the Twiddler's tilt sensors. Although there is quite a bit more variation in the values than is present in the manually created graph, the majority of nearly-straight segments exist around the 500 area. Checking for a majority of time spent at 500 ±20 would probably yield correct results.

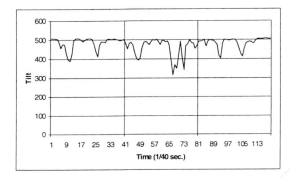

Figure 2. Real-life usage data

2.2. Individual step detection

A natural progression of detecting periods of values around a certain point is to combine this measurement with measurements of minimum values and attempt to detect individual steps.

Looking at Figure 1, very clear hills and valleys are recognizable. In Figure 2, they are not as well defined, but are still recognizable. A basic algorithm would watch for a minimum value (defined as the smallest measurement encountered in some interval that is lower

than some value, both interval and value probably user defined), and then watch for several values in a row with close to the same values. When another minimum is hit, a step would be registered.

One of the possible problems that could be encountered with this method is represented on the graph in Figure 2. At just under 2 seconds, there is a large spike in the graph, caused perhaps by a misstep or twitch of some kind. By watching for several values in a row near each other, rather than just one maximum, spikes are ignored. Another potential problem is erroneous detection; for example, if the user stood still for several seconds, that could be registered as a step. By specifying a minimum value for the steps to be detected, however, this could be avoided.

2.3. Other methods

One possible method for greater accuracy in detecting steps is to apply a Fourier transform to the collected data; when a strong low-frequency oscillation is detected (around 2 Hz?), it could be interpreted as walking. This could also lead to an easier method of detecting other locomotive activities, such as walking down stairs or running.

Another possibility is to analyze data from both the horizontal and vertical sensors of the Twiddler; however, since there appear to be few side-to-side movements in most peoples' walks, there is some doubt as to whether this would prove practical.

Further improvements to these ideas would definitely be helped by research into walking patterns of different people, as well as data collected from various users of wearable computers.

The WristCam as Input Device

Andrew Vardy, John Robinson, Li-Te Cheng
Multimedia Communications Laboratory, Faculty of Engineering and Applied Science
Memorial University of Newfoundland, St. John's, NF, Canada
vardy@engr.mun.ca, john@engr.mun.ca, lcheng@engr.mun.ca

Abstract

We show how images of a user's hand from a video camera attached to the underside of the wrist can be processed to yield finger movement information. Discrete (and discreet) movements of the fingers away from a rest position are translated into a small set of base symbols. These are interpreted as input to a wearable computer, providing unobtrusive control.

1 Introduction

We are investigating the use of a wrist- or forearm-mounted camera for wearable computer applications. As shown in Figure 1, the WristCam attaches to the underside of the forearm and views only the front of the hand and fingers. Typically it is invisible to other people, being concealed by the wearer's sleeve and connected up the sleeve to the remainder of the system.

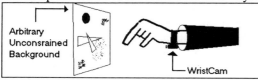

Figure 1. Camera position and expected background conditions

Foreseen applications for the WristCam include a hand's-eye-view key frame recorder (useful for storing sequences of gestures like keystrokes on a dial pad), hand scanning of documents, and active vision tasks that can combine input from a static head camera and a dynamic wrist camera. However, our main interest is to develop a virtual input device that allows chorded character input by tracking certain coarse finger movements or gestures. To do this, we need to track and interpret finger motions as seen by the WristCam, in the wide range of illumination conditions and backgrounds encountered as the user moves their hand around. Typically, the user will tap fingers against a handy table top or their clothing, or simply move their

fingers freely. Recognizing these motions and converting them efficiently to system input makes it possible for WristCam users to interact with their wearable computers unobtrusively. Although head-mounted displays are becoming less encumbering and obvious to others (non-wearers), existing input devices such as chord keypads are very visible and distracting to others. The WristCam will allow input to be subtle (or even covert) and therefore not distracting. Also, when the system is not in "input" mode the user's hands will be instantly free for other uses.

The basic system operation is as follows: A process on the wearable computer is dedicated to interpreting the movements of the user's fingers to determine if the user is attempting to communicate. If the process determines that the user's fingers are in a predefined "start" position then the communication will begin. From this point on, movements of particular fingers and combinations of fingers away from the start position will correspond to individual symbols. These symbols may themselves comprise direct commands, or subsequent symbols may be aggregated together to form "words". In this manner, the user can send not just rudimentary commands such as "UP", "DOWN", and "CONTINUE", but also regular text.

The same system could also be employed to receive a continuous range of input values from the user's hand to use as a control mechanism for some continuous-motion type virtual device such as a scroll bar. This, however, is not the focus of this paper.

2 Methodology

We first identified a set of general requirements for a WristCam input device. Then, for an initial prototype, we established a simple syntax for communication using finger gestures. This syntax drove the detailed design and was used for the testing reported here.

General requirements for a WristCam input device are: robustness, speed, ease-of-use, and covertness.

The system must operate with a very high degree of reliability in a wide variety of environments. Thus, the background and illumination remain unconstrained. A wearable computer user is likely to be found in virtually any environment and should not be expected to hold themselves frozen in front of a featureless background. Thus, the system must work when presented with an arbitrary moving background.

Clearly, an input device must be able to accept user input in real-time. A slight delay may be acceptable, but if the system is not capable of almost immediately responding to a rapid chain of gesture inputs then it will fail as a general-purpose input device.

The system must be easily usable. Gestures corresponding to "inputs" to the wearable computer must be comprised of simple comfortable gestures. This constraint, in conjunction with the robustness constraint, also implies a certain degree of latitude in terms of camera positioning. The system should be resilient to changes in camera position and orientation. It is unrealistic to expect a wrist-mounted camera to stay perfectly rigid and stable.

The covert operation requirement is borne largely from the desire to utilize this system in a social context. Finger movements corresponding to system input symbols must be fairly subtle and unobtrusive.

A simple base alphabet of seven possible gestures was derived from the eight possible combinations of three fingers with each finger being in a state of movement from the rest position. Figure 2 illustrates this alphabet.

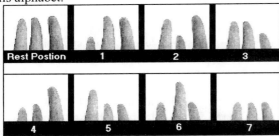

Figure 2. Space of possible 3-finger gesture positions

The static gesture positions shown above do not themselves constitute gestures. We define a gesture as a dynamic change from the rest position to one of the gesture positions, and then back to the rest position. Note that the rest position has the fingers extended, and that the actual gestures are finger lifts. This allows the hand to be rested on a flat surface and taps to be interpreted as gestures. The three-finger alphabet was used because of the relatively high dexterity and close physical proximity of the first three fingers. Also, these three fingers tend to appear parallel to a camera mounted on the underside of the wrist. The system was designed to sense this small set of gestures.

3   System Operation

The system as a whole is a state machine. The following sequence of steps provides a simplified description of normal system operation:
1. The user initiates finger tracking by turning the wrist inwards to blacken the camera's input.
2. The user now places their hand motionless in clear view of the camera. An audible tone will notify the user if the current hand position is unsuitable.
3. The user then begins gesturing. The system is returned to idle by blackening the camera's input.

4   High-Level Design

Two key features of the expected hand-viewing conditions have been exploited in this system. The first is that the hand normally takes up most of the bottom of the image area. Due to the often complex distribution of skin color in color space [1-3], we will find that selection of the "most common color" will often not yield good segmentation of the hand image. However, the assumption that "skin color", however it is defined, is relatively frequent in the source image underpins the approach discussed below.

The second feature to exploit is the parallel nature of the fingers. From the camera's vantage point at the underside of the user's wrist, the fingers, having been bent inwards, all appear approximately parallel in the source image. This suggests converting the source image into a one-dimensional representation according to the average finger angle.

The two motivational assumptions given above provide the basis for our high-level design.

We map the color coordinates of each pixel of the incoming video stream into a 3-dimensional (3 color components) quantized color histogram. We find points of maximum density in the histogram and treat these as candidate skin colors. The learned skin color (the prototype) from previous frames is compared with the candidates and the prototype is incrementally updated towards the most likely current skin candidate. The rate at which the prototype changes is under control of a parameter, which is set so that movement, shading and illumination effects, such as movement of a single finger, that cause transient changes in the histogram, do not cause the prototype to jump. The consequence of this would be a sudden difference in segmentation not only for the finger that moved, but for all of the other fingers as well, thus masking the appearance of a moving finger.

The method used to divide the image into skin and non-skin pixels is a linear color segmentation algorithm developed specifically for real-time skin finding applications. The segmented image is then filtered. Figure 3 illustrates the result of the segmentation process.

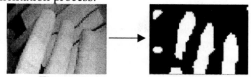

Figure 3. Image segmentation

We now return to the original image and attempt to determine in which direction the fingers are pointing. The parallel assumption allows us to take this as a single direction. We find the angle-to-vertical of the single line which is most closely parallel to the fingers in the source image. We first obtain a thinned contour image from the original bitmap. Next, a sequence of bins is created where each bin corresponds to a range of angles between –45° and +45°. Each contour point with an angle in this range is placed in the appropriate bin. The largest bin is found and the average of all its contour points is taken. This average is taken as the desired angle. Some inertia is required in this quantity in order to stabilize the process. Clearly, this is a simple process. It is also robust and very fast.

Once the angle of fingers is found, we can reduce the source image to the more compact representation desired. The 2-D segmented image is transformed into a 1-D histogram by taking each point in the histogram as the number of skin-color pixels in the segmented image counted by summing along slanted columns of the segmented image parallel to the finger angle line. This histogram is then smoothed. Figure 4 illustrates the histogram constructed from the image above.

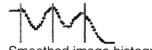

Figure 4. Smoothed image histogram

The histogram is analyzed to determine the heights and locations of the peaks. Each peak should ideally correspond to a single finger. However, in order to combat against temporary periods of poor image segmentation, and thus a poor histogram, three horizontal points along the histogram are assigned to each of the three fingers. If the correct number of peaks are present (i.e. three) then the three horizontal points will be moved incrementally towards those positions. If the number of peaks in the histogram is not correct then the three horizontal points will stay stationary unless they are in the immediate vicinity of a peak in the histogram, in which case they will be moved incrementally towards such a peak.

At this point we have three horizontal points that correspond to three of the slanted columns used to transform the segmented image into the image histogram. These three columns are parallel lines that should roughly bisect each of the fingers in the original image. Thus, three lines are extended from the top of the image down along these three slanted columns. The lines extend down to the point where the fingertips are encountered. This point is determined when a threshold number of skin-colored image pixels are found on a short line (just a few pixels long) called the "test" line which is perpendicular to the downwards extended line and which is fixed at its center to the bottom of that line. Figure 5 shows a close-up of the point at which a fingertip is "found".

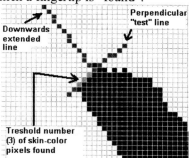

Figure 5. Close-up of "test" line encountering fingertip

The quantity produced by this process is simply the length of the downwards extended line from the top of the image until the point where it encounters the fingertip. Tracking these three quantities (one for each finger) over time generates a third set of histograms. Each of these histograms corresponds to a single finger. To stabilize the process these histograms are continuously smoothed. Also, they are inverted so that peaks become valleys. Finally, by looking for peaks in these histograms we can determine if a finger has moved significantly from the rest position. At this point the finger(s) being moved describe the input symbol. Note that it is necessary to introduce a small delay upon finding a peak in one of the histograms. This delay allows time for another peak in a different histogram to "arrive". That is, in a multi-finger gesture we allow the movements of each moving finger to peak slightly out of phase.

5 Results

We present some numerical results of trials of this system attempted in a variety of environments. The first two environments shown are relatively ideal. A plain background was used and care was taken in the positioning and orientation of the fingers. The other environments employed arbitrary backgrounds and less constrained finger positioning. It should be stated that the results for each new environment were taken after the new position had stabilized (i.e. the camera was allowed to self-adjust its brightness, the finger orientation angle was allowed to settle, and the three histogram peaks were reliably detected). In each environment each of the seven gestures were attempted (see Figure 2). The following table gives the system response to these seven gestures:

Table 1. Tabulated results in seven settings

Setting	Correct	Right time – wrong gesture	Gestures missed entirely	Non-existent gestures
Ideal	7	0	0	0
Ideal	7	0	0	1
Non-Ideal	7	0	0	1
Non-Ideal	5	2	0	1
Non-Ideal	6	1*	0	0
Non-Ideal	7	0	0	0
Non-Ideal	6	1*	0	1
Average	6.43	1.33	0	0.57

* - In these cases a multiple-finger gesture was intended, yet the system interpreted these as two single-finger gestures.

The results for each setting are single trials. No system parameters were adjusted between the tests shown above.

The average delay between the actual completion of a gesture and the time that the system indicates that a gesture has occurred is approximately one second. The average rate of processing is approximately 9 frames per second on a Pentium II 400 MHz PC with 64MB of RAM and a Vista ViCam Digital Camera.

6 Discussion

The results given above are for a single user making single, well-separated, gestures. Although they do not characterize the performance of the system in decoding continuous natural movement, they demonstrate the reliability of the underlying image processing algorithms. They show that correct operation can be reliably achieved if the user is careful about the background seen by the camera. However, in the case of an arbitrary and moving background, i.e. in the context specified by the design requirements, the system exhibits errors. Primarily, these occur when portions of the background are misclassified as skin. Such areas often display frequent alternation of classification, causing spurious gesture detection.

Errors from color misclassification illustrate the persistent difficulty of discriminating fingers from arbitrary backgrounds. The method used to determine skin color by adaptive clustering is robust and fast, but does not disambiguate well against skin-toned backgrounds. We attempted to fix this problem by attaching red illuminants to the camera pointing at the hand. Unfortunately this causes mutual illumination from the hand onto white surfaces (e.g. table tops) resulting in more non-finger areas matching skin color.

The overall frame rate of the system is quite high (9 fps) but the high delay time (one second) makes interactive usage difficult. This delay is incurred through a combination of processing lag and the window of time allocated to wait between the peaks of movement for each finger involved in a multi-finger gesture. We may improve the accuracy of detecting multi-finger gestures, but only at the cost of increased delay. A partial solution to the delay problem, as well as an increase in accuracy, could be achieved by eliminating multi-finger gestures from the alphabet.

7 Conclusions

This paper has described a new kind of input device for wearable computing. Its design gears it towards unobtrusive use in a variety of environments.

The system is completely adaptive and requires no prior training in terms of skin color or expected background conditions. This adaptability is the key strength of this design. It allows the system its robustness and ability to operate in real-time. However, there may be reliability advantages to be gained by equipping the system with some pre-defined notions of what colors to define as skin colors and what colors to define as background.

The next step in development is to develop a more sophisticated input language. This will be designed to be partially error correcting.

The prototype system described here proves the potential for using a WristCam as an input device. By freeing the user from the bonds of a tactile interface and affording them the benefit of discreet operation, this system allows invisible wearability to extend to input and control.

8 References

[1] Pavlovic, V.I., Sharma, R., Huang, T.S., "Visual Interpretation of Hand Gestures for Human-Computer Interaction: A Review", *IEEE Transactions on Pattern Analysis and Machine Intelligence*, July 1997, Vol. 19, No. 7, IEEE Computer Society, Los Alamitos, pp. 677-696.

[2] Kjeldsen, R., Kender, J., "Finding skin in color images" *Proceedings of the International Conference on Automatic Face and Gesture Recognition*, Killington, VT, October 14-16, 1996, pp 312-317.

[3] Saxe, D., Foulds, R., "Towards Robust Skin Identification in Video Images", *Proceedings of the International Conference on Automatic Face and Gesture Recognition*, Killington, VT, October 14-16, 1996, pp 379-384.

Combining Positional Information with Visual Media

Neill Campbell   Henk Muller   Cliff Randell

Department of Computer Science, University of Bristol, UK
cliff@cs.bris.ac.uk, http://wearables.cs.bris.ac.uk/

Abstract

By integrating visual media with positioning information obtained with our wearable computer, we create new opportunities for using visuals both in the field and at the workstation. The position information we store with each visual is direction, pitch, roll, location, focal length, and zoom. This information allows any system to reconstruct the frustum of the visual, and, if height data is available to reconstruct which parts of the earth are visible in the visual. This enables position based lookup and 3D mosaicing of visuals to reconstruct a 3D model.

1 Introduction

We are interested in the association of media files with contextual information gathered by our wearable computer. We have previously explored the combination of audio notes, or reminders, with locations [1]. In this paper we turn our attention to visuals.

Classic photographs and videos store only visual information. Recent advances in photo and video technology have increased the amount of information which can be stored with visuals. As an example, Advanced Photo System (APS) cameras store information about the lighting conditions on a magnetic strip with the photo, and digital cameras store focal length, and shutter time with each photo.

In this document we extend this idea, and annotate each visual (that is: each still, or each frame of a video) with positional information. We have supplemented our wearable computer system, which was already equipped with a GPS receiver, by mounting an electronic compass on a digital camera. The positional information obtained allows us to uniquely identify *where* a photograph was taken, and in which direction, thereby enabling us to develop applications which include indexing; and, in the near future, compositing; image reconstruction; and creation of 3D worlds.

The availability of images indexed by location to the users of wearable computers can provide them with different perspectives of the surrounding environment, and the development of a standard format also enables us to progress towards applications involving augmented reality.

2 Information stored with each visual

We have chosen a set of attributes which will enable us to precisely determine the theoretical field of view contained in each visual. In addition we have selected readily available data which may also have some relevance e.g.time/date. With each visual we thus store the following information:

- Absolute position (Latitude, Longitude, Altitude; from GPS location sensor)
- Direction (horizontal direction, pitch, roll from an electronic compass, or alternatively obtained from solid state accelerometers),
- Absolute Time/Date (also from GPS).
- Focal length and Depth of Field (which part of the scene is in focus),
- Zoom (the Field of View; the horizontal and vertical angle of the visible scene),
- Flash (whether the flash is used; indicates that only the first few metres are visible).

To store this data, we have extended the PNG format [2] with a chunk for position information. The chunk (tentatively named pOSd for position and direction), consisting of a 22 byte block storing the above information as fixed point numbers. This is more restricted and far simpler than the EXIF format [3].

3 Determining the frustum

The basic operation that can be performed using the positional information is to reconstruct the frustum of the camera. The frustum is the part of space which is covered on the visual. This process is shown in Figure 1: the absolute position of the camera (for example a triple X,Y,Z or latitude

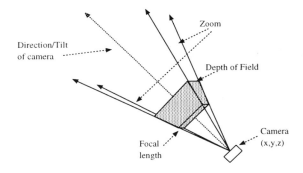

Figure 1. Determining the frustum

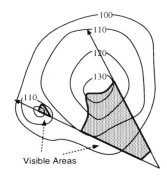

Figure 2. Clipping the frustum using a height map

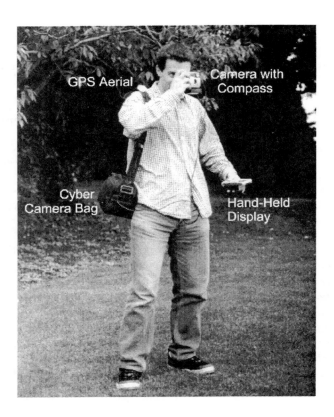

Figure 3. Using the 'Cyber Camera Bag'

4 Configuration

longitude, altitude) determines where the photograph was taken from; the zoom, direction, pitch and roll information determines the field of view; and the focal length, with the depth of field, determines how much of the scene is on the photograph, in terms of depth.

The above process does not use any knowledge about the environment in which the photograph was taken. If more information is available, for example an altitude map of area where the photograph was taken, then the frustum can be clipped further. This is especially useful in outdoor scenes, where the depth of field is probably infinite. First of all, the frustum can be intersected with the elevation map, indicating which areas can be visible. In this case, the altitude map can be used to clip the visible area to exclude anything which is behind, say, a mountain range. Figure 2 shows how to clip the frustum with altitude information. The camera's absolute position together with an altitude map allows us to calculate which parts of the map are visible. We cannot do a precise clip, for parts of this area may be occluded by objects which are not on the map, for example a building, tree or person in the field of vision.

For development purposes our wearable computer (a PC104 based 486, GPS Receiver with differential correction, and LiIon batteries) was installed in a "Cyber Camera Bag" (a heavy version of our unconsciously wearable "Cyberjacket"). This is worn by the photographer in a similar manner to a conventional camera bag into which a digital camera with electronic compass is connected. Figure 3 shows the equipment in use.

Focal length, Zoom, and Flash are already provided by existing digital cameras [4]. We retrieve the geographic position and magnetic variation from the GPS receiver. The prototype digital compass uses Hall Effect sensors and is mounted on the camera to retrieve directional information. Pitch and roll information will be supplied by three accelerometers.

Images are either stored in the camera, or added to the database on a remote server using a GSM 'phone link. A wireless hand-held web browser display [5] can be used to remotely search for, and display, the images also using the 'phone link.

5 Applications

5.1 Positional photo album

The first application is to create a photo album database with position based lookup. All frustums are stored, and given a location on earth you can query all photographs covering that point. Using the camera position data we are able to select the particular images which interest us. This allows the user to quickly collect, for example:

- photographs which show the whole of Stonehenge, yet exclude all the photographs taken *from* Stonehenge;
- photographs of the south face of the Everest - only those taken from the south.

A simple version of the photo-album can be stored locally on our wearable computer by downloading the images of the area we are interested in visiting. We are also currently investigating a web based version where an alta-vista type robot could create a location based index of photographs which can be searched remotely using the hand-held web browser.

The photo album stores the information by calculating the frustum for each photo (as outlined before), and storing it in a quad-tree. The root of the quad-tree spans the whole of the earth (using latitude and longitude information). For as long as the photo spans few cells in the quad tree, the quad tree is extended. Eventually, the frustum will be approximated by a number of squares in the quad-tree. The user can navigate by pointing at an area of a map, the software will navigate through the quad-tree and select appropriate photographs. (An octree would allow height information to be stored, but this adds little information.)

5.2 Intelligent compositing

The second application will be to give feedback to the wearer while taking the photograph, and to improve the composition of the photograph. The wearable will know where the horizon and sun are, and can therefore instruct the wearer that the photograph may be better if taken from a different angle. Alternatively such feedback could be used to automatically control the camera e.g. with a fill-in flash when facing towards the sun.

5.3 Reconstructing 3D images

A more challenging application which we are investigating at the moment is the reconstruction of a 3D model of the environment using the images collected. This 3D model can be used to create a virtual walk-through [6, 7].

Purely vision based 3D reconstruction techniques are now emerging [8]. A set of 2D images of an object are used to build up a 3D model. This reconstruction process requires only approximate positional information of the camera; the precise position and direction of the camera are calculated as part of the reconstruction process. We may be able to construct a mountain range given a set of photographs.

A simpler reconstruction technique will use an elevation map of the area concerned. The photograph can be analysed to produce a texture map, and the height map provides the 3D info. Although neither the position information nor the directional information will be a perfect match, we expect that we will still be able to reconstruct the original image and potentially create images from other viewpoints.

6 Other Formats

Positional information can also be stored with photographs from non-digital cameras or videos. It is possible to store the additional information on the magnetic strip of an APS camera. The incorporation of the 22 bytes of data into each frame of a video sequence could provide the basis of a system to enable the viewer to track the image source in real time. If multiple video sources are available this system could be used by a viewer to select different viewpoints of live action e.g. a football match.

References

[1] R. Hull, P. Neaves, and J. Bedford-Roberts. Towards situated computing. In *Proceedings of The First International Symposium on Wearable Computers*, pages 146–153, October 1997.

[2] T. Boutel. PNG (portable network graphics) specification. *http://www.w3.org/TR/REC-png.html*, October 1996.

[3] ISO technical committee 42. Photography - electronic still picture cameras - removable memory - part 2: Image data format - TIFF/EP. Technical Report ISO/DIS 12234-2, ISO, Nov. 1997.

[4] K. Murata. Kodak digital camera. *Software Developer's Kit Reference Manual*, pages 40,50,120, April 1997.

[5] P. Neaves and J. Bedford-Roberts. Dynamic connection of wearable computers to companion devices using near-field radio. In *Proceedings of The Second International Symposium on Wearable Computers*, pages 156–157, October 1998.

[6] L.-T. Cheng and J. Robinson. Dealing with speed and robustness issues for video-based registration on a wearable computing platform. *Proceedings of The Second International Symposium on Wearable Computers*, October 1998.

[7] S. Mann. Lookpainting: Towards developing a new camera user-interface. *http://wearcam.org/monet/node8.html*, April 1999.

[8] D.P. Gibson, N. Campbell and B. Thomas. The generation of 3D models without camera calibration. *Computer Graphics and Imaging*, pages 146–149, June 1998.

— *Notes* —

IEEE Computer Society Publications

The world-renowned IEEE Computer Society publishes, promotes, and distributes a wide variety of authoritative computer science and engineering texts. These books are available from most retail outlets. Visit the Online Catalog, *http://computer.org*, for a list of products.

IEEE Computer Society Proceedings

The IEEE Computer Society also produces and actively promotes the proceedings of more than 141 acclaimed international conferences each year in multimedia formats that include hard and softcover books, CD-ROMs, videos, and on-line publications.

For information on the IEEE Computer Society proceedings, send e-mail to *cs.books@computer.org* or write to Proceedings, IEEE Computer Society, P.O. Box 3014, 10662 Los Vaqueros Circle, Los Alamitos, CA 90720-1314. Telephone +1 714-821-8380. FAX +1 714-761-1784.

Additional information regarding the Computer Society, conferences and proceedings, CD-ROMs, videos, and books can also be accessed from our web site at *http://computer.org/cspress*